Persons and
Valuable Worlds

Persons and Valuable Worlds

A Global Philosophy

Eliot Deutsch

ROWMAN & LITTLEFIELD PUBLISHERS, INC.
Lanham • Boulder • New York • Oxford

ROWMAN & LITTLEFIELD PUBLISHERS, INC.

Published in the United States of America
by Rowman & Littlefield Publishers, Inc.
4720 Boston Way, Lanham, Maryland 20706
www.rowmanlittlefield.com

12 Hid's Copse Road, Cumnor Hill, Oxford OX2 9JJ, England

British Library Cataloguing in Publication Information Available

Library of Congress Cataloging-in-Publication Data Available

ISBN 0-7425-1214-2 (cloth : alk. paper)
ISBN 0-7425-1215-0 (paper : alk. paper)

Printed in the United States of America

∞ ™ The paper used in this publication meets the minimum requirements of
American National Standard for Information Sciences—Permanence of Paper for
Printed Library Materials, ANSI/NISO Z39.48-1992.

*For Marcia—an exemplar of creativity,
with whom my life is joyously shared*

Contents

Preface

A t a time when the end of philosophy has been announced in the Anglo-American analytic world by many who now call themselves pragmatists and, somewhat ironically, joyously heard by many professors of philosophy, and when, on the Continent, much philosophy is being done with an eraser rather than with pen and pencil (or their electronic equivalents), and when at the same time postmodernist pundits in literary, artistic, and political circles have carried out unrelenting attacks on all traditional notions of thought and rationality, and when in an actual world largely gone mad in the twentieth century, with its cataclysmic wars, genocides, and other unspeakable horrors, it might seem inopportune to engage in an effort to put forth a comprehensive account of what it means to be a genuine, creative person who crafts oneself and one's worlds, and to engage in a further conversation about what philosophy itself is—or should be. Nevertheless, the call for creativity in our thinking about ourselves as spiritual and social beings in the world that I will try to make here, is, I think, always timely and is, as I will try to show, essential to the realization of what it means to think rightly and thereby to live properly.

This work argues for a kind of pluralistic, but not relativistic, philosophical anthropology, ontology, ethics and epistemology in a cross-cultural context. It is my conviction that any discussion of topics in these areas that has breadth as well as depth necessarily involves an effort to understand the nature of various forms of rationality, articulacy, and ways of being within a broad range of human experience and cultural activity.

It is widely recognized today that there is a crisis in contemporary Western philosophy arising out of the progressive sundering, since at least the seventeenth century, of moral or value considerations from our various notions of rationality and the nature of reality. Unlike, say, the Greeks who generally saw an intimate relationship obtaining between the appropriate ends of human thinking and action and the very nature of rationality, and unlike as well, the Chinese—and the Indian, in their distinctive way—who understood a moral quality as inhering in what could only properly be regarded by them as rational, we have come to believe strongly in a value-free explanatory and instrumental rationality; one that celebrates science in such a way as to lead, as with computational models of the mind, to a new form of scientism and some form or other of naturalized epistemology. Many persons, however, in very different fields have become increasingly aware of the tremendous cost, socially as well as intellectually, that we have paid for what has become a value-less epistemology and impoverished metaphysics. Accordingly, my work here represents an effort to reintegrate value considerations into philosophy throughout the domain of its inquiry.

This work includes a number of substantial revisions and reorganizations of materials in my book *Creative Being: The Crafting of Person and World*, published in 1992, and the addition of five new chapters focusing on the nature of rationality and related epistemological issues. As with the writing of the earlier book, I have had the good fortune of being invited to present materials from this revised work at various universities in Asia, Europe, and the Americas—especially to colleagues at the University of Cambridge where I was a visiting fellow in 1998 at Clare Hall. As in the past, I have also had the opportunity to offer a number of graduate seminars at the University of Hawai'i dealing with the topics and themes discussed here. I am immensely grateful to the many friends, colleagues, and students who have encouraged me in this endeavor and who have given so generously of their time, critical intelligence, and wisdom. I am also very grateful to Michael Krausz for his persistence in helping to bring this work into publication.

I am most grateful, though, to my wife, Marcia, to whom this work is dedicated, for continuing to show me so many new possibilities of creative being.

PART I

1

✳

On Being a Person

Two dimensions or domains of our human being are clearly given to us: first, all the universal, general and particular conditions, materials and features that constitute our individual being; second, that spontaneous vitality, the essential spirituality, that is the ground of our being. I call these the human being as *an individual* and as *the Self,* respectively. *A person,* I want to argue, is not a given, but an achievement. A person is a creative articulation, in varying degrees of rightness, of his or her individuality within the matrix of social community and within the enduring reality of the Self.

I

An individual, as I use the term (in keeping with considerable philosophic usage), is a meeting place of universal conditions (e.g., the "words" of the genetic code, shared by all forms of life);[1] general conditions (e.g., the nature and functions of the human brain unique to the species); and particular conditions (e.g., those resulting from the accidents of one's birth, language, culture, environment). An individual thus becomes identifiable by us as a human body with its own distinctive physical features, as a functioning human mind with its own special capacities, as a social or economic being belonging to a certain class or having a certain economic status, and so on. An individual, as I use the term, is the locus of whatever is objectifiable in and of a human being and is explainable in terms of those given conditions, materials and features. An individual is thus a concatenation of universal, general and particular empirical constituents that interact with each other and the world in continuous patterns of experience.[2]

3

The Unity of an Individual

The Buddhist doctrine of "no-self" (*anātman* in Sanskrit; *anattā* in Pali), to which we might profitably first turn because it typifies, in a rather extreme way, an empiricist tendency in human thought,[3] claims that I am nothing but a causal series of impersonal and impermanent elements that constitute my empirical being. I am a pattern of experience, but there is no "I" who experiences. Rather there are five groups (*pañca-skandhas*) of unowned and transitory elements: (1) perception (*samjñā*), (2) feelings or sensations (*vedanā*), (3) volitional dispositions or impressions (*saṁskāras*—all the impulses, emotions, and memories that are associated with past experience and that influence present and future experience), (4) consciousness or intelligence (*vijñāna*), and (5) the body (*rūpa*). At death nothing persists save the psychic continuity, produced by *karman*, that gives rise to, or forms a continuity with, a new empirical pattern.

In the *Milindapañha*, the famous dialogue between the Buddhist monk Nāgasena and the Greco-Bactrian king Menandar, Nāgasena analyzes a chariot into its constituent elements (pole, axle, wheels, etc.) and concludes that "the word chariot is a mere empty sound," not signifying anything over and above—or underlying—the elements so arranged that constitute it. He then argues: "In exactly the same way, your majesty, Nāgasena is but a way of counting, term, appellation, convenient designation, mere name for the hair of my head . . . form, sensation, perception, the predispositions and consciousness [the *skandhas*]. But in the absolute sense there is no Ego here to be found."[4] Now although it is not clear historically just what *ātman* doctrine Buddhism at the time was opposing, its *anātman* teaching—in what appears to be its essential import as a denial, not of a nondual *ātman* (a denial, that were it made, could not, as later Mahāyāna Buddhist thinkers recognized, be sustained), but of any kind of empirical soul-substance doctrine—is, I believe, philosophically efficacious when applied to the individual human being qua empirical self.[5]

Psychē; anima—the animating principle: but when it is viewed as a substance—in the classical sense as that which, in differentiated modes, underlies and supports various qualities or attributes (e.g., the Aristotelian soul, which must, he says, "be a substance in the form of a natural body having life potentially within it"[6])—it must be acknowledged to be a fiction:

1. It is never knowingly experienced as such; that is, as individuals we never experience ourselves as a substantial entity detached from all other experience. Epistemologically, as subjects we cannot be pure objects to ourselves. Our experience of ourselves at this level, as Kant

and the entire empiricist tradition have shown, is always of some aspect or other of what we take to be ourselves—an idea, an emotion, an impression, a feeling, a memory, and so on.

2. A substantial self or ego cannot be logically inferred only from the bare presence in the individual of physical or mental characteristics; such a nonempirical causal or inhering substance is not in any way entailed by the mere fact of empirical qualities or attributes. The characteristics can just as well be seen to be of, or to be regularly associated with, strictly empirical (yet identifiable) dynamic configurations.

3. A substantial empirical self is not necessary as a postulate to account for what would otherwise be inexplicable—namely, the feeling of self-continuity—for this can be accounted for just as well by a consciousness of oneself as a conditioned pattern of ongoing experience. In other words, we are able to recognize ourselves as temporal, empirical individuals within the structures of experience itself without our having to have recourse to some kind of independently existing, atemporal ego.

But if the *anātman* or no-self teaching is pushed, as it was in Buddhism (e.g., by the Sautrāntikas), to an extreme theory of momentariness (*kṣaṇa*), or to a Humean conception of the self as a *mere* collection of distinct existences, then the teaching seems to preclude the possibility of acknowledging any kind of real synchronic unity or diachronic identity to an individual human being—a unity and identity that, I will argue, is necessary for the achievement of personhood. By virtue of our being conscious, we are not to ourselves an additive sum of separable elements or aggregates. The analogy with the chariot breaks down because of, at least, the *skandha* of consciousness. A chariot or any manufactured article is ontically exhausted, as it were, by an accurate characterization of the elements and relations that constitute it. There is no thing underlying or unifying as such the elements as given in their relations. With human beings, however, consciousness functions not just as one factor or aggregate among others but rather as a central, dominant fact of our experience. With the reflexivity power of consciousness, we have the experience of ourselves not as a *collection* of empirical elements but as a centered, unified conscious being (albeit, as we will see, this holds only within an empirical framework that is on this side, as it were, of the reality of the Self).[7]

This does not mean, though, as it has often been believed, that we are then called on to affirm within ourselves some kind of radical dualism between the mind (consciousness) and the body. We are not, in our normal consciousness of ourselves as individuals, constituted of separable physical and mental processes; that is, we are not normally aware of ourselves as being a conjunction of disparate and opposed orders of being any more than we are aware of being a mere collection of aggregates.[8] Phenomenologically we are neither Buddhists nor Cartesians. Unexciting as it may be, at this level of experience each of us is aware of himself or herself, it would seem, simply as a unity in and of itself. Ineluctably in our ordinary, primitive self-consciousness we have simply an awareness of ourselves as an I and a me to which various qualities and characteristics may be ascribed.

What this amounts to is saying that I am aware of myself as a subject that can be objectified and explained. At this level of experience I am aware of myself as a locus of various qualities and characteristics. Although I may use the possessive with respect to the physical and mental (e.g., my body, my mind), and in ordinary language even identify myself with one or the other (e.g., I am beautiful or ugly; smart or dumb), I am not aware of myself as being just a body or a mind or any other isolable thing.[9]

So far we have approached the unity of an individual primarily in phenomenological or experiential terms. It is also the case, I believe, that a straightforward analysis of the meaning of "individuality" commits us to affirm the unity of individuals; for when we ascribe individuality to anything we mean the thing precisely as a distinct particular, that is, we acknowledge that the object appears to us as a unified entity. We would not recognize a mere association or collection of things as an object or thing in itself. On a table, for example, there might be a pencil, a coffee cup, a bowl of fruit, and a newspaper. Taken as elements (of a visual whole), these things would not together constitute a distinct particular or ontological entity, and although the elements might persist unchanged in their relations to one another, one would not in the least be tempted to ascribe thinghood to the collection in virtue of the persistency of the spatial relations obtaining among the individual objects that make it up. Unless one is able to construe the elements as parts of some ontologically (and not merely perceived) whole entity, one would not ascribe particularity to the perceived gestalt, to what is simply perceived as being together. One must, in short, presuppose a unity before one can recognize or ascribe ontic particularity to a thing, or, to put it another way, the acknowledgment that something is a particular thing entails that it is a unified thing. It would make no sense to say that I see X as a distinct particular but I don't believe that it has a unity.

But surely, it might be objected, what distinguishes a mere visual whole from an ontic particular is the kind of relatedness that obtains between the elements that respectively constitute them. With the visual whole we have only (contingent) spatial relatedness of a quantitative (i.e.,

strictly measurable) kind. With ontic particulars we have, as with manufactured things such as a chair, a functional relatedness of legs, seat, back
and so on, or, as with created things such as a painting, an aesthetic or
qualitative relatedness of elements such as line, colors, and shapes
according to a sense of their right or appropriate placement, or, as with
animate things such as a dog, an organic dependency that allows the
thing to bark, eat, run, and exercise a certain control of, and response to,
itself and its environment. Unity, therefore, is not primitive; it is analyzable in terms of the kind of relatedness of the elements that constitute
what is taken as a unified thing.

But it is clear that a distinction must here be made between the *meaning*
of unity and the *test* for unity. If one is in doubt about whether a certain
visual whole has ontic particularity, one would indeed look closely at just
the kind of relatedness of the elements that constitute it. The difference
between a collage and the things on my desk (as making for a visual
whole) would be determined by my ability to note the qualitative, created
relations obtaining among the selected elements of the collage. But this
would be testing for unity when one is confronted with a doubtful case.

The meaning of unity does not call for our breaking something (actually or analytically) into pieces and then seeing how they are put together.
Unity is primitive: a transcendental condition (in the Kantian sense), if
you will, for the possibility of identifying an object as a particular entity
or process.

The things of the world nevertheless are not usually delivered to us as
merely simple unified things; rather their unity or numerical identity is
often a matter of negotiation, as it were, between consciousness and
world. Some things, to be sure, assert their individuality in rather clear
ways (a chair); other things in very uncertain ways (a distant mountain—
Where does it begin and end?), and yet other things in ways that make
doubtful their status as nominal substances (e.g., the collection of paper
clips in my drawer). When we ascribe unity to something, we clearly do
recognize certain features of the world as belonging precisely there; but
this recognition always takes place within and from a particular standpoint of interest and purpose. In his *Elements of Metaphysics*, A. E. Taylor
speaks of this negotiated unity nicely in these terms: "What particular
interest we consider in pronouncing [anything] . . . one, in what interest
we attend to it, may be largely independent of the qualities of the group,
but the fact that the group does function as one in respect to this interest
is no 'fiction' or creation of our own thought; it is the expression of the
nature of the group itself."[10]

It is thus possible and meaningful to affirm the unity of an individual
human being without being committed to a substantialist metaphysics—
for we are not arguing that the unity is a bearer of qualities, that attributes

inhere in it, and so on—or to a naive realist ontology that sees all physical objects as if they were independent givens of an external world. The unity is not a Lockean substantial "I know not what." It is, in this rather dull way, merely a basic content of our self-awareness and a condition by which we identify something qua thing; it is what we mean by ascribing thinghood to some appearance or other. This unity is philosophically important, however, because it can be seen to be the locus of our various depictions, or of what I will call portrayals of an individual, and, most importantly, as it is a condition for the achievement of personhood.

The Portrayal of an Individual

P. F. Strawson has argued effectively that the concept of a person (an individual) is "primitive." It is to be understood, he writes, "as the concept of a type of entity such that *both* predicates ascribing states of consciousness *and* predicates ascribing corporeal characteristics . . . are equally applicable to an individual entity of that type."[11] Rejecting the very basis for the so-called problem of other minds by insisting that one can intelligibly ascribe states of consciousness to oneself only if one is prepared to ascribe them to others, Strawson tries to show that

> the condition of reckoning oneself as a subject of such predicates is that one should also reckon others as subjects of such predicates. The condition, in turn, of this being possible, is that one should be able to distinguish from one another, to pick out or identify, different subjects of such predicates, i.e., different individuals of the type concerned. The condition, in turn, of this being possible is that the individual concerned, including oneself, should be of a certain unique type, namely, such that to each individual of that type there must be ascribed, or ascribable, *both* states of consciousness *and* corporeal characteristics.[12]

Strawson rejects any dualistic or (what he calls) no-ownership account of experience. The dualist cannot show why states of consciousness should be ascribed to anything at all: the holder of a no-ownership (physicalist) view—the view that experiences are not owned by anyone except in the loose sense that they are causally dependent on states of a particular body—cannot state his position coherently without appealing to the very notion of possession that he wants to deny.

Strawson goes on to argue that for the ascription of states of mind to others to be possible the behavioral expressions of states of mind must be more than just signs; they must count rather as logically adequate criteria.

A. J. Ayer, who takes considerable exception to Strawson's view, especially to his notion of logically adequate criteria, nevertheless sums up Strawson's position nicely:

Not everything that we want to say about persons [individuals] can be construed as a statement about the physical objects which are their bodies; still less, when we refer to persons, are we referring to mental substances, or to collections of experiences. Neither, in Mr. Strawson's view, can it be maintained that persons are compound; that they are the product of two separate entities, or sorts of entities, one the subject of physical characteristics and the other the subject of consciousness. He holds, on the contrary, that the subject of which we attribute the properties which imply the presence of consciousness is literally identical with that to which we attribute physical properties.[13]

But how then do we get at the mental and physical in the face of the existential and logical unity of an individual? We do ascribe physical characteristics to an individual (M-predicates in Strawson's terms) in a straightforward enough way for purposes that concern us, and we also employ mental terms to refer to processes with which we are quite familiar—perceiving, conceiving, remembering, imagining—in rather clear and meaningful ways. The answer, I believe, is that we get at the mental and the physical, and perhaps other yet to be disclosed dimensions of individuality, by means of what I would like to call a process of portrayal.[14]

An individual is viewable in an indefinite number of ways. Like any object, she may be perceived from a variety of perspectives that reflect the needs and interests of the perceiver. She may be viewed in mentalistic perspectives (with the categories of psychology or in everyday mentalistic terms); she may be viewed in physicalistic terms (with the concepts of physics and biology, as well as everyday bodily terms); and she may be viewed in other, still-to-be-formulated perspectival frameworks.

An individual, again like any object, is responsive to certain perspectives; that is, she is amenable to being viewed in certain ways. A perspective to which an individual is responsive is a portrait. A portrait is *of* the object; it refers to the object; it is a representation without being a copy. An individual qua individual is portrayed physically, for example, when one is viewed in a physicalistic perspective to which one is responsive— that is, when one is isolated perspectivally as a physical being, is seen as a body, and is able to be dealt with successfully (say, in a scientific, medical analysis) because one can be rightfully represented in that way: empirically one lends oneself to such a perspective. A distorted or simply erroneous perspective is one to which the object is unresponsive: it does not, in the case of an individual, yield a portrait.

Now it is simply a fact that an individual is responsive to portrayal as physical and as mental in a variety of appropriate symbols, models and concepts. His unity is nevertheless preserved, for the individual qua individual defies reduction to any of its portraits. A portrait is at once a perspective upon and a representation of; it refers to its object but does not mirror the object in such a way as to exhaust its possible richness. A portrait is not a duplication, and no mere addition of portraits can fully represent the object: its past is infinitely rich, and future (i.e., as yet unformulated) perspectives are possible.[15] Our empirical knowledge, in short, is always and necessarily incomplete.

We have, then, a unity of an individual, with an individual being portrayable in various ways—namely, but not necessarily exhaustively, in mentalistic and physicalistic terms. The unity of an individual is not a transcendental ego, as no underlying unifying functions as such are ascribed to it. The locus of the unity is neither the mental nor the physical, taken as portraits; rather it is the individual, as primitive, as irreducible to any single portrait or any addition of them.

This analysis of an individual's unity and of the mental and the physical as portraits is not put forward as a solution to the traditional mind-body problem. This problem starts with the dualistic assumption, logically and historically, and although various physicalist identity theories and so-called eliminative materialistic ones, as well as some traditional idealist ones, want to collapse the dualism into one or the other of its terms, they are nevertheless bound up with the assumption in their formulation of the problem.[16] I am not arguing, as identity theorists do, that the meaning (sense) of mentalistic language can be maintained while its reference is in fact the physical; I am arguing, rather, that mentalistic conceptual frameworks and physicalistic ones may well be adequate portrayals insofar as they succeed in doing what is intended by them. I am also not arguing for any Spinoza-like double aspect theory, which would hold that the physical and the mental are both aspects of something that is neither physical nor mental as such—the something being conceived as an underlying substance that is viewed or considered under different attributes. As I have indicated, the unity of an individual is regarded logically just as the condition for identification of something qua individual thing and experientially as the locus for our attributions of qualities and characteristics. At this empirical level of analysis and being we have unified appearances that are portrayable in various ways, some of the portraits proving to be adequate for the purposes intended by them. A portrait theory of the physical and the mental is close to a double-aspect theory in its perspectival dimension; but it differs from it rather radically in its rejection of any claims about the substantiality of the individual. It is enough, I believe, to say that portraits, like ascriptions of attributes, refer to a single subject—whose singleness as individual is unanalyzable into other categories. A portrait in physicalistic terms is the individual as rendered in certain observable (directly or indirectly by instruments) characteristics of a quantifiable sort. A portrait in mentalistic terms is the individual as depicted through certain cognitive, emotional, and volitional dispositions and capacities. A portrait refers to the individual, but it does not exhaust her. An individual, we say, is responsive to a variety of perspectives; the resultant portraits are of her, but no single portrait or mere addition of portraits captures her. Unity is preserved, as it is not portrayable as such. This brings us to the question of an individual's identity.

Individual Identity

Sydney Shoemaker has allowed that "it is obvious that the existence of a special problem about the nature of persons, and the nature of personal identity, is somehow connected with the fact that persons have minds."[17] He goes on to say that "it is primarily the ways in which first-person statements are made and known, not the ways in which third-person statements are made and known, that give rise to a special problem about the nature of persons and personal identity."[18] And Bernard Williams states that "there is a special problem about personal identity for two reasons. The first is self-consciousness—the fact that there seems to be a peculiar sense in which a man is conscious of his own identity. . . . The second reason is that a question of personal identity is evidently not answered merely by deciding the identity of a certain physical body."[19] Terence Penelhum, on the other hand, finds the genesis of the problem of personal identity in reidentification. "To reidentify someone is to say or imply that in spite of a lapse of time and the changes it may have wrought, the person before us now is the same person we knew before. When," Penelhum asks, "are we justified in saying such a thing and when are we not?"[20]

In his *A Treatise of Human Nature*, David Hume answers this way: "It must be some one impression, that gives rise to every real idea. But self or person is not any one impression, but that to which our several impressions are suppos'd to have a reference. If any impression gives rise to the idea of self, that impression must continue invariably the same, thro' the whole course of our lives; since self is suppos'd to exist after that manner. But there is no impression constant and invariable." He goes on in a famous passage to say that "for my part when I enter most intimately into what I call *myself*, I always stumble on some particular perception or other, of heat or cold, light or shade, love or hatred, pain or pleasure. I never catch *myself* at any time without a perception, and never can observe any thing but the perception." And concludes that he can venture for mankind "that they are nothing but a bundle or collection of different perceptions, which succeed each other with an inconceivable rapidity, and are in a perpetual flux and movement."[21]

The question then naturally arises as to why and how we ascribe identity to these successive perceptions. Hume answers that we simply confound the notion of identity or sameness of an object "that remains invariable and uninterrupted through a suppos'd variation of time" with the idea of diversity, of "several different objects existing in succession." Resemblance, he says, is "the cause of the confusion, and makes us substitute the notion of identity, instead of that of related objects." To prove this position he has then "to shew from daily experience and observation, that the objects, which are variable or interrupted, and yet are suppos'd to continue the same, are such only as consist of a succession of parts, connected together by resemblance, contiguity, or causation."

After supposedly doing this, Hume goes on to show the importance of memory in contributing to identity. "Had we no memory," he writes, "we never shou'd have any notion of causation, nor consequently of that chain of causes and effects, which constitute our self or person." He is then able to claim,

> The whole of this doctrine leads us to a conclusion, which is of great importance in the present affair, viz., that all the nice and subtle questions concerning personal identity can never possibly be decided, and are to be regarded rather as grammatical that as philosophical difficulties. Identity depends on the relation of ideas; and these relations produce identity, by means of that easy transition they occasion. But as the relations, and the easiness of the transition may diminish by insensible degrees, we have no just standard by which we can decide any dispute concerning the time when they acquire or lose a title to the name of identity. All the disputes concerning the identity of connected objects are merely verbal, except so far as the relations of parts give rise to some fiction or imaginary principle of union, as we have already observ'd.[22]

Hume was undoubtedly right in not being able to find a substantial enduring self within a mere succession of perceptions as such, but he was wrong to look for it there in the first place. And he was also wrong conceptually (or grammatically, as he might want to call it) in assuming that on the empirical level some kind of internal invariance is the standard of, or is what we mean by, "identity." Although there might not be a single criterion for it, "identity," as we use the term, is a relational and transactional category. Something is identical or is the same only in a context of its relationship to something else. The Mississippi River, once so identified, is the same river even though it is forever changing (and, contra the popular view of Heraclitus, we can step into it twice or more) because it bears continuing spatial relations with other things in a larger geographical context. This is what we mean when we say that it is the same river.

Identity and sameness thus do not refer to completely unchanging inner states of an object, and especially not to its materiality as such. All sorts of changes are compatible with the identity of something *for us.* I emphasize the words "for us," because our recognition of identity is, just like our acknowledgment of unity, very much a function of our interest in the object; that is to say, to ascribe identity to an object, or to withhold the ascription due to a number of changes in the object, is a matter of judgment relative to our interests and not a matter of identifying a certain essential attribute that must abide in some particular substance or of stipulating that certain names be "rigid designators." Although most of the time most persons do agree on when changes are such as to call for a different thing, it is quite possible to have a persisting identity ascribed to something even when we have radical changes indeed.

Suppose, to take an extreme (Humean) example, that a village church is destroyed by fire and that a new one is built on the exact model of the old building. To the architect and builder, and to many others, the new building is clearly a different building than the original; but one can well imagine the local pastor, and at least some members of his congregation, so emphasizing the continuity of the community in relation to its building that they regard the new building as the same as the old one. The changes made, radical as they are, are still compatible with an ascription of identity. The different structures would for them simply be stages in a single process, the life of the church (qua church building).

With this understanding of identity, an individual can indeed be said to be the same in a number of ways. Each individual can be identical, depending on the maintenance of his or her basic relationships with other beings and modes of being. An individual, in other words, may have an identity, be the same over time, as he or she maintains some core of sustaining relationships with friends and with family, with the natural environment, with a divine being and so on. The I retains itself, by this use of sameness, as a relational being and not as a thing having an isolable and recognizable essence or invariant materiality.

Moreover, at the empirical level the phenomenon of memory when approached in a special way, provides another (more phenomenologically grounded) basis for establishing individual identity. I recognize and acknowledge that it is indeed arguable whether it is possible to demonstrate any kind of individual identity without referring in one way or another to the physical as we know and experience it from portraits. Many philosophers, however, from Locke to Thomas Nagel would insist that our concept of individual identity is one that need not make any specific appeal to the somatic. Locke believed indeed that one was accountable only for those actions which one could recognize by way of remembrance as one's own: "For it is the same consciousness that makes a man be himself, personal identity depends on that only, whether it be annexed solely to one individual [material] substance or can be continued in a succession of several substances. For as far as any intelligent being can repeat the idea of any past action with the same consciousness it had of it at first, and with the same consciousness it has of any present action so far it is the same personal self.[23]

Thomas Nagel believes that our concept of the self, if it refers at all, "must refer to something essentially subjective . . . which is the persisting locus of mental states and activities and the vehicle for carrying forward familiar psychological continuities when they occur."[24] Although Nagel goes on to argue that this concept does not tell us what the self actually is and that this would necessarily involve an appeal to one's having a brain (for it would be inconceivable how we could be the same person now and in the future with its absence or replacement), he nevertheless asserts that "it is clearly part of the idea of my identity that I could have led a completely different mental life from birth. This would have happened, for example, if I had been adopted at birth and brought up in Argentina."[25] Now apart from the awkward question-begging here, we seem to have, for Nagel, a kind of disembodied identity that has nothing to do with experience or with the kind (and quality) of actions that we perform.[26] As we will want to show later, however, who I am is very much related to what I do and how I do what I do—psychophysically. Individual identity can never be properly divorced from an individual's actual experience, and this clearly involves somatic as well as purely mental considerations.

The traditional bias for the mental over the physical in demonstrating personal identity, however, is quite understandable; for (1) we tend to identify ourselves at least, if not others, by the consistency and continuity of our mental capacities, states, and dispositions as relationally determined (albeit we would be duly shocked in the morning to see someone else looking back at us from the bathroom mirror); (2) we know that our bodies can undergo radical changes without causing a complete loss of individual identity; and (3) we can at times dissociate consciousness from any awareness of the physical without losing a sense of ourselves (e.g., when concentrating intensely on something or other). In any event, in arguing for individual identity on the basis of memory I do not claim that this is the only way to establish that identity; I want only to argue that memory, when approached in a special way, is able to provide one basis for it.

Commenting on *Brahmasūtra* II.2.25 (*anusmṛteh ca*), Śaṃkara (ca. 788–820), the leading philosopher of the nondualistic (Advaita) Vedānta school of Indian philosophy, proffers an interesting (Lockean) argument against the Buddhists. He argues that the phenomenon of memory or remembrance (*smṛti*) implies a kind of personal identity that is incompatible with the Buddhist doctrine of momentariness.

The [Buddhist] philosopher who maintains that all things are momentary only would have to extend that doctrine to the perceiving person (*upalabdṛ*) also; that is, however, not possible, on account of the remembrance which is consequent on the original perception. That remembrance can take place only if it belongs to the same person who previously made the perception; for we observe that what one man has experienced is not remembered by another man. How, indeed, could there arise the conscious state expressed in the sentences, "I saw that thing, and now I see this thing," if the seeing person were not in both cases the same.[27]

Śaṃkara is saying that remembrance and the activities of memory are based on past experience and that a necessary condition for remembrance is that there be a same individual who has the experience and who makes the recollection. Experience gives rise to memory, and the fact of memory implies an identical individual who is carrying out the memory act and who had the original experience. One does not have direct memories of another person's experience. If it were not the same I who had the experience and who remembers it, memory itself would be completely unintelligible.

Some of the well-known difficulties in this argument (e.g., How are we to decide between a genuine and an apparent memory in any given case? It is too stringent to restrict personal identity to cases where a person can actually recall his past actions or experiences) can be overcome and the argument from memory strengthened considerably if we argue not so much from the fact that we have memories of past experiences as from the manner in which we, in fact, remember. One of the most striking things to note in most discussions of individual identity that involve an appeal to memory is the almost simple-minded understanding of memory that is exhibited. Memory seems to be understood as if it were essentially a mere projection of images on a mental screen. Hume states, "For what is memory but a faculty, by which we raise up the image of past experience."[28] And from this we get all the fanciful discussion in analytic philosophy about what it would mean to have another person's memories (or quasi-memories). Derek Parfit, for example, in his bold if slightly crazy analysis of personal identity (which notion is finally dispensed with in favor of the idea that we are but serial selves that connect with one another in greater or lesser degree of strength and continuity: a modern day Buddhism *sans* karma), conjures up the idea of a quasi-memory. "I have," he says, "an accurate quasi-memory of a past experience if (1) I seem to remember having an experience; (2) someone did have this experience; and (3) my apparent memory is causally dependent, in the right kind of way, on that past experience."

He goes on to say, "We do not quasi-remember other people's past

experiences. But we might begin to do so. The causes of long-term memories are memory-traces. . . . Suppose that . . . neuro-surgeons develop ways
to create in one brain a copy of a memory-trace in another brain. This
might enable us to quasi-remember other people's past experience."[29] The
account of memory he then gives in a science-fiction-like example is once
again Humean in its sole reference to images (and sounds).

> *Venetian Memories.* Jane has agreed to have copied in her brain some of Paul's
> memory traces. After she recovers consciousness in the post-surgery room,
> she has a set of vivid apparent memories. She seems to remember walking
> on the marble paving of a square, hearing the flapping of flying pigeons and
> the cries of gulls, and seeing light sparkling on green water. One apparent
> memory is very clear. She seems to remember looking across the water to an
> island, where a white Palladian church stood out brilliantly against a dark
> thundercloud.[30]

But memories are extraordinarily complex phenomena, having strong
affective dimensions and involving various kinds of evaluative features
built into the selectivity (the presencing and forgetting) that is always
operative. Depth psychology, of which writers like Nagel, Williams, and
Parfit seem to be unaware, teaches us that on the one hand we retain too
much, even aspects of primordial, ancestral experience, and on the other
have available in our waking consciousness too little, by way of all the
defense mechanisms of repression we employ. In any event, subconscious
or not, we clearly remember (with contents that bear on questions of personal identity) not as isolable image projections that are shorn of all emotive content and value but in terms of selected frames of reference. When
one refers to a series of past experiences, to a memory-gestalt, one necessarily sees it from a particular point of view in one's past experience, with
this standpoint becoming constitutive of the memory act carried out in
the present. One constitutes memories from the standpoint of an important (to the experiencer) aspect of the memory gestalt. When you look
back over, say, the last few months of your experience, you order the flow
of events, reactions, feelings, thoughts, dreams—the contents of your consciousness—selectively in terms of one or more dominant event(s), reac-
tion(s), or feeling(s), and you see all other contents in relation to it. All
memory acts that range over a series of events occur in reference frames
of this sort, and it is this constitutive power of reference frames to order
past experience that makes for the possibility of affirming individual
identity at this level of experience.

I cannot constitute your experience. I cannot select the reference frames
by which you order, in a constitutive way, the contents of your consciousness, and the selection for myself, and this is a crucial point, is never

wholly self-conscious or voluntary. The dominant patterns or aspects of experience are dominant not because I arbitrarily decide they will be but because they in fact are, within the complex fabric of my past experience itself. Often we are disturbed by dominant patterns that have become reference frames constitutive of our experience and that are disclosed so sharply in dreams; we want to shake ourselves free from them, and we become pathological when we are utterly their victims; when, at any given time, we feel unable to order, to constitute, our experience in any other way, and when we feel driven to dwell on past experience in terms of a particular event, reaction, or happening. Most often, though, the frame of reference that is operative is a matter of both choice and necessity; that is, we can choose among several competing dominant features of our experience and can move easily from one to another.

This process could not take place, however, unless the individual who has the feelings, the thoughts, is the same individual who makes them coherent to himself. One is able to recognize oneself in oneself at any given moment, so to speak, only because one is the same individual.

This argument from memory, unlike a Śaṃkara-Lockean one, is not essentially circular. Joseph Butler pointed out some time ago that memory presupposes, and does not constitute, personal identity. More recently it has been stated that "something can be a genuine memory of an earlier mental event only if the earlier event was experienced by the same person. Thus, memory already presupposes the concept of the mind and cannot be used to explain that concept."[31]

By arguing that it is the manner in which we are predisposed at any present moment to structure past experience that assures our individual identity, we are not dependent on the accuracy of a subject's memories or even on his being aware of remembering. It is the private and partly involuntary character of the selection of reference frames that ensures the sameness of the remembering subject and not the fact that one has (reliable or otherwise) memories of one's past experience.

Social Individuality

So far I have discussed the concept of an individual as an insubstantial locus of empirical attributes that is nevertheless unified, that is portrayable in diverse ways—namely, the physical and the mental—and that has an identity that can (Hume notwithstanding) be understood analytically in terms of the constancy of relations it maintains and can be demonstrated phenomenologically in at least one way by the manner in which memory functions. All this might suggest that we can conceive of an individual as an asocial, autonomous concentration of various indifferent conditions. This, of course, is not the case. Any adequate analysis of indi-

viduality—and this has been presupposed throughout the discussion—
discloses clearly that various social dimensions of experience are constitutive of that very individuality.

Alasdair MacIntyre has argued, quite effectively it seems to me, that a
person (what he calls a character) is one who embodies and lives a narrative history that is uniquely his or her own but which at the same time is
thoroughly grounded in the social. He writes: "I am forever whatever I
have been at any time for others—and I may at any time be called upon
to answer for it—no matter how changed I may be now. There is no way
of *founding* my identity—or lack of it—on the psychological continuity or
discontinuity of the self. The self inhabits a character whose unity is given
as the unity of a character."[32] MacIntyre goes on to say that "The narrative
of any one life is part of an interlocking set of narratives."[33] He adds that
"The story of my life is always embedded in the story of those communities from which I derive my identity . . . The possession of an historical
identity and the possession of a social identity coincide."[34]

Another way of putting this would be to say that one's social relations,
especially close and intimate ones, are part and parcel of one's facticity,
one's objectifiable individuality. We cannot even conceive of an individual apart from others, for the interactions between a human being and his
world are always socially mediated. One's native language clearly enters
into the very fabric of one's perceptual experience; the conventions, man-
ners, and expectations of one's society obviously inform one's behavior,
and so on. A human being in his social individuality is ineluctably a
bearer of his culture.

II

But not in his pure spontaneity. The Self, the deepest level of our human
being, knows nothing of an other. It is undifferentiated, without time or
space, and thus cannot be known as an object of thought. Nevertheless it
can—as testified to by many throughout history—be fully realized as a
state of conscious being, as a surpassing value, as a plenitude and joy of
being.

According to Kant, whose problem of the self is instructive, the self
("myself as I am") cannot be either known or realized directly in experience. The self, as the synthetic or transcendental unity of apperception, is
just a condition for knowledge; it is that by which continuity and order
are sustained in experience as the very possibility of experience. Conscious to itself, as it were, this self is nevertheless unrealized in experience
and cannot be known as an object of direct knowledge. Kant writes, "If . . .
we admit that we know objects only in so far as we are externally affected,

we must also recognize, as regards inner sense, that by means of it we intuit ourselves only as we are inwardly affected by ourselves; in other words, that, so far as inner intuition is concerned, we know our own subject only as appearance, not as it is in itself."[35] And continues: "I have no knowledge of myself as I am but merely as I appear to myself. The consciousness of self is thus very far from being a knowledge of the self."[36]

The "I think" that, according to Kant, "expresses the act of determining my existence"[37] and that "accompanies all of our representations," cannot itself be perceived and thereby be known. Nothing permanent, no unification of all categories, can be delivered by an inner intuition. Insofar as I think myself I can see myself only temporally, as a succession of states, as a phenomenon. Although it is the basis for making all other experience intelligible, the thinking self (myself as I really am) thus remains unintelligible.

For Kant, then, I am not to be reduced to my experience and yet I do not have the qualities and characteristics that allow me to be known independent of my experience. Hence the problem of the self. But if the empirical or phenomenal self has as its ground reality itself and is simply misperceived when taken to be an ultimate reality by one who is lacking genuine knowledge, then there is no longer a *problem* of the self, but only the (immense) difficulty of tearing aside the misidentifications that we make of ourselves as empirical beings. The epistemological problem becomes psychological and ontological and is confronted successfully only when, through arduous mental discrimination and discipline, the Self as pure spontaneity is realized to be identical to reality in and through immediate spiritual experience.

III

A Person as an Achievement

A human being, I argue, realizes himself as he ought to be to the degree to which he becomes a person. On this account personhood, then, is an achievement; it is not simply given to us in virtue of our being human. The word "person," then, as I use it, is not synonymous with "mind" or an "individual rational human being." Boethius' classic definition— *Persona est substantia individua rationalis naturae*—that was so influential in medieval thought and indeed remains typical of much modern thinking (e.g., Locke's definition of a person as "a thinking, intelligent being, that has reason and reflection and can consider self as itself"[38]) grants personhood to everyone (except perhaps idiots and very young children) as a given of being human. But if apart from some possible, and no doubt considerable, advantages that might be had for legal purposes, we collapse all that is obviously achieved in our human development to givens, an enormous gap will exist between what we recognize to be psychological facts and our philosophical concepts. It would seem quite obvious that our fundamental notions about who and what we are need to take into account the readily observable phenomena of person development: that we are not just a set of given conditions that bear a simple unity and identity but that, from within those conditions and the spiritual depth of being we develop and fulfill, in varying degrees, our several (cognitive, physical, emotive, etc.) capacities and acquire our own styles of being. We become, in short, distinctively crafted social, historical, cultural beings.

As an achievement term, then, "person" necessarily involves a sense of ideality—which is to say, the explication of what it means to be a person will involve a mapping out of ideal possibilities that are realizable along a continuum of achievement. Some among us approach full personhood, whereby we exhibit a rich articulation of the potentialities of our nature. Others among us border on being mere individuals dominated by our thinghood, our identification of ourselves only as products of historical, social, economic, and political forces (or, in extreme cases, as their victims). Without underestimating the importance of these forces (for indeed they play a crucial role in the attainment of, or failure to attain, personhood), we can readily acknowledge that a human being qua an individual is unrealized; she fails to exhibit her own nature as the person she potentially is.

A person, as I use the term, is a dynamic integration of the particular conditions and universal features of her individual being, an integration that is articulated in a manner that, while allowing for multiple appearances, is appropriate for herself. She is a person, in varying degrees, who realizes the Self and makes the conditions of her individuality opportunities for nonegocentric, socially informed growth. Let me explain.

Apart from the bare unity that we enjoy as individuals, each of us—as a full-bodied human being—strives for a psychophysical unification of the diverse raw materials of our individual being; what developmental psychologists call a striving for integration. It does seem clear enough that, through complex functions of learning, of adaptation and acculturation, we become socially informed organizations of various traits and habits that yield a personal *identification* (not just identity) that we call "me." Among the givens of our individual human being are precisely the power and capacity to transform the brute conditions of individuality by way of ongoing dynamic integrations of these conditions into higher-order sustaining configurations. We become centered in and through certain dominant values and interests that, while often partly imposed upon us, are nevertheless selected by us—and are often created by us—within the framework of our culture. We become differentiated into identifiable personalities with our own characteristic ways of acting and reacting.

A person, then, must appropriate his individual being in order for him to rightly articulate that being; he must acknowledge and assimilate that which he is as an individual. This sounds simple enough, perhaps almost simple-minded, until we realize that most of the time most of us are at best only part owners of what we are: we are dissociated in varying degrees from our minds, which seem so often to have independent lives of their own, running as they do in all directions and filled as they are with involuntary contents; we are alien and hostile to ourselves as physical beings, believing as we do that we simply either have or are bodies. A person, on the other hand, appropriates the given mental and physical conditions of his individuality in such a way that, while subject to continual alterations, they become his own. One can be self-creative only with the materials of "own being." A fully developed person, in short, cannot be divided and alienated from himself.[39]

Masking: A Person qua Persona

We have said that personhood is an articulation of one's being. Articulation, I believe, is a special kind of masking, as is suggested by the etymology of the word "person" which, we are frequently told, derives from the Latin *persona*, originally referring to the theatrical mask used in Greek and later Roman theater.[40] The term was apparently used (e.g., by Cicero)[41] in several distinct ways, including references to one's appearance to others, one's set of individual qualities, and one's social role or function. Personae were thought to conceal as well as to reveal. Psychologically they are partly voluntary (as artifice) and partly involuntary (as faithful presentation). To be articulated rightly as a person, I want to argue, means essentially to create masks that fit properly.

Many masks fit too tightly and thus are utterly transparent. When masking, as an articulation, is completely coextensive with individual personality development, one simply becomes the appearances that are formed. The mask reveals too much: the person is exhausted by his or her appearance. Many masks, on the other hand, fit too loosely and thus are altogether opaque. Here there is a marked discrepancy between one's inward life, as it were, and one's actual presentation. The mask conceals too much: the person hides from himself and others. When the mask fits rightly it becomes the articulation of a genuine person. When the mask fits rightly, then, one becomes the mask insofar as it is the presentation of an integrated personality; one does not become it, however, insofar as there remains a distance between the wearer in his or her self-transcendence and what is worn. This vital space is possible and necessary because of the subsistence of the Self.

It is from an awareness of the incommensurability of reality (the Self as pure spontaneity) and appearance (an individual qua individual) that genuine masking is possible, for without that awareness there are only earnest egos striving fanatically to be something or other. With consciousness of the Self we have person development as a kind of play. Masking becomes a creative undertaking that is aware of itself and its ground. The consciousness of the Self involves an awareness of a surpassing reality and value and consequently an awareness of the pretension in all other value schemes. It yields then a detachment that carries along with it the recognition of the illusory character of all that is not, or is taken to be in some way independent of, the Self. When the mask fits rightly, when there is the detachment and recognition consequent on self-realization, one is aware that one is not exhausted by one's presentation. One is aware of the opportunity and freedom to be creative of personhood.

But the creativity, the masking, is not arbitrary. A person is not like a professional actor who can convincingly assume any role; the mask must relate closely to, in order for it to be medium for, the expression of the integrated person. A person is always playing a role, for to be maskless is not, as some gurus of self-improvement would have us believe, to be most natural; it is rather to be nonformed, undeveloped—to be maskless is to be naïve, as distinct from having a richly formed innocence.

When the mask fits too tightly, then, at the extreme, there is no room for creative play; the actor is unaware of being his or her role. When the mask is too loose, it has no relation to the personality of the wearer; the actor becomes a poseur. When consciousness of Self is absent, we have either stubborn individuality or empty artificiality. When masks fit properly, on the other hand, when there is consciousness of the Self and creative play, the masks are like the personae of the trinity: each has an integrity of its own while remaining identical with that which it presents. A mask thus need not essentially hide one's "true being." The presentation that is rightly articulated is not something that is deceptive to others and alien to oneself; it is a proper showing. It is the person in action.

The term "personhood" is thus at once substantive and adverbial; it refers to the actor and to the way she acts, and, although a person has a characteristic rhythm that governs her actions, one of course acts in many ways: as a social being one is called on to play many roles. A secondary masking occurs when, from the primary persona, we form temporary, organized presentations that serve various functional ends. We show multiple appearants; we become, as it is said, multiple, functional selves. But these too may—indeed must—be carried out with that creative play associated with the articulation of the persona proper. A developed person does not purposively manipulate himself in order to manipulate others (to do so would be to be only for the other); rather he assumes specific stances or postures that are appropriate for the situation at hand and that continue to present his primary persona. Multiple appearances thus need not be disconnected, autonomous systems, a sign of pathological disunity; rather they may be natural expressions of the primary persona.

Personhood, we have said, is a process of articulation; it is a forming, a shaping, a making evident a possibility of human being—and it thus involves the inarticulate or nonarticulated as well. An articulation of a possibility forms the contexts within which it is itself defined and determined. There is the unsaid, the silence, that belongs with what is shaped and formed. The articulate carries its background, as it were, along with it as part and parcel of its being. The mask that fits rightly shows itself as continually drawing from the spiritual richness of its being.

Articulation is thus a kind of self-cultivation (in the best Confucian sense) or crafting of person. It is a reaching into the depth of human being—a sending down of the roots, a forming of one's being in an explicit fashion with care and concern. It is a vital state of standing in openness to being. Crafting is thus a kind of imitation. But this imitation must be sharply distinguished from simple copying. Copying deals with mere appearance; imitation with that which is grounded in reality. Copying is a mere assumption of form; imitation is a forming that gives rise to what is unique and right for itself.[42]

Trustfulness: A Person as a Loving Being

A person who is right for herself is one in whom we are inclined, in the most natural way, to place our trust. The truthful is the trustful.[43] What makes a person trustful?

We recognize in a person whom we trust the presence of a wholeness—a sincere affirmation of herself as she ought to be according to the conditions, both individual and universal, of her own being—and an openness to our own being. The authentic, the true, is the honest—but not so much in the moral sense of honesty (as truth telling) as in the ontological sense of being-in-honesty, of being expressive of one's spiritual potentialities to be a loving human being.

The authentic, the trustful, differs from the reliable in this: to trust someone is to recognize the love in the other, while to rely on someone (to believe that he is reliable) is merely to recognize his competence in the matter at hand and to believe that he has no reason to be harmful to me. A genuine person is a loving being. One is, by virtue of the strength of one's own being, harmless; that is, one stands confidently in one's own being and in recognition of the valuable being of the other.

It is important to emphasize this relation between a person and his ontological ground, for views of personhood qua development and realization are often accused of harboring a peculiar amorality; they allow, it is argued, for there to be no incompatibility between being a fully developed person and being able to commit heinous acts. A Hitler, a Ghengis Khan, or your everyday pedestrian murderer could be true to himself. But by insisting that the content of personhood is grounded in our spiritual being we have as sharp an incompatibility as is possible between person realization and acts of destruction and exploitation. To be a fully developed person means to be a loving being, not in a sentimental, self-centered, romantic way, but in a manner that exhibits a sensitivity, informed by knowledge and understanding, which expresses an affirmation (celebration) of own-self and other.

Nonegocentricity

This brings us to the question of the ego, for one of the key factors in the development of personhood is the maturation of the ego—from being an appropriating center for narrow possessiveness to being a vital locus for creative power.

William James once pointed out that "no more fiendish punishment could be devised . . . than that one should be turned loose in society and remain absolutely unnoticed by all the members thereof."[44] Without the recognition accorded to us by others we become quite literally nothing to ourselves. Dependent on others for its very being, the ego, in its natural development, becomes thoroughly social; that is, it functions in contexts where the other is seen as a potential threat to me or as that which might aid me in fulfilling some purpose or end of my own.[45]

The ego then becomes protective and aggressive—and constructs various defenses. I am not speaking here of the elaborate defense mechanisms that psychoanalytic theory tells us we constantly employ, rather of something more elemental, more basic to the life of an individual. I am referring to the manner in which one sets boundaries to one's identification (what one identifies with) and consequently limits to one's experience. With egos we become egocentric; the I extends to what it possesses or what it invests with itself. One of the most distinctive characteristics of the ego—of ourselves as egocentric—is its delimiting function. By compelling an individual to relate only to that which proves useful, the ego closes off a vast world of potential experience.

The Buddha was right: a personal life grounded in ego desire (*tṛṣṇā*) leads inevitably to a narrowly circumscribed life of incompleteness, of running around incessantly on that circle that leads nowhere (*saṁsāra*), of suffering and frustration (*duḥkha*). But as the Buddha also insisted, egocentricity can be overcome and this overcoming is very much a factor in the development of what I call a person.

The term "nonegocentricity," as I use it, however, does not mean the utter destruction or annihilation of the ego; it means rather its transformation so as to allow for a simple ease and assurance of personal being. A total transcendence of the ego might very well be demanded for the full realization of the Self as pure spontaneity, that is, for the realization of the deepest level of one's being; but, for person development, what is required is that one achieves, from that deepest level, a certain spiritual indifference—not an indifference of callous disregard or disinterest but one that assures a sense of community with others. It is an indifference that allows a full openness to experience, for the indifference associated with nonegocentricity is never selective, as is the case with one who uses the appearance of indifference to avoid a conflict that might, were he to enter it, injure his own standing and influence. Such a person quickly abandons even the pretense of impartiality when his own immediate interests are at stake. Spiritual indifference is just that state of basic harmony that gives a person a quiet confidence, a genuine self-assurance, that allows him to be fully sensitive to the other. A flagrant disregard for the reactions and feelings of others, which is so often exhibited by those who masquerade as nonegocentrics, is most often egocentric to an alarming degree. Not caring is thoroughly egocentric and is to be sharply distinguished from that spiritual impartiality associated with the achievement of personhood.

Autonomy of Person

Once a bare unity and a bare identity is ascribed to something, making then a perceptual-conceptual configuration into an individual thing, we immediately have as well qualitative determination, for all perceiving-conceiving is inherently evaluative. We do not see just bare qualities that we assume are attached to substratums, nor do we see something as it is a bare lonesome thing. Rather, we see things relationally as better or worse in the manner and degree to which they exhibit a rightness that we take to be appropriate to them; we see something as it has its own realized being.

Clearly, however, not only do things of the same kind achieve their appropriate realization in varying degrees but also different kinds of things have different capacities or potentialities to achieve a higher unification and identification. Things vary in their capability to be other than they are in their givenness—and surely we recognize that in our perception of them. Individual human beings, we believe, enjoy the possibility of person-making in ways very different from stones and trees.

One of the classic (Aristotelian) definitions of "substance" has to do with independent existence, a substance being precisely that which can exist independently. But nothing in actuality does or can exist in total isolation from a sustaining environment and other individual things. Without air and water, organic being as we know it would be impossible; without other persons and cultural forms of life, no civilized human being would be possible. The independence that is attributed to substance is thus clearly a logical Cartesian-like one (something conceived in and of itself); it is not an existential possibility.

It is, then, perhaps better to speak of someone attaining a higher unification and identification—personhood—not in terms of his achieving some kind of static, lonely independence but of realizing an ongoing, dynamic autonomy. To be independent, especially in its negative sense of not being dependent upon others, oftentimes involves a foreclosing of possibilities, a shutting of oneself off from growing through relationships, and relationships of a very special kind, namely those wherein one strives to bring the other to his or her own appropriate autonomy. The autonomous person is one who transforms social dependencies into care-filled relationships where one's own autonomy is seen to be realized only as one promotes as well the autonomy of others. The word "autonomy" thus suggests not only particularized wholeness and integrity, a self-governing capacity—as though when autonomous one could be self-enclosed, churning away at and with oneself in a presumed isolated splendor—but also a state in which one is at once centered and open, availing and available.

Schleiermacher defined religion as the feeling of absolute dependency upon God—by which he meant not only ontological dependency (God being the primal source of, and sustaining ground for, one's being), but also axiological dependency (God being the value-bestowing center of experience).

The phrase "I am nothing" is either one of the most daring and sublime of human utterances, because it recognizes the ultimate illusion of individuality, or it is one of the most pathetic despair-laden cries to be heard, if it arises from one who fails utterly to recognize that illusion.

Absolute dependency, then, ought to mean the realization of the fullness of being. When the little I or ego is seen to be nothing in itself, a person can then be what he or she ought to be, an autonomous being in play.

Freedom of Person

Maturation is a matter not of discovering who I am but of creating the socially informed sensitive person that is right for me. A person who is right is like a work of art; he or she is a simplification that is richly constituted. As with artworks, it is not the case that there is only one right articulation from within the conditions of individuality. This predetermination of being is antithetical to the very nature of creativity. In both art and life there must be self-determination of being.

The term "freedom," then, as applied to a person qua rightly articulated persona, is simply part and parcel of the meaning of personhood.

The Self, being fully spontaneous, is completely without limit. It is never other than itself.

A person—the integrated, articulated, particular human being—is free to the degree to which he or she realizes the Self and allows that spontaneity to be a determining factor in the creative forming of an appropriate persona.

Freedom is thus a quality of achieved personhood. It is less a condition that allows for something else (e.g., moral responsibility) than simply a property or feature of what is achieved. I am free only insofar as I am as I ought to be—with that ought itself dynamically established within the particular, general, and universal conditions of my being.[46]

In sum: a human being, I have tried to show, must be seen in terms of his or her individuality, Selfhood and personhood.

The Buddhist rightly denies any substantiality to the empirical self and sees the human being as constituted by various groups of impersonal and impermanent elements (the *pañca-skandhas*). He rightly denies substantiality, for it is never experienced as such, it cannot properly be inferred from observable qualities, and it is not necessary as a postulate to account for what would otherwise be inexplicable. But he wrongfully, I argue, regards the human being as just a collection or group of distinguishable elements. With consciousness we are not to ourselves a sum of aggregates. We are, rather, unique subjects, with a spiritual ground of our being.

An individual, we have seen, is the meeting place of empirical possibilities. He or she is the locus of whatever is objectifiable and explainable (particularly, generally, and universally) in and of the human being. An individual has a unity and an identity. The unity is logically primitive, being the condition for the possibility of particularized identification, and is experienced simply as such; which is to say, that as an individual, one is aware of oneself as a subject that may be objectified. Although this awareness is irreducible, it does not foreclose other kinds of depictions. On the contrary, it makes intelligible how mentalistic and physicalistic portraits of an individual are possible. The term "a portrait," as I use it, denotes a perspective to which an individual is responsive. It is a representation, conceptually or symbolically, of him or her; but it is not a copy, an exhaustive presentation. New portraits are always possible, and refinements will no doubt be made in those mental and physical ones we already have.

The identity of an individual can be established in diverse ways. The empiricist's (Humean) difficulty in establishing identity rests, first of all, on a mistaken notion of what is meant by the term "identity." Identity need not imply some kind of internal invariance but rather only the persistency of a thing's relations with other things. What changes (relational and internal) are compatible and what changes are incompatible with a thing's identity become then a matter of decision, with the decision being relative to the decision maker's own interests as well as to the condition of the object as such. At the empirical level of mentality, the phenomenon of memory, when approached in a somewhat un-Humean way, also establishes individual identity, for, when we examine the manner in which we in fact remember, we find that we frame our memory acts with those selected events, reactions, feelings that were of special importance to us, and these become constitutive of our memory acts. The identity of an individual must then be presupposed, for one cannot constitute another's experience. It must be the same individual who has certain feelings and thoughts who can make them coherent to himself. It is thus our predisposition at any present moment to structure past experience in certain distinctive ways that guarantees our identity as individuals.

The Self, I have affirmed, is a nondual state of spiritual being. Beyond temporality, it is pure spontaneity. Unlike the Kantian thinking self which remains forever unknowable, lacking, as we are said to, that intellectual intuition that alone makes self-knowledge possible—the Self as pure spontaneity can indeed be realized; for it is recognized, when the empirical self is no longer misperceived, to have been one's own most proper state of being. The Self is the content of the conscious identity between subject and being.

A *person*, on the other hand, has an identity only as a creative achievement. A person is one who is grounded in spiritual being, in the Self, and who realizes his or her own ought as it is dynamically established, qua personae, within the limiting conditions of his or her individuality. A person is grounded in spiritual freedom and becomes a loving being in virtue of this grounding. A person is an articulation, a crafting, of a unique subjectivity whose rightness is secured through the affirmation and creative transformation of the constraints and conditions of his or her individual being. One realizes oneself as a social being and develops that non-egocentricity that allows one to function in society with integrity, autonomy, and freedom.

NOTES

1. It is often pointed out that "The three-letter words of the genetic code are the same in every creature. CGA means arginine and GCG means alanine—in bats, in beetles, in beach trees, in bacteria. . . . Wherever you go in the world, whatever plant, animal, bug or blob you look at, if it is alive, it will use the same dictionary and know the same code" (Matt Riley, *Genome: The Autobiography of a Species in 23 Chapters* [New York: HarperCollins Publishers, 2000], 21–22).

2. There is, of course, considerable controversy between behavior geneticists and evolutionary psychologists regarding the relative importance of the universal and the particular and the relationships between them. As Riley points out: "behaviour seeks variations between individuals and seeks to link the variation to genes. Evolutionary psychology seeks common human behaviours—human universals, features found in every one of us—and seeks to understand how and why such behaviour must have become partly instinctive. It therefore assumes no individual differences exist, at least for important behaviours. This is because natural selection consumes variation: that is its job. If one version of a gene is much better than another, then the better version will soon be universal to the species and the worse version will soon be extinct. Therefore, evolutionary psychology concludes that if behaviour geneticists find a gene with common variation in it, then it may not be a very important gene, merely an auxiliary. Behaviour geneticists retort that every human gene yet investigated turns out to have variants, so there must be something wrong with the argument from evolutionary psychology" (Riley, *Genome*, 105).

3. The empiricist tendency in Buddhism is most evident in its earliest periods but, with regard to its teachings on the nonsubstantiality of the self or empirical ego, this tendency runs throughout its historical development. It should be noted, however, that the various philosophical teachings of Buddhism form a coherent and interconnected body of doctrine. For our purposes I am isolating (and thereby doing some injustice to) its *anātman* teaching—a teaching which is properly understandable only in connection with other Buddhist theories such as *pratītyasamutpāda* ("dependent co-arising").

4. "The Milindapañha," trans. by Henry Clarke Warren in *Buddhism in Translations* (Cambridge: Harvard University Press, 1953), 133.

5. There has been a good deal of discussion in recent times by scholars of Buddhism regarding whether or not the mainline Buddhist *anātman* teaching should be characterized as a "reductionist" or "eliminist" account of the self. According to Mark Siderits, the reductionist, unlike the eliminist, allows for the meaningful-

ness of what he calls "the personhood convention," that is, that empirically we rightfully refer to an individual as a unified being provided we do so with the understanding that this is only a conventional designation which is useful for a number of reasons, foremost among them being "because it is more conducive to overall welfare than the readily available alternatives" insofar as it allows one "to see one's life (the events in the causal series) as a kind of self-authored narrative." ["Relativism, Objectivity and Comparative Philosophy: Seeing Parfit Through Buddhist Eyes," *The Journal of Indian Philosophy and Religion*, vol. 3 (October 1998), 1–15.

6. See *De Anima*, Bk. II, Ch.1, 422ᵃ in *The Basic Writings of Aristotle*, ed. with an intro. by Richard McKeon (New York: Random House, 1941), 555.

7. When taken seriously as a pragmatic teaching, the *anātman* theory can be acknowledged to be of immense value in breaking attachments to the superficial and petty ego (for who would knowingly be attached to the nonexistent?), which attachment is recognized to be a prime hinderance to spiritual realization. See *Sanyutta-nikya*, iii.66: "Thus perceiving [the truth about the insubstantiality of the *ātman*] . . . the learned disciple feels loathing for the body, for feeling, for perception, for the aggregate, for consciousness. Feeling disgust he becomes free from passion, through freedom from passion he is emancipated."

8. It is, it seems, only when there is a striking disruption (or crisis) that the mental and the physical emerge for us as separate fields or domains of being which, we might believe, additively constitute ourselves as individual beings. To be sure, we learn mentalistic and physicalistic language at an early age, and we are capable of directing attention to either mental or physical phenomena, but a dualism as such of mind and body arises for us only when we are disturbed in such a way that either the one or the other is called upon to engage the disruption and be recognized as a separable functioning process. Existentially it would be pathological to be in a continual dualism. In colloquial English we say "he has cracked up" to suggest such severe mental disturbance, or that "he had a breakdown." The extremely neurotic or psychotic, we might say, tends to a radical pluralism of self; one simultaneously inhabits several worlds (physical, cognitive, emotional and so on) without being grounded existentially in the natural unity or simple ease of his or her individual being. Disjunctiveness (born out of a conjunctive dualism) rather than disunity as such is characteristic of an individual who is situated existentially in a mind-body problem. Descartes himself pointed out that we cannot conceive of a person or a mind as other than indivisible: we know what half of a body might mean and be, but not a half of a self or person. Apart from his metaphysical dualism, however, Descartes was primarily concerned with the existence, not the constitution, of the self and showed how there is no possibility of denying intelligibly one's own existence. It should be pointed out, though, that customarily one asks "Who am I?" and not "Am I?" Were someone to pose the later question seriously we would not know how to answer him, for any answer of a rational sort would have to appeal to just that kind of self-consciousness which is presumably lacking.

9. One can, of course, identify "the body" or "the mind" without reducing the person as such to either of them, just as one can talk about the branches of a

tree without assuming that a tree is nothing more than its branches. In short, we can talk about a thing as a unity and still distinguish different of its features—understanding as well, as we will see with the *portrayal* of an individual, that the features do not have independent, self-sufficient ontological status.

10. A. E. Taylor, *Elements of Metaphysics* (London: Methuen & Co. Ltd., 1903), 126.

11. See P. F. Strawson, *Individuals: An Essay in Descriptive Metaphysics* (Garden City, N.Y.: Doubleday, 1963), 100.

12. Ibid.

13. A. J. Ayer, *The Concept of a Person: And Other Essays* (New York: St. Martin's Press, 1976), 86.

14. I will elaborate on this concept of "portrayal" in some detail in chapter 9, "Epistemic Portraiture."

15. As we will see further in our discussion of the body and consciousness, there is no reason for us to assume that the language, conceptual symbols (and all that is implied with and by these) of the "physical" and the "mental" will be seen always to be the only two primary discourses appropriate to human experience. It is arguable that already with psychoanalytic ideas of the "unconscious" and the "subconscious" raw materials for a new kind of portrait might very well be in the making insofar as the phenomena associated with these domains of experience do not seem to lend themselves very neatly or nicely to usual physicalist or mentalistic language and conceptions. Freud certainly struggled to bring the whole of this language under "instincts," "energies," "motives," "intentions," and the like, but over the long run a new kind of language and conceptualization might be developed that is more appropriate to the experience. The new is always initially stated in terms of the old (and certainly partially distorted thereby). In any event, it would be foolish indeed for us to assume that we have with the "physical" and the "mental" the right overall conceptual scheme that only for the rest of time needs filling out and refining.

16. Derived as it is from Cartesianism, the mind-body problem was traditionally formulated against the background of mechanistic notions of causality, notions that we now know to be inadequate. With a more organic model of causality—based, as I will try to show, on more fundamental forms of empirical experience—new ways of formulating the issue may become apparent.

17. Sydney Shoemaker, *Self-Knowledge and Self-Identity* (Ithaca, N.Y.: Cornell University Press, 1963), 8.

18. Ibid., 9.

19. Bernard Williams, *Problems of the Self* (Cambridge: Cambridge University Press, 1963), 8.

20. Terence Penelhum, "Personal Identity," in *The Encyclopedia of Philosophy*, ed. Paul Edwards (New York: Macmillan and The Free Press, 1967), vol. 6, 95.

21. David Hume, *A Treatise of Human Nature*, I,4.6, ed. L. A. Selby-Biggs (Oxford: Clarendon Press, 1988), 251–52.

22. Ibid., 262.

23. John Locke, *An Essay Concerning Human Understanding* (New York: Valentine Seaman, 1824), 303.

24. Thomas Nagel, *The View from Nowhere* (New York/Oxford: Oxford University Press, 1986), 40.

25. Ibid.

26. Derek Parfit also believes, that "there is no reason to suppose that being transplanted into a very different body would disrupt my psychological continuity." See his *Reasons and Persons* (New York/Oxford: Oxford University Press, 1986), 253.

27. Śaṃkara, *Brahmasūtrabhāṣya*, II.2.25, trans. George Thibaut. *The Vedānta-sūtras with the Commentary of Śaṅkarācārya*, in vol. 34 of *Sacred Books of the East*, ed. Max Muller (Oxford: Clarendon Press, 1890).

28. Hume, *A Treatise of Human Nature*, 260.

29. Derek Parfit, *Reasons and Persons*, 220.

30. Ibid.

31. Jerome Shaffer, "Mind-Body Problem," in *The Encyclopedia of Philosophy*, vol. 5, 337.

32. Alasdair MacIntyre, *After Virtue* (Notre Dame: University of Notre Dame Press, 1981), 202. Much postmodernist thinking, however, has challenged the very idea of a unified self, psychologically grounded or otherwise, in favor of "an open, changing, growing, multiplicity of selves or self-descriptions" which, according to Richard Shusterman, "makes the whole idea of an integral enduring self seem completely empty and suspect." Shusterman goes on, however, and rightly so it seems to me, to remark that "But without such a self [person] that is capable of identity through change or changing description, there can be no self capable of self-enrichment or enlargement and this would nullify the Rortian aesthetic life of self-enrichment by rendering it meaningless." " 'Ethics and Aesthetics are One': Postmodernism's Ethics of Taste," in *After the Future: Postmodern Times and Places*, ed. by Gary Shapiro (Albany: State University of New York Press, 1990), 125.

The crafting of personhood, I have suggested, is made possible by the unity and identity of an individual (conceived in non-substantialist terms) and by the spontaneity of the Self. The postmodernist argument is that our status as individuals, rather than involving numerical or specific identity, is a highly de-centered and fragmentary one. Further, rather than our enjoying an initial psychophysical unity from which we then strive to create a higher unification and identification, what we have to begin with are disparate functional systems with at best only a nominal or analytical unity. Unification, insofar as it is desired and attainable, is thus itself only a temporary achievement and is, in any event, open at all times to new and radically different re-configurings.

Apart from the considerations suggested by Shusterman, the answer to this, I think, is that if the bare unity and identity we have argued for was in fact illusory then one could never make the first move toward the achievement of personhood, for one's energies would be exhausted, as it were, in establishing oneself as some kind or other of functioning unified individual. Without an integrated individuality, it seems to me, we simply could not become, in varying degrees (as indeed we do) the persons that we are. Unconnected, radically contingent, ever-changeable constellations cannot have a narrative history, cannot achieve an appropriate style of being, cannot be a moral agent, and could not begin to make sense of themselves.

33. MacIntyre, *After Virtue*, 203.

34. Ibid., 204. It is with classical Chinese thought more perhaps than with any other tradition that the social dimensions of individuality are recognized and are given central importance. According to mainline Confucian thinking an individual is the center of a network of relationships: I am as I am the son/daughter, the brother/sister of; living here, at this time, and so on. There is simply no way open to a human being to be other than within a family, a community, drawing from and contributing to an ongoing tradition.

Although this stress on the social determinants of individuality rests on the supposition of a rather stable, cohesive social order (traditionally in China hierarchically structured) and might thus appear to be irrelevant to much of modern experience, East or West, we have, I think, much to learn from the Chinese regarding the social nature of humankind and especially how the social factors can be seen not so much as constraints but as opportunities for self-cultivation. Among recent discussions, see especially Herbert Fingarette, *Confucius: The Secular as Sacred* (New York: Harper & Row, 1972); Tu Wei-ming, *Centrality and Commonality: An Essay on Chung-Yung* (Honolulu: University Press of Hawaii, Monograph No. 3 of the Society for Asian and Comparative Philosophy, 1976); Donald Munro, *The Concept of Man in Early China* (Stanford: Stanford University Press, 1967); and David L. Hall and Roger T. Ames, *Thinking Through Confucius* (Albany: State University of New York Press, 1987).

35. *Critique of Pure Reason*, "Transcendental Deduction," B156, trans. Norman Kemp Smith (New York: Humanities Press, 1950), 168.

36. Ibid., B158, 169.

37. Ibid., 169n.

38. See Locke, *An Essay Concerning Human Understanding*, 312.

39. It is important to emphasize once again, as it will have considerable bearing on the phenomenon of person-deception, which we will see to be one of the primary obstacles to the attainment of personhood, that the very notion of a "fully developed person" is set in terms of its being an ideal limit along a continuum of development. The concept of personhood, in other words, holds out the possibility (but very seldom, if ever, the completely realized actuality) of one's having a unity of character wherein all aspects of one's individuality are so happily in accord with each other that one becomes a thoroughly integrated vital whole. Psychologically, the task of integration, especially for persons of considerable complexity, is usually too demanding, if for no other reason than the fact that one is comprised of various dynamic tensions between opposing desires, hopes, and aspirations that cannot readily be reconciled. Rather than this situation closing down the effort to achieve high levels of integration, however, it should make the creative striving for integration, enabling a right articulation of one's being, all the more interesting and exciting.

40. "The roots both of the Japanese and of the European words for masks," Graham Parkes interestingly notes, "lead us back to the face." The origins of our word *mask* are, appropriately, veiled in obscurity; several dictionary entries

report: "derivation disputed." A relatively young word (not appearing in French and English until the sixteenth century), it is presumed to come from the Latin *massa* meaning "paste"—whence "mascara"—and *masca* meaning "demon" or "sorcerer." (With the face apparently transformed and transfixed by a mask, the gestures of the rest of the body can become demonically expressive.) The word's Latin and Greek equivalents connect immediately with the idea of the person. In Latin the image is acoustical, insofar as the components of the word *persōna*, meaning "mask," "character," "person," mean literally "through sound." The Greek *prosōpon* means "front," "facade," or "face"; whence "mask," "character" (in a drama), and "person"—in the original, legal sense. The image is optical, *pro-sōpon* meaning "at the eyes': as front or facade, that which the eyes meet; as mask that too, but also something held or worn in front of the eyes.

The Japanese word for mask, *kamen*, is composed of two characters; *ka*, meaning "temporary," or "provisional," and *men* meaning "surface," "front," or "face." It thus signifies the provisional front one presents to the world, the face one puts on, and on things. As with *prosōpon*, to introduce an optical element by adding the graph for eye, *moku*, produces *menmoku*, meaning "face" in the sense of honor, dignity, reputation. That most horrendous of catastrophes for the Japanese, losing face, is *memoku o ushinau*; to lose the mask that fronts and confronts the eye. Graham Parkes, "Facing the Self with Masks" in *Self and Deception: A Cross-Cultural Philosophical Enquiry*, ed. by Roger T. Ames and Wimal Dissanayake (Albany: State University of New York Press, 1996), 289–90.

41. See Max Müller, *Biographies of Words* (1858), 35.

42. See my *Essays on the Nature of Art*, chapter 1 (Albany: State University of New York Press, 1996) for an elaboration of this notion within an aesthetic context.

43. It is interesting to note that the present English word "true" comes from the Middle English *trewe*, which comes from the Old English *treowe*, meaning "trustworthy," "loyal."

44. William James, *The Principles of Psychology* (New York: Henry Holt, 1890), vol. 1, 293.

45. A great deal of work has been done in contemporary psychoanalytic theory (see, for example, Erik Erikson's *Childhood and Society*, 2d ed. [New York: W. W. Norton, 1963], pt. 3, chap. 7) to describe and mark the various stages and natural crises that an individual endures in the development of ego. It is now widely recognized that there are certain natural turning points in the movement from childhood to adulthood around which distinctive conflicts, aspirations, needs, and frustrations in the development of one's identification tend to revolve. These steps are at once "natural" (they are correlated with an individual's physical-mental maturation and decline) and "social" (they are conventionally determined in their specificity by the requirements of the society in which the person lives). For example, every culture, it seems, has found ceremonial ways to mark an initiation into manhood for its young men. The specific time and manner of initiation vary, as do the precise modes of behavior expected of the initiated, but the variations occur within margins that are predetermined, as it were, in the developmental

process. The young man is initiated around the time of puberty and is expected to set aside certain childish attitudes and actions in favor of those of the adult members of the community.

46. See chapter 13, "Causality, Creativity, and Freedom," for a more detailed account of this meaning of "freedom" as it applies directly to human actions.

2

Person-Deception

There is no royal road to the achievement of personhood and freedom. Rather there are innumerable obstacles, the most insidious of them being the pervasive phenomenon of what I will call "person-deception" (rather than the usual "self-deception"). I employ this designation because I want to focus specifically upon that perplexing situation of a person so divided within himself that he is severely thwarted from embarking successfully on anything like a proper crafting of his personhood. One is in person-deception whenever there is a fundamental discrepancy between what one (believingly) avows to be the case about oneself as a person and what is patently the case about the state of one's achieved personhood. Person-deception represents a refusal to acknowledge who I am and what I am doing, not out of simple ignorance, but from what appears to be a kind of unselfconscious willful perversity. I am in person-deception whenever, while having the opportunity for self-knowledge and person development (and especially when confronted with that opportunity), I refuse to acquire the knowledge and undertake the development, all the while claiming that I have done otherwise.

There is a vast literature now on self-deception which engages the phenomenon from standpoints of, among others, philosophy of mind, behavioral psychology and social psychology.[1] A rich variety of descriptions and explanations have been put forward, some of which, because of the alleged hopelessly paradoxical nature of the phenomenon (especially when self-deception involves the holding of what appears to be contradictory beliefs), have even been bent on denying its very existence.

One point is immediately evident, and that is that differing accounts of self-deception rest on different fundamental views regarding the nature of the self. For those of a psychoanalytical persuasion, the picture of the self in general is one grounded in conflict—in some fundamental division or other within the self (e.g., between ego and id) so that one domain of selfhood is able to keep quite purposively, if not intentionally, something of a threatening importance from another domain of that very self. Philosophers such as Robert Audi are thus able to argue that self-deception can be understood rationally only as a conflict of unconscious and conscious experience as this is supported by a particular "want."[2] Others with a more epistemological-analytic approach assume that the self is an autonomous truth-and-knowledge seeker and thus tend to see self-deception precisely in terms of someone's holding what appears to be irreconcilable beliefs. Some social-psychological treatments of self-deception, on the other hand, go so far as to allow that one can "assume that all of the self-deceptive procedures . . . can be effected without benefit of consciousness."[3]

In his intriguing book entitled *Self-Deception*, Herbert Fingarette points out accurately enough that "philosophical attempts to elucidate the concept of self-deception have ended in paradox—or in loss from sight of the phenomenon itself."[4] Fingarette goes on to offer a brilliant critique of various analytic efforts to understand self-deception and argues that what is needed is a "volition-action" account instead of a "cognitive-perception" one. His own view of self-deception is that the deceiver is one who refuses to spell out, to avow, some feature of his engagement with the world. Adhering to a policy of nonrecognition, the self-deceiver persistently avoids articulating what would otherwise be obvious about his manner of being in the world. Fingarette thus claims that "self-deception turns upon the personal identity one accepts rather than the beliefs one has."[5] I want to take Fingarette's claim seriously, for he seems to me to be on the right track, and try to develop the "personal identity" side along more thorough *ontological* as well as "volition-action" grounds.

There are, it seems, several domains or levels of person-deception that need to be distinguished. The first, and most basic, revolves around the refusal of someone to allow the spontaneity of the Self to be a creative force in his life. To disallow spontaneity means to occupy oneself completely with a certain particularized world. It means to fill oneself up, as it were, with the nonself. Submitting to the distractions (and what at times seems to be the compelling necessities) of the world, one no longer becomes available—one is no longer poised—to realize the Self. This making oneself unavailable is, in the last analysis, due to the preoccupation of an individual with his own ego. One makes of the little "me" the center and way of being of his or her world. Gabriel Marcel once noted that to be concerned with oneself is not so much to be concerned with a particular object as to be concerned in a particular manner. It is the manner of "busyness" which constitutes a flight from the Self. One seeks every opportunity to avoid having to be, in the fullest sense, who one is. And one does this, it seems, out of fear—fear of losing oneself, fear of ego anni-hilation, fear of encountering an abyss and nothingness. *We hesitate to awaken out of fear of losing our dream.*

The turning away becomes deceptive and inhibits the development of personhood, then, when one either denies, in the face of one's immediate experience, the reality of the Self or claims, while living in opposition to it, that one is indeed vitally grounded in it.

This *root* person-deception, if we may call it that, is quite obviously a pervasive phenomenon. It touches almost everyone in fundamental ways and makes for the spiritual atrophy which so often resides in our being. Allowing ourselves to be conditioned to an alarming degree, we then deceive ourselves that we are free (where we are not), having denied our-selves as we are genuinely free.

A more recognizable, but also fundamental, second domain of person-deception occurs when one refuses to acknowledge the possibility of achieving personhood by insisting that one is only one's individuality, that one is reducible to (at least some of) one's objectifiable, historical con-ditions, or that one is exhausted by one's not fully developed persona. Now it is clear that not everyone has equal opportunity to be rightly cre-ative of their being. The oppressed, the exploited, the enslaved, those who have lacked completely the chance for education, leisure, the cultivation of their sensibilities, obviously have considerable justification for regard-ing themselves as victims. Historical conditions have so constrained their possible field of action that these conditions actually function as determi-nants of their being. Also there are many instances where, apart from social exploitation, an individual is determined in his personality devel-opment to a considerable degree by others, especially in childhood by parents, and is faced then with an enormous task of working creatively with those determinants. But in these various cases it is usually not a mat-ter of person-deception at all, but rather a recognition of the harshest of empirical realities. Person-deception presupposes an individual's having the liberty, the opportunity, to develop as a genuine person. One must *refuse* to do so—and on the grounds that one is (and can be) only what circumstances have made of one, or that one is (and can be) only what one happens to be qua persona at the present. One deceptively maintains that others not only have set limits (and opportunities) for one's develop-ment but have so determined one's being as to rule out possibilities of change.

This kind of person-deception clearly becomes a convenient way to avoid responsibility (and the risk of failure, and so on). If who I am is involuntary, then I cannot be held responsible for myself. I can always look elsewhere (where it is much easier) to excuse myself. The development of personhood suffers then by the individual's disavowal of the possibility of undertaking it in one or more crucial dimensions of his being.[6]

Closely related to this kind of person-deception, and in a way its opposite side, is the rather common phenomenon of someone refusing to affirm (even to acknowledge) certain conditions that clearly are the raw material of his being. Someone denies his background, parentage, race, color or whatever; he says "this is not me" about that which obviously is him—the human being qua individual. This refusal to accept something of oneself is usually centered on those (minority) conditions which, in a given sociocultural context, are denigrated in that (majority) context. They are "socially unacceptable"—the majority attitude here being internalized in such a way that the individual disavows something of himself, believing he is not that which he is. Now it is of course true that there can often be a significant discrepancy between one's identification of another and that person's own identity, with the discrepancy owing to error in one's judgment rather than to the other being in person-deception. In a number of cases it might be that the individual concerned does not so much reject something obviously the case about himself as reveal an indifference to that condition, seeing it of no (or very little) importance for who he is and who he might become. In other words, what is not acknowledged might, in certain cases, be irrelevant. But when person-deception of this kind is present we obviously do have a restricting of an individual's being, of his potentiality to be what he ought to be—for one can develop as a person only within and through the available raw material of one's being, one's situation as an individual.[7]

The most common and readily recognizable third domain of person-deception, and one that requires the most extensive analysis, is closely related to the domain just discussed and has to do with the refusal to affirm (acknowledge or accept) various specific qualities or traits of one's personality. Person-deception here seems to be of two basic kinds: in the first, I either (believingly) affirm what is not the case about myself ("I am generous") or (believingly) deny what is the case about myself ("I am not envious")—that is to say, in the first, I either claim to be what I am not or refuse to acknowledge what I evidently am; in the second, I claim that I can always be other than I am if I choose to in situations where this seems to be impossible.

Person-deception of both kinds—as indeed of all forms as well—is, as we have noted, often regarded as involving a conflict of knowledge or belief: a person holds irreconcilable views about herself, or keeps something hidden from her own awareness. In any event person-deception is regarded primarily as a phenomenon of consciousness, but, however so regarded (epistemic or otherwise), person-deception implies the hopelessly paradoxical situation, as Sartre clearly recognized in his trenchant criticism of Freudian psychoanalysis, that a person somehow is already aware of what she is hiding from herself, that a person must somehow be on both sides of the deception, that there is an I who knows the truth (the deceiver) and an I who is ignorant (the deceived). Referring to the Freudian censor who, in psychoanalytic theory, acts so as to repress those id-contents which the ego refuses to accept, Sartre writes:

> If we reject the language and the materialistic mythology of psychoanalysis, we perceive that the censor in order to apply its activity with discernment, must know what he is repressing. . . . But it is not sufficient that it discern the condemned drives; it must also apprehend them as *to be repressed*, which implies in it at the very least an awareness of its activity. In a word, how could the censor discern the impulses needing to be repressed without being conscious of discerning them? How can we conceive of a knowledge that is ignorant of itself?[8]

But instead of looking at person-deception at this level as a phenomenon of consciousness, as a conflict of awareness (or in Sartre's own *mauvaise-foi* terms) suppose we regard it as an experience of will, as a conflict—which does of course involve cognitive acts of recognition—of desires. When seen in this way, however, person-deception is not simply a matter of wanting to be other than one is, or a disguised wish to be what one claims to be (generous, not envious); on the contrary, person-deception, I want to argue, is *the expression of the desire to be precisely what one already is*. The conflict arises because one recognizes that the appropriate social values run directly counter to that wished-for acceptance.

In the first kind of person-deception, when John, who is extremely self-centered, says "I am generous," he is in fact expressing the desire to be self-centered and ungenerous *and to have others affirm that quality or characteristic*. He knows, however, that generosity and not self-centeredness is the prevailing social value and will control the judgment of his character. He is claiming (and believing) to be what he evidently is not, while all the time wanting to be what he is. If he did not want to be what he is he would acknowledge what he is with the hope that others might excuse him or affirm him in spite of this quality, or he would acknowledge what he is as the first step in a process of seeking to change himself.[9]

Person-deception as involving a "wanting to be what one is" implies, then, that one does not truly own "what one is" so long as, in the absence of other overriding values, others withhold their assent from it. Now we cannot deny that there often exists a tension between the claims of person development and societal values. Often indeed the "herd values" of mediocrity, mere conformism, and so on, as Nietzsche so clearly saw, become serious obstacles to the creative becoming of a person, but usually there is no problem of person-deception here, as the tension is very much engaged in and recognized for what it is. Also, not infrequently a person may reject a particular social value (e.g., patriotism) and want nothing less that the approval of others with regard to it. For this reason we have the qualification "in the absence of other overriding values." The person-deceiver, at this level of being and action, is one who possesses fully to himself only what is approved by others, with one's person-deception being a disguised plea for the acceptance from others of what one is. When other, overriding values are present, we do not have a person-deceptive situation; we have simply an acknowledged conflict of values.

In the second kind of this form of person-deception one gives direct expression to the desire (but one that is not factually grounded here because of the very logic of person-deception) that "I can always be other than I am if I choose to be." In these cases a person, at a particular time, is unable to be other than he is, because he actually wants to be what he is, while claiming that he can indeed be other than he is if he so decides or desires. He claims to have an option which, in fact, is nonexistent. The conflict in will is between wanting to be "what one is" and wanting to have the power to change so that one can conform to a given social standard. The process of deception in this second case is thus one of my wanting to retain myself as I am while—instead of calling for others to affirm me as I am—claiming that I can always meet the social standards which would allow me to be affirmed by others. The deception is not so much a disguised plea for affirmation as an expression of a desire which would, so to speak, be neutralized by its being in direct conflict with another contrary desire. The claim to, and belief in, having the power is thus vacuous.

In person-deception of this form, then, it is not so much that something is being hidden from oneself (a conflict in consciousness) as that one is subject to irreconcilable wantings (a conflict in will). In the first kind of deception one wants in fact to be what one is while wanting an approval from others that cannot be offered; in the second kind, one wants, once again, to be what one is while claiming the power to conform to what others believe one should be, which power, were it present as such, would be nullified by the contrary desire to be what one is.

This account of a third domain or level of person-deception still leaves unanswered questions concerning the actual psychological mechanisms of person-deception (the "psychic correlates" of desire) and fails also to resolve the paradox of person-deception, which here takes the form that the deceiver must somehow desire what he does not desire in order that he not desire it (i.e., put it out of reach through person-deception). Like Freud's censor, the deceiver must again, in some way be on both sides of the deception. But whereas the paradox, when it is located in the domain of knowledge appears to be self-contradictory, rendering the phenomenon unintelligible, it can, when it is placed in the domain of desire, more readily be tolerated (and ameliorated considerably), for as so often with desire ambivalence already reigns. Incompatible urgings do seem to coexist in our emotional life (love-hate dualities and the like) and provide many of the interesting complexities of that life. We do desire and not desire something simultaneously, and not just with respect to different qualities of the thing; we want and do not want something of ourselves. A paradox remains but becomes more acceptable.[10]

The last domain of person-deception to which we need to attend is closely related to the third in its dynamics, and has to do primarily with a person's actual relations in the world as they are reflective of his being. This most prevalent and particularistic form of person-deception involves one's refusal to acknowledge the nature of one's actions (or lack of them) and, because of one's commitment to remain blind, as it were, to allow any contrary evidence to alter that refusal. Harry infuriates his coworkers by his complete lack of respect for their privacy, while uttering to others and to himself, "They never leave me alone; I'm not the least interested in what they do." When confronted with the obvious facts of his behavior Harry may reply, "Well, when I do inquire about others I'm only expressing my concern for their welfare."

To the person-deceiver his action is entirely rational. He fully believes that had he different reasons for what he does his actions would be different than they are; and he also believes that there is no discrepancy between what he intends to accomplish by what he says and does and what (to others) would be the predictable consequences of these actions. It is precisely here that the rich variety of those mechanisms identified in psychoanalytic theory come into play to defend the deceiver from his own deception. The person-deceiver "projects" and "transfers" in order to keep himself from himself.

Person-deception in all its many forms—forms which intermingle and interfuse and in any event are found together in the same person—thus tends to become a characteristic style of a person's behavior rather than isolated episodes of his or her experience. Person-deception, in short, becomes habitual; it becomes the basis for a certain consistency (and precarious harmony) in a person's life; patterns of deceit are constructed and become constitutive of the person's being.

This habituation means, then, that person-deception is the manner in which the deceiver is as a person. With the root deception being a refusal to affirm Self-spontaneity or to affirm it while living in opposition to it (and carrying this out by means of various and innumerable strategies), the deceiver sets upon a course of person development that is certain to be highly restrictive. Without the creative dynamism afforded by the Self one is bound closely to the conditions of one's individuality while all the time refusing, out of fear of losing the empirical self, to realize one's true Self. One could, to be sure, for whatever peculiar reasons, consciously choose certain limitations and thus not be in person-deception. Person-deception is present when there is that "willful perversity" and "discrepancy" between what is avowed to be the case and what is in fact the case.

The second domain of person-deception—wherein the deceiver, in the one case, claims to be only her empirical conditions, her given historical being, her determined persona, and in the other claims not to be some of those conditions—obviously constrain personal identity in many ways as well. One who (erroneously) believes oneself to be a victim will tend toward that peculiar passivity that so often rules out initiative and creativity. If, essentially to avoid responsibility, I embark on a program of consistently denying opportunities for development, then I shall surely succeed in that venture; I will largely be what others would have me be. Similarly, when I deny certain important conditions of my individuality I will simply have less to work with and will never be fully integrated. Something of myself will remain alien to me, and I will be unable thereby to be immediately reflective or expressive of my nature.

The same holds true for the other empirical forms of person-deception which have to do with one's personality and one's actions. In both forms the deceiver is at cross-purposes with himself. He is able to function in a coherent way, to be sure, but he is out of joint with himself and with reality. He is, we must say, "deluded"—but not to the point of the psychotic who seems no longer to have the opportunity for overcoming his delusion through any act of recognition on his part. The person-deceiver, unlike the psychotic, does not compress his entire being, as it were, into those traits or actions about which he is deluded; he is able to function "normally" in most everything he does—but not as an integrated person with an achieved identity. The person-deceiver, to some extent, is always "deformed"—and is accordingly unfree.[11]

Our discussion until now has been carried out in what might appear to be a cultural-neutral context. A basic problematic must, however, be articulated, which is: Do we have different phenomena of person-deception in different cultures in virtue of their varied social practices as these are themselves informed by different social values and ways of interpretation? or, Is the phenomenon the same, but is only conceptualized in different ways in virtue of different styles of argument, criteria of rationality, and the like, which are employed? In whatever way the problematic is most properly addressed, it might be that by looking how a non-Western philosophical tradition, here mainly the Indian, would treat person-deception we might be able to clarify and deepen the analysis so far given. I will concentrate once again on Vedāntic thought in its nondualistic (Advaita) form, the mainline philosophical tradition most often associated, rightly or wrongly, with Brahmanic or Hindu thought in general.

To begin with, it should be noted that, at least to my knowledge, there is no explicit philosophical treatment of the problem of self-deception in Vedānta as this is formulated typically in the West.[12] Vedānta does nevertheless concentrate on what we have called "person-deception," and it is quite possible to reconstruct its way of treating various forms of empirical person-deceit in terms of its doctrine of levels of consciousness and the accepted notions of *karman* and *dharma*.

According to Śaṃkara, our root person-deception is a basic and pervasive person-confounding of our own making. We incessantly and quite naturally misidentify ourselves and wrongly attribute to the Self characteristics which properly belong only to our empirical individuality; we "superimpose" (*adhyāsa*) attributes of the non-self onto the Self and of the Self onto the non-self. In our ordinary consciousness of ourselves we are thus subject to a profound ignorance (*avidyā*). In his oft-quoted introduction to his commentary on the *Brahma-Sūtras*, Śaṃkara writes:

It is a matter not requiring any proof that the object and the subject, whose respective spheres are the notion of the "Thou" (the Non-Ego) and the Ego, and which are opposed to each other as much as darkness and light are cannot be identified. All the less can their respective attributes be identified. Hence it follows that it is wrong to superimpose upon the subject—whose Self is intelligence, and which has for its sphere the Ego—the object whose sphere is the notion of the Non-Ego, and the attributes of the object; and vice versa to superimpose the subject and the attributes of the subject on the object. In spite of this it is on the part of a man a natural procedure.[13]

For example:

Attributes of the body are superimposed on the Self, if a man thinks of himself [his essential self] as stout, lean, fair, as standing, walking or jumping.[14]

In other words, we quite naturally misidentify ourselves by attributing to our real Self, which is, in essence, identical to reality itself, qualities and characteristics that belong only to our empirical individuality. When one conceives of himself as—when he believes that he really, as distinct from only empirically, is—of a certain height and weight, carrying out various physical actions, he is subject to *avidyā*, to ignorance, or is engaged in *adhyāsa*, superimposition.

For Vedānta, then, person-deception, in its most fundamental form, is more of a (universal) metaphysical affliction than a (personal) epistemic condition. For Vedānta, person-deception at its root involves not so much a division within oneself as a break between an individual and reality. When a person comes to realize his true identity with a non-differentiated reality, when, that is to say, self-understanding and freedom (*mokṣa*) are obtained the very possibility of empirical person-deception is eliminated.

Turning to the empirical forms of person-deception, which those of who have failed to achieve full self-understanding are prone to be a victim of, Indian thought in general, as disclosed in its rich mythology, often depicts cases of these deceptions as a kind of self-forgetfulness (as one comes under the power of *māyā*) losing one's memory, as it were, of who one once was and empirically more truly is—say, one is in fact a noble prince who forgetfully plays the role of a dissolute wanderer. For Indian thought, it is not so much that there is a person-deceiving and a person-deceived, or a split personality of some sort, but a person who is asleep, as it were, and the (same) person who is awake.

For Vedānta, this is expressed philosophically in terms of its doctrine of levels of consciousness. Four such states are identified: waking (*jāgarita*), dream (*svapna*), deep-sleep (*suṣupti*) and a fourth (*turīya*), transcendental condition. Person-deception of at least one empirical form would be interpreted as a confounding of the dream-state (with its desire-driven modalities) and the waking state; which is to say, that a person in deception would be one who, while awake empirically, functions as though he were in dream as far as being clouded by involuntary desire, while all the time claiming and believing that he was acting quite rationally. This is perhaps the closest Vedānta would come to a Western-like kind of analysis which would understood self-deception as a conflict within consciousness as based on desire.

For the most part, though, Vedānta would appeal to two of the most axiomatic (and interrelated) notions in Indian culture to account for empirical forms of self-deception, mainly *karman* and *dharma*. For Indian thought generally, in the domain of human social life each person is said to have his or her *dharma* or "law" or "duty" to oneself and to others, and this is determined by one's station in life (one's *varṇa* or "class," one's *āśrama* or stage of life, and one's *puruṣārtha* or aim of life), which is itself the result of one's past action. One's law or duty is thus self-made.

Karl H. Potter has shown, quite convincingly I think, that the best way to understand *karman* in traditional Indian thought is in terms more of "making" than of "action," as we understand these terms in contemporary Western thought. Words based on the Sanskrit root *kṛ*, Potter argues, call up expectations in Sanskrit users

that it will be possible to identify a maker (*kartṛ*), some materials out of which the making is intended, a purpose or purposes (*puruṣārtha*) being served by the making, an operation (*vyāpāra*) by which the making is carried out, and of course a resulting thing made (*karman*), which will serve the purpose or at least perform a function conducive to the eventual satisfaction sought. . . . So, for example, when in Indian thought we hear of something *kṛta*, we should understand the reference is not only to some deed, something done, completed, but further that it refers to something made, produced from some material by someone for somebody's purpose.[15]

Purposive making, Potter goes on to note, always yields results that are frustrating or satisfying in varying degrees. We make ourselves purposively, then, with varied degrees of success. Person-making, within the traditional Indian conceptual scheme also requires indefinite time spans, with one's present making affecting incrementally what one may become—and most importantly what others will also become. This social dimension of *karman* is often overlooked in philosophical analyses of the concept, but it is central to the doctrine insofar as it recognizes fully that human actions or makings do not occur in some pristine private space but are embedded in the social order and have ramifications beyond the forming of individual dispositions to act. The doctrine of *karman* teaches us that as beings in process we are fully responsible for whatever we do, and whatever we in fact do impacts on all persons, present and future, who fall within the compass of our actions.

Person-deception, then, for Indian thought generally, would involve some kind of fundamental confusion about one's karmic-based *dharma*; a confusion about the kind of person one has made oneself to be. In person-deception one might thus attribute to one's empirical self various roles for which one is ill-equipped to perform. Person-deception here would be a kind of deluded performance—an enactment of a role for which one is mis-suited. In the West, we often see this as a kind of comic situation (à la Molière); for India it would be somewhat more tragic.

Further, in this context, person-deception might also be said to consist in one's believing that one can alter fundamentally one's *karman* while lacking the means or even the will to do so, and/or announcing that one's *karman* determines, rather than only conditions, one so as to render one helpless to do anything about one's person-making. According to Indian teaching, *karman* does condition, but it does not determine. One might be conditioned by the accidents of birth to speak Hindi, but this does not mean that one is determined as such to say whatever one does say in that language. One is, to be sure, predisposed, by the acquisition of various habits (*saṁskāras*), to say certain things, and especially in certain ways, but this does not preclude one from altering one's habits and developing new ones. In any event, in these cases one is confused about one's *dharma* and refuses to avow, to spell-out (in Fingarette's terms) that very confusion.

Contrast this, if you will, with the thought of Béla Szabados who, accepting the argument that because of its logical paradoxical nature self-deception cannot possibly exist, asks "then why did we nevertheless have to invent it?" And answers:

> The answer given is that self-deception is really [only] a game we play with and for other people. We all partake in a conspiracy by having an unspoken treaty with each other to play this game. The aim of the game is to confuse people so as to make them unsure how to judge us. To deceive oneself is really to pretend that one is self-deceived in order to confuse others so that one gets away scot-free or with little blame for what is a blatant lie or pretense.[16]

Person-deception, when understood in role terms, does indeed become a kind of game, but not in the superficial sense described by Szabados. The ever-popular Indian text, the *Bhagavadgītā*, insists that persons must perform various roles, fulfill their *dharma*, but with the understanding that the performance is a kind of play, a *creative* undertaking. In its teaching on *karmayoga*, the *Gītā* urges us to act with non-attachment to the fruits of our action, with devotion (*bhakti*) and knowledge (*jñāna*) and thus act freely. This is what it means for a person to be without deception while functioning within the social order. One acts with a reverential spirit in the knowledge that one is intimately bound-up with nature and yet, at the same time, is identical to an essential freedom that allows for—indeed calls for—a creative person-making.

NOTES

1. See, for example, the bibliography in Mike Martin's *Self-Deception and Morality* (Lawrence, Kans.: University Press of Kansas, 1986) and the bibliography compiled by Uma Narayan in *Perspectives on Self-Deception*, ed. Brian P. McLaughlin and Amélie Oksenberg Rorty (Berkeley: University of California Press, 1988).

2. See his "Self-Deception and Rationality," in *Self-Deception and Self-Understanding: New Essays in Philosophy and Psychology*, ed. Mike W. Martin (Lawrence, Kans.: University Press of Kansas, 1985), 169ff.

3. See Daniel T. Gilbert and Joel Cooper, "Social Psychological Strategies of Self-Deception," in *Self-Deception and Self-Understanding*, 76.

4. Herbert Fingarette, *Self-Deception* (New York: Humanities Press, 1969), 11.

5. Ibid., 67.

6. In its most primary forms, self-deception may appear to be a neurotic breakdown of an individual's capacity to be responsible, to be able (and not just unwilling) to acknowledge the actualities of his personal identity-making and to exercise one's inherent powers to strive toward integration and freedom. When it comes to questions of moral judgment (of condemnation and the like) of the self-

deceiver, this issue might be of considerable importance. We are not so much concerned here, however, with determining moral responsibility, and the conditions for it, as we are with recognizing the manner in which the self-deceiver clearly surrenders, voluntarily or not, his potentiality to achieve a full measure of personhood.

7. The phenomenon of masking that is too tight or too loose in person-making, which we have previously discussed, can be seen now to have direct bearing on this form of person-deception. When masking is "completely coextensive with individual personality development," we have the possibility arising that the person will claim that, in order to avoid responsibility, his being has been so determined by others and involuntary circumstances that he cannot help being what he is. When masking, on the other hand, serves primarily to conceal one's inner life from others, it may in turn function so as to conceal oneself from oneself by one's refusing to acknowledge who in actuality one is. In either case, we have a stultifying inhibition at play in one's person-making.

8. Jean-Paul Sartre, *Being and Nothingness*, trans. Hazel E. Barnes (New York: Washington Square Press, 1966), 93.

9. It might be argued that self-deception need not always involve the deceiver's having oneself as the object of one's deception. A parent, for example, might refuse to recognize some obvious deficit in her child, and so on. This is assuredly the case, but the self-deceiver's having another as the object of her deception does not imply that it is any less her state of being or that it is any less analyzable, *mutatis mutandis*, as a conflict of her desires.

10. It should be pointed out here that this phenomenon of having "incompatible urgings" is intimately related to that struggle for personal integration that we previously called attention to and makes for the removal of person-deception at this level always a matter of degree. Most of us, most of the time, lack the strength of character or power of insight to reconcile and bring to full integration the many conflicting patterns of desire that arise in the process of our becoming persons and which then take up residence in our being. Some degree of person-deception seems, in this context, inevitably to become part and parcel of one's being. This situation, however, ought not to invite despair so much as to be seen as an ongoing opportunity for creative self-engagement. A lack of complete integration at this level of personhood may very well keep one creatively alive.

11. One would, I think, have to allow that there are times when person-deception is clearly preferable to what would seem to be the actual alternatives. Person-deception, although a kind of delusion, is also often a protection against psychic disintegration. (O'Neill's *The Iceman Cometh*). It allows, as we have seen, for a certain consistency and style of behavior. It is certainly better to be in person-deception than to lack a stable center completely. Person-deception, however, is certainly never better than the attainment of a genuine personal identity or full integration.

12. In Karl H. Potter's extensive *Bibliography of Indian Philosophies* (Delhi: Motilal Banarsidass, 1970), for example, there is not a single entry under any recognizable category of self-deception.

13. Śaṃkara, *Brahmasūtrabhāṣya*, 3.

14. Ibid., 8–9.

15. Karl H. Potter, "Metaphor as Key to Understanding the Thought of Other Speech Communities," in *Interpreting Across Boundaries: New Essays in Comparative Philosophy*, ed. Gerald James Larson and Eliot Deutsch (Princeton: Princeton University Press, 1988), 26.

16. Béla Szabados, "The Self, Its Passions and Self-Deception," in *Self-Deception and Self-Understanding*, 144.

3

✳

The Performance of Emotions

Amélie Oksenberg Rorty has pointed out that

Emotions do not form a natural class. After a long history of quite diverse debates about their classification, emotions have come to form a heterogeneous group: various conditions and states have been included in the class for quite different reasons and on different grounds, against the background of shifting contrasts. Fear, religious awe, exuberant delight, pity, loving devotion, panic, regret, anxiety, nostalgia, rage, disdain, admiration, gratitude, pride, remorse, indignation, contempt, disgust, resignation, compassion (just to make a random selection) cannot be shepherded together under one set of classifications as active or passive; thought-generated and thought-defined or physiologically determined; voluntary or involuntary; functional or nonfunctional; corrigible or not corrigible by a change of beliefs. Nor can they be sharply distinguished from moods, motives, attitudes, character traits.[1]

By "the emotions" I mean to designate those occurrent affective states (actions or processes) that typically get labeled as fear, joy, anger, and jealousy, and that intend specifiable (albeit often highly complex and confusing) objects. An emotion, as I use the term, is thus an intense, episodic affective state that, while closely related to moods (e.g., depression, anxiety), desires (sexual, gustatory), motives (for revenge, for success), and dispositions (to be cheerful, to be morose), can indeed (if not sharply at least workably) be distinguished from them—and especially from what we might call raw emotive responses with which they are so often confounded.

A raw emotive response, in contrast to a full-fledged emotional act, is often based on identifiable neurobiological conditions (e.g., when the initial shock of fright one has at a loud, sudden, unexpected noise, may be traced to primitive survival needs) and most often on what appears to be compelling psychological forces (e.g., the bursting into a rage over some trivial affront, the outburst being accounted for in terms of frustrations arising from unfulfilled wants, repressed desires or traumatic childhood experiences). With raw responses we tend to look for causal explanations; with emotional states we tend to look for rational justifications—and for the fitness of the response to its object. Raw emotive responses exhaust themselves; emotional acts strive to complete themselves. One is, with raw responses, very much their victim (as with the emotionality of the senile, with its wayward anger and despair); with emotional acts there is the drive to achieve understanding through their appropriation and eventual transformation. Although many people might believe that emotionality in general consists mainly of raw emotive responses, it seems clear enough that they are at one end of an affective-spectrum which runs to the other end of appropriate feeling activity, with the emotional life of most persons with some measure of an alert consciousness (the vast majority of us) consisting of our exercising a variety of emotional acts that we strive to perform correctly and rightly.

My thesis is that *emotions are those ego-based, affective processes that typically intend objects (states of affairs—real or imagined—other persons and oneself) in relationships of relative frustration and hence as value-foci; that exhibit, and are intimately bound-up with, one's dispositional character or personality structure; that are often experienced bodily as felt involuntary changes expressed in standard symptomatic ways and as disorganizing forces; that are thoroughly temporal (involving a present object, drawing upon and restructuring past experience, and influencing future behavior); that are performed in socially informed ways so as to intensify themselves, and thereby to clarify their intentionality and preserve situations, the more effectively to deal with them, whether actually or fantastically; and that can be performed correctly—and rightly.*

Emotions are those ego-based, affective processes . . .
    The emotions, as we know, have often been denigrated by those philosophers, puritans, and ascetics who see emotional states as essentially body-based and as standing either in the way of the mind's ability to know things clearly or of the spirit's capacity to be purely.[2] Emotions as passions were thought to reflect just that passivity associated with the word and thus to be in sharp opposition to that controlled activity which was genuinely expressive of one's rational, spiritual being.[3] This disvaluing of the emotions as so understood may have had considerable justification; but more often than not the disvaluing was based on some kind of radical mind-body or spirit-flesh dualism and accordingly involved at the start an inadequate conception of the emotions.

Although emotions oftentimes do seem to be body based, at least insofar as emotional states often involve involuntary body changes, the body (qua object-body) is in fact more their victim than their source or center. The physical as such (albeit there might be strong genetic determinants at play) has no cares or concerns than get expressed as remorse or compassion; it is the *person* driven by ego who has them. As Descartes himself noted, "The objects which move the senses do not excite diverse passions in us because of all the diversities which are in them, but only because of the diverse ways in which they may harm or help us, or in general be of some importance to us."[4] I have, I am, emotional states to the degree to which I am ego-centered (which is not, of course, the same thing as being egoistic: I might be highly ego-centered and still have a very low opinion of myself). It is only when I have an interest at stake (and not necessarily restricted to only the narrow, selfish ones) that I have emotions. Indignation at some horrible case of child abuse that one might have witnessed, although exhibiting genuine concern about the child, is nevertheless directly indicative of one's interest in preserving, promoting certain values and modes of behavior—with these values not only informing one's emotionality but oftentimes getting disclosed to one primarily in and through one's emotional states or actions. One discovers a good deal about how one "really" values other persons, situations, actions by the various emotions one has when involved with them. Being ego-based, then, does not preclude emotions having a reference; on the contrary it calls for one. The point here is that the primary locus of emotions is the person as an ego-bound being. I suffer or enjoy emotional states in virtue of my seeing myself as separate, regard myself as important, and constrain my being into a posture that faces the world (defensively/ aggressively) with interest. I am my emotions at the time of their occurrence. I own them and they own me: we become identified. Being emotional (about something or other), is then, a kind of self-indulgence. I dwell in my emotions. They become my power of being. They announce my importance—to me.[5]

that typically intend objects (states of affairs—real or imagined—other persons and oneself) . . .

Emotions, unlike moods (e.g., of anxiety) it is often said, are always about something; which is to say, that they *intend* objects and thus involve judgments. As phenomenologists are fond of noting, the intentional object need not be objectively real. What one is emotional about may, in fact, not be the case. Jones is angry about being insulted by Smith, where no insult was meant. Jones simply misunderstood the situation. In any event, there is always an interpreted occasion for one's emotion; something which brings one into vivid relationships with one's world and oneself.

Emotions, however, are seldom experienced by us as singular, easily identifiable states; rather they are experienced as complex, containing a rich variety of ingredients. One's anger about something is usually not about that something in a narrow, exclusive way, rather the anger was built-up over a period of time with reference to a variety of situations (which is why emotional states, in their intensity, so often appear to be out of proportion to the situation at hand). Related to this, we also have what might be called historical emotion. Encapsulating the agonies, triumphs, aspirations and disappointments of an era or epoch, monuments often serve as a focus of historical experience, with viewers responding to them in those terms. Long-standing family or tribal feuds often persist long after the actual origins of the feud have become meaningless to the present participants but where the accumulation of passion over (sometimes) generations is very much a living reality.

Patterns of emotionality which develop in intense interpersonal relationships also often seem in many ways to be enduring. Years after a husband and wife separate and meet again the same old emotions assert themselves. Each party believed, mistakenly, that the whole business, as it were, between them was over and done with.

It is clear from this that psychologically the subject is not only the bearer of his emotion, but (in complicated ways) the object as well. Oftentimes, as subsequent reflection shows, when responding emotionally to some negative quality that another persons exhibits one is as well responding to that same quality as it is possessed by, or recognized to be potentially acquirable by, oneself. Inherent in certain emotional states is the recognition of, and consequent judgment concerning, one's having deep-seated attitudes of a kind incommensurate with one's self-image. Jones in hating Smith discovers a hatefulness within himself that he deplores.

One of the most interesting and baffling features in the psychology of emotions is just this manner in which so many of one's emotional states reveal not just a lack of self-control but a lack of regard for others, which in turn signifies a lack of regard for oneself. Intense emotions often betray a lack of self-esteem; they show our need to be recognized; they exhibit a sense of our inferiority. One gets wrapped up in oneself not when one is pleased with oneself but rather when one is highly displeased. When there is a healthy self-confident ease of being one is open to, is sensitive to, the world.

in relationships of relative frustration and hence as value-foci;

If emotions do belong to a person in a fundamental way then it is not surprising that they involve wants and wishes—the whole range of what was once called the conative. When we are emotional we want something or some state of affairs to be the case, even when we enjoy a temporary satisfaction with what is the case. (The so-called positive emotions such as joy have, as poets have told us through the ages, their own frustration in virtue of, if nothing else, their transiency).[6] There is, to be sure, a wide difference between those emotional states, often characterized as childish, that seem to translate intense desires directly and immediately and those that involve a richer variety of judgmental elements. One can, of course, want something without being emotional about it (those would be rather abstract wants or wishes—for example, for universal peace with respect to which the wanter might nevertheless be rather passive), but, when one is emotional, there is always an active wanting present, with most such wantings promoting and informing various identifiable emotional acts.

It is this wanting dimension of emotionality that perhaps contributes so significantly to the contagion effect of emotion. Emotions in one person often ignite emotions in another; there is, it seems, a pervasive wanting ready at any time to find an emotional expression and embodiment, with mass hysteria, group panic and the like being among its extreme manifestations.

The intentional objects of emotional states are not, of course, mere neutral data of consciousness, rather necessarily, they are, as we have seen, objects of interest, sources of frustration, and therefore value-foci. Emotions invest objects with importance and significance. And it is here that the question about the cognitive dimension of emotions often arises, for values presuppose judgments, and judgments in turn presuppose a recognition of various qualities—a recognition that is essentially cognitive in character.

A good deal of the current literature on the emotions in both philosophy and psychology is concerned with this cognitive character, with some (e.g., Solomon) arguing that the cognitive-judgmental aspect is at the very heart of what the emotions are.[7] Others (e.g., de Sousa) argue that it is sufficient to note how they are "in part patterns of attention" and "underlie our rational processes."[8] Some psychologies (e.g., Stanley Schachter and Jerome E. Singer) have held that beliefs actually cause emotions; while some philosophers (most recently those associated with common language analysis) have argued that the logic involving the use of emotion terms (their correct application) shows that emotions necessarily presuppose various beliefs and judgments. It would not make sense to say (without considerable elaboration and explication), "I'm afraid of Henry, but I don't believe that he will or can harm me." In any event it is clear that certain emotions such as hate, hope, pity, fear, and envy do involve beliefs about objects and that in any explanation or justification that would be offered for an emotional state, various pronounced judgmental features would be included. The more interesting, and less obvious, cognitive functions of emotionality, however, are disclosed, I believe, in emotions as performances. As I will try to show, a cognitive struggle takes place within the emotional state itself, and various imaginative activities are brought forth and become integral to that state.

that exhibit, and are intimately bound-up with, one's dispositional character or personality structure;

One of the reasons why many emotional states are profoundly disturbing is that they disclose oneself to oneself—and often in ways and with contents that one would prefer not to have to acknowledge. Emotions clearly do not arise in a vacuum. An occurrent emotional state is always closely related to a broader dispositional structure or pattern.[9] If Mary exhibits fear at something in her present experience, her doing so is obviously indicative of her past fear-laden experience; it is related to what she has been and will likely be fearful of.

When persons are characterized in terms of broad personality traits they are often so characterized in generalized emotion or mood terms such as cheerful, melancholy and so on. There is some considerable agreement among writers on the emotions that although the distinction between episodic emotional states and moods cannot be drawn very sharply, emotions, in contrast to moods, as we have indicated, always have specifiable objects. Moods are global states, generalized emotions, which involve a pervasive attitude toward the world and one's life as a whole. What is of interest here is the manner in which moods seem to be entirely expressive of one's dispositional character or personality structure and thus are compatible, as it were, with only a restricted range of emotions. My being in a certain mood, which is reflective of what kind of person I am, precludes my having certain emotions. Yet, on the other hand, the strength of certain episodic emotional states that occur suddenly may alter my mood so as to make the mood supportive of the emotion. The relationship between emotion and mood is thus dynamic, interactive. And emotions themselves often become mood-like in their pervasiveness. One's grief over the loss of a loved one may become a rather long-lasting sorrow, a depression that infects one's entire being and action.

The dispositional tendencies that constitute character are themselves often influenced at the outset by elemental emotional experience (childish fears, resentments and disappointments) and get constantly reenforced by subsequent emotional states—while at the same time providing a selective range of experience wherein emotions operate. One is always disposed emotionally in certain ways.[10]

that are often experienced bodily as felt involuntary changes . . .

We have said earlier that the body as such has no cares or concerns that get expressed emotionally and that emotions, therefore, are not strictly body-based as was sometimes thought to be the case (with the old James-Lange theory allowing that emotions are nothing but our awareness of involuntary body changes[11]); nevertheless as lived experiences, many of our emotional states are felt as involuntary body changes, especially those powerful emotions such as fear and anger or rage. What does this tell us about the nature of the emotions?

We must, I think, leave to the experimental sciences the question of what kind of causal relationship might obtain between various emotional states and various bodily conditions. It seems to be the case that certain emotions, at least as behavioral manifestations, can be physically induced (by chemicals and by electrical shocks), and also, from the other side, that certain psychological reactions to situations affect bodily conditions, but these are strictly empirical matters, however difficult they might be to resolve.

One meaning element that is disclosed in the lived-experience of involuntary bodily-changes often accompanying, or being correlative with, or giving rise to, emotional states is its contributing to the confusion in emotional consciousness about the appropriateness of the state. I am my emotions; they are part and parcel of my personality, and yet they often appear as alien intrusions, especially at the physical level. How then can they be mine? One of the central features of emotions as performances, I will argue, is the struggle within emotional consciousness itself to gain clarity with regard to its object and the right manner of engaging the situation. Inherent in the having of emotions is the effort to appropriate them, to make them one's own, and to achieve appropriateness in their direction and intensity. It is not a matter of reason controlling the emotions, but of emotions themselves seeking a clarity that allows for their rightness.

expressed in standard symptomatic ways . . .

Certain emotional states are often exhibited behaviorally in standard ways, both in terms of what appears to be biological necessity and social regimentation. Darwin, for one, noted various correlations between emotional states in animals and their typical behavioral manifestations. With human beings, too, there seems to be natural correlations between sadness and slowness, exhilaration and rapidity. Smiling seems universally to be a sign of friendliness. Most important for human beings, however, is the socialization of emotionality which may differ significantly from one culture to another.[12] In fact the very permissibility of showing emotion differs markedly. For whatever reasons, in northern European countries an extensive and expansive display of emotion is thought to be in bad taste, if not barbaric; in some southern European countries, on the other hand, it is the accepted and expected norm. It is also arguable that cultural conditions (especially moral values and codes) determine to a considerable extent just what emotions an individual will and can experience. In certain societies, for example, the having of the emotion of bodily shame would be inconceivable. Envy, one suspects, is hardly known or seldom experienced in a tribal society. In any event, as we shall see in closer detail, emotions do have their scripts which are written largely in social terms.[13]

and as disorganizing forces;

We often experience emotional states, especially at their inception, as powerful forces that seem to disrupt that normal mental-vital-affective rhythmic whole that constitutes our functional integrity. While recognizing that emotions often give substance and richness to our psychic vitality, and may themselves be symptomatic of a kind of psychic dissociation (so that they sustain a divided person), they oftentimes have an initial disorganizing shock value. They disrupt and distort, compress and constrain; they are experienced often as a violation of the integrity of our being.

Emotional states nevertheless also serve to mobilize otherwise disparate psychic energies, as well as sometimes to immobilize them. Occasionally they seem to do both simultaneously.

Accordingly, it is one thing to ridicule a hydraulic model that regards emotions as essentially (nothing but) a complex of irresistible forces pressing tirelessly for expression; it is another to neglect the phenomenological fact that emotions are indeed often experienced by us as compelling, consuming energies, and to fail to realize that this fact contributes significantly to the possibilities (and difficulties) that one has in dealing correctly with them.

that are thoroughly temporal (involving a present object, drawing upon and restructuring past experience, and influencing future behavior);

That we speak of emotions as occurrent or episodic states suggests that temporally they are present bound. Emotions do, as we have seen, involve a present object—that of which they are about—and they obviously have a present duration, a now of their happening. They also have a backward-looking and forward-orienting function.

Emotional states, relative to dispositional structures, as we have noted, draw upon past experience, and they also restructure that experience in diverse and subtle ways. Larry is angry at his wife for being rude to a friend whom he brought home unexpectedly for dinner. He responds from the basis of his attachments, expectations, sense of obligation, and so on, and in the process of responding adds a new dimension to that range of experience, an addition that is not just an adding to but is a restructuring, an alteration, a reorganizing of it. Except perhaps in those rare instances when an emotional state is nothing more than an expression of one's dispositional structure (Cheryl tends to be remorseful and, for no apparent present reason or occasion, simply exhibits remorse as an occurrent state) our emotions change us—sometimes enriching, sometimes impoverishing our personhood by way of reordering our past.

Remembrances themselves are emotion laden, and it might even be the case that all instances of emotionality are a kind or remembrance or, at the least, imply a bringing of an intensified past to bear on a present situation.

Emotions also clearly influence future behavior in many subtle and complex ways. My reactions to Y for doing Z will inevitably affect my future relations to Y. One may forgive and forget, but the relationship will not be the same. Once distrust, for example, arises (justifiably) the same kind of intimacy is no longer possible.

Emotions are thoroughly temporal.

that are performed in socially informed ways so as to intensify themselves, and thereby to clarify their intentionality and preserve situations, the more effectively to deal with them, whether actually or fantastically;

Emotion, for Sartre, is a form of unreflective consciousness that exhibits the bearer's inability to deal directly and effectively with some situation that frustrates her expectations or inhibits her desires, and thus becomes a kind of magical substitute for action. An emotion, Sartre writes, "is a transformation of the world. When the paths traced out become too difficult, or when we see no path, we can no longer live in so urgent and difficult a world. All the ways are barred. However, we must act. So we try to change the world, that is, to live as if the connection between things and their potentialities were not ruled by deterministic processes, but by magic."[14]

But emotional behavior is often surprisingly effective. My anger at X frightens him and he alters his conduct accordingly. Strong passion often motivates both thought and action (especially social and political, as Sartre well knew). Also emotional states are often induced for their sheer excitement value, such as when one attends horror movies, and thus are regarded as something positive.

Sartre's "emotional consciousness" makes the person—and rather surprisingly indeed—a victim. With strong Freudian overtones (compare Freud's notion of sublimation and his explanation of the function of neurotic symptoms), Sartre claims that, "the origin of emotion is a spontaneous and lived degradation of consciousness in the face of the world. What it cannot endure in one way it tries to grasp in another by going to sleep, by approaching the consciousness of sleep, dream and hysteria. And the disturbance of the body is nothing other than the lived belief of consciousness, insofar as it is seen from the outside."[15]

For Sartre, then, all emotions are negative in virtue of their being "degradations" of consciousness—their purpose being "to negate a problematic world" so that "the emotions which appear positive are only superficially so; only as *descriptions* are they positive. Their purpose is to trick us, by magical incantation, into believing that the negative situation does not exist."[16] What kind of magic is it though wherein the magician is himself deceived by it?

Sartre points out that emotional consciousness is originally unreflective (e.g., "fear is not originally consciousness of being afraid"), that is, emotions are not in the first place reflexive. It is arguable, however, that emotional consciousness does indeed have a pronounced reflexive dimension just insofar as its bearer struggles to give form or meaning to that consciousness. Inherent in the having of an emotional state, we shall try to show, is the drive toward clarification of it. Except in those instances wherein one is consumed utterly by an emotional state (and it is then something of a raw response), there is a consciousness of the emotion as well as the consciousness in the emotion of that which it is about. It is this very tension in consciousness that makes for emotional states to strive for a formal expression, to be reenactments or performances.

The essential feature of an emotional state, as an occurrent episode, I argue, is its being a kind of performance. Emotions thus have, as it were, their scripts. Emotions may, then, be said to be imitative as well as expressive or symbolic.

Ronald de Sousa speaks of this imitative or learned depiction of emotions in terms of "paradigm scenarios"; that "we learn our repertoire of emotions, much as we learn some of our verbal repertoire—our vocabulary of concrete predicates—by ostensive definition. . . . Once learned, it is correctly 'applied,' like a learned predicate, to situations that are relevantly similar to the paradigm scenario in which it originates."[17]

Performances are repetitive in principle; albeit each performance will have its own special qualities. Like renditions (interpretations) of the same musical score, emotions may have similar structures and yet exhibit unique features. Much of the scoring of emotions, as we have seen, appears to be instinctual insofar as there are symptomatic bodily expressions associated with different emotional states. On the other hand, much of the scoring, as we have also noted, is socially informed insofar as in every society there are characteristic ways in which emotions get exhibited or performed.

But what does this performance of emotions as ritualized action accomplish? What is the *telos* of emotions? The answer seems to be that an emotion does not so much transform a situation magically as it intensifies itself in order to clarify its intentionality and preserves the situation in order to reconstitute it.

In their inception emotions tend both to be intrinsically complex, in virtue of their complicated intentionality, and to confuse their beholder. Emotions thus cry out for clarification and elucidation, which is precisely what their performance allows. Emotions tend to feed on themselves; to become stronger and more focused as they get performed, which makes it then easier for their intentionality to get disclosed. Intensification brings the intellect into play and makes it part and parcel of the emotion itself. Sartre, I believe, rightly notes that "In organizing itself with knowledge into an imaginative form, desire projects outside itself its object. It thereby becomes conscious of itself."[18] It is as though in the very development of emotional consciousness one wants (sometimes rather desperately) to know just "what is going on"—with this inquiry then becoming integral to the emotional state itself. Emotion as performance has always its cognitive elements. Emotions involve a recognition of their objects and one's attempt to understand them in relation to oneself.

It is this cognitive activity that enables one to distinguish most readily a full-fledged emotional state from a raw response or instinctual reaction (e.g., the immediate sense of fright one has when, while walking down the familiar quiet street to one's home, a snarling dog suddenly jumps out at one. The fright no doubt rather quickly enough becomes the emotion of fear. When fear is present the mind is already rather fully at work).

Emotional states as performance, we have said, both intensify and preserve. They preserve the very tension inherent in the situation that occasioned the emotion so that imagination can do its resolving work. Emotional states do not easily or readily let go of the situation that occasioned them; they seek rather to complete themselves through an active resolve. Imagination here works sometimes in the direction of fantasy, conjuring up make-believe resolutions of conflict situations (the swift annihilation of one's enemies) and has something of the magical sense which Sartre (over-) emphasizes; it works too in the direction of creativity, in reconstituting situations in order to deliver realistic strategies to deal with them. These imaginative activities are not simply reflections generated by some emotional state, rather they are integral to that state. The emotion would not be the emotion it is in their absence.

As performances, emotions thus allow for their appropriation. In the working out of an emotion a person strives to reestablish and reconstruct that rhythmic normality characteristic of his being, and to do so he must either expel the emotion and the dispositional tendencies toward it or assimilate the emotion to his overall experience. But whereas expulsion is well-nigh impossible (the emotion and tendency were not there voluntarily in the first place), assimilation is only very difficult. More often than not we have in our emotionality failed performance—or better only partial success. We achieve a measure of clarity and imaginative handling of the situation, and some degree of appropriation, but neither formal correctness in performance nor rightness in the full realization of the emotion's telos.[19]

and that can be performed correctly—and rightly.

Emotions, then, are reenactments and not bare acts. They have, as it were, a ritual quality—and thus they can be performed correctly or incorrectly. Aristotle long ago noted that "The man who is angry at the right things and with the right people, and, further, as he ought, when he ought, and as long as he ought, is [rightly] praised."[20] This suggests that an emotion is performed correctly when and only when there is (1) a true belief about the intentional object; (2) a proportionality of response (in intensity) to that object; and (3) an appropriate behavioral expression.

We have said before that there is an "aboutness" in emotionality—that emotional states have intentional objects, however complex they might be and however difficult it might sometimes be to specify clearly what they are. It is necessary in this context, then, to draw distinctions between the *actual object* of an emotion (what the emotion is actually about), the *occasion* for an emotion (that which triggers the emotional act), and the *target* of an emotion (that toward which the emotion is directed).[21]

Let us contrive a rather trivial, yet surely not atypical, example. Mary and John, both in their early thirties, have been married for eight years. Because of financial hardship they decided not to have children. John has had a series of jobs, but cannot seem to find his way vocationally. He knows more what he does not want to do than what he wants to do or is capable of doing. He is nevertheless concerned about his future and wants to do everything he can for Mary, whom he loves very much. Mary, who is usually even-tempered, has become irritable and impatient. She wants, and thought that by marrying John she would have, children and a secure family life. She gave up the possibility of having a career of her own by leaving school when she first met John. After talking with a friend one afternoon, who told Mary how fulfilled her own life has been with children and a successful husband, Mary confronts John at dinner that evening, accusing him of not caring, of being childish and selfish, shouting that she despises him.

The actual object of Mary's emotionality is her own existential situation; herself as the bearer of her history of choices, lost opportunities, and so on. Her emotional act was triggered by her talking with her friend and was directed to her husband John, the target of her emotion.

In emotional states there is more often than not a discrepancy between the actual object of the emotion and that to which it is directed. Object and target, in other words, do not coincide. When this happens, targets usually serve as a way of displacing emotions, and thus some degree of self-deception is involved. One cannot bear to accept the actual object, which is usually oneself to a considerable degree, and accordingly targets someone or something else. In any event, apart from elementary psychological description, it is obvious that when there is a significant disparity between the actual object and the target of an emotion, the bearer of that emotion does not have a true belief about the intentional object. One might be simply mistaken in spite of every reasonable effort to secure adequate evidence or one might be subject to some inner compulsion to believe apart from all question of reasonableness and evidence. Indeed the more incorrigible the belief, despite all evidence given to the contrary, that sustains an emotion, the more likely there is a significant disparity between the actual object and the target of the emotion. If I persist in believing—with this belief sustaining an emotional situation—some state of affairs to be the case (that Jones is my enemy and is plotting against me; that my wife is having an affair, etc.) when it is patently not the case, I undoubtedly have some overriding need to believe that so and so is the case. In these instances, whatever the basis for the erroneous belief, my emotions get misdirected and are thus performed incorrectly. In correctly performed emotion the actual object and the target are identical; that is, the emotion is directed toward that of which it is actually about. Ideally, then, for complete correctness, one should recognize some state of affairs as it is, with one's emotion then being directed to that state of affairs as such.[22]

Oftentimes, as we have also noted, there is a lack of proportionality in the intensity of emotionality relative to the situation at hand, a lack that often betrays precisely that discrepancy between actual object and target mentioned above but not restricted to it. More often than not we overreact (and sometimes underreact) emotionally. Instead of a normal fear we suffer terror; instead of distaste we experience revulsion (e.g., at some minor instance of vulgarity).

We measure proportionality in terms of our (socially grounded) values, values that enable us to discriminate between what we take to be relatively trivial and relatively important situations, incidents, and states of affairs, with the assumption that the important properly calls for a different kind of intensity than the trivial. We know that something is askew in our own emotionality and in that of others whenever we are aware of disproportionality, an awareness that contributes to the drive within emotional consciousness itself to gain clarity and proportionality.

Finally, correctness in performance does naturally involve correctness of expression (when an emotion is overtly expressed) at the direct biological and the more complex social level. Something is wrong if when I am happy about something I mournfully drag myself about, or if when I want very much to have someone know how much I care for them I scowl at them and show disgust. Social correctness is, of course, culturally informed, although universal features, or at least features that are widely shared among diverse societies, may obtain.

We have then a kind of affective continuum from that of raw emotive responses that tend to expend themselves and to which we look for causal explanations, to emotions as performances that strive to complete themselves—and are, accordingly, performed, in varying degrees, correctly or incorrectly—and where we look for rational jusitifications.

Emotional states are, it seems, ineliminable at the level of separative, interactive experience. Although ego based, they are essentially intersubjective, centered on one's relationships with other persons and situations in the world. Hence, as Spinoza saw so clearly, emotions betray our dependency. They bind us to others—and to ourselves.

The trick then is to have emotions which fulfill their telos without our being bound by them—which means, I believe, to perform emotions not only *correctly* but *rightly*. An emotion that is performed rightly is an expression of what we might call a "feeling sensitivity"—an active state of affective awareness that discloses the fundamental qualitative character of things. Feeling sensitivities are not so much inner sensations as they are outward-facing affective states or actions. We have feelings *toward* which, in their intentionality, are radically unlike the so called feelings *of* (e.g., pain). Feeling sensitivities participate *with* that which they intend and thereby generate an atmosphere, as it were, that suffices a situation in much the same manner as transformed aesthetic emotion gives unity and integrity to an artwork. A feeling sensitivity, then, is not a sense but a sensibility: it belongs to a person who has achieved a certain disinterested openness, a loving, concerned responsiveness, and is thus able to relate to the world aesthetically, with creativity.

Chinese philosophers, for example, the Taoist Wang Pi/Wang Bi, distinguished clearly between those persons who are attached to their emotions and those who "have emotions without ensnarement." Fung Yu-lan has stated that "The Neo-Confucian method of dealing with the emotions follows the same line as Wang Pi's. Its essential is the disconnecting of the emotions from the [narrow egocentric] self."[23] He goes on to quote the Neo-Confucian philosopher Ch'eng Hao/Cheng Hao who taught that

> The normality of the sage is that his emotion follows the nature of things, yet of himself he has no emotion. Therefore, for the superior man nothing is better than being impersonal and impartial, and responding to things spontaneously as they come. . . . When the sage is pleased, it is because the thing

is there which is rightly the object of pleasure. When the sage is angry, it is because the thing is there which is rightly the object of anger. Therefore the pleasure and anger of the sage are not connected with his mind, but with things.[24]

This conscious "connection with things," rather than with one's ego-centered self, represents precisely the transformation of a correctly performed emotion into a feeling sensitivity that intends a harmonious resolution of the disruptive situation which occasioned the emotion. The exercise of a feeling sensitivity is a kind of cofeeling experience; it not only intends a valuable world, it participates with that world in heartfelt intimacy.

A rightly performed emotion, then, is one that shows correctness in a manner or style of artful performance. No longer an indulgence, emotionality becomes an affective discernment. Its attainment requires a profound shift away from the centering of oneself around obsessive ego-concerns to the realization of the essential freedom of one's being. With this freedom, emotionality as such becomes transformed into its being an affective mode of value discernment and a creative responding to one's world.

NOTES

1. Amélie Oksenberg Rorty (ed.), *Explaining Emotions* (Berkeley: University of California Press, 1980), 1.

2. In recent times this denigration has continued under new epistemological forms with the positivist alignment of the emotive with the evaluative (as set sharply against the superior cognitive with the factual and descriptive). But this alignment unwittingly assigned the emotions a central place in the basic areas of human experience. Most of the time, most persons clearly experience the world and themselves in the evaluative terms of ethical and aesthetic judgment rather than in the factual, assertive terms of truth-seeking empirical discourse.

3. "The term *emotion*," we are told, "is derived from the Latin, *e* + *movere*. It originally meant to migrate or transfer from one place to another. It was also used to refer to states of agitation or perturbation, both physical (e.g., the weather) and psychological. . . . The term *passion* is derived from the Latin, *pati* (to suffer), which in turn is related to the Greek *pathos*. Also derived from *pati* are such expressions as *passive* and *patient*. At the root of these concepts is the idea that an individual (or physical object) is undergoing or suffering some change, as opposed to doing or initiating change." (James R. Averill, "Emotion and Anxiety: Sociocultural, Biological, and Psychological Determinants," in Rorty [ed.], *Explaining Emotions*, 38.)

4. René Descartes, *The Passions of the Soul*, article LII, in *Descartes*, ed. Ralph M. Eaton (New York: Charles Scribner's Sons, 1927), 379.

5. Harry Frankfurt for one denies this ownership aspect of emotions in favor

of the more traditional view that regards (at least many) emotions as alien intrusions. It is only in the (superficial) sense as a matter of identification that in all cases emotions belong to part of someone's ongoing history. Many emotions, Frankfurt argues, are essentially external to the person. They are in certain respects analogous to involuntary bodily movements, like being pushed from behind. See his "Identification and Externality," in A. Rorty (ed.), *The Identities of Persons* (Berkeley: University of California Press, 1976), 239–51. Whenever ownership of the emotions in the strict sense is denied, however, it is simply impossible for the person to come to grips with them, to appropriate them, to bring them into the fabric of his identity so as to allow for their completion and possible transformation. Although it is the case, as we will discuss, that many emotional states are felt by us to be foreign to what we take to be our real selves or true personalities, they nevertheless inescapably are part and parcel of our own dispositional nature and always exhibit something of oneself to others and to oneself.

6. It might also be argued that so-called positive emotions such as sympathy are not so much emotions, at least as I have defined them, as they are affective attitudes. They are, to their beholder, self-evident as to their object and source, unlike with emotions per se that need to be acted out in order to be understood.

7. See Robert C. Solomon, *The Passions: The Myth and Nature of Human Emotions* (Garden City, N.Y.: Doubleday, Anchor, 1979).

8. Ronald de Sousa, "The Rationality of Emotions," in Rorty, *Explaining Emotions*, 141.

9. Gilbert Ryle, in his well-known *The Concept of Mind* (New York: Barnes and Noble, 1949), goes so far as to argue (albeit inadequately) that emotions themselves are essentially dispositional, in contrast especially to feelings which he takes to be primarily body sensations.

10. And it is here, of course, that various "superego" constraints may profoundly affect the manner in which, and the degree to which, emotional dispositions get fulfilled, the constraints giving rise to conflicting voices within the emotions, especially those that are intimately bound-up with sexual desires.

11. William James states succinctly that "Our natural way of thinking about these standard emotions [surprise, curiosity, rapture, fear . . .] is that the mental perception of some fact excites the mental affection called emotion, and that this latter state of mind gives rise to the bodily expression. My thesis is that the *bodily changes follow directly the perception of the exciting fact, and that our feeling of the same changes as they occur is the emotion*" ("What is an Emotion?" *Mind*, 9 [1884]; reprint in *The Emotions*, ed. Knight Dunlop [Baltimore: Williams & Wilkens Company, 1922], 13). This notion, which came to be developed as the James-Lange theory, was, it is now believed, rather thoroughly refuted by W. B. Cannon, who (in 1927) showed experimentally that similar physiological changes accompanied quite varied emotional states and that one could induce those changes without at the same time producing the appropriate emotions.

12. See for example, Catherine A. Lutz, *Unnatural Emotions* (Chicago: University of Chicago Press), 1988.

13. These social dimensions of emotion contribute often as well to the fundamental confusion in emotionality where emotions sometimes get aroused against

the very emotion being experienced. This seems to have particular force with gender-differentiated situations. Men are not supposed to have certain emotions (e.g., those associated with sensitive caring); women are not encouraged to exhibit what are otherwise deeply felt states (e.g., those involved with aggression, ambition and the like), and, when these emotions and states are present, they may give rise to strong reactions of disapproval within their bearer.

14. Jean-Paul Sartre, *The Emotions: Outline of a Theory*, trans. Bernard Frechtman (New York: Philosophical Library, 1949), 58–59. Sartre later recognizes that a different form of emotion is present when the world itself presents itself in wholly unexpected ways. The sudden experience of a face in one's window horrifies, with the world itself becoming horrible.

15. Ibid., 77.

16. Joseph P. Fell, *Emotion in the Thought of Sartre* (New York: Columbia University Press, 1965), 25.

17. Ronald de Sousa, "Self-Deceptive Emotions," in Rorty, *Explaining Emotions*, 286.

18. Jean-Paul Sartre, *The Psychology of the Imagination*, trans. Bernard Frechtman (New York: Philosophical Library, 1948), 210.

19. We also of course do have on occasion a rather complete failure in performance. In close interpersonal situations we often find a mild initial emotional response soon developing into a fulfledged paroxysm. Lovers' quarrels oftentimes exhibit this pattern. The performance is over (temporarily) only when the actors are exhausted.

20. Aristotle, *Nicomachean Ethics*, 1125^b.

21. The occasion and the target of an emotion are, of course, oftentimes identical (that which triggers the emotion being at the same time that toward which it is directed—tragicomically sometimes as when the bearer of bad news is maltreated).

22. In causal terms, the intentional object may be said to be the cause (and not just a possible occasion) for an emotion when a coincidence between actual object and target does obtain. When there is a significant discrepancy between object and target we do not look to the target as the primary basis for causal explanation, but rather to some nexus involving the actual object—which, as indicated, more often than not has something intimately to do with the subject, the bearer of the emotion. This is especially the case, as we have seen, with raw emotive responses. The closer an emotional state is to the raw response, the greater will be the likely disparity between the causes of the emotion and that to which the emotion is directed and the greater the coincidence between the occasion for the emotion and its target.

23. Fung Yu-lan, in *A Short History of Chinese Philosophy*, ed. Derk Bodde (New York: The Macmillan Company, 1960), 238. Romanization is given throughout first in the older, standard Wade-Giles system followed by the contemporary *pinyin* system.

24. *Ming-tao Wen-chi*, chuan 3, in ibid., 287.

4

✳

The Body of a Person

At birth each individual human being is a unique configuration of
various physical, psychical (and perhaps other yet to be determined)
conditions.[1] These conditions, which are indefinite in number and clearly
embody biological and cultural processes, are not, of course, simply
heaped-up together like bits of dirt on a pile, rather they are given as constitutive of a unified being. An individual is a psychophysical being.[2]

At birth each individual nevertheless can be weighed and measured;
she can be examined closely by an attending physician for physical "birth
defects"; hair and skin color can be noted, and so on. Some of the given
physical conditions are universal; others are general or particular (what
an older terminology quaintly called "accidental"). I have a nervous system which is the "same" as yours; I have various instinctual drives which
define my organic being and that of others; and certain of my other physical characteristics may also be similar to those of others of the same
national, ethnic or racial origin. I also have my own peculiar physical features. No one looks exactly like me. As an individual I am an identifiable
physical being embodying universal, general, and particular conditions. I
can be explained by a scientist or physical anthropologist and I can be
depicted by an artist.

An individual, then, does not so much have a body as she is her physical (and other) conditions. "The body," I want to argue, is an achievement
concept. *Persons* have bodies to the degree to which they appropriate the
physical conditions of their individuality and become active, integrated
psychophysical beings.[3]

THE BODY AS AN ACHIEVEMENT CONCEPT

Several metaphors have dominated and controlled much of philosophical
and popular thinking in the West about the body. The body, it has been

said, is among other things a "prison house," a "temple," a "machine," an "instrument." The metaphors obviously contain and mix together descriptions, attitudes and theories.

The (Platonic) prison-house metaphor is essentially a complaint which relates the awareness of the possibility of, and difficulty in attaining, pure rational consciousness. The body is seen not only as the principle that differentiates and restricts the possibilities of one's being but also as the principle of containment—as that which hinders and becomes an obstacle to that (knowing) consciousness that wants to be everywhere and nowhere. The body, according to Plato, makes incessant demands, driving us toward "evil pleasures and desires, causing war and faction and fighting."[4]

The great body-despisers of history, as Nietzsche would call them, have all at one time subscribed to this metaphor, which so powerfully expresses the recognition of the physical as the seat of restlessness, of sexual desire, of distraction, and especially of sickness and decay.

The prison metaphor, however, points to a divided self and can, in the last analysis, when believed in only yield a frustrated will. Experience, as exemplified in the ascetic who struggles to deny the body while all the time feeling its compelling presence, clearly testifies to the fact that waking consciousness can be dissociated from the physical conditions of our being only at the cost of those conditions seeking their revenge, working through that division to demand and take their due. This is especially the case with sexuality, nicely characterized as "the complex conscious and unconscious desires and interdictions that shape human's conceptions of themselves as desiring creatures."[5] Sexuality is in fact often experienced as pervading one's physicality, exhibited most fully in the adolescent whose entire physique seems at times to get compressed into a sexual bodily presence and self image.

The temple metaphor (1 Cor., 6:19), on the other hand, is not so much a description of how we so often experience our bodies as the locus of restlessness and desire but a prescription that tells us how we ought to regard our bodies. It finds its intelligibility within a religious framework of values that sees the possibility of a reverential attitude toward all things in virtue of their divine origin and grounding. The body can be a holy vessel enshrining a divine spirit. Not to be taken as a mere source of pleasure and pain, the body is to be counted among things potentially sacred.

The temple metaphor has always had a rather limited acceptance. It obviously points for some to a noble ideal, but tends to overlook too strongly just those features of the prison-house metaphor that have given it its enduring appeal. Within Christian thought itself the metaphor had to be Aristotelianized and integrated into a doctrine of resurrection, in which the physical body as such becomes, quite obscurely, a spirit-body.[6]

The machine metaphor, which at least since Descartes has been so pervasive in modern Western thinking, is essentially an explanation that purportedly shows us what the body actually is functional and the place it occupies in the natural scheme of things. Grounded in seventeenth-century mechanistic science, the machine metaphor intends to bind human physicality entirely to nature, the human body being but one kind of physical system among many others.

Although crude machine models have been largely abandoned in most thinking people's image of the body in favor of more organic and cybernetic ones, the basic intent of the metaphor for many people still stands. A human being qua physical being is utterly a part of nature. His mental being is an autonomous (thinking but unextended) order set over and against the physical, yet somehow interacting with it.

The machine metaphor does capture something of the sense we have of the centrality and priority of consciousness in our experience of ourselves and the world. Part of us might be reduced to lawlike forces, but with our minds we nevertheless—in our folk ways of thinking—transcend the physical as such. Our nobility, we believe, demands our being able to differentiate ourselves sharply from the rest of the animal world. Our bodies might be machine-like and inextricably a part of an objectified order but our minds (consciousness, soul) are immaterial, not having as such a specifiable spatial location.

The instrument metaphor is closely related to the machine metaphor and is, in many ways, an extension of it. It is essentially a description of how human beings control and employ their (machine-like) bodies in innumerable ways (without, of course, their knowing how physiologically they are able to do so). The metaphor presupposes that human beings have independent wills and the like that enable them to use their bodies to carry out various tasks. A tool requires a user.

There is an undeniable force to the instrument metaphor, as living things do indeed seem to have, in varying degrees, the wondrous capacity to initiate all sorts of body-based purposive actions. This, quite naturally, gives rise to the sense that somehow I am other than my body and can use it as a vehicle or carrier to fulfill some conscious purpose in much the same way that I can employ a hammer, a saw, a screwdriver to make a table—although reflection ought to show that the I who uses a body is already constituted bodily in a certain way.

Now these dominant metaphors, in addition to being dualistic in character,[7] presuppose that the meaning of "the body" can be spelled out in principle in purely descriptive or factual terms. This is characteristic of the logic of formulating many of our most basic concepts. Let me explain.

Philosophers (still somewhat under the sway of positivism) often distinguish between evaluative and descriptive (or classificatory) uses of conceptual terms and insist that "meaning" as such belongs exclusively with the latter. Morris Weitz, for example, in his well-known article "The Role of Theory in Aesthetics," writes,

> "Art" is construed as an evaluative term which is either identified with its criterion or justified in terms of it. "Art" is defined in terms of its evaluative property, e.g., successful harmonization. On such a view, to say "X is a work of art" is (1) to say something which is taken *to mean* "X is a successful harmonization" (e.g., "Art *is* significant form") or (2) to say something praiseworthy *on the basis* of its successful harmonization. Theorists are never clear whether it is (1) or (2) which is being put forward. Most of them, concerned as they are with this evaluative use, formulate (2), i.e., that feature of art that *makes* it art in the praise-sense, and then go to state (1), i.e., the definition of "Art" in terms of its art-making feature. And this is *to confuse the conditions under which we say something evaluatively with the meaning of what we say.*[8]

There are, however, I firmly believe, a range of concepts that have their meaning only in evaluative or (better) achievement terms, which is to say that certain concepts have no clear or exhaustive descriptive content apart from their evaluative or achievement sense. Personhood, as we have seen, is just such a concept. To be a person means to have achieved a certain kind of integration and quality of being; it means, among other things, to have achieved a sensitivity and openness to the being of others. Persons, on this account, are not givens of nature. The meaning of personhood is not reducible to a set of descriptive features available to a presumed everyday value-free sense perception. There is no way that one could spell out the sufficient conditions for personhood and then impose evaluative properties on the otherwise presumably clear-cut descriptive meaning. These evaluative properties are simply built in to those conditions.

Frank Sibley has argued that aesthetic terms function much in this same way. For their application they require a certain perceptiveness or taste, for "there are no non-aesthetic features which serve in *any* circumstances as logically *sufficient* conditions for applying aesthetic terms."[9] There may indeed be negative conditions that govern the application of aesthetic concepts—if, for example, a painting were of pale colors and was highly geometric, one can be certain that it is not "fiery or garish or flamboyant." But, and this is the main point, no description of a painting as being of X color, Y shape, and so on, can ensure that it will be serene or graceful.

The same, I think, holds true for the concept of a person's body. I have/ am a body, in the primary sense of the term, to the degree to which I have appropriated and integrated the given physical conditions of my being (which conditions as such can indeed in principle be described). *My* body *is* only as it is articulated within my being as a person. The isolable physical conditions of my individual being, in other words, are not "my" body. What I recognize as integral to me qua person is not this configuration but what, in a way, I have made of it as my own. To appropriate the physical means to acknowledge the given conditions—the physical structures, drives, powers, capacities—and to bring them firmly into the fabric of my achieved identity. A body always belongs to someone. The primary meaning of the concept is its achievement sense.[10]

Achievement terms, then, are not condition-governed. The aesthetic, moral, or spiritual quality to which they apply is not reducible to a set of features that admits of simple sense recognition. Nor does knowledge by description help: knowing that a young man has paid great attention to the care of his physical body does not guarantee that he has appropriated rightly the physical capabilities of his individual being. He might, with all this attention and care, become entirely one-sided, a "mindless muscle-man."

It is then a peculiarity of achievement terms that one cannot specify at what (quantitative) point they admit of application. Just when an individual becomes a person cannot be stated; at exactly what time-space the given physical conditions get rightly appropriated as a body cannot be indicated—precisely because they are qualitative achievements. In short, when something is an achievement, it has taken on a qualitative character that is different in kind from the raw materials that constitute it.

THE APPROPRIATED BODY

Sartre insists that we choose the constitution of our body as given to us. The cripple, Sartre says, chooses the way he constitutes his disability "as 'unbearable,' 'humiliating,' 'to be hidden,' 'to be revealed to all,' 'an object of pride,' 'the justification for my failures,' etc.)."[11] But this analysis, too, presupposes that the body is the physical conditions of an individual, not what is appropriated by a person. It also assumes that body constitution is primarily volitional.

Self-consciousness of the body, however, starts from the standpoint of psychophysical unity. It is simply not the case that some separable I adopts an attitude toward a pregiven body, for that I is already what the person has created qua persona out of the raw materials of his or her being. A person *is* his or her achieved identity. We are not chosen by ourselves but are created in a more fundamental ongoing way.

Body appropriation—the bringing of the physical conditions of one's individual being into the matrix of one's personal identity and self-image—proceeds, quite obviously, through various stages. The child must struggle through to an initial assimilation of the physical in order to accept the raw material of her bodily-being as her own—the physical, at this stage, often subject to rapid change and growth. The appropriation process from childhood to adulthood is largely unself-conscious: a personal I continually develops (and sometimes disintegrates) autogenetically, as it were, and precariously. At every stage a person has a kind of unfinished completeness. A unified I stands forth, a unique personality is announced, subject to change, alteration, and development.[12]

Appropriation is thus at once an acknowledging-integrating and a selecting process. It is an acknowledging-integrating of the conditions of individuality (as being my limitations and opportunities) and it is a selecting from among the conditions those (in pattern, combination, configuration) that will be educated for disciplined action. The selection process is not, of course, entirely voluntary. In the development toward maturity one is trained to do certain things (and not others) in certain ways—things and ways which are part of the larger society's ways of doing things. Body education is both personal and social. At various stages of one's life one is able to decide to acquire certain body skills and to devote the necessary time and energy to that acquisition. Body appropriation thus sets the stage, as it were, for one's potential actions. Personal identification is as much a matter of what I am *able to do* as it is *who* I am; or, to put it another way, who I am involves very much what I am able to do and in what manner or way.

The body as appropriated can never then, as Gabriel Marcel puts it, be "exterior to a certain central reality of myself."[13] As a person I am as I have created myself in and through the raw materials of my being. A disparity may, of course, exist between the manner of one's body appropriation (one's personal identification) and the actualities of one's given physical conditions. A person might indeed believe herself to be (in bodily terms) other than she in fact is; Jane might think of herself as being physically beautiful but command little agreement from others on that score (albeit her believing so would no doubt affect positively the total self-image she presented to others). In any event, a kind of person-deception in somatic terms is always possible, and is no doubt rather prevalent.

It is also the case that when circumstances disallow or make it extremely difficult to achieve the having of an appropriated body in a full, integrated way, there will oftentimes be a corresponding diminution or deprivation of personhood. By rejecting significant parts of the conditions of its being, the I will necessarily be divided within itself. And just as at the level of person presentation, where multiple appearants of a unified self are brought forth in a variety of functional roles, so at the somatic level multiple body-appearants may be said to derive from the integrated appropriated body; one might exhibit an athlete-body, a lover-body, a laborer-body and concentrate one's bodily being, as it were, into one or more of these functional syntheses.

Also, the manner in which individual body appropriation takes place will indeed vary enormously in different historical and cultural contexts. Women no doubt appropriate their bodies in ways (with content and style) different from men; and individuals within each gender as well—depending upon everything from social-class distinction (especially for those who have had to use their bodies as laborer-bodies in primary ways) to health care opportunities—will appropriate their bodies differently. For some persons the physical conditions of their being become a happy source for personal identity; for others they become an oppressive burden. When one is identified by various physical features (e.g., skin color) in contexts that are derogatory (racist), the achievement of a secure personal identity is an extremely difficult task: there is always considerable psychological resistance to appropriating what others take to be negative.

Person-consciousness, then, does not say in any exclusive sense that I am my body anymore than it says that I am not my body, for the body is here part and parcel of the very condition of identification. Pathological disunity and one-sided identification are always possible—but they are recognized precisely as pathological.

"Who or what then carries out the appropriating process?" it might well be asked. And the answer must be that no one or no thing as such can be specified as the agent behind the process, rather the means and conditions of appropriation emerge in the process itself and are constantly modified thereby. We are so accustomed to think in terms of independent agency that it seems almost self-contradictory to conceive of a process, creative or otherwise, as setting the conditions for its own direction and fulfillment; however, it seems clear to me, that is its nature. The person who appropriates his or her experience and the terms of his or her individuality is the same person who creatively comes forth. As Merleau-Ponty noted in a different context: "In so far as the content can be readily subsumed under the form and can appear as the content *of* that form, it is because the form is accessible only through the content."[14] The wearer creates the mask; the mask becomes the wearer. Person-making, albeit socially grounded, is throughout autogeneous in character.

The question that is often raised, then, of whether or not I am contingently related to *this* body is thoroughly misguided. It is simply inconceivable for a person whose achieved appropriation of the physical is constitutive of his personhood to be other than himself. He cannot, without contradiction, think of *himself* as someone else: He can imagine what it might be like to have certain qualities that he does not have; but the I who does the imagining is already constituted *qua* persona in a certain way.[15]

This does not mean, however, that a person *owns* his or her body in any literal sense of the term. The concept of ownership with respect to the body lacks a precise literal meaning, albeit it has rich metaphoric possibilities. To own something in the literal sense means to be separate from it and to have some special claim upon it. Ownership usually implies possessionship of some kind—either directly or by having a "right of." I might own the house I live in and have the right of possession to the apartment I own elsewhere. As a social, legal concept having essentially to do with property, ownership has nothing literally to do with the relationship between a person and his body (qua appropriated). A person cannot exchange his appropriated body for another without ceasing to be himself; he cannot decide to occupy it or not. His "body language," his unself-conscious gestures, facial movements, express and signify uniquely *his* emotional states, desires, anxieties and the like.

But people do identify with what they own, and hence a vital metaphor of "ownness" does arise in the context of personhood. I own my body as a person most powerfully in the sense of affirmation and identification. Psychologically the metaphor carries the sense of being the opposite of disowning. To disown something of what I obviously am involves some kind of person-deception. The term "ownness" here means a lucid self-togetherness: it means a "belonging with." I own my body insofar as it belongs to me and for which, without my possessing it as a commodity, I assume a special responsibility.

The primary consciousness of ourselves qua body is, then, we are suggesting, from the standpoint of a unified state of the psychophysical. We do not start with a disembodied I who suddenly discovers that he or she has a body of a certain kind. That I is what it is in terms of somatic as well as mental appropriation.

In speaking, as we have done, of the appropriated body as a personal achievement, one might get the impression, which would be erroneous, that the appropriated body as we understand it is a private something or other to which I alone have privileged access. The appropriated body, I believe, is basically an interpersonal phenomenon, for the simple reason that the very concept of a person—to which the appropriated body contributes in such a significant way—is throughout social in character. I am a person only in relation to others. I am a person only as a cultured being. The persona that I present myself as being is seen by others precisely in terms of the achieved unity of my mental and physical powers, such as they might be. The appropriated body, in short, is perceived by others as a matter of course in their perception of me and is what it is in virtue of the complex process of relationships that constitute my historical experience as a human being. Each of us may be profoundly alone, but there is no solitary person.

The primary meaning of the term "body" then, is the physical conditions of individuality become part and parcel of an integrated (social-grounded) person. In Marcel's words, this body is not so much an object but "the condition for objectification." The body may though become an object for consciousness, and then we may properly speak of an "object-body." It may also be experienced by a person as the locus of his activity, as a "subject-body."[16]

THE OBJECT-BODY AND THE SUBJECT-BODY

A child first sees himself qua body as others see him; as tall or fat or good-looking, and so on. The child's body may, in this sense, be said to be a "social construction," an identification constituted by various social inputs. This "object-body," as we will call it, is, however perspectivally objective as well as socially public. It is what we see of the physical from the perspective of an appropriated body consciousness when we isolate the physical and treat it precisely as an object. The object-body, in short, is noetically the developed physical conditions of one's being as brought into a portrait.

A portrait, as we have seen, is a perspective to which a person is responsive. It refers to an object without being a copy of it. It is a representation that rightly shows an object without exhausting it. Persons may be viewed in physicalist perspectives (through a variety of scientific descriptions, models, theories and explanations and in more everyday bodily terms) to which they are responsive; empirically, we would have to say, they lend themselves to just such perspectives. The portraits successfully represent the body as an objective and public phenomenon.

If one had a complete knowledge of the physical, the object-body and the developed physical conditions would be exactly the same. We would have, then, not a portrait but "the truth." Lacking that complete knowledge, as we now do and no doubt forever will, the object-body will always be presented by an incomplete representation.

It is the object-body as such, then, that we take to be subject to generation and degeneration and to be therefore thoroughly temporal.

The object-body is the materiality of the individual as objectified. It establishes the *place* of a person's body. An embodied person must always be someplace in an environment.

Being the temporally laden, objectified content of a portrait does not, however, make the object-body any less real than the appropriated body. The object-body is secondary only in the order of meaning and in the givenness of experience. Its content is given to us necessarily from the standpoint of person consciousness, which is to say we are able to discriminate an object-body (our own and that of others) only through an appropriated body-mind consciousness: an object-body content is accessible to us only as formed (by portrayal).

Sartre has argued that "the body is the point of view on which there cannot be a point of view."[17] If this were so, then there would be no way by which a person could constitute his "facticity"—or, in our terms, form a portrait of oneself and others qua body, which we obviously do. It is however certainly the case that we do not actually perceive other persons as bodies having minds or simply as bodies that may or may not be mind-informed (as a strict empiricist might want to have it); we perceive other persons as the persona they present themselves as being.

Sartre has shown brilliantly (and vividly, with examples such as that of the voyeur) the manner in which we are beings-for-others (*être-pour-autrui*); that is, the manner in which we objectify others and press that objectification on to their own self-consciousness. The man looking through the keyhole alone in a deserted hallway is to himself merely perceiving a certain scene; it is when someone appears in the hallway that he becomes and recognizes himself to be a voyeur. "Hell is other people," Sartre announces in his play *No Exit* (*Hui Clos*). The other always makes of me what I am but not what I am to myself.

All of this is perhaps only a dramatic way of saying that the object-body is a richer social phenomenon than what is simply given by a portrait of the physical conditions of one's being. In our everyday experience the object-body of another is always perceived meaningfully. Except when, as medical scientists, we perceive another human being in bodily terms, we do not just perceive bare anatomical structures and the like and what we understand about their functioning; we perceive the other bodily in complex qualitative ways (aesthetically, ethically, etc.). In the last analysis, as already indicated, we do perceive the other in fact as an appropriated body. We move, it seems to me, quite readily from simple behavioral perception of the other's object-body to an apprehension of the other as he is to himself. This brings us to the subject-body.

Max Scheler, and others in the phenomenological tradition, distinguish a "lived body" (*der Leib*) from a "thing body" (*der Körper*). Scheler calls the lived body the immediate "hereness" of body; it is "that of which we have an inner consciousness."[18] The lived body, then, is simply "a totally uniform phenomenal fact" that "is independent and, in the order of givenness, prior to any special so-called organic sensations and special kinds of outer perception."[19] The lived body's relationship to these organic sensations is "one between *form* and its *content*. In the same sense as all psychic experiences are only together in an 'ego' and conjoined into a unity of a special kind, all organic sensations are necessarily given as 'together' in a lived body."[20] The thing body is the "outer perception" of this primordial lived body.

The lived body, as Scheler characterizes it, however, becomes something of a convenient fiction; it is not directly known in experience. "In the same sense as the 'ego' must accompany all our (psychic) experience (as Kant pointedly said) so also," according to Scheler, "our lived body must accompany all organic sensations."[21] The unity of self, for Kant, though, is not itself a content of experience. The relation of lived body to thing body, as well as their respective natures, remains then a mystery. Scheler lacks that third central term, what we have called the appropriated body, which provides the ground for the distinction that may be drawn between the subject-body and the object-body.[22]

The subject-body as phenomenon is, as I define it, the immediate sense one has of one's physicality primarily as it is a seat of potential activity. The subject-body is what I experience myself to be physically (not simply in terms of an immediate sensation, proprioceptive or otherwise, which seems to ground many later phenomenological analyses, but as an ongoing source of activity).[23] One is normally aware of oneself physically not in terms of all that one might know about one's object-body (which is usually very little), but in those terms that are required for successful action. As a subject I am aware of certain primitive possibilities of body action, of the repertoire of actions that I have acquired and learned: first of all, those that come quite naturally within my physical capacities and that I perform in instinctive ways (e.g., basic bodily functions like digesting); then, those that require a learned effort and consequently get performed in habitual ways (like riding a bicycle). The subject-body, we might then say, is for us a locus of body habits, of body *saṁskāras*, or dispositions to act in certain ways.[24]

The subject-body, by virtue of its being action oriented, is thus always grounded in an environment with which it interacts. It inhabits a world with which it is in constant negotiation and becomes, so to speak, that world insofar as it is in a continual process of engagement with it.

Gabriel Marcel writes, "my body is only properly mine to the degree to which I am able to control it. But here, too, there is a limit, an inner limit; if as a consequence of some serious illness, I lose all control of my body, it tends to cease to be my body, for the very profound reason that, as we say in the common idiom, I am 'no longer myself.' "[25] The inability to control one's body, as with one who is incontinent, means that one is no longer integrated as an agent in an environment; one is reduced, as it were, to being one's object-body. In our normal functioning, though, as Merleau-Ponty notes, "The body is the vehicle of being in the world, and having a body is, for a living creature, to be intervolved in a definite environment, to identify oneself with certain projects and to be continually committed to them."[26]

In short, the subject-body, we are suggesting, is essentially our awareness of ourselves as an active and as a potentially active being co-present with an environment. I experience myself physically primarily in terms of the actions I do and can perform. The body as activating telos is the way we live our bodies as persons.[27]

If the essence of our consciousness of ourselves as a subject-body is as it is a seat of potential activity and not merely as it is a congeries of inner sensations or a passive "being-here," then it follows that our subject-body, like our appropriated and object bodies, is an intersubjective or social phenomenon, for the repertoire of actions that is the content of that consciousness is itself largely social in character. Much of what I am able to do—and especially in the manner in which I do what I am able to do—is, as we have already noted, learned behavior. I am educated to do a rich variety of actions. The vast majority, in fact, of my everyday actions, from eating to talking, reflect my learning how to do these things in socially determined ways in a context of interaction with, and reaction to, others in an environment.[28]

We are not three different bodies: there is only a unified person. We speak of a person's having or being an appropriated body as this is part and parcel of his or her constitution as a unified being. The given physical conditions of individuality are taken up, to the degree to which they are, as integral to person-consciousness and identity. From that standpoint, the natural standpoint of a mature consciousness, one is then able, in a derivative way, to see and conceptualize the physical as an object-body, as that which, albeit social in character, is strictly objectifiable. We form portraits of the physical, amenable perspectives, conceptual and symbolic notions and models which, when successful, do the descriptive and explanatory jobs intended by them. We do have medical science, and we are able to view others and ourselves quite readily in ordinary language physical terms. At the same time we do have that primitive sense of ourselves as a physical presence capable of action; we are a subject-body, the consciousness of our object-body as it is for us.

NOTES

1. As I have noted before, I see no reason why we should assume that what we perspectivally regard now as physical and as mental necessarily exhausts what we may know about the raw material of our individual being. Radical new

ways of regarding human beings are certainly a logical possibility and, if the history of science is any indication, an empirical likelihood.

2. The physical conditions of our individual being, in their bare normal functioning, are apparently entirely commensurate with, and allied with, various mental functions. Most of our body-based actions are at once physical and purposive. It is the psychotic who is the walking dualism; his body-movements seemingly unrelated to any purposive activity. The restiveness of the physical—without restraint!

3. Another way of putting this would be to say that the unity of a person as a psychophysical being shows or implicates itself in every domain of personhood that one might, for whatever reason, care to discriminate. A person's body is *his* body only insofar as it is informed by and is constitutive of the psychophysical unity of his being.

4. Plato writes: "must not genuine philosophers find themselves holding the sort of belief which will lead them to say, one to another, something like this: 'It would seem that we are guided as it were along a track to our goal by the fact that, so long as we have the body accompanying our reason in its inquiries, so long as our souls are befouled by this evil admixture, we shall assuredly never fully possess that which we desire, to wit truth. For by reason of the nurture which it must have, the body makes countless demands upon us, and furthermore any sickness that may befall it hampers our pursuit of true being. Then too it fills us with desires and longings and fears and imaginations of all sorts, and such quantities of trash, that, as the common saying puts it, we really never have a moment to think about anything because of the body. Why, what else is it that causes war and faction and fighting but the body and its desires?" (*Phaedo*, 66:b, trans. R. Hackforth.)

5. Peter Brooks, *Body Work* (Cambridge: Harvard University Press), 6.

6. See Etienne Gilson, *The Spirit of Medieval Philosophy*, trans. A. H. C. Downes (London: Sheed & Ward, 1950), chapter IX. "Christian Anthropology," for an interesting historical-theological discussion of this issue.

7. The machine metaphor is explicitly so, for it forthrightly excludes the mental from that extended (Cartesian) realm of materiality of which the body is inextricably a part. The prison-house and temple metaphors likewise see the human body in some kind of radical dissociation from the spirit, at least initially, and seek to come to terms with that dissociation in their own ways. The instrument metaphor splits the willful person and his acting body and, like the other metaphors, must find a way to establish some kind of intimate relation between them.

It should also be pointed out that the different metaphors are no doubt understood and accepted by different persons relative to their own personal experience. The slave who is constrained to be identified primarily as a thing body would probably recognize the instrument metaphor as closest to his experience; the holy ascetic either the prison-house or temple metaphor.

8. Morris Weitz, "The Role of Theory in Esthetics," *The Journal of Aesthetics and Art Criticism* 15 (1956): 33 (last italics mine).

9. Frank Sibley, "Aesthetic Concepts," *The Philosophical Review* LXVIII (October 1959): 354.

10. By the primary meaning or sense of a concept I mean that which has priority in an axio-noetic way (and not that which is most widely used in ordinary language; although the two may, of course, coincide). The meaning of "the body" in the primary sense is what our physical nature is for us most intimately in our value experience and which is thereby presupposed in other uses or senses of the term—and this, it seems clearly to me, is what I will call the "appropriated body." It is primitive not because it is undefined but because it is only from its standpoint, as I will try to show, that other somatic distinctions can be drawn.

11. Jean-Paul Sartre, *Being and Nothingness*, trans. Hazel E. Barnes (New York: Washington Square Press, 1966), 432.

12. Traditional societies, more so than modern ones, seem to give full recognition to the stages in body appropriation that a young person typically undergoes. Various and oftentimes elaborate rites of passage are articulated which map out both natural changes and how those changes are to be negotiated within the social fabric. The rites guide the young person, making clear what it expected of him or her qua body appropriation.

13. Gabriel Marcel, *Metaphysical Journal*, trans. Bernard Wall (Chicago: Henry Regnery Co., 1952), entry November 9, 1920.

14. Maurice Merleau-Ponty, *Phenomenology of Perception*, trans. Colin Smith (New York: Humanities Press, Inc. 1962), 102.

15. Our "object-body," as we will call it, does of course have a sort of ontological contingency, for the physical conditions of individuality as such do not, as given, bear any necessary reason for their being; albeit they are given within a causal nexus which many would regard as bearing some sort of empirical necessity.

16. One of the conceptual niceties of the very idea of the appropriated body is its subverting of any dualism that might otherwise be buried in the object-body/subject-body distinction or, as in other formulations that separate the lived body from a thing body where, as with Sartre, the dualism is quite explicit.

17. Sartre, *Being and Nothingness*, 403ff.

18. Max Scheler, *Der Formalismus in der Ethik und die materiale Wertethik*, trans. Manford S. Frings, in *The Philosophy of the Body: Rejections of Cartesian Dualism*, ed. Stuart F. Spicker (New York: Quadrangle, The New York Times Book Co., 1970), 161.

19. Ibid., 163.

20. Ibid., 165.

21. Ibid.

22. In what follows, I will not be going into elaborate phenomenological detail regarding the functions of the subject-body as this has been spelled out, in lived body terms, quite thoroughly in the now rather large literature on the subject. I will concentrate only on those general features that have conceptual bearing on the idea of a person's body.

23. Gabriel Marcel, for example, writes: "my body, in so far as it is properly mine, presents itself to me in the first instance as something felt." (*The Mystery of Being: I Reflections and Mystery*, trans. G. S. Fraser [Chicago: Henry Regney Company, Gateway Edition, 1960], 125.)

Now the subject-body as phenomenon does of course involve our "inner bodily sensations" (our felt-awareness of various happenings carried out with and upon the body, from love making to being hit by a car), but these sensations, by their very nature, tend to be intermittent and short-lived. Sensation-wise we experience ourselves physically for the most part only when we meet resistances or obstacles to our performing various actions or are inhibited in our ability to carry out chosen tasks by various bodily conditions. Physical pain, for example, forces an awareness and acknowledgement of our brute physicality. It can be consuming. Painful sensations are, however, not merely subjective mental events, for they tend rather immediately to announce their physical locations ("my head hurts," "I have a toothache") so that they appear at once as mine and as "other." The essential, rather more enduring sense we have of ourselves physically is as the body is a locus of our potential activity. This sense is not an abstraction, but is rather the experiential realization of our power to act. This awareness of aliveness, of vitality (such as it is) tells us that we *can* act: the subject-body, in short, is our awareness of our power of doing within the conditions of our object-body.

24. And thus there appears to be a notable somatic dimension to all subwaking consciousness; which is to say that one is not normally aware of the way and extent to which one's body has assimilated and retained various action forms (skills such as riding a bicycle or typing), which nevertheless influence strongly the purposive actions that are performed at the level of waking consciousness. The body as educated has its capacities and its habits. It becomes its actions insofar as it is always influenced by what it does and in what manner of doing.

25. *Mystery of Being*, 119.

26. *Phenomenology of Perception*, 151.

This is borne out by the fact that one of the most terror-laden experiences one can have is the sudden, unexpected inability to control oneself physically. This inability threatens the very existence of the I. A straight-jacket might help restrain a madman, but if suddenly imposed upon an ordinary person it might well render him quite deranged.

27. Lacking an habitual environment from which he might be exiled, the nomad, the wandering *sadhu*, is subject-bodywise severely restricted in the possibilities of actualizing his person-development. His radical dissociations, albeit offering opportunities for person-transformations, lead him to regard his body primarily as an instrument and to represent it to himself as primarily an object, and therefore as not truly his own.

28. We will explore later in our discussion of causality and creativity how, in a person's "acting freely," the body may be regarded as taking on qualitative determinations.

5

✳

The Consciousness/
Mind of a Person

Searing heat and desert-rock dust: the tribe, its camels heavy-laden,
gathers its black tents and whitish goats and moves on across the bar-
ren Persian hills. It knows where there is water.

Dependent upon nature for the satisfaction of his needs, the nomad
believes, nevertheless, that he is free, for his needs are so few—and
there is always another place to go.

Consciousness is nomadic when it has no ground other than its own.

I

Human consciousness is a power the being of which is to be bound
or boundless. The distinctive achievement of person-consciousness,
I maintain, is its ability to engage the world freely.

Consciousness is bound whenever it is in virtue of its objects. (My) consciousness is bound whenever I discern objects perspectivally through
dynamic modes of selectivity (and enable them to be for me). (My) consciousness is bound when reflexively I am aware of being aware of a certain content. (My) consciousness is bound whenever it is in virtue of an
intersubjective community of awareness and is dependent upon an other.
(My) consciousness is bound when, as an organic temporality, it is
informed by an irrevocable history. (My) consciousness is utterly bound
when its desire-laden contents are completely involuntary.

Consciousness is boundless when, without memory, it is attentive solely to reality. Consciousness is boundless when, as a power of being, as an essential feature of the Self, it is without determinate content. Consciousness is boundless when, unselfconsciously, "I" am at one with reality.

There are thus two primary states or modes of consciousness: in its bound state consciousness is selective, reflexive, temporal, dependent, and anticipatory; in its unbounded state it is unified, undifferentiated, and timeless. When bound, consciousness is personal, it always belongs to someone. When boundless, consciousness is non-personal, it ceases to belong to anyone, being an essential quality of being.

But these two primary states of consciousness do not make for a duality; they are so radically unlike one another as to be incommensurable. A multi-leveled view of consciousness (with various sublevels to be distinguished) is thus necessary:

1. Experience itself dictates that the features of bound consciousness are not simply opposed by boundless consciousness but are radically negated and are overcome by it. For example, we do not have a different and opposing kind of temporality and memory in boundless consciousness; we have rather a timelessness and no-memory. Boundless consciousness simply annuls or utterly contradicts the contents of bound consciousness. When "I" am completely liberated the bound is no longer for me.

2. Linguistically the terms and criteria appropriate to one state cannot meaningfully be employed with reference to the other state. We have, for example, a variety of procedures for determining the accuracy of our perceptions in bound consciousness (we can see whether, under the appropriate conditions, they are repetitive, whether they gain public consent, whether they are pragmatically efficacious, enabling us to negotiate in the world), but these procedures are clearly of no avail in that state of fullness of being wherein no distinctions obtain between perceiver and perceived.[1]

3. Explanatorily we are unable to account for one state or mode of consciousness in terms of the other or to reduce one to the other. Although in practice various conditions within bound consciousness may need to be realized in order to attain boundless consciousness, no causal (or other alleged internal connection) between the bound and the boundless is possible. If the boundless were merely an effect of conditions fulfilled in bondage, then it would be a member of that series and would lose thereby precisely its character as the limitless freedom that it is.

Whether as a faculty of awareness or the locus of various mental activities (such as conceiving, perceiving, and imagining), and whether bound or boundless, consciousness, like that of the unity of an individual, has most often been conceived of as something substantial—as some kind of thing that underlies, supports, or otherwise unifies various elements, relations, or functions.[2] But as William James (and indeed innumerable Buddhist philosophers long ago)[3] convincingly argued, this awareness, this mentality we call "consciousness" is more an activity than a substance—it is a *function*, not an *entity*—for it does not endure (that is to say, it has no *svabhāva* or "own-nature") apart from its distinctive power.[4]

Thus, although we are constrained (and conditioned) by language usage and linguistic structure to make of consciousness something substantial, as in the very expression "acts *of* consciousness," the term "consciousness" ought to function more as a verb and less as a noun. We should be able to refer to "consciousing," rather than to "acts of consciousness."

In any event, we want to understand consciousness as an activity or power—in its bound state as a power of discernment, and of reception and retention (as it becomes then an "appropriated mind" and derivatively an "object-mind" and a "subject-mind"), in its boundless state as a power of being—and in its distinctive functioning in a person as a power of being creatively.

II

To begin with the bound: two fundamental states of bound consciousness, or modes of consciousing that are given to us as individual human beings, need to be distinguished—the waking and the subwaking. These states or modes are commensurate with one another, for they frequently interfuse and commingle and, in their varying degrees of intimacy, constitute a continuum from the utterly bound to the borderline, as it were, of the boundless.

Waking Consciousness

Waking consciousness, I want to argue, is essentially a power to discern. It is a power to discriminate among objects, to sort out mental contents reflexively, and, most importantly, to recognize qualitative differences.

Waking consciousness was associated for the Greeks, as it still is for many of us today, with perception as well as reason.[5] Plato insisted that "sight is the keenest mode of perception vouchsafed us through the body."[6] And the most fundamental character of this awareness is noetic; it enables us to know the world. Plato thus compared the light of the sun, which at once causes vision and is seen by the vision that it causes, to the relation that obtains between the idea of the Good and human intelligence and intelligible objects.[7] Reason was a light; consciousness, a lamp that illumines an otherwise dark and abysmal world.

But a lamp indifferently illumines whatever comes within its field, while consciousness is highly selective—and reflexive. We are predisposed at any moment to select various objects for attention and to invest them with meaning as well as discover meaning in them. Consciousness, being a power of access to objects, cannot be an object to itself, yet it nevertheless functions reflexively—which is to say that, unlike a lamp, I am aware of my own mental activities in varying degrees of intensity.

Following the Greeks, and in many ways continuing their thinking, we have, it must be noted, a number of other rationalistic models of consciousness. Descartes, for example, who radically restricted consciousness to the human (he regarded, thoughtlessly one might say, animals as mere physiological automata), also related consciousness (*conscientia*) closely to light. His whole notion of clarity and distinctness, which played so great a role in his theories of knowledge and truth, is informed by the illumination model. Descartes writes:

> A clear perception I call that which is present and open to the attending mind; just as we say that those things are clearly seen by us which, being present to the regarding eye, move it sufficiently strongly and openly. But that perception is distinct which is not only clear but is so precise and separated from all others that it plainly contains in itself nothing other than what is clear.[8]

But consciousness does, for Descartes, become highly reflexive: "By the word thought (*cogitatio*), I understand all that which takes place in us that we of ourselves are immediately conscious of."[9] And we still say, "I see the light," when we understand something, although most of us might hesitate to affirm, as did Descartes, that when we are conscious we are always conscious of our own cognitions.

Rationalistic models of consciousness, nevertheless, tend to take consciousness as something determinate, complete and universal, informed as it is thought to be by various (innate) ideas, principles, categories, or structures, and to neglect thereby the dynamic and developing nature of consciousness. They assume that categorical features of mind are fixed forms (Kant) or a predetermined structural nexus (Hegel), and thus overlook the possibility of radical changes and evolutionary developments.

Also with their obsession with the universal, with what holds for everyone's consciousness, rationalistic models fail to pay attention to the particularities of individual consciousness. With respect to possible contents, intensities, qualitative differentiations, the question "Whose consciousness?" is never seriously addressed.

Similarly, they neglect what we might call the "nether side" of consciousness. The nothingness that infects consciousness (Sartre), its grounding in forces beyond rational determination (Freud), and so on are set aside in favor of an exclusive attention to sunlit intelligence.

The classical British empiricist model of consciousness, which conceived of consciousness as a kind of theater without a stage and therefore as inherently passive, is also inadequate. Hume writes:

> The mind is a kind of theatre, where several perceptions successively make their appearance; pass, re-pass, glide away, and mingle in an infinite variety of postures and situations. There is properly no simplicity in it at one time, nor *identity* in different; whatever natural propension we may have to imagine that simplicity and identity. The comparison of the theatre must not mislead us. They are the successive perceptions only, that constitute the mind.[10]

This sensualistic conception of consciousness asserts then that "every distinct perception which enters into the composition of the mind, is a distinct existence, and is different, distinguishable, and separable from every other perception, either contemporary or successive."[11]

For Hume, consciousness is thus a mere accumulation of sensory data and images. No real internal connections exist between these atomic elements; no substantial entity underlies or supports them. The theater is the drama being performed.

But consciousness is active from the start; it is continually engaged in the world and has its own organizing principles. William James, in his critique of the classical empiricist view, saw this clearly, but then went on in what he thought was a more radical empiricist manner and asserted that consciousness was a kind of stream. Each element in the stream, James argued, is bound together in a continuous unity which is for us "suffused with a warmth and intimacy." Accordingly, "consciousness . . . does not appear to itself chopped up in bits."[12] What both Hume and James failed to notice, however, is that the stream of experience has these peculiar features: its temporality is organic rather than linear; every moment of consciousness is a kind of new beginning as well as part of an ongoing history; and it is chameleon-like, taking on the form of whatever it experiences.

Empiricist accounts of consciousness, with their emphasis on the successiveness of perceptions, tend to reduce consciousness to a strict sort of linear temporality. But the temporality of consciousness is clearly one of fits and starts, sudden achievements of attentiveness and discernment, and just as sudden retreats and lapses into vague distractedness. It is the time-world of growth, development and decay, such as they might be, rather than the temporality of a train moving steadily down a track.

Whenever I am consciousing (thinking, perceiving and the like) it is as if it were initially a fresh start. I do not have immediately available all that I might previously have thought (or perceived) about the issue (or object) at hand. Consciousness is at once old and new. Each act is, in a way, a new beginning. At any time it takes a certain effort to bring one's capacities into play as they have been shaped throughout one's experience; that is to say, it takes a certain effort not to have to begin all over again. At any moment we attend, then, as though for the first time, but not from a bare structure or as part of a simple, ongoing stream. We attend as a child with an older person's history.

It is perhaps the selective character of memory itself that makes for this peculiar freshness of consciousness. Memory keeps things out of consciousness as much as (if not more than) it brings a history to it. This selectivity, this forgetting, insures a certain naïveté to our thinking and perceiving; it guarantees that we will not see in terms of all that we may know.

But this, of course, does not mean that we are thereby enabled to see more clearly objects "as they are"; it means only that we are constrained to see things, and think about them, without the immediate burden or benefit of all our past experience.

The stream metaphor of consciousness also is deficient in its nonrecognition of the fact that consciousness not only anticipates but "becomes" its contents and does not merely flow indifferently in, around, and through them, as though these contents were rocks and pebbles on a riverbed. I have said that consciousness is chameleon-like, that it takes on the form of whatever it experiences—but what does this mean? It means that in perception there is an assimilation of a perceived gestalt *in* consciousness, and not just a simple illumination of an alien content. The perceiver becomes the perceived in the sense that what is "meant" in perception, the *noema* as Husserl calls it, is constituted in consciousness in virtue of the essential intentionality of waking consciousness to be *of* something. There is no waking consciousness that can be referred to apart from its contents. This is one of the most fundamental intuitions of phenomenology: that "no mental state is to be conceived only and exclusively as a real and temporal event in the stream of consciousness, without any reference to a sense."[13] Husserl says, "Each cogito, each conscious process, we may also say, *means something or other* and bears in itself, in this manner peculiar to the *meant*, its particular cogitatum."[14] And hence, "If one admits that all consciousness is consciousness-of-something, it is evident that nothing can be said about consciousness unless attention is paid to that of which one becomes conscious in the various acts."[15]

This suggests further that consciousness is not some kind of neutral or disinterested container into which contents are placed; rather consciousing, in this its waking state of boundedness, is a power to discern and intend contents, and to be those contents.

But this does not mean that consciousness creates its contents or can be indifferent to their objectivity. Husserl is surely misguided in his "envisaging a science that is, so to speak, absolutely subjective, whose thematic object exists whether or not the world exists."[16] For consciousness, as a power to discern, is sensitive to *qualitative* differences; it is able to recognize value as well as intend meaning, and this discrimination calls indeed for the objectivity of objects—that a world exist. We do not just perceive our perceptions. We do not simply see things as they become *noemata* for us; rather we discern their quality as well as their rightness. And this discernment is something more than what the phenomenologists call the prospect of an object, which is essentially a judgment as to the object's instrumental value, for it seeks to be aware of, to recognize, the object as a qualitative thing in its own terms. Consciousness, in short, is value discerning: it notices one thing as it may be better or worse than another, and as it may have a radiant intrinsic value.

Hegel writes, "Self-consciousness exists in itself and for itself, in that, and only by the fact that it exists for another self-consciousness; that is to say, it *is* only by being acknowledged or recognized."[17] Hegel argues that self-consciousness is achieved through a process of one ego seeking dominance over another ego. Recognizing an other as claiming independence—"of wanting to be all of reality"—one must seek that other's subordination, its reduction to a mere reflection of oneself, but in such a way that the other is not destroyed. One does not dominate a corpse. The other must be as an object for one, which is to say in total obedience or slavery. As dominant ego I attain self-consciousness because the other ego is then only a reflection of myself.

But a kind of ironic reversal takes place, for in the development of the master-slave relationship the master's self-consciousness turns out to be dependent upon the acknowledgment by the slave of the other's mastery, and, by relying upon the slave's labor, the master comes to lose his own autonomy. The slave who, through fear, is initially dependent upon the master, and is reduced accordingly to having a mere consciousness of objects, is thus able, through his labor with objects, to make them subservient to his will and to regain self-consciousness and attain self-reliance. Hence "just when the master has effectively achieved lordship he really finds that something has come about quite different from an independent consciousness."[18]

Jean Hyppolite, with reference to Hegel, writes, "Self-consciousness is not confined somewhere within a biological organism. It is a relation, and a relation to the other. But it is related to the other on the condition that the other be I: related to me on condition that I be the other."[19] Hyppolite thus characterizes Hegel's analysis of the development of self-consciousness in dependency as a kind of mirror play: "By making the other appear, I also lose myself. I am out of myself, in a certain sense, since I see myself as another."[20]

Autonomy, as Hegel inadvertently shows, is thus *not* achieved in a dominance-subordination framework of relationship; rather it is only when one is capable of recognizing the other as a being with dignity (not as a "reflection of myself"), of acknowledging his or her personhood, that a confidence in consciousness of oneself as a person who can be enhanced by the other is possible, and thereby an autonomy appropriate to consciousness at this level be achieved. The autonomy can never be absolute or complete, for an intersubjective dependency, rather different from that conceived by Hegel, does seem to obtain in experience.

Although one is always strongly tempted to solipsism—my consciousness is so central a reality for all my experience, with the reflexivity of consciousness in particular being so intimate to me, that there is a natural tendency to believe it is sufficient unto itself to account for all experiences—at every moment in a person's conscious life there is an (implicit, at least) acknowledgment of a community of consciousness, a realization that one is not utterly isolated in the world and that one is sustained by the consciousness of others. I am aware of myself—I can attain to self-consciousness in the first place—only with this prereflective background awareness, as it were, of community consciousness, for without it there would be no way open for me to seek meaning, to communicate, to articulate—a seeking which is essential to my being a person. A person cannot be as if he were entirely a single one. Without community consciousness, I would be burdened with alone maintaining my experienced world, and this would be an intolerable burden indeed.

Sartre, who was often unafraid of heavy and intolerable burdens, has written that "consciousness is a being the nature of which is to be conscious of the nothingness of its being."[21] This nothingness (*néant*) is not, of course, to be confused with that spiritual emptiness (*śūnyatā*) which admits of no distinction and which finally turns out to be a kind of ontological fullness or plenitude. Sartre's nothingness is rather a kind of "indeterminacy," a "lack," a "negation" and "that which by definition will never be given." Although Sartre constantly jumbles together noetic, ontical and psychological usages of key terms ("nothingness" is at times an epistemic lack, an ontical negation, a psychological absence), it is clear that for Sartre consciousness does not have a determinate structure or content, and by its own power to recognize incompleteness (e.g., the recognition that objects are revealed to us only in successive profiles, and not in the full richness of their possible determination) it introduces a nothingness at the heart of being. But this, then, calls for a split in consciousness between its functioning as a medium of access to the world (to the en-soi, which is "full of itself") and its functioning reflexively, its turning upon itself (as a pour-soi). Sartre is asking for a self-consciousness so extreme that it must annihilate itself, as it were, in order to be. "The being of consciousness qua consciousness," Sartre writes, "is to exist at a distance from itself as a presence to itself, and this empty distance which being carries in its being is Nothingness. Thus, in order for a self to exist, it is necessary that the unity of this being include its own nothingness as the nihilation of identity."[22]

So a self cannot be itself—for a conscious coincidence of self with self "causes the self to disappear"—and "neither can it not be itself, since the self is an indication of the subject himself. The self therefore represents an ideal distance within the immanence of the subject in relation to himself, a way of not being his own coincidence."[23]

But perhaps more fundamental to subject disappearance is the movement of consciousness toward its own extinction. The being of consciousness, we have already seen, involves a certain effort—one that strives against deep-seated indolence (tamas, as Indian philosophers call it), which seems to be part of the very structure of consciousness. Freud saw this drive toward extinction as the expression of a death wish (Thanatos), a willingness to reduce excitation to a minimal point, an attempt to revert back to an inorganic state.

Waking consciousness seeking oblivion, a diminution of its being as a power. Waking consciousness unable to sustain its incessant changes, unable finally to be among the contents it becomes. Oblivion haunts consciousness not as a prereflective cogito so much as a postreflective dismissal of thought. Nothingness is negativity without transcendence.

Tedium, ennui—like a secure animal you give up the struggle to stay awake; but then you find yourself only in another sphere of ceaseless activity.

Conscire: the inescapable other of consciousness.

In sum: as a power of discernment, waking consciousness is:

. . . selective and reflexive . . . It is predisposed to attend to various objects and to invest them with meaning as well as discover meaning in them. It functions then so as to be aware of being aware in varying degrees of intensity. Hence the inadequacy of the classical lamp metaphor of consciousness, for a lamp indifferently illumines its objects and is blind to itself.

. . . active with an organic temporality and continuity . . . Consciousness always involves a new beginning as well as an ongoing history. With its discriminating forgetfulness it perceives and conceives freshly, but within an ongoing experience that becomes constitutive of consciousness itself. Consciousness is chameleon-like; it takes on the form of what it experiences. Hence the inadequacy of empiricist accounts of consciousness— those that see consciousness either as a passive theater or as a flowing stream, for consciousness is not an indifferent, passive container or a simple temporal continuity; it is more like the history of something, where the events in that history become constitutive of the bearer of it.

. . . qualitatively discriminating . . . It recognizes value (both intrinsic and instrumental) as well as intends meaning, and thus can never be properly conceived as a self-enclosed subject-object situation wherein the subject is indifferent to the object's mode of being, as would be the case with the Husserlian intentionality thesis of consciousness.

. . . socially dependent . . . Consciousness, although often strongly disposed toward solipsism, is always sustained by the consciousness of others and acknowledges its dependence upon this community awareness. Unlike the Hegelian dependency of consciousness, which casts persons, in at least one stage of their development, in a relentless struggle for dominance with one consciousness compelled to reduce the other to mere objectivity, the sociality of consciousness is supportive of the possibility of achieving an autonomy of consciousness, appropriate to the person at this level of experience, through the recognition by consciousness of the intrinsic value and being of an other.

. . . and driven toward a kind of extinction.

Subwaking Consciousness

According to Freud, waking consciousness is a battleground: the ego is driven by the *id*, which is blind to itself, confined by the *super-ego*, which lays down its moral laws, and repulsed in its self-aggrandizing activity by the real world. An incessant struggle goes on in the psyche between the demands of the unconscious and the needs of the conscious self to adapt to the (primarily social) world.

But in discussing the structure of the psychic personality, Freud recognized clearly enough various conceptual difficulties in the notion of the unconscious. He asserts, to begin with, that "it is indeed the case that large portions of the ego and super-ego can remain unconscious and are normally unconscious, that is to say, *the individual knows nothing of their contents and it requires an expenditure of effort to make them conscious.*"[24] He goes on to say, "It is a fact that ego and conscious, repressed and unconscious do not coincide,"[25] and then distinguishes two kinds of unconscious:

> One which is easily, under frequently occurring circumstances, transformed into something conscious, and another with which this transformation is difficult and takes place only subject to a considerable expenditure of effort or possibly never at all. . . . We call the unconscious which is only latent, and thus easily becomes conscious, the preconscious and retain the term unconscious for the other.[26]

The distinction between a preconscious and an unconscious is made, then, according to the availability of certain contents to waking consciousness. But this is not the end of the matter, for, according to Freud,

> unluckily the work of psychoanalysis has found itself compelled to use the word unconscious in yet another, third sense and this may, to be sure, have led to confusion. Under the new and powerful impression of there being an extensive and important field of mental life which is normally withdrawn from the ego's knowledge so that the processes occurring in it have to be regarded as unconscious in the truly dynamic sense, we have come to understand the term 'unconscious' in a topographical or systematic sense as well; we have come to speak of a 'system' of the preconscious and a 'system' of the unconscious and have used the word more and more to denote *a mental province rather than a quality of what is mental.*[27]

C. G. Jung, on the other hand, who felt it was "impossible to explain the subliminal nature of all [unconscious] material on the principle of repression,"[28] argued that it is necessary to distinguish a personal from a collective unconscious. "The materials contained in this [personal] layer," Jung writes, "are of a personal nature in so far as they have the character partly of acquisitions derived from the individual's life and partly of psychological factors which could just as well be conscious. . . . We recognize them as personal contents because we can discover their effects, or their partial manifestation, or their specific origin in our personal past."[29]

On the basis of our having various images, symbols, ideas that are exhibited in analysis and that do not seem to have significant personal elements, Jung then maintains that "we must assume that the uncon-

scious contains not only personal, but also impersonal, collective components in the form of inherited categories or archetypes."[30]

It is, I believe, rather evident that two different sorts of things are being
talked about in the psychoanalytic theories of Freud and Jung (as indeed
in other analytic theories of the unconscious). On the one hand, we have
certain identifiable mental phenomena associated with Freud's preconscious and Jung's personal unconscious—phenomena involving specifiable contents, meanings, values with their attendant emotional actions
and reactions. On the other hand, we have conceptual models and
descriptions of a system or topology of forces, drives and the like which
has, as it were, an autonomous (and universal) life of its own. With this
latter system we have, as we have suggested, the apparent need to formulate a new portrait of the individual, a perspective that is not reducible to
the usual mental and physical ones and that allegedly describes an
entirely different domain of our being. A portrait, we may recall, and as
we will see in detail later on, is a kind of theoretical model, a perspective
to which the object is responsive. It remains to be seen, of course, if any
of the psychoanalytic perspectives will in fact yield a new portrait. We
are probably seeing the development of one in only its most rudimentary
stage.

Philosophically, however, our concern must be with the first area of
experience—that is to say, with those mental functions of an unconscious
character which can be recognized and analyzed without making reference to an unconscious system or topology. The topology, which attempts
to answer different sorts of questions, would, if it were correct, tell us
something about the distinctive content of the unconscious and its (possible) effects upon waking experience, but it would not necessarily tell us
about those nonreflexive functions of mental life that seem nevertheless
to inform waking experience in various fundamental and pervasive ways.
We may conveniently refer to this dimension of consciousness, to these
functions, as "subwaking consciousness."

Subwaking consciousness, then, comprises those functions that have a
distinctive mental or intentional character (hence their belonging to consciousness) yet are not ordinarily accessible to waking consciousness
(hence their designation as subwaking). Subwaking functions as we deal
with them, therefore, are not mental structures that constitute a subterra-
nean domain of mentality, but mental activities that are not subject to
what Augustine calls our inner sense—that is to say, we are not normally
aware of their occurrence. Subwaking mental activities, unlike waking
ones, in short, are not open to immediate recognition. This does not mean,
however, that these activities are only inferred or are postulates to
account for what might otherwise be inexplicable in our experience, for
we certainly can recognize directly their role in constituting some of the

limiting conditions of our individuality and thereby contributing to the boundedness of our phenomenal experience.

Two basic functions may be seen as involving the subwaking: (1) a function or power of reception and (2) a function or power of retention.

Unlike waking consciousness, which is, as we have seen, primarily a power of discernment, subwaking consciousness, as an impressive amount of analytic data shows, strives, without any objective value discrimination, to gather to itself everything that has a possible emotional meaning for the ego. In its receptive function subwaking consciousness assimilates those aspects of experience (and those experiences) that seem to be potentially as well as actually significant to the experiencer. The subwaking does not discern quality as intrinsic to the objects that it intends; rather it blindly takes in (what to waking consciousness is) the trivial as well as the important. In short, whatever is received is of value to the ego, irrespective of the values that inform waking consciousness as such. What makes something valuable to the ego is no doubt a very complex matter, but one which happily is for the psychologist and not the philosopher to answer. Philosophically it is enough to notice that there is an enormous range of mental contents that have been assimilated by the ego (as clearly evidenced by anyone, for example, in dream experience) that have no grounding in the reflective, discerning functions of waking consciousness. We are often surprised to encounter these contents (in our fantasies or daydreaming as well as in dream experience), for we cannot imagine what importance they had (or have) for us. We are quite content, in our full waking consciousness, to dismiss them as utterly insignificant.

The receptive function of subwaking consciousness does, however, play an extremely important role in our mental lives, for in many ways it provides the raw material, as it were, to be developed by other mental functions of waking consciousness. Thinking, imagining and so on are not activities which deal only with presently given objects; they clearly do their work from within a rich matrix of unselfconsciously appropriated contents available to the thinker—contents the connections between which remain an enigma to the rational powers of waking consciousness but which have value to the ego. Thus the subwaking, through its receptive functions, is also the seat of our emotional life.

Now although specific emotions, as we have seen, usually have conscious aims (I am angry at X for having said S to Y) and are in this way intelligible to us as conscious intentional activities, emotional states generally have their primary function, as it were, as modes of structuring consciousness by way of informing its interpretations and judgments. Loving, hating, raging, being vengeful or respectful, for instance, develop from the totality of one's (appropriated) experience and strongly condition the value-discernment capability of waking consciousness.

As a retentive function subwaking consciousness, although it is atemporal in the sense that it is so thoroughly imbued with temporality that is indifferent to historical order or sequence, is a kind of pure immediacy. The subwaking is not a transcendence of time; rather it is at the other extreme from timelessness. The past is as present to it as the moment of any specious now. But what is retained through this function of subwaking consciousness is not be thought of as memory traces or repressed contents; rather what is retained in our experience at the subwaking level is precisely those appropriated contents that, as emotional values, become constitutive of certain conditions of individuality itself. The retentive function, in other words, goes to form those dispositional tendencies (the *saṃskāras* of traditional Indian thought) which so strongly influence our waking experience.

Consciousness, as we have noted, has its own kind of history: each individual consciousness is predisposed at any moment to select various objects for attention and to relate meaningfully to them in certain distinctive ways. These dispositions informing consciousness clearly have a dynamic, developing character of their own. An individual might lose parts or pieces of his history that once were significant influences upon him; but he is also constantly adding to that history in terms of the contents of his ongoing experience.

Whereas in boundless consciousness there is no memory and in bound consciousness, in its waking state, there is a plurality of memory functions—(1) those memory acts that accompany every temporal act of consciousness (consciousing) which exercises the capacity for integration (i.e., the retention of prior elements in a mental process); (2) acts of remembering, whether of learned content (remembering some piece of information) or of past experience (reliving the emotional value or meaning of a previous experience), which occur as specific mental episodes; (3) the objectification of remembered contents so as to imbue one's world with a meaning; and (4) acts of reminiscence, as an escape from present experience, an indulgence with remembered contents, and so on—in the subwaking state of bound consciousness there is just a retentiveness of those contents which become constitutive of our (psychic) individuality. This function, then, is less a repository of past waking experience than a formative retention of appropriated experience.

The subwaking thus becomes a basis for psychic determinism (which we will see later, involves a lack of causal efficacy on the part of the agent) and is the ground for an individual's impulsive action. In his or her portrait as mental the individual represents a set of psychic conditions that include not only native mental capacities but various appropriated-retained contents. In subwaking, the individual is therefore bound to a greater extent than in waking. If one were entirely in that state (which rarely, of course, happens) one would be utterly bound to these desire-need contents. One's consciousness would be entirely involuntary.[31]

The Appropriated Mind, the Object-Mind, and the Subject-Mind

Human consciousness is not simply a given that one possesses in virtue of being human; rather it is most fundamentally, like the body, an achievement—something that each person realizes uniquely from within and through the rich intricacies of his or her experience. Persons appropriate their various mental capacities, their power of discernment as reflected in and exhibited by their perceivings, their reasonings, their evaluatings, and so on, in ways that make these capacities, in varying degrees, their own. Our consciousness, in its waking and subwaking modes, becomes in short an appropriated mind. And, as with the somatic, persons, we need say, have minds (and not just bare functioning brains) to the degree to which they appropriate the mental conditions of their individuality and become integrated psychophysical beings.

Mental appropriation is thus the bringing of the mental conditions of one's individual being into the matrix of one's personal identity and the educating of those conditions for disciplined awareness. And it is here, of course, that the social dimensions of consciousness become so evident. The maturation of the mental is informed to a considerable, if not thorough, extent by cultural factors. What and how one sees and thinks is largely a shared experience within any culture, albeit there are always unique features present in any particular experience, and, if it is the case that consciousness gets shaped and formed, as it were, by its contents, that what one experiences in the present always influences how one experiences in the future, then it is readily apparent that the appropriated mind at once belongs to a person as his or her own achievement and to the culture as part of its world.

Consciousness as mind is usually conceived and treated, however, not as an appropriated mind but as either an object-mind or a subject-mind, that is, as it may be characterized and explained objectively as a given thing or phenomenon among other things or as it may be described in first person terms as the locus of one's lived thoughts and feelings.

The object-mind is the raw material, the given mental functions and capacities, of our individual human being as this may be known (in whatever appropriate way) through a perspective to which we are responsive. In short, the object-mind is the mental functions of our individuality as objectified in a portrait. It is what we know, believe, and assume the mind to be in objectified terms—whatever they may turn out to be.[32]

In our actual perception of other persons we do not, of course, perceive them in terms of bare brain functions or other accounts of their raw mental acts, but as they are culturally and socially informed beings who exhibit what we call mental behavior. We do not look for or see mental functioning apart from the person whose functioning it is. The object-mind, in short, is both logically and experientially an abstraction from the whole psychophysical person—the person who is aware, to the degree that he or she is, of his or her own thoughts, sensations, feelings: hence the subject-mind.

Traditionally, consciousness has been defined largely in introspective terms—e.g., from Locke's definition of our having an internal sense, the perception of what passes in our own minds, to Merleau-Ponty's assertion that "all thought of something is at the same time self-consciousness, failing which it could have no object. At the root of all our experience and all our reflections, we find, then, a being which immediately recognizes itself. . . . Self-consciousness is the very being of mind in action."[33]

Now, introspection has been given a rough time for many decades, summed-up nicely by Searle: "Any introspection I have of my own conscious state is itself that conscious state . . . the standard model of observation simply doesn't work for conscious subjectivity."[34] Nevertheless, it seems self-evident that we do have a sense of a wide range of mental activities in their lived, nonobjectified quality—the thoughts, attitudes, imagings that are part and parcel of our power of discernment and disclose to us the potentialities of our mentality. The subject-mind is simply the locus of our grasping ourselves, as it were, in both the immediacy of our lived or vital experience (Husserl's *Erlebnis*) and in the projection of future possibilities.

While it is certainly the case that we are aware (of thinking, perceiving, and evaluating), it is, however, also the case that, as Sartre points out, the I that carries out this reflexive activity *is* only on the reflected level of consciousness.

> When I run after a streetcar, when I look at the time, when I am absorbed in contemplating a portrait, there is no I. There is consciousness of *the streetcar-having-to-be-overtaken*, etc., and non-positional consciousness of consciousness. In fact, I am then plunged into the world of objects; it is they which constitute the unity of my consciousness . . . but *me*, I have disappeared. . . . And this is not a matter of chance, due to a momentary lapse of attention, but happens because of the very structure of consciousness.[35]

Even when we are self-reflective I's, our awareness of the subject-mind is highly limited, not only with regard to the activities of subwaking consciousness but to the continued, ongoing thoughts and feelings of the waking. We never quite catch-up with ourselves so long as we remain lively, waking beings.

Madness

What does it mean to be psychotically? What is the being of madness?

No theory or account of consciousness can pretend to be comprehensive in scope if it neglects to mention, if not analyze in depth, that nether side of life that we call madness, for madness is the great destroyer of the possibility of spiritual being, while seeming at times to have a close kinship with it, and stands as a constant threat to, while revealing the fragility of, ordinary waking-subwaking being. Freud writes:

> The difference between nervous health and nervous illness (neurosis) is narrowed down . . . to a practical distinction, and is determined by the practical result—how far the person concerned remains capable of a sufficient degree of capacity for enjoyment and active achievement in life. The difference can probably be traced back to the proportion of energy which has remained free relative to that of the energy which has been bound by repression, i.e., it is a quantitative and not a qualitative difference.[36]

But the difference between mental health and (neurotic) illness and surely between unbounded consciousness and madness is precisely qualitative insofar as differing ways of being are afforded the bearer of the one and denied the bearer of the other, ways that are fundamentally different in terms of openness, creativity, and play.

Mental disorder and personal identity: Can there be an active sense of not being the same person over time?

Why are the insane almost never represented in art? Is the being of the artwork fundamentally hostile to that of madness?

We would certainly be deluding ourselves if we thought we could answer these and similar questions from within the state of madness itself. Writing on Foucault's widely heralded *Madness and Civilization: A History of Insanity in the Age of Reason* (*Folie et déraison: Histoire de la folie à la âge classique*), Jacques Derrida nicely argues that we cannot, in speech and thought, have an inner access to madness.

> It is a question, therefore, of escaping the trap or objectivist naïveté that would consist in writing a history of untamed madness, of madness as it carries itself and breathes before being caught and paralyzed in the nets of classical reason, from within the very language of classical reason itself, utilizing the concepts that were the historical instruments of the capture of madness—the restrained and restraining language of reason.[37]

He goes on to say that "Foucault's determination to avoid this trap is constant. It is the most audacious and seductive aspect of his venture, producing its admirable tension. But it is also, with all seriousness, the *maddest* aspect of his project."[38]

There are, however, two intertwining avenues that seem to be open to us by means of which we can find something of a way into the understanding of the being of madness: the one through the recognition of shadow or twilight forms of derangement (such as fits of rage, paranoia, terror, fanatical pursuits of unreachable goals, flights of fantasy), dislocations that show us ways of being both what one is and is not; the other through the recognition of precisely what madness is not—a kind of *via negativa* by which we come to see, without actually reaching, something of its essential character.

There are obsessions that are a kind of shadow madness to which one escapes from an otherwise unbearable normality. This twilight madness appears as a place to be when clarity is unendurable.

One can become obsessed, potentially, with anything—fame, fortune, a woman, a man, this car, that flower, the weather, one's children's education, a political leader, a book, an idea—and, when so obsessed, one can be incapable of seeing clearly the values appropriate to these things.

One becomes one's obsessions; one does not just have them, and yet one is not completely lost to them, as the insane are in their delusions.

There is a kind of twilight madness associated with the obsessive that emerges from a deep-seated frustration of not having what one feels entitled to, or not being what one believes one ought to be in terms of accomplishments that are so recognized and duly celebrated by others. This pathological condition often exhibits itself as a consuming envy of those who have and are what is wanted. Inordinate demands for attention and approval are made, with nothing satisfying the demands. Consciousness becomes distorted, no longer being available to what is.

There is a kind of madness in dreams when the displacement is severe enough to call into question the range of reason itself. Taunted by the Eumenides, pursued by prancing furies, the soul abandoned to itself discovers its profound vulnerability, its inability to disallow that madness is not something alien to it but a presence able to announce itself as it pleases.

Don Quixote's delirium is sheer folly so long as he is unaware of the gross disparity between his images and the actual things of the world. Does real madness always contain at least a hint of its own nature?

There is a kind of arrogance exhibited in the many forms of romantically inspired madness, a rather pathetic assertion of superiority (Nietzsche before he actually went mad), which enables one to dwell in a private world, forsaking all the fools constrained to their smug, meaningless normalities.

But one pays a high price for this arrogance, as it is purchased with a loss of whatever inspires genuine community with others and wonderment toward being. Safe as one might be in a world where one cannot be disturbed, there still remains a profound dependency which belies any claim to freedom. In twilight madness, as with the real thing, one cannot act spontaneously, only compulsively in greater or less degree—the very antithesis of acting freely.

One seriously deludes oneself, then, in thinking that one can deny the limitations and constraints of waking-subwaking consciousness while remaining within its territory—that is, without achieving genuine personhood. We become mad at the edges of consciousness, as it were, whenever—through what we believe to be an exercise of will—we seek to overcome radically all the tensions and contradictions, the pain and stress of waking being at the level of waking being alone.

Person-deception, as we have seen, is also a kind of shadow madness, a division of one's being into apparent and actual selves. A person in deception is, other conditions being ordinary, able to function as an agent in an environment with various projects and the means to carry them out, but she does so torn (although usually unaware of it except in some dim fashion) between the need to deny something of herself and the need to have it at the same time acknowledged and affirmed by others.

If time and space, as we will see, are as articulate temporality and spatiality, then madness is precisely a derangement of that articulation or a total failure to make and sustain it. Madness lacks the capacity for creativity, and is thus more a failure of imagination than of free will (the ability to do and be otherwise than what is felt to be compelled).

One is thus mildly mad when one sinks into one of the other of the raw materials of time and space—living either completely in a time-space world of one's own making (a lived space-time independent of a public space-time) or within a space-time world governed entirely by a publically agreed upon mode of measurement: the wayward eccentric and the linear automaton.

Consciousness is an embodied history—in some cases highly organized, like an artful narrative, and in other cases, wildly inchoate, and as such closer to the actualities of everyday experience. In either event, madness means to be without a history that can be shaped and appropriated.

The mentally disordered are incapable of performing emotions correctly (let alone rightly); their affectivity is involuntarily that of raw response.

Having become severely dissociated from themselves, the insane are incapable of appropriating their bodies, of making them their own, of having them be the locus of integrated purposive activity.

Twilight or shadow forms of madness, negative as they are in their fundamental inhibition on attaining freedom, nevertheless do reveal a great deal about the being of madness and disclose as we have noted, the vulnerability of ordinary consciousness to a breakdown in its power of discernment. They reveal that madness does not transcend but locks one into the conditions of individual being; that madness is a dwelling in a disorganization of those conditions, a derangement of the possibilities to be realized.

To be mad is to no longer have an appropriated mind and thereby to lack a personal destiny.

The (real) opposite of madness, however, is not normality but being able to engage the world freely.

I am free in consciousness when I am able to exercise fully my native and cultivated capacities of intellect and feeling; when nonegoistically, unselfconsciously, I am my activity in virtue of my being attentive to reality. Freedom of consciousness is always a disciplined play of one's integrated mental and sentient capacities in concentrated openness to reality. Further, by being available, attentive, and thereby obedient to reality, personconsciousness is not so much a freedom from something or other, but a freedom to: a freedom to bring forth new meaning and value. In short, he enjoys the greatest freedom who does what he most essentially is; he is free who is able to perform, as it were, his own being in relation to reality. Freedom is thus integral to what it means to achieve personhood. Freedom of consciousness is precisely that of becoming a realized person.

NOTES

1. See Margaret Macdonald, "Sleeping and Waking," in *Essays in Philosophical Psychology*, ed. Donald L. Gustafson (Garden City, N.Y.: Doubleday, 1964), for an interesting analysis of the philosophic (logical) incommensurability between sleeping and waking states, an analysis which applies *mutatis mutandis* to the linguistic incommensurability of the bound and the boundless.

2. Two senses of the word "consciousness" (or *conscientia; cit; conscience; Bewusstein*) are often distinguished, only to be recombined into a broad meaning of the term: (1) consciousness as a faculty of awareness, and (2) consciousness as the locus of various mental activities (such as conceiving, perceiving, imagining);

in this latter sense, often simply identified with "mind." "The term 'consciousness,' " we are told "has a broad sense to designate whatever is about a state which makes it mental" (Charles Landesman, Jr., "Consciousness," in *The Encyclopedia of Philosophy*, ed. Paul Edwards [New York: Macmillan and The Free Press, 1967], vol. I, 193.

3. See William James, "Does Consciousness Exist?" in his *Essays in Radical Empiricism* (New York: Longmans, Green and Company, 1912).

4. However, the Buddhists, as we have seen, were not predisposed to identify self with consciousness in the first place.

5. Although Greek philosophers did not develop a concept of consciousness that corresponds closely to the sense of the term as a power or process of awareness, it is evident that they developed rather elaborate concepts of mind, and, as it has been pointed out, "with the 'psycho' in 'psychology,' 'psychosomatic,' or 'psychophysical,' Greek philosophers, said to lack the concept, have given us the words which best express it" (W. F. R. Hardie, "Concept of Consciousness in Aristotle," *Mind* 85, no. 339 [July 1976]: 388–411).

6. *Phaedrus*, 250D.

7. *Republic*, VI.508. This epistemic bias, which runs subsequently throughout so much of Western thought, needs to be disturbed, as I will try to show, in favor of other ontologic possibilities.

8. René Descartes, *The Principles of Philosophy*, I.45.

9. Ibid., 1.9.

10. David Hume, *A Treatise of Human Nature*, 1.4.6.

11. Ibid.

12. William James, *The Principles of Psychology*, vol. 1, 239.

13. Aron Gurwitsch, *Studies in Phenomenology and Psychology* (Evanston: Northwestern University Press, 1966), 134.

14. Edmund Husserl, *Cartesian Meditations: An Introduction to Phenomenology*, trans. Dorian Cairns (The Hague: Martinus Nijhoff, 1960), 33.

15. Joseph J. Kockelmans, "Intentional and Constitutive Analyses," in *Phenomenology*, ed. Joseph J. Kockelmans (Garden City, N.Y.: Doubleday, 1967), 139.

16. Husserl, *Cartesian Meditations*, 30.

17. G. W. F. Hegel, *The Phenomenology of Mind*, trans. J. B. Baillie (New York: Harper & Row, 1967), 229.

18. Ibid., 235.

19. Jean Hyppolite, "Hegel's Phenomenology and Psychoanalysis," in *New Studies in Hegel's Philosophy*, ed. Warren E. Steinkraus (New York: Holt, Rinehart and Winston, 1971), 62.

20. Ibid., 63.

21. Jean-Paul Sartre, *Being and Nothingness*, trans. Hazel E. Barnes (New York: Washington Square Press, 1966), 86.

22. Ibid., 125.

23. Ibid., 123–24.

24. Sigmund Freud, "The Dissection of the Psychical Personality," in *New Introductory Lectures on Psychoanalysis*, trans. and ed. James Strachey (New York: W. W. Norton, 1965), 70 (italics mine).

25. Ibid., 71.

26. Ibid.

27. Ibid. (italics mine).

28. C. G. Jung, *Two Essays in Analytic Psychology*, vol. 7 of *The Collected Works of C. G. Jung*, trans. R. F. C. Hull, Bollingen Series 20 (New York: Pantheon Books, 1953), 124.

29. Ibid., 133.

30. Ibid., 135.

31. It is interesting to note, however, that like the dream state (*svapna-sthāna*) of consciousness identified in classical Vedānta philosophy, the subwaking may be seen as an advance in the direction of free consciousness in virtue of its scope and relative freedom from the constraints of an external world. In subwaking one can (believe oneself to) be anywhere one desires. Nevertheless, because of its desire-laden character, the subwaking is a diminution of the power to discern. Lacking reflexivity (and not yet being *of* reality) the subwaking is a deepened bounded-ness.

32. Philosophy of mind, in both its analytic and materialistic or naturalistic per-suasions, has been concerned primarily with *the individual*, not *a person*, and his mental states and activities as these relate to various brain states or neurological conditions, and thus with what we are calling the object-mind. Some philosophers have gone so far to argue (see for example the work of Paul M. and Patricia S. Churchland) that we can properly eliminate all "folk-psychological" characteriza-tions of mental life—our having such things as beliefs, thoughts, sensations, desires and the like—in favor of attending only to descriptions of our neuro-physiological processes. John R. Searle, in his controversial *The Rediscovery of the Mind* (Cambridge and London: The MIT Press, 1992) wants, he says, first of all "to bring consciousness back into the subject matter of science as a biological phe-nomenon like any other" (85), while at the same time, however, insisting that "Conscious mental states and processes have a special feature not possessed by other natural phenomenon, namely subjectivity" (93). Searle rants against all forms of materialism and traditional mind-body dualisms, yet his view seems very much like a "property dualism" that holds that conscious experience always involves irreducible personal properties that go beyond or supervene on causal physical properties. Brain processes may very well be the physical source of con-scious awareness, causing our mental states, but what they give rise to are higher-level subjective processes.

In any event, it seems clear that we still have at best only a rudimentary under-standing of the relationships or correlations between brian processes and con-scious mental states and, if Colin McGinn is at all correct, we might never be able to determine the connection that would provide an adequate explanation of mind-body connectivity within the existing conditions of our rational cognitivity. (See his *The Mysterious Flame: Conscious Minds in a Material World* (New York: Basic Books, 1999.)

33. *Phenomenology of Perception*, trans. Colin Smith (London: Routledge & Kegan Paul, 1962), 371.

34. Ibid., 97.

35. Jean-Paul Sartre, *The Transcendence of the Ego*, trans. Forest Williams and Robert Kirkpatrick (New York: The Noonday Press, 1957), 49.

36. Sigmund Freud, *Introductory Lectures on Psychoanalysis*, trans. James Strachey (New York: W. W. Morton & Company, 1966), 465.

37. Jacques Derrida, *Writing and Difference*, trans. Alan Bass (London: Routledge & Kegan Paul, 1981), 34.

38. Ibid.

PART II

6

✳

The Nonrational and Contemplative Rationality

I cannot think reality; albeit consciousness, in its depth, can realize reality directly.

What does it mean to realize reality? It means to awaken fully to the spirit that one already is, which awakening involves precisely the negation of that I who would presume to stand over against reality, subject to object, and the affirmation of that nothingness, that fullness, which is at the center of one's being. The realization of reality shows, then, epistemically, and hence for us metaphysically, an unbridgeable chasm between the content of awakened consciousness and everything else in our ordinary experience.

Reality, for awakened consciousness, is timeless and spaceless: all other modalities of experience are for us temporal and spatial.

Reality is undifferentiated: all other modes of existence are distinction-laden.

Reality is utterly simple: all other ways of being are multiple and complex.

Reality and everything that is discriminated in bound consciousness—let us call this, borrowing older terminology, "the phenomenal"—cannot thus be put into relation with one another. When reality is for us, the phenomenal is not. When absorbed in the phenomenal, reality for us ceases to subsist.

The phenomenal—and here we need a sharp departure from what is carried in the older terminology—is, then, not an appearance which at once discloses and obscures reality, rather the two, reality and the phenomenal, are for us incommensurable. The one order "contradicts" the other in just this sense, that for us when the one is the other is not. There is, then, a *radical discontinuity* in being.

What is meant by "discontinuity"? One state of being or object X may be said to be ontologically discontinuous with another state of being or object Y if and only if (a) the presence of X as a content of consciousness precludes the presence of Y and the presence of Y precludes the presence of X, (b) because the qualities of X, in principle and in fact, negate those of Y or the qualities of Y negate those of X, and (c) no causal relations can be established between X and Y.

This definition of discontinuity, it should be noted, does not call for empirical spatial-temporal breaks in some ongoing process or other; rather it simply points the way toward a multi-leveled ontology, with each level, when confined to itself, having its own integrity. Also the definition does not refer to any inability on our part to predict the exact location of some element in a process, as is usually the case with mathematical definitions of discontinuity, it calls rather for a basic incompatibility between states of being, objects, contents of consciousness. X precludes Y when it is not possible to be conscious of—or simply to be—both X and Y at the same time. A quality negates another quality not when one is just different from, or opposite to the other, but when one is different in kind from the other and is incompatible with it. A timeless state of being would negate a temporal one; it would drive out the other from consciousness and utterly replace it.

And even if X and Y were fundamentally incompatible, if the one gave rise to the other causally, then X and Y would clearly be continuous with each other just insofar as they bear this relationship. Where there is ontological discontinuity between X and Y no causal relations can be established between them.

Jones is walking along a river bank in the Florida everglades at dawn, watching the sun filtering through the mist rising from the water. Suddenly, terrified, he stops, for lying directly in front of him is a huge alligator, half in the water. Jones is too scared to move and stares dumbly at the alligator. But the alligator too does not move and seems utterly indifferent to Jones' presence. Then, in a flash of recognition, Jones realizes that the object before him is not an alligator at all—it is only an old misshapen log.

Now as contents of consciousness the alligator and the log are incompatible. The one precludes the other. One cannot be conscious of the log as log and the log as alligator at the same time. The capacity of an alligator to move, to attack, is negated by the inertia of the log. The inanimate here negates the seemingly animate—indeed the alligator exists only until it is replaced by a right perception that contradicts it; the alligator exists for the perceiver, in other words, only so long as it is misperceived. And the alligator certainly does not cause the log; and the log does not cause the alligator. The alligator, we might say, is dependent upon the log; the log being a necessary, but not a sufficient, condition for the alligator. There are, to be sure, causes for both the log and the alligator, but no causal relation as such obtains between the two.

The essential features of this kind of illusory experience, then, are that the alligator appears positively in experience and depends for its existence on the log but disappears when a correct perception of the log is attained. The alligator is thus a temporary creation of the perceiver's ignorance. The alligator is not describable as "real," for it is contradicted by the perception of the log, nor as totally "unreal," for it actually appears, if only briefly.[1]

Assume, from the standpoint of enlightenment, that there is a state of being, of silent being, which is different in kind from all relative, pluralistic, changing things and conceptual impositions upon them, and when realized annuls all other pretensions to full knowledge and truth. Reality, then, as the Vedāntin would say, is that which cannot be contradicted by anything else—there being in fact nothing external to it.

All sense-mental experience is stamped with dependency, with contingency, and is open to contradiction. Every empirical thing, idea, belief, judgment, or perception is open to possible falsification, to replacement in future experience by some other thing, idea, belief, judgment, or perception.

If our consciousness were coincident with reality, we would no longer be aware, in the way in which we ordinarily are, of particular things, events, processes. Consciousness of reality would drive out consciousness of existence. To claim otherwise would be to assert that our ordinary modes of perception and conception, even as refined in scientific practice, disclose or present the *ding-an-sich*, the thing in itself, the noumenal world.[2]

Reality is silence, the home of the unsaid and the unsayable, but with very much a positive quality of its own. This silence is the very core of our own being and, when realized, becomes for us a supreme and incomparable value.

Reality, the utter silence of being as disclosed in nondual spiritual experience, is thus nonrational. It cannot be characterized properly through any form of determination, for any determination is only a negation (*omnis determinatio est negatio*); nothing positive can rightly be asserted about reality without at the same time allowing the possibility of its opposite. Only a *via negativa*—as in the Vedāntic assertion that reality (Brahman) is *neti neti*, not this, not that, or in the repeated calls of Western apophatic theology that no speech can speak rightly of, no words can rightly refer to, the divine[3]—is, in the end, appropriate for the finite mind anxious to know what is inherently unknowable to it.

And further, insofar as we take our stand entirely in the phenomenal we face the paradox of our not being able to grasp the nature of that very deficiency that drives us to deny the nondual nature of reality. As Heinrich Zimmer notes with reference to the Vedāntic view:

> It [ignorance, *avidyā*] cannot be demonstrated by reasoning, since reasoning itself can never stand apart from ignorance. Analyzing ignorance by reasoning is like searching darkness with the help of darkness. But neither can it be demonstrated by knowledge; for with the awakening of knowledge no trace of ignorance remains. Analyzing ignorance by knowledge is like studying darkness with a blazing light.[4]

And thus the glorious *absurdity* of being shines forth.

Two kinds of absurdity need to be distinguished: let us call them "existential" and "spiritual," respectively.

Existential absurdity, of the sort made known to us by mid-twentieth-century *philosophes*, holds that there is no meaning or significance that is simply given to us in life: the world, in essence, is incomprehensible and human nature entirely indeterminate, and consequently a radical choosing of oneself and one's manner of being is necessary. Existential meaninglessness or absurdity is itself comprehensible, however, only against the background of what it denies, namely traditional theism where the possibility of a meaning-grounded transcendence was affirmed. The meaninglessness of existence comes from the lack of meaning otherwise sought for, and claimed to be had, by theism (Sartre). Whatever freedom is to be had must come, then, from the very consciousness of the absurdity of one's situation ("Sisyphus"), and not from any other source. Existential absurdity is thus a form of radical humanism.

Spiritual absurdity, on the other hand, does not involve a frustrated expectation of meaning; it involves rather a joyous recognition of the "no-meaning" that shines forth consequent upon the realization of a radical discontinuity in being. With the overcoming of ego-centeredness, a person simply finds herself at home with what she is in her essential fullness.

Spiritual absurdity is not, then, merely a cognitive recognition; it is a liberated letting-go of the very search for rational and moral certitude. Spiritual absurdity, in other words, is an acknowledgment of phenomenal limitations, but differs from that propounded by the existentialist, as the acknowledgment is at the same time a freedom or release from the very conditions of limitation. The realization of spiritual absurdity, somewhat ironically perhaps, thus makes possible the achievement of a form of rational contemplation that becomes a source for all subsequent value-grounded reasoning and, in the end, as we will see, a liberated creativity that is revelatory of being.

*   *   *

This, then, which gives to the objects of knowledge their truth and to him who knows them his power of knowing, is the Form or essential nature of Goodness. It is the cause of knowledge and truth; and so, while you may think of it as an object of knowledge, you will do well to regard it as something beyond truth and knowledge and, precious as they both are, of still higher worth.[5] (Plato)

Nature does not lack; it creates because it possesses. Its creative act is simply its possession of its own characteristic Essence; now its Essence, since it is a Reason-Principle, is to be at once an act of contemplation and an object of contemplation.[6] (Plotinus)

This activity [contemplation] is the best (since not only is reason the best thing in us, but the objects of reason are the best of knowable objects) . . . And the activity alone would seem to be loved for its own sake.[7] (Aristotle)

He who knows in essence this glory and power of Mine is united by unshaken discipline; there is no doubt of that.[8] (*Bhagavad Gītā*)

Our thoughts will not be unstable, going to and fro from one thing to another; but we shall see all we know at one glance.[9] (Saint Augustine)

We delight in whatever we understand by the third kind of knowledge (*scientia intuitiva*) [which proceeds from an adequate idea of certain attributes of God to an adequate idea of the essence of things], and our delight is accompanied with the idea of God as its cause.

From this kind of knowledge arises the highest peace of mind . . . the highest joy.[10] (Spinoza)

To investigate principle [*li*] to the utmost means to seek to know the reason for which things and affairs are as they are and the reason according to which they should be, that is all. If we know why they are as they are, our will will not be perplexed, and if know what they should be, our action will not be wrong.[11] (Chu Hsi/Zhu Xi)

[R]eason shows such a pure spontaneity in the case of ideas that it far transcends everything that sensibility can give to consciousness and shows its chief occupation in distinguishing the world of sense from the world of understanding, thereby prescribing limits to the understanding itself.[12] (Kant)

There is a state of knowing consciousness that is directed toward and participates in an aesthetically ordered unity of being. "Contemplative rationality," as we may designate generically this mode of knowing consciousness that has been given innumerable characterizations throughout human history, differs fundamentally from the I-centered consciousness of an empirical knowing subject, as it is without determinations of particularity. Contemplative rationality is *impersonal*.[13]

Plato, who perhaps more than anyone else set Western philosophy on its rationalistic course, understood contemplative rationality at once in participatory and objective terms, as did other Greek philosophers generally who adhered to the notion of the *logos* as that which united the soul with the cosmos. Contemplation involved precisely the participation of the knowing human mind in the rational order of being, with *nous*, the highest activity of the soul, reaching the supreme Idea of the Good and thereby seeing and evaluating everything else in relation to it. Reason, for Plato, it has been rightly noted "is our capacity to see being, illuminated reality. Just as the eye cannot exercise its function of seeing unless there is reality there and it is properly illuminated, so reason cannot realize its function until we are turned towards real being, illuminated by the Good."[14] Thus: "To be ruled by reason means to have one's life shaped by a pre-existent rational order which one knows and loves."[15]

Theōria—the contemplation of the rational order of reality—becomes then for Plato, and for Aristotle in his own way, the highest aim of life. Through a purified loving and knowing consciousness, the vision of the value-bestowing order of the whole of reality is realized, with everything else seen in relation to it.[16]

Throughout the history of Western thought, most rationalists, as Brand Blanshard points out, "were confident that by the use of reason they could travel from point to point in *the* conceptual framework of the world, moving along lines of logical necessity to truths that were genuinely new."[17] Today, however, we have lost confidence in the idea that our human reason can be wholly commensurate with a rational structure of being that embodies a necessary causal order operating, as with Spinoza, on the one hand, among things that are and perish temporally, everything there being what it must be in virtue of its connectedness with other things, and, on the other hand, among eternal objects whose very nature follows deductively, as it were, from the necessity of the divine nature itself.[18]

We are prepared to acknowledge that there may be necessary features in our ways of talking about things (*de dicto*), but we are no longer inclined to believe that there are necessary features of things themselves (*de re*). In so far as it obtains at all, analyticity or logical necessity resides, we believe, in statements which are true in virtue of the definition of their terms or in virtue of their relationships with other statements in a given system of stipulated formal connections, not—as Blanshard would have us believe—in the connectedness of things as they are part of a necessary order of relations in being. In short, the fundamental mistake of rationalism, we have come to believe, is its assumption of the possibility of translating the recognition of value vouchsafed contemplative consciousness to a knowledge of nature given by a movement of thought along lines of necessity in nature. It is one thing to see *sub specie aeternitatis*, it is quite another thing to think through an order of necessary truths presumed to be grounded in reality and to reside in nature.

Further, although Spinoza, following Plato here, understood deeply the relation between his "third kind of knowledge" and "love,"[19] later, even more pretentious, forms of rationalism (e.g., Hegelian Idealism) tended to sunder the two in favor of a one-sided emphasis upon the coincidence of an absolute mind and the human mind as it is said to return to its own full power of transcendent self-consciousness. The affective, value-bestowing dimensions of contemplative rationality were lost sight of.

For Western (and to a considerable extent as well for Asian) theistic traditions, on the other hand, contemplation was most generally understood as a kind of beatific state, graciously proffered by the Divine as a vision (at least partially) of His own supreme and wondrous mind. While setting epistemic limits to itself, theism presents at the same time a strong implicit critique of any rationalistic claim to possess a knowledge of divine being. Saint Thomas Aquinas writes:

> Everything is knowable according to its actuality. But God, whose being is infinite . . . is infinitely knowable. But no created intellect can know God infinitely. For a created intellect knows the divine essence more or less perfectly in proportion as it receives a greater or lesser light of glory. Since therefore the created light of glory received into any created intellect cannot be infinite, it is clearly impossible that it should comprehend God.[20]

Paul Tillich, on the other hand, while accepting Thomistic-like limitations of reason, follows a somewhat more Augustinian tradition of inwardness, and understands human reason itself to be deeply grounded in divinity. "The depth of reason," he writes, "is the expression of something that is not reason but which precedes reason and is manifest through it."[21] Further, Tillich insists on an intimate relationship between love and knowledge. "In every act of grasping truth, truth itself is grasped implicitly, and in every act of transforming love, love itself transforms implicitly. . . . The depth of reason is essentially manifest in reason."[22]

Asian philosophical traditions, with few exceptions, were not inclined

in the first place to interpret contemplative experience along strict rationalistic lines, favoring instead somewhat of a conflating of spiritual knowing and contemplative consciousness (as in Advaita Vedānta in its analysis of that state of being designated as *saguṇa* Brahman[23]) and
emphasizing precisely the value dimensions of the contemplative (as in
the *Bhagavadgītā*, and in Buddhism, Taoism and Confucianism, in their
own ways).[24]

In our own time and place, the affective value-bestowing dimensions
of contemplative rationality may be retrieved, I believe, through understanding the nature of contemplative rationality as involving primarily a
realization of a unity and harmony of being which gives rise, through a
principle of rightness, to innumerable rational expressions of value. Contemplative rationality does not involve so much strict logical necessity as
it does what we may call "aesthetic necessity." Let me explain.

In rational contemplation, consciousness finds itself fully integrated.
Knowing and loving, intellect and feeling, become thoroughly conjoined
and an awareness of a profound unity in and of being is attained. Rational
contemplation is thus an awakened state of freedom that is realized positively as a harmony of being. And it is at the same time a spontaneity, in
Kant's terms, that realizes the limits to discursive, rational comprehension insofar as it recognizes that the "content" of contemplative rationality as such can never be logically demonstrated. The reasoning mind
would have to separate itself out completely from the very experience
which grounds, enables, and supports it and thereby make of the content
of that experience an object of a kind which it can never be. In short, in
rational contemplation the mind becomes aware of its own being as
freedom in such a way as to preclude its having a determinate content. It involves nevertheless the recognition of spiritual power as value-
bestowing and as grounding a principle of rightness.[25]

Just as in a work of art where the relations between elements appear to
aesthetic consciousness as inevitable in the dynamic ordered unity that
emerges contextually, so, in the order of being as vouchsafed rational contemplation, an infinite potentiality for intelligible relations to be brought
creatively into emergent orders that are appropriate to their constituent
elements is realized. Rightness means, for consciousness, that what
appears is as it should be according to its own conditions of being. It
involves, in short, an exercise of *taste*.

In recent times, a renewed interest in the concept of taste has been kin-
dled, primarily by philosophical hermeneutics, where it has been recognized that the concept has both epistemic and aesthetic components.
Gadamer, for example, writes:

> The concept of taste undoubtedly implies a mode of knowing. The mark of
> good taste is being able to stand back from ourselves and our private prefer-

ences. Thus taste, in its essential nature, is not private but a social phenomenon of the first order. . . . The decisiveness of the judgment of taste includes its claim to validity. Good taste is always sure of its judgment—i.e., it is essentially sure taste, an acceptance and rejection that knows no hesitation, no surreptitious glances at others, no searching for reasons.[26]

He goes on to note that

taste not only recognizes this or that as beautiful, but has an eye to the whole, with which everything that is beautiful must harmonize. . . . Against the tyranny exercised by fashion, sure taste preserves a specific freedom and superiority. This is its special normative power, peculiar to it alone: the knowledge that it is certain of the agreement of an ideal community. . . . It follows that taste knows something—though admittedly in a way that cannot be separated from the concrete moment in which that object occurs and cannot be reduced to rules and concepts. . . . Both taste and judgment evaluate the object in relation to a whole in order to see whether it fits in with everything else—that is, whether it is "fitting."[27]

The necessity that is made evident in contemplative rationality is thus essentially aesthetic insofar as it involves a sense of rightness, of taste, and is the source for all value-grounded reasoning and for that creative play which brings forth new formed contents. Contemplative rationality becomes, then, less a matter of apprehending perfect Platonic forms or various kinds of rational necessity thought to reside in the world and more that of simply recognizing a splendor and harmony of being that informs the loving rational mind with a profound sense of rightness. It also directs reason to set universal exclusionary boundaries and justifying criteria for various diverse rational practices.

NOTES

1. See chapter two of my *Advaita Vedānta: A Philosophic Reconstruction* (Honolulu: East West Center Press, 1969) for the way in which classical Vedānta analyzes this kind of experience—an analysis to which I am clearly indebted.

2. Thomas Nagel nicely states that in our ordinary world of experience "since we are who we are, we can't get outside of ourselves completely. Whatever we do, we remain subparts of the world with limited access to the real nature of the rest of it and of ourselves. . . ." *The View from Nowhere*, 6. Nagel, though, does not allow for, or at least he does not take into account, the possibility of enlightenment; nor does he concern himself with radical discontinuity as such.

3. *Bṛhadāraṇyaka Upaniṣad*, II, 3, 6; and, for example, Dionysius the Areopagite, *The Divine Names* or the anonymous *Theologica Germanica*.

4. Heinrich Zimmer, *Philosophies of India*, ed. Joseph Campbell (Cleveland and New York: The World Publishing Company, 1956), 42.

5. Plato, *The Republic of Plato* (VI, 508), trans. with intro. and notes by F. M. Cornford (New York and London: Oxford University Press, 1945).

6. Plotinus, *The Enneads*, III, 8. 3, trans. Stephen MacKenna, 2d ed. rev. B. S. Page (New York: Pantheon Books).

7. Aristotle, *Nicomachean Ethics* (Bk. X, Ch. 6, 15–20) trans. W. D. Ross in *The Basic Works of Aristotle*, ed. Richard McKeon (New York: Random House, 1941).

8. *Bhagavad Gītā* (X, 7), trans. with intro. and critical essays by Eliot Deutsch (New York: Holt, Rinehart and Winston, 1968).

9. Saint Augustine, *De Trin.* XV, 16, quoted in *Saint Thomas Aquinas*, ed. with intro. by Anton C. Pegis (New York: Random House, 1948), 90.

10. Spinoza, *Ethics* (Part V, Propositions XXV and XXXII), ed. with intro. by James Gutman (New York: Hafner Publishing Company, 1955).

11. Chu Hsi, in *A Source Book of Chinese Philosophy*, ed. Wing-tsit Chan (Princeton, N.J.: Princeton University Press, 1963), 611, 638, 640.

12. Kant, *Foundations of the Metaphysics of Morals*, trans. with intro. by Lewis White Beck (New York: The Liberal Arts Press, 1959), 71.

13. Michael Polanyi, in his rather remarkable work *Personal Knowledge*, interprets this ancient insight in a somewhat different way when he remarks that "The impersonality of intense contemplation consists in a complete participation of the person in that which he contemplates and not in his complete detachment from it, as would be the case in an ideally objective observation" (*Personal Knowledge: Towards a Post-Critical Philosophy* [Chicago: The University of Chicago Press, 1958], 197).

14. Charles Taylor, *Sources of the Self: The Making of the Modern Identity* (Cambridge: Harvard University Press, 1989), 124.

15. Ibid.

16. As Gadamer notes: "The primitive meaning of *theoria* is participation in the delegation sent to a festival for the sake of honoring the gods. The viewing of the divine proceedings is no participationless establishing of some neutral state of affairs or observation of some splendid demonstration or show. Rather it is a genuine sharing in an event, a real being present. Correspondingly the rationality of being, this grand hypothesis of Greek philosophy, is not first and foremost a property of human self-consciousness but of being itself, which is the whole in such a way and appears as the whole in such a way that human reason is far more appropriately thought of as part of this rationality instead of as the self-consciousness that knows itself over against an external totality." (Hans-Georg Gadamer, *Reason in the Age of Science*, trans. Frederick G. Laurence [Cambridge: The MIT Press, 1981], 17–18.)

17. Brand Blanshard, *Reason & Analysis* (LaSalle, Illinois: Open Court Publishing Company, 1962), 283–84.

18. Spinoza writes: "Things are conceived by us as actual in two ways—either in so far as we conceive them to exist with relation to a fixed time and place or in so far as we conceive them to be contained in God and to follow from the necessity of the divine nature. . . . *Ethics*, Note to Proposition XXIX, Part 5.

19. See Ibid., Proposition XXXII: "We delight in whatever we understand by the third kind of knowledge, and our delight is accompanied by the idea of God as its cause.

Demonstration. From this kind of knowledge arises the highest peace of mind, that is to say, the highest joy.

Corollary. From the third kind of knowledge necessarily springs the intellectual love of God [*amor intellectualis Dei*].

20. Thomas Aquinas, *The Summa Theologica*, Q. 22. Art. 7., in *Saint Thomas Aquinas*, ed. with intro. by Anton C. Pegis (New York: Random House, 1948).

21. Paul Tillich, *Systematic Theology*, vol. I (Chicago: The University of Chicago Press, 1951), 79.

22. Ibid., 80.

23. See my *Advaita Vedānta: A Philosophical Reconstruction* (Honolulu: East-West Center Press, 1969), chapter 1.

24. See, for example, Takeuchi Yoshinori, *The Heart of Buddhism*, trans. by James W. Hsig (New York: Crossroad Publishing Company, 1983), chapter 2. "The Stages of Contemplation," and A. C. Graham, *Disputers of the Tao: Philosophical Argument in Ancient China* (LaSalle, Ill.: Open Court, 1989), 95–105.

25. Another way of putting this would be to say that rational contemplation, representing as it does a dramatic shift away from the I-centered consciousness of a thinking subject to that of a mind unself-consciously participating in a value-bestowing reality, becomes, in virtue of its ahistorical timefulness, inexpressible as such. This, however, does not negate the epistemic force of contemplative rationality. When Hegel, in his critique of Kant, asks "How can we critically investigate the cognitive faculty prior to knowing?" we can thus answer that an understanding grounded in awakened and contemplative consciousness is able indeed to see the inherent finitude of all empirically based rational practices and to show the limitations of reason that follow from an analysis of these practices.

26. Hans-Georg Gadamer, *Truth and Method*, translation revised by Joel Weinsheimer and Donald G. Marshall (New York: Crossroad, 1989), 36.

27. Ibid., 37–38.

Although John Dewey would have little or nothing to do with what we call "contemplative rationality" and would thus no doubt be suspicious of talk about evaluating an object "in relation to a whole in order to see whether it fits in with everything else," he nevertheless was able to write that "The word 'taste' has perhaps got too completely associated with arbitrary liking to express the nature of judgments of value. But if the word be used in the sense of an appreciation at once cultivated and active, one may say that the formation of taste is the chief matter wherever values enter in, whether intellectual, esthetic or moral. . . . Taste, if we use the word in its best sense, is the outcome of experience brought cumulatively to bear on the intelligent appreciation of the real worth of likings and enjoyments. . . . The formation of a cultivated and effectively operative good judgment or taste with respect to what is esthetically admirable, intellectually acceptable and morally approvable is the supreme task set to human beings by the incidents of experience." (*The Quest for Certainty*, 1929, chapter 10.)

7

The Universality of Reason and Epistemic Irrationality

Hilary Putnam has observed that

> Bereft of the old realist idea of truth as "correspondence" and of the positivist idea of justification as fixed by public "criteria," we are left with the necessity of seeing our search for better conceptions of rationality as an intentional activity which, like every activity that rises above the mere following of inclination or obsession, is guided by our idea of the good.[1]

Built, it seems, into the very idea of the good is the drive to be evaluative, or, to put it another way, one cannot hold to an idea of the good and at the same time deny the meaningfulness of making value judgments; and so it is entirely natural, even if futile, that as rational beings we strive to formulate universal conditions for rationality that allow us to set timeless standards for truth and knowledge.[2]

Now it has been a commonplace in Western thinking throughout much of its history that there is a single conception of rationality or a universal rational standard which is normative for all humankind and is essential and central to all human knowledge. Reason, as the Cartesian-based Enlightenment-like rationalist still among us would have it, is a capacity or power latent in all human beings to make legitimate inferences, provide reasons for one's beliefs, and aim to secure various nonrelative truths. Although, because of various social factors, reason may be inhibited or underdeveloped in certain individuals and groups, it is in principle essentially the same in all persons. As rational beings, no one among us is special: reason is simply ingredient in human nature.[3]

Further, for this so-called Enlightenment project, it is believed that reason ought not to be controlled or determined by tradition, revelation, or any other kind of external authority. Reason is a self-sufficient power which enables us to explain the natural world in universal nomic terms and to order and give meaning to our human actions and social relations. In short, so-called autonomous rational men of good will should in principle be able to come to agreement on, if not full understanding about, any conceptual issue of importance.

Prompted by this Enlightenment way of thinking, and by subsequent developments in the scientific revolution itself toward ever-greater non-observational abstractions, a great divide in modern conceptions of rationality came about between theoretical (mainly mathematical) and practical (mainly action-oriented) forms of reasoning. Representations of a mechanized Nature in abstract mathematical formulae became radically separated in actuality from the less certain, often tentative, means to ends ways of accounting for human actions. In any event, the dominant modern understanding of human beings as rational celebrated—even, as with Kant, when restricting its metaphysical aspirations—the power of reason to explain the natural and engineer the social for the benefit of all humankind.

Now, of course, there have been many reactions to, and rejections of, this rationalist "pretension" that extolled a universal reason and its self-appointed centrality in our experience. Nineteenth-century Romanticism, especially in its Germanic form with its ties to the ancient Dionysian, culminating perhaps in Nietzsche, argued instead for the superiority of the power of imagination and feeling, of the strength of will and intuition of the godlike genius in the attainment of truth; and most recently, with the development of psychoanalytic theory, the rationalistic pretension has presumably been exposed at its roots: "We rationalize rather than reason"—so the slogan goes. The practitioners of the sociology of knowledge, a number of feminist philosophers, as well as Foucault and his epigoni, have also shown how many rational activities in Western culture have been inextricably part of various social practices and power relationships which severely limit any rationalist claim to impartial objectivity.[4]

Nevertheless, in spite of the diversity of views about, or conceptions of, rationality on the scene today, and especially its denigration in various postmodernist perspectives,[5] few of us are prepared to sacrifice reason (however this is to be understood) on the altar of some other phenomenal "faculty" or capacity, and indeed—as though this were the only alternative—many among us continue to struggle to establish a universal, culture-free conception of what it means to be human and rational. In a rather tongue-in-cheek manner, Clifford Geertz has remarked that

> moves toward restoring culture-free conceptions of what we amount to as basic, sticker-price *homo* and essential, no additives *sapiens* take a number of

quite disparate forms, not in much agreement beyond their general tenor, naturalist in the one case, rationalist in the other. On the naturalist side there is, of course, sociobiology and other hyper-adaptationist orientations. But there are also perspectives growing out of psychoanalysis, ecology, neurology, display-and-imprint ethology, some kinds of developmental theory and some kinds of Marxism. On the rationalist side there is, of course, the new intellectualism one associates with structuralism and other hyper-logicist orientations. But there are also perspectives growing out of generative linguistics, experimental psychology, artificial intelligence research [and so on].[6]

Within the more restricted problematic of rationality as such, at present three kinds of effort to establish universality of one sort or another seem to be dominant, namely (1) to demonstrate a naturalized necessity of thinking, grounded either in neurobiological-based cognitive processes which determine the ways we think and establish the limits or parameters of rational thought, or in a universal generative grammar that involves controlling linguistic principles which set conditions for all intelligible discourse; (2) to show the inescapable necessity of a minimal set of restraints on all rational thinking that derive primarily from the laws of (Aristotelian) logic; and (3) to insist on there being a form of free communicative discourse presupposed in and required for all genuine rational argument and hence the possibility of universal rational agreement.

The first of these efforts may indeed in good time disclose a number of features of human thinking, identified to be emergent from biological evolutionary development and to be categorical for various functions of our rational thinking, that have hitherto been hidden; but neurobiological conditions and/or structural grammatical patterns, with their abstract constraining structures, can in principle tell us very little, if anything, with appropriate specificity, about the many forms and contents of rational thought and, most importantly, the appropriate ways in which to evaluate them. Questions regarding the truth or validity of ideas and beliefs have a hard time finding resolution in lawlike accounts of how we think and speak. As Putnam rightly observes:

> A physiological or psychological description of vision cannot tell us whether seeing bands in the rainbow counts as seeing "correctly" or not. Even less could a physiological or psychological description of the brain-process which goes on when one "grasps" the Principle of Mathematical Induction tell us whether that principle is *true* or not. Once one sees this, it should be no surprise that a description of the brain process which goes on when one "sees" that an action is unjust cannot tell us whether the action really *is* unjust.[7]

Put quite simply: no descriptive account of brain processes by itself can reveal the meaning of or justify our various truth-claims and valuediscernments. Michael Polanyi makes the interesting point that "it is meaningless to represent mind in terms of a machine or of a neural model. Lower levels do not lack a bearing on higher levels; *they define the conditions of their success and account for their failures, but they cannot account for the success, for they cannot even define it.*"[8] Reductive explanation *in certain contexts* itself becomes then a kind of "quasi-irrational" procedure insofar as it would shut out and dismiss from the scene potentially richer and more robust forms of explanation and understanding.

It can also be said that no grammatical pre-wiring of the mind can in itself determine any universal logically necessary features of a natural language. Chomsky himself states that: "The properties of universal grammar are 'biologically necessary,' but in the interesting cases not logically necessary elements of what someone might choose to call a language."[9] More importantly he goes on to say:

> Two individuals with the same genetic endowment and common experience will attain the same state, specifically, the same state of knowledge of language (random elements aside). But this does not preclude the possibility of diversity in the exercise of this knowledge, in thought or action. The study of acquisition of knowledge or of interpretation of experience through the use of acquired knowledge still leaves open the question of the causation of behavior, and more broadly, our ability to choose and decide what we will do.[10]

In other words, possessing identical biological endowments does not determine the rational choices we make as individuals nor, most assuredly, the justifications we offer on their behalf. Further, as Thomas Nagel—here from a phenomenological standpoint—points out:

> Behavioristic reductions and their descendants do not work in the philosophy of mind because the phenomenological and intentional features that are evident from inside the mind are never adequately accounted for from the purely external perspective that the reducing theories limit themselves to. . . . The internal perspective of consciousness dominates any attempt to subordinate it to the external perspective of physiology and behavior."[11]

Also, as Nagel tirelessly argues—here from a highly rationalistic perspective—the very conceptions we have of reason and truth can never be derived from, or delivered by, a causal or purely descriptive account of rational thought as such, but are presupposed in any such account and would need to be justified philosophically, if it were at all possible, by other non-reductive means or forms of non-circular argument. "Thought," he says, "always leads us back to the employment of unconditional reason if we try to challenge it globally, because one can't criticize something with nothing; and one can't criticize the more fundamental with the less fundamental."[12]

The second effort which deals with specific logical constraints on our thinking has had the longest history and, for many, still has the greatest force, for it seems that without the "laws of logic" or universal fixed criteria of rationality "anything goes," and communication involving the expression of beliefs—especially across different societies—would be impossible. Steven Lukes, for example, while taking very seriously the fact of a plurality of rationalities in different cultures, argues that "some criteria of rationality [by which he means a rule specifying what would count as a reason for believing something or acting in a certain way] are universal, i.e., relevantly applicable to all beliefs, in any context, while others are context-dependent, i.e., are to be discovered by investigating the context and are only relevantly applicable to beliefs in that context." These universal criteria are, he says, "the ultimate constraints to which thought is subject." He finds this in the assumed fact that "if S (society) has a language, it must minimally, possess criteria of truth (as correspondence to reality) and logic, which we share with it and which simply *are* criteria of rationality." In short: "the very fact of a society's having a language entails that it has some features of rationality identical to our own."[13]

In a somewhat later account, Lukes reiterates his position "that in the very identification of beliefs and *a fortiori* of belief systems we must presuppose commonly shared standards of truth and of inference, and that we must further presuppose a commonly shared core of beliefs whose content or meaning is fixed by application of the standards."[14] Barry Barnes and David Bloor take up this claim, and as also made by Martin Hollis, "that there are simple forms of inference [e.g., *modus ponens*] which all rational men find compelling," and argue rather convincingly in turn that "for the rationalist there is little that he can offer by way of reasoned argument in favor of adherence to deductive inference forms"[15] for, in the last analysis, as we have already pointed out in the most general way, "Justifications of deduction themselves presuppose deduction. They are circular because they appeal to the very principles of inference that are in question."[16]

But, it might very well be argued, this inability to get outside of a logical form in order to justify it hardly matters insofar as appeals can always be made to the consequences that would follow for our very ideas of truth and knowledge if adherence to certain conditions or forms of inference were abandoned—for example, if the "law of non-contradiction"— something is not both f and non-f, or (for propositions) that both P and not-P cannot be true—were not adhered to there would be no way open to distinguish logically the true from the false. As Aristotle nicely pointed out, if someone persists in talking inconsistently, it is impossible to argue with him, for whatever he says may be contradicted by him. In any event, the "features of rationality" which, according to Lukes, are "criteria of rationality" clearly involve what we might call a narrow sense of rationality, the paradigmatic activities of which are usually thought to be traditional logic and mathematics.

There is, however, a wider sense of the term where questions of material truth and its relation to value-issues reside. The narrow sense might indeed call for certain universal features of rationality to be operative in logical and mathematical practices, insofar as anyone who participates in the exercises is compelled to admit the validity of what correctly follows and unfolds therein; the wider sense, on the other hand, which involves the enormous range of actual human cognitivity in its various instrumental, critical and substantive, as well as formal, types of rational practice, clearly shows the presence, and perhaps desirability, of a richer plurality. Lukes himself seems aware of this when he allows (the other half of his claim) that "there are (obviously) contextually-provided criteria of *meaning*. Again," he says, "there are contextually-provided criteria which make particular beliefs *appropriate* in particular circumstances. There are also contextually-provided criteria which specify the best ways to arrive at and hold beliefs. In general, there are contextually-provided criteria for deciding what counts as a 'good reason' for holding a belief."[17] And so we have come, as it were, full circle.

There is also a somewhat expanded, but still rather narrow, sense of rationality elaborated in traditional epistemology which is closely related to this kind of universalistic view where, when setting forth necessary and sufficient conditions for "S knows that P," an idealized objectivity which entails universality is laid claim to: "S" is *anyone* who knows, without reference to historical context, gender, culture, stage of life, class, education, and so on. Justified as this narrow sense might be for a restricted range of epistemic practice involving statements of empirical fact, and central as this was thought to have been for scientific methodology, it clearly does not embrace the many other kinds and forms of knowing that constitute so much of our human experience where the irreducible particularities of "located" knowers clearly come into play. It is surely rather ironic that for many traditional empiricist notions of rationality, a procedure or method becomes ideally rational to the degree to which the knower *qua* person is absent.[18]

And to make the picture somewhat more complicated, it is obvious that other philosophical-cultural traditions see the whole enterprise of explanation, at least on its "formal" side, rather differently. For example, although classical Indian philosophy does not depart radically from traditional Western thought regarding the need to fulfill various conditions for correct thinking, one very important difference needs to be noted. For the Indian view, any valid reasoning must be bound to actual experience by an appeal to a concrete example or exemplifying instance (*dṛṣṭānta*). What this comes down to, without going into detail, is the denial of any kind of strictly formal reasoning or formal validity as opposed to material truth. Reasoning, as inference (*anumāna*), must always be informed by concrete experience. Distinctions between analytic and synthetic statements, or necessary and contingent truth, so dear to classical Western rationalism and empiricism, do not therefore emerge. Somewhat more pragmatically than in traditional Western philosophy, Indian thought insists that all cognition must find its justification in practical action.[19]

In addressing the notion that "The concept of deductive or logical necessity which is paradigmatically illustrated by proofs in mathematics and formal logic and the allied notion of *a priori* knowledge seem to be simply missing from the entire arena of Indian philosophical disciplines," Arindam Chakrabarti, on the other hand, points out that "two different sorts of response have been made to this crucial complaint. First, that in recognizing very clearly the law of non-contradiction *nyāya-vaiśeṣika* logicians do display adequate sensitivity to the concept of logical truths or necessity; and that in Buddhist logic deductive inferences find a place: and finally that the role of hypothetical reasoning (*tarka*) as buttressing evidence for universal generalizations shows that Indian logic has room for the modal notions of necessary connections between non-actualized possibilities."[20] Nevertheless, referring to Mohanty's not being "baffled by this apparent lack of interest in purely formal necessity/possibility on the part of Indian logicians," Chakrabarti notes:

> Since Indian logic arose out of two different contexts—namely, as a science of adjudication of actually happening debates and disputations, and as part of a general epistemology in which inferential cognition as a form of veridical awareness had to be normatively thematized—it was natural that component sentences of a valid argument were usually confined to those which were materially true."[21]

In short, Indian *pramāṇa* theory, which seeks to articulate the valid means of knowledge—a "valid means" being the identifiable cause of an irreducible kind of *pramā* or "truth"—understands logic more as an ordering of cognitions than of propositions as such. We think rightly and attain truth(s) when our cognitions are generated in a way appropriate to the objects to be known.

It should also be noted that in other non-Western traditions, namely the Chinese, even sharper differences with the West regarding models of reasoning seem to obtain. Going back to Marcel Granet's work *La pensée chinoise* (1934) A. C. Graham, Joseph Needham, and others have called attention to a "correlative model" of thinking which was characteristic of various cosmological speculations in the Han dynasty (mainly between 206 B.C.E. and 220 C.E.) and became a general feature of much traditional Chinese philosophy. Graham writes that "We do get pure analytic thinking in the Sophists and Late Mohists. But it is notable that even the later Mohists offer no forms of argumentation which we would regard as belonging to logic; the discipline which they do recognize as requiring formal procedure is the one we have called the 'art of discourse.' "[22] While perhaps overstating the difference between Western and Chinese styles of conceptuality, with his insistence that "causal thinking dominates in Western culture," David L. Hall points out that "correlative thinking involves the association of concept-clusters related not by physical causation but by meaningful disposition. Correlative thinking is a species of spontaneous thinking grounded in necessarily informal analogical procedures, presupposing both association and difference."[23]

Hall, in collaboration with Roger T. Ames, elaborates further the difference between Chinese correlative thinking and the causal reasoning dominant in Western experience by noting,

> In contrast to the rational mode of thinking which privileges univocity, correlative thinking involves the association of significances into clustered images which are treated as meaning complexes ultimately unanalyzable into any more basic components.
>
> Concepts based on correlative thinking are image clusters in which complex semantic associations are allowed to reflect into one another in such a way as to provide rich, indefinitely vague, meaning.[24]

Although, as A. C. Graham has repeatedly pointed out, a type of "rationalism" did appear in China, namely in the *Kung-sun Lung tzu/Gongsun Long Zi* ascribed to the third century B.C.E. "sophist" Kung-sun Lung/Gongsun Long, and in the later Mohists where, for example, it is argued that "the [logically] necessary is the unending" and "Being this or not this is necessary" (see *Mo-tzu/Mozi*, Canon A51 and its Explanation), what is centrally characteristic of classical Chinese thinking is a style of correlative thinking supported by critical judgment. This is neither a type of anti-rationalism which simply denies that reason can deliver things as they are (and is thus not to be confused with "irrationalism," which finds no place at all in Chinese philosophy), but a subtle and complex *art* of thinking that concentrates on the particularities of experience as they emerge and develop in intricate patterns of relationships which become evident to an appropriately sensitive philosophical mind.

It should also be pointed out that the core of laws or principles of logic that is held to be required for all rational cognition, and/or the necessary and sufficient conditions for "S knows that P" in traditional epistemology, if taken in isolation, not only remain entirely formal and abstract insofar as they are content-neutral and person-indifferent, but most importantly do not in themselves accommodate different cultural values. In fact, to be rational, according to narrow (modern, if not classical) conceptions has nothing to do with moral or cultural values. Reason is value-neutral insofar as it can be employed properly by anyone for whatever purpose. The scoundrel as well as the saint can correctly deduce conclusions from premises, recognize a good argument, and know that S is P—which brings us to Habermas and his theory of communicative action where, recognizing with Lukes the fact of a plurality of cultural expressions, he nevertheless aspires to a single universal rationality which excludes cultural values.

"The central presupposition of rationality," according to Habermas, is that "they [expressions and actions of whatever kind] can be defended against criticism."[25] Although he understands well enough that there are indeed different norms or standards (of taste, etc.), Habermas seems to presuppose that "criticism" itself is univocal—that it adheres to some set of noncultural-specific criteria. He wants, in other words, to exclude cultural values from discourse aimed at securing "universal validity claims." He writes:

> Cultural values do not appear with a claim to universality, as do norms of action. At most, values are *candidates* for interpretations under which a circle of those affected can, if occasion arises, describe and normatively regulate a common interest. The circle of intersubjective recognition that forms around cultural values does not yet in any way imply a claim that they would meet with general assent within a culture, not to mention universal assent. For this reason arguments that serve to justify standards of value do not satisfy the conditions of discourse.[26]

He later elaborates on this notion by stating:

> Cultural values do not count as universal; they are, as the name indicates, located within the horizon of the lifeworld of a specific group or culture. And values can be made plausible only in the context of a particular form of life. Thus the critique of value standards presupposes a shared preunderstanding among participants in the argument, a preunderstanding that is not at their disposal but constitutes and at the same time circumscribes the domain of the thematized validity claims. Only the truth of propositions and the rightness of moral norms and the comprehensibility of well-formedness of symbolic expressions are, by their very meaning, universal validity claims that can be tested in discourse.[27]

But, one must ask, does not this exclusion of cultural values place in jeopardy the possible validity of the very range of propositions, moral claims and other symbolic expressions that Habermas sets forth, insofar as this range is in fact informed by those cultural values? Surely cultural values are not simply untouched meta-entities occupying their own logical space; rather they give color and shape to, and become part and parcel of, all forms of cognition—and thus provide a basis, as we shall see, for "alternative rationalities."

Habermas does not believe that this is the case. In the context of discussing Peter Winch's criticism of the work of anthropologists such as Frazer and Tyler who commit "the error of simply imposing the supposedly universal rationality standards of one's own culture upon alien cultures," he avows that

> This methodological position does not at all result in a prior decision on alternative standards of rationality. . . . What counts in any instance as a good reason obviously depends on criteria that have changed in the course of history. . . . The context-dependence of the criteria by which the members of different cultures at different times judge differently the validity of expressions does not, however, mean that the ideas of truth, of normative rightness, of sincerity, and of authenticity that underlie (only intuitively, to be sure) the choice of criteria are context-dependent in the same degree.[28]

In his discussion of Weber's characterization of "Occidental rationalism," Habermas then lets the cat completely out of the bag when he rhetorically asks,

> if . . . we take as our point of departure the rationalization of worldviews that results in a decentered understanding of the world, then we have to face the question, whether there is not a formal stock of universal structures of consciousness expressed in the cultural value spheres that develop, according to their own logics, under the abstract standards of truth, normative rightness, and authenticity. Are or are not the structures of scientific thought, posttraditional legal and moral representations, and autonomous art, as they have developed in the framework of Western culture, the possession of that "community of civilized men" that is present as a regulative idea?[29]

In order to appreciate, and even celebrate, a plurality of rationalities and of different rational expressions within diverse modalities of reason we do not, it seems to me, need to insist, as does Habermas, that the Western way of articulating "structural properties of modern life forms" constitutes its basis. Rather, we can, I believe, articulate an idea of "exclusionary principles" that universally informs rationality, setting as it does the boundary between the rational and the irrational, and in such a way as to point the way to an appropriate plurality of rational expression.

In the context of explicating his notion of virtue as "a state of character concerned with choice, lying in a mean, i.e., the mean relative to us, this being determined by a rational principle, and by that principle by which the man of practical wisdom could determine it," Aristotle allows that

> not every action nor every passion admits of a mean; for some have names that already imply badness, e.g., spite, shamelessness, envy, and in the case of actions adultery, theft, murder. . . . It is not possible, then, ever to be right with regard to them; one must always be wrong.[30]

Following Aristotle's lead, in the context of moral judgment it can, I believe, be convincingly argued that we have "exclusionary principles" at work which deny admittance, as it were, into the arena of positive moral value of certain kinds of behavior in virtue of their being utterly violative of the core values of personhood and freedom.[31] The torture, the humiliation, of another person are destitute of intrinsic moral value (albeit in some exceptional circumstances one might be strongly inclined to justify them prudentially) and hence cannot be accorded the possibility of having inherent moral worth. And so with certain epistemic practices: there are those that by their very nature could not possibly be truth-knowledge producing and are thus void of cognitive value. Exclusionary epistemic principles set the boundaries between the rational and the irrational and, like Aristotle's rejection of certain moral practices, they do function *universally*.[32]

Take once again the law of non-contradiction, now as a kind of foundational exclusionary principle. Positivists were at one time convinced that the law was not about the way things are in the world (the law as such was not capable of empirical verification), rather it functioned somewhat like a rule of etiquette, it *regulated* a kind of pre-existent cognitive behavior (the application of words/sentences/statements to facts or states of affairs) but did not necessarily *constitute* rational thought as such. But quite clearly the law of non-contradiction is—or at least strongly appears to be—foundational for rationality insofar as any rational practice must abide by it.[33] If self-contradiction, as already noted, were not prohibited, there would be no way to distinguish the true from the false by any criteria whatsoever.

However, as Kant astutely observed, the law of non-contradiction, while functioning as a "universal and completely sufficient principle of all analytic knowledge," provides only a negative criterion for synthetic knowledge: a synthetic statement that contradicts itself cannot be true (or false)[34]—or, as we want to put it, cannot at the outset enter the domain of the true or false. The principle of non-contradiction, or any other of the "laws of logic," however, can tell us nothing regarding what statements are materially true or false. It functions like the skeletal structure of a building that requires to be filled-out with walls and windows and the rest in order for the building to become livable—and livable in many different ways. With respect to any particular epistemic practice (e.g., nomic explanation or instrumental determination), in addition to not violating the laws of logic, one needs always to understand those general principles of thought or action whose violation would preclude the possibility of fulfilling the intentionality of that particular rational undertaking. One would be irrational epistemically if one claimed to be playing a truth/falsity-conducive game but was dwelling cognitively in the realm of the exclusionary.[35]

Although it might sound somewhat disquieting to speak of irrational explanations or beliefs as being incapable of being true or false rather than being simply false, this way of speaking has the added advantage of enabling one to see truth and falsity across a continuum within the rational. For a belief to be false (or lack truth to whatever degree) it must be formed in such a way as to be capable, at least in principle, of being true. Exclusionary principles that preclude ways of thinking and acting from entering the arena of the true and false altogether, must thus also allow us to distinguish them from various rules that regulate particular rational practices, the violation of which would only lead to falsehood or inadequacy.

In short, just as in Indian logic/epistemology where a "fallacy" (*hetvā-bhāsa*) is not so much an error in formal reasoning (which would bring it into the domain of the rational) as it is a deficiency in cognition which disallows at the outset the possibility of attaining a right cognition (*jñāna*),[36] so across the range of rational activity various ways of thinking and acting can be identified which would constitute a domain of the irrational, for if followed they would preclude the attainment of the ends to be sought.

The irrational does have epistemic force or meaning, then, only in the context of the rational, which is to say that, on the subject side, one always presumes a capacity for rationality in that person to whom one would ascribe (epistemic) irrationality. The psychotic, the deranged, indeed a very young child or anyone else lacking linguistic or intellectual competence, is outside the pale, as it were, epistemically, albeit in common language this distinction is not often made. Indeed, we refer to both persons and their actions as irrational when there appears to be a breakdown in a person's ability to exercise self-control, when her actions are obsessive, and so on. Also we are inclined to attribute irrationality to someone who turns his back on the whole rational enterprise, either from some kind of sheer perversity or by claiming possession of some other allegedly superior power that is opposed to, rather than being qualitatively different from, the rational, and to someone as well who, at the other extreme, comes across as a kind of rational automaton wholly lacking in spontaneity and determining by calculation every step and move in her behavior. In any event, it is necessary to distinguish at least roughly between what we might call epistemic and psychological irrationality; the former having to do with one's adhering to a program/method/policy that would preclude the attainment of truth(s) and knowledge or disallow the possibility of fulfilling one's ends or purposes[37]; the latter with being incapable of acting or thinking coherently in the first place.

And it is here that the need for a distinction between "relativism" and "pluralism" becomes evident. According to Barry Barnes and David Bloor:

> For the relativist there is no sense attached to the idea that some standards of beliefs are really rational as distinct from merely locally accepted as such. Because he thinks that there are no context-free or super-cultural norms of rationality he does not see rationally and irrationally held beliefs as making up two distinct and qualitatively different classes of things.[38]

For the pluralist, on the other hand, "exclusionary principles" do make possible a clear separation between epistemic rationality and irrationality, for they serve as universal conditions for the very possibility of having truth(s) and knowledge. Ian Hacking draws a distinction between "those propositions that have a sense for almost all human beings regardless of reasoning" [for "there is a common human core of verbal performances connected with what people tend to notice around them"] and "those that get a sense only within a style of reasoning,"—a mode of reasoning that has "a specific beginning and trajectory of development" and which, he argues, determines what counts as true-or-false rather than what counts simply as true. Styles of reasoning, Hacking believes, open a way toward a pluralism which is not just a subtle form of relativism.[39]

W. Newton-Smith, however, insists, erroneously I think, that

> Hacking has sought to give sense to a *form of relativism* [my italics] by arguing that what can vary from age to age or from social group to social group is the availability of propositions. That is, a proposition which is for us a candidate for being true or false may be a proposition which the Herns cannot entertain. The reason for this, according to Hacking, is that the sense of a non-observational proposition is in part fixed by the style of reasoning used in relation to the proposition. Given that styles of reasoning change, as

Hacking argues, one cannot grasp the sense of a sentence used in one style of reasoning without grasping the style of reasoning.

Newton-Smith goes on to say:

> There is nothing particularly relativistic about this claim. However, Hacking then proceeds to give an account of styles of reasoning which generates an exciting relativism [*sic*, "pluralism"]. Hacking's claim is that "the propositions which are objectively found to be true are determined as true by styles of reasoning for which in principle there can be no external justification. A justification would be an independent way of showing that the style gets at the truth, but there is no characterization of the true over and above what is reached by the styles of reason itself."[40]

But as long as "truths" do get generated, Why, one might very well ask, is there the need for this kind of justification in the first place? It is sufficient, I think, to understand how exclusionary principles are constitutive of various rational practices (if you do not follow them you are not engaged in the practice) and how they then make possible, at a next step for us to determine, truths and falsities along a continuum within the rational order. And further, unlike the regulative rules of etiquette or, say, the constitutive rules of chess, rational exclusionary principles have a special force in our lives. It is not at all necessary, as it is with being rational, that one play chess in order to survive or to knowingly negotiate one's way in the world or to lead a flourishing life.

Let us look at this in somewhat greater detail. A general schema for epistemic rationality/irrationality might, I think, look something like this.

Figure 7.1.   Beliefs

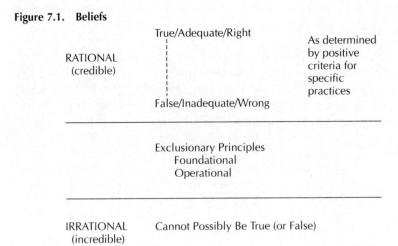

By "Beliefs" we mean here any statement, hypothesis, theory . . . that is held or asserted however fallible its truth-value may be. Beliefs are credible or incredible, depending on the possibility of their being justified. Rational beliefs are credible because they abide, at least nominally or intentionally, by rules of inferences, and are substantively true or adequate or right along a continuum, the lower end of which would be the false, the inadequate, or the wrong.[41] These designations are appropriate relative to particular discourses or subject matters (e.g., we usually speak of the truth/falsity of empirical statements, the adequacy/inadequacy of theories or general viewpoints, the rightness/wrongness of various kinds of aesthetic and moral judgments), these designations being subject to changing fashions of use.

Exclusionary principles, as indicated, are those which if adhered to preclude the possibility of certain ways of thinking from entering the arena of the credible. They are of two kinds: the "foundational" and the "operational." *Foundational* exclusionary principles are those which if adhered to would not allow a person to even get started in any rational practice whatsoever (e.g., again, the rejection of the law of non-contradiction, or perhaps of any accepted "law of logic"). As we have noted, although laws of logic are not by themselves productive of substantive knowledge, their rejection would simply and effectively shut one off from the possibility of attaining truth or knowledge in our thinking and therefore from the domain of the rational. *Operational* exclusionary principles, on the other hand, consist of those conditions that demarcate rational practices, and which, while taken to be universal at any one time, are in principle subject to historical revision under changing circumstances. Foundational exclusionary principles are for us invariant—we can not imagine epistemic situations in which they would not be effective; operational exclusionary principles are historically variant, for any set of which we can imagine situations where some of the principles could be subtracted from the set while others could be added.[42]

For example, for us today any set of operational exclusionary principles would surely include the demand for coherence, falsifiability, and shareability. A belief must in principle be part of a web of belief that is otherwise sustainable as a background corpus of knowledge so that the belief coheres with that structure and is not asserted in a manner that radically deviates from it. One would be irrational if one were to affirm—rather than simply suspend judgment regarding—a belief that was utterly incompatible with everything else one felt justified to believe. Rationality calls always for at least the possibility of there being systematic coherence in experience.

A belief must also be framed in such a way that it is always potentially subject to revision and defeat. It must in short be fallible. Although one might rightly hold to the initial validity of one's perceptions and conceptions, they must always be acknowledged to be, in principle, subject to being false at that very time and be open to revision in the light of future experience. By this exclusionary principle we would regard as epistemically irrational X's holding a belief Y when, for whatever psychological factors, X is compelled to hold Y and would accept nothing to count against it. Avoiding the so-called genetic fallacy, we would have to allow that Y might be true, but that X nevertheless is in no position to justify Y and in this instance would not be thinking rationally in affirming it.[43]

We also hold today that a belief and the reasons given for it must be sharable and such that they could, in principle, be convincing to another belief-practitioner. One would not be playing the belief-affirming game if one claimed that one's belief could not, in principle, be communicated to another or seen by him to be justifiable. In short, although one may reason to oneself, as it were, about the validity of one's beliefs, for a belief to be rational it must be inherently inter-subjective in character.

These operational principles, while universally binding for us at this time, are nevertheless susceptible to alteration and elimination under very different epistemic situations. It is conceivable (albeit barely), for instance, that falsifiability might be dispensable in some possible world because the state of knowledge in that world was so complete that all beliefs held there were incorrigible.

In the meantime, in this actual world, criticizing or evaluating beliefs (of one's own and those of others) is a two-stage affair: first, examining the belief and reasons allegedly supporting it in terms of seeing if the belief enters the arena of the rational by way of its crossing over the exclusionary boundary by not violating its foundational and operational principles; second, on the positive side, determining, on the basis of various positive criteria adhered to by a given community of practitioners, the degree to which a claim is warranted. The first stage or test determines whether a belief has the possibility of being true (or adequate or right) in terms of its not violating the conditions that are accepted as defining the practice as rational; the second determines the degree of truth, adequacy or rightness of the belief in terms of its fulfilling the set of conditions that are accepted by the appropriate community as necessary for truth attainment within the context of various general criteria.

This appeal to the epistemic standards of communities of practitioners in justifying various substantive beliefs is not, of course, to be construed as telling the whole story of justification, for as we will try to show there are "givens" of our experienced world which must be taken into account in any claim to justified belief. There is, in other words, a conventional dimension or element in all justificatory rationality, but it does not bear the entire weight of what is called for in justification. We need always to show that there is some strong connection between the positive criteria we employ in our practices of justifying belief and the belief being "true."

It should also be noted that the general positive criteria, as well as specific ones accepted by a given community of inquirers at any one time, are never set in stone. Their social character is such that they are always subject to changing cultural conditions, to advances in methodologies, to new kinds of self-understanding, and so on, as well as to the nature of the different subject-matters to which they apply. Further, as we have seen, beliefs are always value-laden, informed by the shifting interests and concerns of the holder of the belief, and are hence subject to change.[44]

It must again be stressed, however, that while telling us that there are necessary conditions for the attainment of knowledge, exclusionary principles do not provide us as such with (formulaic) sufficient ones. Exclusionary principles, in their universality, are essentially negative in import. They tell us more about what we cannot do than about what we should positively do in attaining truth and knowledge. A kind of pernicious absolutism arises when, ignoring "styles of reasoning" and the positive criteria for various belief-producing practices, we transform an exclusionary principle into a single, positive program—of action, of thinking, of political organization—where a one, correct pattern of behavior and a one right way of thinking gets announced that has a presumed enduring, universal reach. Exclusionary principles, when properly understood, provide I believe a basis for acknowledging the possibility (and indeed desirability) of there being many right ways of acting and thinking.[45] They make possible, and indeed call for, a creative bringing forth of diverse rational expressions.

This understanding of the role of exclusionary principles as universal and yet leading to a plurality of rational expressions must also be seen to be able to accommodate the fact of there being *alterative* rationalities among diverse cultures with respect to different ideas regarding the relationship between moral and strictly cognitive values. What may be regarded as irrational in this context may differ markedly from one culture to another, and at different periods within the same culture. For example, for the traditional Chinese, "irrationality" could very well mean sundering reason from morality in such a way that one would think wrongly and act inappropriately within the knowing conditions of *li*: that there would be something irrational about the very assertion of the absolute authority and autonomy of a disengaged reason. For the traditional Indian, on the other hand, irrationality could very well mean willingly or self-deceptively remaining in—or returning to—the state of *avidyā* (of a kind of ontological "ignorance") and of thinking and acting accordingly.

In our own time and place, it is beginning to be recognized (however dimly) that irrationality may very well incorporate moral-value as well as strictly cognitive-value concerns; that, for example, it would be entirely appropriate to regard as irrational the employment of correct instrumental reasoning dedicated to the pursuit of evil ends. Integrating the moral with the cognitive in the very definition of rationality remains for us today a major philosophical challenge and task.

NOTES

1. Hilary Putnam, *Realism with a Human Face*, ed. James Conant (Cambridge, Mass.: Harvard University Press, 1990), 139.

2. The term "universal" unfortunately, for some, suggests that which is invariant as well as (biologically or logically) necessary. But, quite clearly, it might very well be the case that at a given time human biology, say, might necessitate that we perceive objects according to recognized (e.g., gestalt) "laws" of perception, so that everyone, everywhere minimally is subject to them; but this does not entail that at some other time evolutionary conditions might be such that these frameworks no longer apply.

3. This indicates rather clearly that Enlightenment thinking in general is not so much a theory of rationality, which is the way it is oftentimes now regarded, as it is a philosophical anthropology—a view of humankind as capable, through the exercise of reason, of perfecting a science of the natural world, of organizing a just social order and of making all experience intelligible. For this kind of anthropology, everything wayward and perverse in human nature is only contingent, the result of misinformed intelligence and malformed institutions.

4. It is also something of a commonplace today to acknowledge that historically there have been, in Western thought alone, a number of different conceptions of what constitutes rationality and what functions reason is equipped to perform, albeit the tendency remains among those adhering to any one of the conceptions to assume its universality. Charles Taylor rather nicely and concisely presents an account of this history when he writes that "Plato's . . . stands at the head of a large family of views which see the good life as a mastery of self which consists in the dominance of reason over desire. . . . And with the development of the modern scientific world-view a specifically modern variant has developed. This is the ideal of the disengaged self, capable of objectifying not only the surrounding world but also his own emotions and inclinations, fears and compulsions, and achieving thereby a kind of distance and self-possession which allows him to act 'rationally.' This last term has been put into quotes, because obviously its meaning has changed relatively to the Platonic sense. Reason is no longer defined in terms of a vision of order in the cosmos, but rather is defined procedurally, in terms of instrumental efficacy, of maximization of the value sought, or self-consistency." (*Sources of the Self: The Making of the Modern Identity*, 21.)

5. It has, however, been recognized that many postmodernist rejections of modern claims regarding the scope and objectivity of reason, on the grounds that all rational practices are embedded in social practices that are dictated by power

relations and manipulations and by linguistic constructions that render all nor-mativity either in science or in social life impossible, is doomed not only to out-right inconsistency (How could such a critique itself be rationally justified?), which situation would not necessarily bother certain deconstructivist postmod-ernists, but to a lifeless sterility of thought where all genuine criticism and creativ-ity would disappear—and this, one would think, ought to bother them greatly.

6. Clifford Geertz, "Anti Anti-Relativism," in *Relativism: Interpretation and Confrontation*, edited by Michael Krausz (Notre Dame: University of Notre Dame Press, 1989), 20.

7. Hilary Putnam, *Reason, Truth and History* (Cambridge: Cambridge University Press, 1981), 146.

8. *Personal Knowledge: Towards a Post-Critical Philosophy*, 382. With respect to scientific practices, Mary Tiles and Jim Tiles also make evident this epistemic limi-tation when they write: "Science claims a non-human standard for its authority, the non-human, material world. But a world conceived as the legitimate object of domination cannot also be the source of knowledge of human nature, including knowledge of what would constitute human fulfillment. Human flourishing is not a possible object of knowledge for a science which has banished teleology" (*An Introduction to Historical Epistemology: The Authority of Knowledge* [Oxford: Black-well Publishers, 1993], 200).

9. Noam Chomsky, *Rules and Representations* (New York: Columbia University Press, 1978), 28.

10. Ibid., 40.

11. Thomas Nagel, *The Last Word* (New York/Oxford: Oxford University Press, 1997), 73.

12. Ibid., 20–21.

13. Steven Lukes, "Some Problems About Rationality," in *Rationality*, ed. Bryan R. Wilson (Oxford: Basil Blackwell, 1970), 208–210. Thomas Nagel makes the same point somewhat differently when insisting that "However much one may try to construe one's concepts and thoughts naturalistically, as the expression of contingent forms of life, the logic [the system of concepts that makes thought pos-sible and to which any language usable by thinking must conform] of the effort will always generate thoughts too fundamental for this, thoughts which one can-not get outside of in this way and which one must employ in trying to view from the outside anything else that one does" (*The Last Word*, 32–33).

14. Steven Lukes, "Relativism in Its Place," in *Rationality and Relativism*, ed. Martin Hollis and Steven Lukes (Cambridge: The MIT Press, 1982), 262.

15. Barry Barnes and David Bloor, "Relativism, Rationalism and the Sociology of Knowledge," in *Rationality and Relativism*, 40.

16. Ibid., 41.

17. Steven Lukes, "Some Problems About Rationality," 211. Thomas Nagel goes much further than this when he claims that "reason produces belief" (*The Last Word*, pp. 31–32). But the belief-making process, once contextuality is prop-erly introduced, is surely more subtle and culture-laden that what is suggested by Nagel's claim. Further, it certainly seems to be the case that reason, in the con-text of belief-formation, functions more often than not in a critical manner, focus-

ing on what we are predisposed to believe on the basis of our accumulated experience as it applies to new anticipations of understanding, than in an originary producing of a new belief.

18. Rational thinking, for some empiricist-minded thinkers, is universal to the degree that it is modeled on some kind of ideal computer program where the same result will always be obtained by anyone and everyone as long as proper procedures are followed. This impersonal algorithmic conception of rationality, to be sure, has happily been roundly criticized (within neo-pragmatic analytic thinking beginning with Quine) with the result being that very little, apart from consensus-building as a result of ongoing inquiry, is left of the very idea of an empiricist-grounded epistemic universality.

19. See J. N. Mohanty, "Phenomenology and Indian Philosophy: The Concept of Rationality," in *Philosophy and Phenomenology*, ed. D. P. Chattopadhyaya, et al. (Albany: State University of New York Press, 1992), 10.

20. Arindam Chakrabarti, "Rationality in Indian Philosophy," in *A Companion to World Philosophies*, ed. Eliot Deutsch and Ron Bontekoe (Oxford: Blackwell Publishers, 1997), 269.

21. Ibid., 271.

22. A. C. Graham, *Disputers of the Tao: Philosophical Argument in Ancient China*, 323.

23. David L. Hall, "Reason and Its Rhyme," *Journal of the Indian Council of Philosophical Research*, vol. IX, no. 2 (January–April 1992): 35.

24. David Lynn Hall and Roger T. Ames, "Rationality, Correlativity, and The Language of Process," *The Journal of Speculative Philosophy*, vol. V, no. 2, 1991.

25. Jürgen Habermas, *The Theory of Communicative Action*, trans. Thomas McCarthy (Boston: Beacon Press, 1984), vol. I, 16.

26. Ibid., 20.

27. Ibid., 42.

28. Ibid., 55.

29. Ibid., 180.

30. *Nicomachean Ethics*, II, 6, 9–14, trans. W. D. Ross.

31. I will elaborate on this moral dimension in chapter 15, "Creative Anarchism."

32. The distinction between the rational and irrational here quite naturally has its grounding in the aesthetic-moral values constitutive of contemplative consciousness. The irrational disallows the attainment of that genuine harmony in thought which underlies and sustains in the end all rational practices. Another way to put this would be to note that the irrational is repugnant to rational consciousness in much the same way that the destructive and disharmonious is to contemplative consciousness and that it is the very awareness of rightness generated in the contemplative that precisely informs the rational in such a way as to provide it with the basis for that repugnance to the irrational. The irrational makes impossible the achievement of genuine coherence, and thus is at odds with the very ontological ground of human reason.

33. A possible exception to this is certain theoretical-epistemic practices in quantum mechanics, but even here this seem to have more to do with indetermi-

nacy or with the principle of excluded middle than with non-contradiction as such. (See, for example, Willard Van Orman Quine, "Two Dogmas of Empiricism," in *From a Logical Point of View* [Cambridge: Harvard University Press, 1953], 44–46.)

34. Kant writes: "The universal, though merely negative, condition of all our judgments in general . . . is that they be not self-contradictory; for if self-contradictory, these judgments are in themselves, even without reference to the object, null and void.

"The *principle of contradiction* must therefore be recognized as being the universal and completely sufficient *principle of all analytic knowledge*; but beyond the sphere of analytic knowledge it has, as a *sufficient* criterion of truth, no authority and no field of application. . . . [I]n regard to the truth of this [synthetic] kind of knowledge we can never look to the above principle for any positive information, though, of course, since it is inviolable, we must always be careful to conform to it." *Critique of Pure Reason*, trans. by Norman Kemp Smith (London: Macmillan 1929), A151, 152.

35. Exclusionary principles may, if one prefers somewhat more positive-sounding rule-language, be said to be *rules of admissibility* for entrance into the domain of the rational. To refer, however, to the law of non-contradiction as an exclusionary principle, the violation of which . . . , rather than as a necessary condition, the fulfillment of which . . . , has the advantage of marking off a clear demarcation between the rational and the irrational and, by insisting on their being nonproductive by themselves of knowledge and truth, of providing a basis for a plurality of truths on the rational side. Violate the principle and you cannot be an articulate knower, follow it and you may, but not necessarily will, be a participant in the producing of knowledge and truth.

36. See J. N. Mohanty's discussion of this in his *Reason and Tradition in Indian Thought: An Essay on the Nature of Indian Philosophical Thinking* (Oxford: Clarendon Press, 1992), 101ff.

37. As Larry Laudan rather mildly puts it, "to adopt a goal with the feature that we can conceive of no actions that would be apt to promote it . . . is surely a mark of unreasonableness and irrationality" (*Science and Values: The Aims of Science and Their Role in Scientific Debate* [Berkeley: University of California Press, 1984], 51).

38. In "Relativism, Rationalism and the Sociology of Knowledge," 28.

39. See his "Language, Truth and Reason," in *Rationality and Relativism*, 51ff, and his *Representing and Intervening: Introductory Topics in the Philosophy of Natural Science* (Cambridge: Cambridge University Press, 1983), especially his chapter 5, "Incommensurability."

40. W. Newton-Smith, "Relativism and the Possibility of Interpretation," in *Rationality and Relativism*, 120–21.

41. And it is here that the role of authority so often comes into play. Most of us do not know first-hand how to justify the vast majority of the beliefs we hold regarding historical events, cultural and physical geography, and so on; rather we rely upon the "expert testimony" of others. Trustfulness is thus built into the very logic of belief. We assume that when a geologist tells us his story about the forma-

tion of rocks and of the earth, a historian gives us her account of the when, where and why certain decisive events occurred, a physicist his description and explanation of subatomic happenings, that we are not being purposively deceived. Education is clearly based on trust of this sort: the tellings, the accounts given may turn out to be wrong, incomplete, or inadequate, but that is another matter.

42. This does not mean, however, that we can relativize operational exclusionary principles to local practices as such, for any such rational practice must presuppose those very principles if it can hope to be effective according to its own positive criteria.

43. It might also be argued that, at the other extreme, any clinging to a radical skepticism regarding the possibility of ever having adequate beliefs about anything would be irrational, on the grounds that such an epistemic attitude would run directly contra to that initial presumption of validity we accord our perceptions and conceptions that is a condition for our sanity. If every time one observed something and judged it to have such and such properties one simultaneously withheld one's assent to that judgment, one couldn't even begin to negotiate one's way in the world. One would be frozen and imprisoned in a contradiction of one's own making. This is not to say, though, that one is disentitled to withhold one's assent to some candidate for belief, for this withholding is not a matter of epistemic skepticism but a realization that at the present time one doesn't have sufficient information to render a proper (justified) judgment. This epistemic attitude presupposes the possibility that one could have or acquire the necessary information.

44. With the explosive achievements and rapidly changing developments in the natural sciences, the proliferation of information in the social sciences about cultural practices in civilizations throughout the world, the profusion of new understandings and interpretations of experience in the arts and humanities, we are in a position now to believe strongly in the impossibility of philosophy to articulate any universal generalizations which would encompass all instances of what we might take to be warranted factual claims or rationally justified beliefs. The positive criteria for justification in the varied rational practices we recognize are themselves too diverse and contingent to allow this: pluralism, it must be acknowledged, once again reigns.

45. The advent of non-Euclidean geometries, for example, nicely shows how exclusionary principles of the most general nature, such as, once again, the law of non-contradiction do not necessitate a single system (of geometry or of logic itself) but can tolerate, indeed promote, diverse systems with their own specific rules and primitive axioms.

8

✳

Moral Values and Justificatory Rationality

It has become rather commonplace in the philosophical literature on rationality to depict "instrumental reason" as the dominant form of rationality in the modern world. From Bacon onward, the notion that to understand something means to know how one can change it (rather than, as with the previous tradition generally to contemplate its essential nature) was quite naturally allied with a conception of causality emerging from the development of the new science. This theoretical conception, as embedded in explanatory accounts of natural events and processes, collapsed all material, formal and final causes into the efficient, and was readily extended to explain human actions in terms of the means by which our purposes were to be fulfilled. Practical reason thus became an instrument for determining the most effective or efficient means to attain a chosen end.

This instrumental conception of reason, however, clearly does not embrace adequately all the various kinds of reasoning that we frequently employ in our effort to make intelligible the primary domains of human inquiry, namely that of explaining natural events or processes, determining appropriate means/end relationships, and accounting for our human actions. I would suggest that the term "justificatory" rather than "instrumental" as such can best designate these various kinds of reasoning. This will become evident as we comment briefly on the respective intentionalities of these rational practices, what these modalities of rational expression primarily aim to achieve, and indicate how these practices may become value-laden and give rise eventually to a plurality of epistemic portraits.

Before turning to an examination of our justificatory practices in the context of their integrating moral values into their very definition, it might be useful to look again at Habermas' notion of rationality, now as set forth in his *The Philosophical Discourse of Modernity*. He rightly, I believe, points out there that

> As long as Occidental self-understanding views human beings as distin-
> guished in their relationship to the world by their monopoly on encounter-
> ing entities, knowing and dealing with objects, making true statements, and
> implementing plans, reason remains confined ontologically, epistemologi-
> cally, or in terms of linguistic analysis to only one of its dimensions. The
> relationship of the human being to the world is cognitivistically reduced:
> Ontologically, the world is reduced to the world of entities as a whole (as the
> totality of objects that can be represented and of existing states of affairs);
> epistemologically, our relation to that world is reduced to the capacity to
> know existing states of affairs or to bring them about in a purposive-rational
> fashion; semantically, it is reduced to fact-stating discourse in which assert-
> oric sentences are used—and no validity claim is admitted besides proposi-
> tional truth, which is available *in foro interno*.[1]

He then argues, however, that

> as soon as we conceive of knowledge as communicatively mediated, rational-
> ity is assessed in terms of the capacity of responsible participants in inter-
> action to orient themselves in relation to validity claims geared to inter-
> subjective recognition. Communicative reason finds its criteria in the
> argumentative procedures for directly or indirectly redeeming claims to
> propositional truth, normative rightness, subjective truthfulness, and aes-
> thetic harmony.
>
>   Thus, a procedural concept of rationality can be worked out in terms of
> the interdependence of various forms of argumentation, that is to say, with
> the help of a pragmatic logic of argumentation. This concept is richer than
> that of purposive rationality, which is tailored to the cognitive-instrumental
> dimension, because it integrates the moral-practical as well as aesthetic-
> expressive domains: it is an explication of the rational potential built into the
> validity basis of speech. . . . Communicative reason is expressed in a decent-
> ered understanding of the world.[2]

The idea of a communicative reason seeking intersubjective agreement with respect to a wide range of validity claims is certainly well and good as far as it goes, but it does not, it seems to me, reach far enough towards fulfilling its desire for integrating the "moral-practical and aesthetic-expressive domains" into a concept of rationality, since it is confined essentially to speech-situations (as understood broadly in terms of speech-act theory in the philosophy of language). Consequently insuffi-cient attention is paid to the actual experimental work of explanatory science and to practical reasonings in determining means/ends relations and in justifying our purposive actions. What is needed is not just an expanding of the list of what can legitimately claim validity, but an integration of the moral-aesthetic into these existing rational practices in such a way as to bring about a re-definition and transformation of those very practices at their core.

There appears among many post-empiricist philosophers of science today a marked change in direction away from an adherence to the traditional notion of science pursuing, and closing-in on, a one, true picture of things in favor of recognizing the historicity of science as a cultural as well as biological and strictly cognitive matter and thus as very much a human affair constrained by innumerable social and political as well as strictly evolutionary and logical factors. Nevertheless, at the same time, there seems to be something of a consensus that the rational practice of science has for its aim to *explain*, in a third-person impartial and objective manner, various selected natural processes and happenings within the framework of nomic or lawlike causal relations, albeit this is understood more in the fallibilist terms associated with warranted assertibility notions of truth than in the apodictic terms related to correspondence theories. As Mary Hesse nicely sums up this post-empiricist account of natural science:

1. In natural science data is not detachable from theory, for what count as data are determined in the light of some theoretical interpretation, and the facts themselves have to be reconstructed in the light of interpretation.
2. In natural science theories are not models externally compared with nature in hypothetico-deductive schema, they are the way the facts themselves are seen.
3. In natural science the lawlike relations asserted of experience are internal, because what counts as facts are constituted by what the theory says about their interrelations with one another.
4. The language of natural science is irreducibly metaphorical and inexact, and formalizable only at the cost of distortion of the historical dynamics of scientific development and of the imaginative constructions in terms of which nature is interpreted by science.
5. Meanings in natural science are determined by theory; they are understood by theoretical coherence rather than by correspondence with facts.[3]

Justificatory rationality as embodied in science, on this view, thus aims to give us *adequate* accounts, but not an everlastingly true theory, of the way things and events are constituted and behave in relation to other things and events in their environments.[4] And it aims to do this so that we may predict phenomena in a variety of ways and thereby manipulate and control them for our own benefit.

There also seems to be considerable agreement that actual scientific practice remains throughout subject to its own cognitive values and exclusionary principles, for it has come to be widely recognized that in science one cannot specify algorithmic rules and procedures the following of which will ensure successful discovery so much as one can show the futility of employing certain means or methods if one's aim is to achieve success. As Michael Polanyi notes: "Theories of the scientific method which try to explain the establishment of scientific truth by any purely objective formal procedure are doomed to failure. Any process of enquiry unguided by intellectual passions would inevitably spread out into a desert of trivialities."[5]

While eschewing consideration of moral values in science, Larry Laudan, nevertheless, endorses a "reticulated model" of justification which allows for the possibility of "several, even mutually incompatible, goals" that may satisfy the constraints it sets forth in the proper relationships between the methods, theories and aims of science. In the reticulated picture, "Justification," he says, "flows upward as well as downward in the [traditional] hierarchy, linking aims, methods, and factual claims. No longer should we regard any one of these levels as privileged or primary or more fundamental than the others. Axiology, methodology, and factual claims are inevitably intertwined in relations of mutual dependency."[6] And thus, "Those who imagine that there is a single axiology that can or should guide investigation into nature have failed to come to terms with the palpable diversity of the potential ends and uses of inquiry."[7]

Laudan goes on to argue that this does not "take the bite out of the demand for rationality," for "beyond demanding that our cognitive goals must reflect our best beliefs about what is and what is not possible, that our methods must stand in an appropriate relation to our goals, and that our implicit and explicit values must be synchronized, there is little more that the theory of rationality can demand."[8]

There is, however, I would suggest, a great deal more that such a theory can demand, not the least of which is the integration of moral-value concerns into the otherwise purely cognitive-value picture presented. It has been characteristic of our thinking about science for several centuries now that science, taken as the very epitome of rationality, is rightfully dedicated to the pursuit of knowledge for its own sake. Struggling to withstand calls by any external authority to limit its investigations, the scientific enterprise—although somewhat ironically seeking justification by its good works—was determined to assert its Baconian-like autonomy. However, as Mary Tiles and Jim Tiles point out:

> In the seventeenth century context it was necessary to argue for the independence of natural philosophy from moral philosophy and theology in order to secure for it a place outside the jurisdiction of religious authorities. By insisting on a sharp division between natural science on the one hand and morals and theology on the other, Bacon hoped to persuade people of the moral neutrality of his project. But to succeed, his own arguments had to straddle that division, and the fact that Bacon's advocacy of his program for acquisition of knowledge does rest on a moral vision [regarding the improvement of the material conditions of life], at the same time as proclaiming the autonomy of science from moral and political jurisdiction, means that there is an inherent source of tension within the project.[9]

And this tension is still very much with us today. It has become increasingly clear to many thoughtful persons that to divorce "the scientist" from the person who happens to be one—that his work as a scientist may be radically sundered from his moral standing as a human being—is patently unacceptable. It makes altogether feasible the caricature of the mad scientist demonically at work in his steamy laboratory creating hideous new life-forms or doomsday machines, for there appears to be nothing in the claim for scientific autonomy that precludes a search for knowledge intending to develop technologies destructive of the most basic human values. Not much has changed since Ralph Barton Perry noted:

> The independent values of science consist of the qualifying attributes of knowledge, that is, those characters of truth, proof and certitude, for which knowledge is esteemed for its own sake. Judgment by those attributes taken as standards constitute the final and internal part of the normative nature of science.[10]

And that

> While science qua science is not obliged to consider its moral relations, society may well consider them, and ask how far science, being what it is, tends to serve or thwart the moral purpose.[11]

Michael Polanyi and Harry Porsch have rightly pointed out, however, that

> Scientific inquiry is . . . a dynamic exercise of the imagination and is rooted in commitments and beliefs about the nature of things. . . . Science is not thus the simon-pure, crystal-clear fount of all reliable knowledge and coherence, as it has for so long presumed to be. Its method is not that of *detachment* but rather that of *involvement*.

Thus the idea of pure objectivity in knowing and in science has been shown to be a myth. It is perhaps a harmless myth if most of its implications are not followed out, but it is certainly a poisonous one if they are. For the implication that the truth about human behavior demands an amoral standpoint is . . . part of what our moral inversions have been made of.[12]

It must be understood, then, that although it is entirely appropriate that public-policy questions regarding the social good that may or may not come out of any given scientific investigation be asked, it is insufficient for moral concerns only to be imposed by society on an otherwise value-free, autonomous rationality, telling it from an external standpoint what it can and cannot do in terms of a calculus of human benefit. What is clearly needed is a fundamental shift in our understanding of the nature of explanatory rationality in a direction that would embody "moral relations" at its very core. This integration of moral considerations with strictly cognitive ones in determining the rationality of a given explanatory inquiry, imposing thereby a special moral burden on science, arises also from the fact that how we regard the objects of explanatory inquiry (e.g., as things out there to be controlled) does impact importantly on how we regard others and organize our social institutions. With the dominance of science, its instrumental viewpoint quite naturally extends outward from science into our fundamental assumptions about ourselves as social beings. The "moral-political," in short, is thoroughly present in science. There is no amoral core in explanatory practices which is untouched by the humanness of the scientist and accordingly it becomes an imperative of science itself to recognize the moral *in* science and its impact on other of our human dealings with each other and our worlds.

This needed self-conscious integration of the moral with the cognitive is, however, in no way intended as a call for some kind of political ideology, masquerading as it so often does as a utopian social vision, to dictate what is true scientific theory (as happened so clearly in the Soviet Union of the 1950s); quite the contrary, such an intrusion would in the view being developed here, be irrational: it would violate operational exclusionary principles of science itself, for example that all explanations be fallible. Ideologically driven explanations in science disallow falsifiability and thus fall outside the rational domain of justificatory rationality.

A *regulative ideal* of scientific practice, presupposed by anyone joining that community of rational inquiry and discourse, would be the adherence to, and the promotion of, a program of developing the basic values of personhood and freedom. In exclusionary terms, the scientist would, by her own commitment to justificatory rationality, be precluded from carrying out research, say, of developing ever more cruel means to torture another human being, that would be violative of those fundamental values. She would also, according to her acceptance of this regulative ideal, and not just by legal constraints, be disallowed from employing certain methods of inquiry irrespective of the subject-matter or object of the inquiry—for example, to act with careless disregard for potential or likely hazards in the experimental process. In short, justificatory rationality in its explanatory modality would be such that certain inquiries and ways of carrying-out various inquiries simply would not be pursued *according to the rational criteria of science itself.* Built then into the very definition of science as a rational practice would be the responsibility of the scientist to adhere to certain basic human values and to be thoroughly accountable for the choices she makes with respect to the what and how of her inquiries. Science, Bernard Williams tells us, "is a complex social activity, and the fact that some branch of science at a given time settles on certain theories or models rather than others is not an outcome straightforwardly determined by perception, but rather by scientist's habits and practices, including their ways of selecting and interpreting observations."[13] This selecting and interpreting function inescapably involves moral-value considerations which need become part and parcel of the core of the very rationality of science. The reasoning of a genuine person demands a cognitive-moral rationality. To sunder the cognitive from the moral would for him itself be irrational. And happily there is nothing that prevents any scientist from being a genuine person.

Justificatory reasoning with respect to means/ends situations aims to bring about the best relationship between the means to be selected and the ends to be achieved, "best" most often, but not always, involving maximal efficiency. Exclusionary-wise, under any circumstances, rationality here clearly calls for commensurability between means and ends. We would, we believe, rightly take an instrumental reasoning that would justify the choice of a means that was either incapable of, or straightforwardly detrimental to, achieving the desired end as irrational—albeit full confidence here is not readily attained, as one could always be mistaken about, or be misinformed regarding, possible connections between the apparently ill-chosen means and the end to be attained. Justificatory rationality here quite obviously allows for disagreement about what constitutes the meaning of "best" in the relationship between means and ends and, for better or worse, acknowledges the extent to which justificatory rationality itself may or may not provide reasons for the goals or ends that it seeks to fulfill.[14]

When the moral dimension becomes integral to instrumental reasoning, however, the choice of ends necessarily becomes a part of that reasoning. Just as with the explanatory, where moral-cognitive exclusionary principles preclude undertaking certain forms and ways of inquiry, so with the instrumental, it would, in this account, be irrational for a realized person to coolly calculate the most efficient means to attain some end that was violative of fundamental values of human decency and dignity.

The exclusionary principles operative in means/end justificatory rationality also, within at least most non-authoritarian societies, already involves the criteria that "the end does not justify the means"; that what we take to be a worthwhile end does not allow us to justifiably select any means whatsoever to realize it. This moral-value, I would hold, belongs as an integral feature in the very criteria for justification in this modality of reason, which is to say, that the violation of the dictum ought to be seen not only as relatively morally wrong but as universally irrational. As Dewey wisely observed, means and ends are not radically separate from one another, the means chosen will inevitably intrude upon and shape the ends to be reached. The very logic of instrumental rationality calls for moral commensurability between means and ends.

On the positive side of judgment, one can with some confidence, I believe, also say that *any* criterial-scheme of instrumental efficiency that might be evoked in justificatory rationality must take seriously into account the social context of a "problematic situation" in such a way as to call for the means employed in the resolution of the situation to be in harmony with that context. By "harmony" we mean that unifying quality that emerges from, and then goes in turn to inform, the mutual adaptation of diverse, and oftentimes contending elements, that participate in a particular situation. This quite clearly involves a kind of *phronēsis* or practical reasoning that seeks not only to promote various accepted existing values or, in Aristotle's terms, "universal principles," within the concrete choices regarding means that one makes, but to bring forth new forms of value as required by the situation at hand. Just as the general social values or rational principles constitutive of *phronēsis* are not such as to be mechanically applied, but serve to guide one's intellectual sensitivity toward appropriate ways of acting in novel situations, so the values that emerge from rational deliberations regarding means/end situations are not in themselves in any way timeless or absolute, they are rather precisely *situational*. This means also that judgments regarding the rationality of an action need attend to the *kairos*-like appropriateness of the action in its social and natural environmental contexts. *Who* does *what* on *which occasion*—whether the doing is ceremonial or not—is part of the "felicity" (to use Austin's felicitous expression) of the action and is constitutive of the action as judged properly with respect to the degree of its rationality.

In spite of the fact that it is often held that "A theory of the rationality of belief will consist in large part of a system of rules which determine, in a given cognitive situation, what a man's doxastic commitments ought to be,"[15] it seems quite clear that there is a great deal more that is central to the rationality of belief as it involves the justification of human actions than our being determined by a "system of rules," for is it not the case that one's ongoing engagements with one's natural, social and cultural environments generate various significance-laden criteria by which we judge the adequacy of our beliefs regarding our actions and those of others? We seek, it would seem, more to *understand* our actions than to *explain* them as such.

As Dilthey, Weber and others around the turn of the twentieth century argued, while explanation has to do with proffering generalizations about predicable phenomena, its natural home being the exact sciences, understanding has to do with what is unique and non-repeatable, as is art and history and other domains within the *Geisteswissenschaften*. Understanding was thought to be essentially teleological insofar as it takes as its primary concern the purposes of an acting human being in his bodily actions and in his manner of participation in social institutions. The search for causes is made subordinate to the recognition of aims and intentions and the significance of those human activities that embody them.

Today, we are not so much inclined to draw a sharp dichotomy between explanation and understanding, in favor of a broader hermeneutic approach that embraces them both, but still it must be allowed that although there might oftentimes be a predictive element in justifying human actions, in contrast to explanatory justification as such, this element is indeed subordinate to grasping the intentionality of the agent and his or her action and recognizing the degree of appropriateness of the action in its full particularity, as well as the worthiness of its end and the manner in which it is sought to be attained.

Also, for the most part, we do not call for the giving of reasons to justify the contents of everyday actions unless we are simply curious about why someone is doing what they are doing, with the "why" not being immediately apparent, or when we notice a seeming disparity between our expectations of what should be taking place and the actual action that is performed.[16] Justificatory reasoning as applied to human actions always involves, at least in principle, levels of rational appeal: one can always ask for higher order justifications which involve appeals to both one's established beliefs and one's fundamental values regarding why a given action is worth performing.

In short, we often have with justificatory reasoning with respect to actions, a first order ready-at-hand announcement of intention (what it is that one is aiming to attain), followed by showing its appropriateness within the given context and indicating its fit or coherence with other of one's established beliefs and fundamental values. There is no necessary closure to the justificatory process here, albeit—with the possible exception of certain heavy moral cases—we would think it rather unseemly to be pressed far up the ladder of justifications and would lose patience with whoever was doing the pressing.

Justificatory reasoning of this sort is obviously subject to various exclusionary principles. We would not accept as rational if someone offered a justifying reason which did not seem to have any relation to the action that was to be justified although, as with means/ends situations, one can, of course, never be certain that one did not miss some connection between them. Also, we should, I think, regard as irrational and not just immoral the offering of reasons for an action which was intentionally violative of basic human values. We rightly look to the intentions and motivations of the actor as well as to the observed action itself in determining its rationality, for intentions and motivations do not stand apart as external causes or occasions for an action; they inform in a variety of subtle ways the action that is performed.[17]

On the somewhat more positive side, justifications of actions ought also to apply not only to the "what" of an action but as well to the "how" it is carried out. We ought to expect justifications to answer to questions regarding the degree to which actions promote social harmony and reflect the ideal of acting freely;[18] in short, to questions regarding the quality or *style* of the performance of actions as this reflects the intentions of the actor and her sense of rightness grounded, to the degree that it is, in aesthetic necessity. In fact, when we discern that an action which is correct in content is performed with rightness in style we see it as precisely value-fulfilling and not standing in need of any further justification.

The acceptance or rejection of a rational justification of an action therefore necessarily involves cognitive judgments that become at once moral and aesthetic in character: the inquirer into the "why" of an action must, in short, discern the action in the full manner of its performance in order to appraise the correctness of the reasons given to justify it.

Determining the relative rationality of an action is thus always an intersubjective affair, even when one is appraising one's own action, for some kind of agreement is being sought between the person as action-performer and the person as action-justifier.[19] But this seeking of agreement by way of questioning and examining reasons is not simply what comes about—or is aimed to come about—by way of a Habermasian ideal speech situation where in a non-dominant attitude the parties to the situation take themselves as equal participants in the inquiry. One might always very well ask, Why should I want to come to argumentative agreement with someone whom I perceive to be grossly insensitive to moral and aesthetic values with regard to judgments about the rationality of an action? One is strongly inclined to *disagree* with that person until such time as one is able to accept him as a genuine rational agent. One need not assume a rational equality—"rational" understood here not as a mere capacity to reason correctly by adhering to certain inferential rules and the like—in advance of recognizing the quality of the person, for the two are inseparable.

Integrating moral values with strictly cognitive values into the operating exclusionary principles and the positive criteria accepted for successful performance in various of the modalities of justificatory reasoning is, it seems to me, a necessary requirement for a theory of rationality appropriate to our times. The integration may help considerably to bridge the gap that has developed so strongly between theoretical (scientific, mathematical) and practical (various kinds of instrumental) reasoning, for both would become transformed into a pursuit of wisdom, guided by the idea of the good, as well as a pursuit of truth.

The realization of the play of moral values into the core of rationality cannot be indifferent to the quality of the knower as the person she is. There is, I think, something fundamentally amiss with any theory of knowing (most often one that defines rationality by the constraints of rules and inferential procedures alone) that assigns, as already noted, ideal reasoning to the mind of a knower absent his or her personhood, for to know the good is, as I have tried to argue, to have become the sort of person who is disabled from doing the wrong—with the possibility then opening up for their being many legitimate ways epistemically to realize the good.

NOTES

1. Jürgen Habermas, *The Philosophical Discourse of Modernity,* trans. Frederick C. Lawrence (Cambridge: The MIT Press, 1991), 416.

2. Ibid., 418.

3. Mary Hesse, *Revolutions and Reconstructions in the Philosophy of Science* (Bloomington: University of Indiana Press, 1980), 172–73.

4. This understanding of the pluralistic nature of science was already clearly set forth at the beginning of the twentieth-century in what may now be called "classical pragmatism." In his *Pragmatism. A New Name for Some Old Ways of Thinking,* published in 1907, William James wrote that "as the sciences have developed further, the notion has gained ground that most, perhaps all, of our laws are only approximations. The laws themselves, moreover, have grown so numerous that there is no counting them; and so many rival formulations are proposed in all the branches of science that investigators have become accustomed to the notion that no theory is absolutely a transcript of reality, but that any one of them may from some point of view be useful. . . . They are only a man-made language,

a conceptual shorthand . . . in which we write our reports of nature. . . ." (Lecture II)

5. Michael Polanyi, *Personal Knowledge: Towards a Post-Critical Philosophy*, 135.

6. Larry Laudan, *Science and Values: The Aims of Science and Their Role in Scientific Debate* (Berkeley: University of California Press, 1984), 62–63.

7. Ibid., 64.

8. Ibid., 64.

9. Mary Tiles and Jim Tiles, *An Introduction to Historical Epistemology: The Authority of Knowledge*, 27. It is also interesting to note, as do the Tiles, that "For those who accept logic as the basis of scientific rationality, this [the "incommensurability of rival theories" á la Kuhn and Feyerabend] would mean that theory choice can never be a matter of rational argument" (163), which is to say that an epistemological pluralism regarding the outcome of theory choice in science is precisely what is alone rationally sustainable.

10. Ralph Barton Perry, *Realms of Value: A Critique of Human Civilization* (Cambridge: Harvard University Press, 1954), 315. In somewhat more recent times, Hans-Georg Gadamer states even more boldly that "It [science] will continue along its own path with an inner necessity, and it will produce more and more breathtaking knowledge and controlling power. It can be no other way. It is senseless, for instance, to hinder a genetic researcher because such research threatens to breed a superman." (*Philosophical Hermeneutics*, trans. and ed. David E. Linge (Berkeley: University of California Press, 1976), 10.

11. Ibid., 316.

12. Michael Polanyi and Harry Porsch, *Meaning* (Chicago and London: The University of Chicago Press, 1975), 63.

13. Bernard Williams, "The End of Explanation," in *The New York Review of Books*, vol. XLV, no. 18 (November 19, 1998).

14. Although wanting to go beyond a simple instrumental conception of rationality, Robert Nozick states that for this conception "rationality consists in the effective and efficient achievement of goals, ends, and desires. About the goals themselves, an instrumental conception has little to say." *The Nature of Rationality* (Princeton: Princeton University Press, 1983), 64. In supporting this he quotes Bertrand Russell and Herbert Simon: " 'Reason' has a perfectly clear and precise meaning. It signifies the choice of the right means to an end that you wish to achieve. It has nothing whatever to do with the choice of ends." Bertrand Russell, *Human Society in Ethics and Politics* (London: Allen and Unwin, 1954), p. viii. "Reason is wholly instrumental. It cannot tell us where to go; at best it can tell us how to get there. It is a gun for hire that can be employed in the service of any goals we have, good or bad." Herbert Simon, *Reason in Human Affairs* (Stanford: Stanford University Press, 1983), 7–8, 64.

15. Marshall Swain, editor, *Induction, Acceptance, and Rational Belief* (Dordrecht: D. Reidel Publishing Company, 1970), 27.

16. For our purposes here we can readily accept the general distinction often drawn in analytic theory of action between behavioral events, which answer adequately to causal explanatory accounts, and human actions *per se*, those for which we look to the purposes of the actor for understanding the meaning of what is

going on—a stock example being the difference between raising one's arm as a result of a nervous spasm (for which we would want a causal account for why it occurred) and lifting one's arm to wave goodbye to a friend (which could not be understood apart from that intention).

17. See my *Personhood, Creativity and Freedom* (Honolulu: University of Hawaii Press, 1982), chapter 5.

18. See my *Creative Being*, 166–74.

19. Martin Hollis has offered an interesting account of what he calls "strategic actions" which points further to the intersubjective or social character of actions. "There are," he says ["with respect to actions] strategic choices if and only if what I expect you to do depends on what I expect you to expect me to do. Strategic action is basic for social life and social science. People could not live together without pooling their interests and coordinating their actions. Nor would their less cooperative activities be possible without taking account of the account which others take." (Martin Hollis, *Trust Within Reason* [Cambridge: Cambridge University Press, 1998], 12–13.)

9

Epistemic Portraiture

Justificatory rationality, I have tried to show, in all its various modalities is, by its very nature, pluralistic. Many "true" or "adequate" or "right" accounts may be given with respect to different nomic schema or "versions" in science and to the wide range of other ways in which we work out our descriptions and understandings of phenomenal experience. Hilary Putnam has, I think, put it nicely this way:

> We don't have notions of the 'existence' of things or of the 'truth' of statements that are independent of the versions we construct and of the procedures and practices that give sense to talk of 'existence' and 'truth' within these versions. Do *fields* 'exist' as physically real things? Yes, fields really exist: relative to one scheme of describing and explaining physical phenomena; relative to another there are particles, plus 'virtual' particles, plus 'ghost' particles, plus . . . Is it true that *brown* objects exist? Yes, relative to a common-sense version of the world: although one cannot give a necessary and sufficient condition for an object to be brown (one that applies to all objects, under all conditions) in the form of a finite closed formula in the language of physics. . . . We have many irreducibly different but legitimate ways of talking, and true 'existence' statements in all of them.[1]

I shall want to question shortly what appears to be an over-emphasis upon the role of language here, but it should be noted that Putnam is careful to observe that the fact that we have "many irreducibly different but legitimate ways of talking" does *not* imply a "cultural relativism" of the sort that allows that "a claim is right *whenever* those who employ the language in question would accept it as right in its context," for all such claims are subject to further rational appraisal by what he calls a "transcendent" function of reason "which we use to criticize the conduct of *all* activities and institutions"[2]—albeit this totalizing criticism itself may be informed by a complex set of cultural considerations. In any event, it is evident that we do have a pluralistic as well as value-laden rationality at work—one that yields what we might call "epistemic portraits."

An epistemic portrait emerges when *human knowers*, as members of epistemic communities, bring those of their *value-laden, belief-bearing organizing perspectives* to the *givens of an experienced world that lend themselves to* the *satisfying of various epistemic expectations*.

human knowers

Human consciousness, like personhood itself, as we have seen, is not simply a given that one possesses in virtue of being human. It is rather a power that each person realizes in a unique manner from within the conditions of her individuality and the rich intricacies of her experience. Persons *appropriate* their various mental and physical capacities and exhibit this appropriation throughout their cognitive experience. Psychophysical appropriation is the taking-up of the mental and physical conditions of one's individuality into the matrix of one's personal identity and involves the educating of these conditions for various forms of concentrated (perceptual, conceptual, imaginative) awareness.

And it is a person (qua her appropriated mind and body) that thinks and knows. Although in recent times there have been many philosophical rejections of mind-body dualism, especially of a Cartesian sort, we are still so accustomed to believe, and to express in everyday language, that it is some isolable mind or pure intellect that thinks and knows that we find the plain assertion that it is not a mind as such but a person who carries out these activities philosophically quite unsettling. Nevertheless, is it not obvious that just as it is a person, a concrete psychophysical, historically placed man or woman, who suffers pain and expresses joy, who talks and walks, writes letters and entertains friends, and not some bit or piece of the person as such, so it is the person who knows, and not some separate disembodied mind? If this is the case then all acts of knowing bear an irreducible particularity. Each and every one of a person's cognition is colored to some extent by her past experience and reflects present interests and future expectations. One's ability to follow an argument out to its conclusion, to concentrate on relations obtaining between things and events, to see intricate connections between ideas—all the factors that define our intellectuality—will, to a considerable extent, be a function of one's basic capacities as they have been disciplined by one. No two knowers will be exactly the same with regard to these factors. Every mental act will reflect what we might call the "mind-style" of the thinker and will involve the degree of her epistemic competency.

Further, although the bodily situatedness of a knower in determining the object that is known and how it is known has in many phenomenolog-ically oriented—and feminist—epistemologists been perhaps over-stated, its affect on one's style of reasoning after all being rather minimal (one takes one's deeper culture-informing history with one *wherever* one goes); nevertheless that situatedness for epistemic portraiture is a factor that must be taken into account. *Where*, quite literally, I stand as a knower con-tributes, while not setting the limits, to what content is brought into the portrait that I employ. One's thoughts, images and memories might roam rather freely from where one happens to be at the moment; one's place-ment as a knower, however, can never be wholly unconstrained by one's spatial-temporal place in an environment. And if Heidegger is at all insightful, the very condition of our being able to form epistemic portraits is that in a rather primordial way we are at the outset engaged prereflec-tively with the world and the things in it and come to grips with it. And this "coming to grips" is always to a significant degree highly personal, which is to say that there are always particular beings to whom what we call the world appears.

Having said this, one must nevertheless recognize that human knowers are not idiosyncratically individual. Knowing *is* particularized—everything that one sees, hears, imagines, thinks about is constituted in an extraordinarily rich variety of ways by factors contributed by the person experiencing—but it is also highly generalized, for, together with com-mon biological functions and structures, the maturation of the mental, especially with respect to linguistic practices, is deeply shaped and formed by cultural factors. What and how one sees and knows is largely a shared experience within any culture and, in many significant and central areas, across different cultures. In short, the psychophysical conditions that get appropriated by persons are similar in many important ways: in spite of particularized factors, culturalization is much the same for most persons during any historical epoch; what we take to be canons of intelli-gibility will be shared widely, the languages we employ will of necessity be public in character, and so on. Rational persons think at once within *universal* conditions of epistemic intelligibility and linguistic competency, *general* features of their cultural-historical placement, and *particular* char-acteristics from within their own life stories and personal development. Human knowers are thus at once constrained by all the biological factors that are involved in cognitivity and by their inescapably being members of epistemic communities, whether as an identified practitioner of a spe-cialized discipline or simply as a culturally placed and placing participant in an inquiring society.

This membership means that the presuppositions that underlie, and the values that inform, a knower's beliefs and inquiries are shared and go to constitute publicly accepted paradigms that enable a community to organize and order their experience coherently in such a way as to bring common *perspectives* to bear upon their worlds.

value-laden, belief-bearing organizing perspectives

The term "perspective" is often employed philosophically as a metaphor derived from our visual experience. We see things and events from various relatively fixed positions that determine to a considerable extent what is included in, and excluded from, what we are able at the time to see. Philosophical hermeneutics speaks often of *horizons*—a horizon, according to Gadamer, being "the range of vision that includes everything that can be seen from a particular vantage point."[3]

A "perspective," as I use the term, is a mode of epistemic engagement with a world of which the knower is a part. It incorporates selectively what one feels justified to believe, albeit often in a non-articulated manner, and brings thereby a presumed knowledge-laden background to its specific focus. An epistemic perspective is an *active* "looking" of a person seeking understanding. Native to consciousness as such, this looking strives rather unself-consciously to recognize order, to bring some kind of initial coherence to experience, and to grasp the meaning of what is seen.

Further, this looking is quite clearly not only a seeing-*of* something or other, rather it is also always a selective seeing-*as*. Every perspective that becomes constitutive of an emergent epistemic portrait is expressive of the experience of the seeing person who brings to his perceptual engagements a special combination of personal, socially informed interests, needs, and capacities. Each molds the contents of experience into his own value-laden, belief-bearing viewpoint. As William James noted:

> Let [several] men make a trip to Europe. One will bring home only picturesque impressions. . . . To another all this will be non-existent; and distances and prices . . . and other useful statistics will take their place. A third will give a rich account of the theaters, restaurants. . . . Each has selected, out of the mass of presented objects, those which suited his private interest and has made his experience thereby.[4]

James does go on, however, to say,

> In my mind and your mind the rejected portions and the selected portions of the original world stuff [the possible contents of perception] are to a great extent the same. The human race as a whole largely agrees as to what it shall notice and name, and what not. And among the noticed parts we select in much the same way for accentuation and preference or subordination and dislike.[5]

What this all comes down to is the realization that all epistemic perspectives are always personally and socially valuative as well as strictly cognitive, involving as they do a wide range and assortment of values that is shaped by historical and cultural factors as well as of beliefs that are based on one's own accumulated experience. To see is to evaluate: the forms of things, the patterns embedded in and constitutive of processes, become foci of judgment reflecting the predispositions of the experiencer to appreciate (or, as the case might be, to repudiate or devalue) their qualities and to discover their meanings.

The active looking of a person seeking order, coherence and meaning is not, therefore, a disengaged value-neutral seeing. An epistemic perspective differs from a strictly cognitive or conceptual scheme in virtue of its emphasis upon the strong and ineluctable valuative factors which contribute to it.

givens of an experienced world that lend themselves to

Every knowing act is unavoidably *about* that which is known. Phenomenally, where there is a subject there is an object, albeit epistemically they are inextricably bound together. Another way of putting this would be to say that human consciousness is always situated in a world that constrains, but does not solely determine, what it engages. At one level of experience, G. E. Moore's old common-sense realism holds sway. When I look out my study window and see a tree (with its particularities) at time$_1$, and return my view there shortly after at time$_2$, I don't—under normal non-hallucinatory conditions—see an elephant. I see the tree.

Worlds are given to us in terms of publicly accessed commonalities and regularities with their own structures of lawlike normality, the very assumption and recognition of which makes possible our practical negotiations with and in these worlds. One does not change the weather by the use of a measuring thermometer (a defective one does not make it any less or more hot or cold outside), although what is *meant* by "hot" or "cold" may very well be influenced by its use.

This little exercise in common sense is not in any way intended as a refutation of the "Myth of the Given" (Sellars). I would agree that no coherent claim can be made that our sense experience provides us with brute items or data which can be foundational in such a way as to allow certainty to our empirical knowledge or science. All that is being claimed is that there are "givens" in experience which lend themselves to restricted, yet highly diverse, rational accounts of their nature or function. In other words, the world as given *for us* has a modal character, as it were, of its own; which is to say that its makeup as we encounter it within the conditions of our being human knowers is such that it makes feasible— and rules out—various possible understandings that we may have of it.

Put very simply, we reside in an *actual* world; it is only cognitively that we entertain contrafactual *possible* worlds. In this regard, the actual world may be said to be like a text which lends itself to various justifiable readings, while excluding as incredible many others.

And hence, a portrait theory of knowing will differ in many important ways from any kind of "internal realism," with which it might be confounded, that stresses an ontic role of language, for it will insist precisely upon that "aboutness" of knowing previously alluded to. Putnam states over and over again that " 'Objects' do not exist independently of conceptual schemes. *We* cut up the world into objects when we introduce one or another scheme of description."[6] But what precisely does it mean to say that " 'Objects' do not exist independently of conceptual schemes"? Suppose I notice a particular plant growing in my neighbor's yard as having a certain shape, color, and placement there in relation to other plants, but without my having any idea of, or interest in, what *kind* of plant it is or how it grows and is tended to, without my having, that is, any vocabulary to knowingly describe it other than in terms of it being identified as a "plant" in virtue of referring to its observable properties. What sense is there in saying its "existence" is dependent upon my—or anyone else's— "scheme of description"? My *knowledge* about the object quite obviously is not independent of what I bring conceptually and linguistically to it, but the existence of the object surely is not dependent upon the way in which I so describe it. Putnam seems to be aware of this difficulty when he further states that "Internalism does not deny that there are experiential *inputs* to knowledge; knowledge is not a story with no constraints except *internal* coherence." He finishes the sentence, however, once again, with the claim that internalism, "does deny that there are any inputs *which are not themselves to some extent shaped by our concepts*, by the vocabulary we use to report and describe them, or any inputs *which admit of only one description*."[7] Yes, "inputs" do not admit of only one description; but no, inputs as such are not shaped in any interesting ontic sense by the "vocabulary we use to report and describe them." In other words, it might very well be the case that we do not have, and cannot have, a theory-neutral language which maps on to the objective givens of experience, but this does not make the givens themselves mind-dependent in any robust metaphysical or ontological sense. Surely what we perceive and relate to in our cognitive and practical actions has something central to do with the being of the objects of our perceptions, even if we are predisposed by our linguistic habits to interpret our experience in specific and varied ways.[8]

In short, the things of the world do not ontologically disappear for us into the vocabularies we employ to describe, explain and interpret them; albeit, we do not have access phenomenally to any *Ding an sich* that stands before us in some pristine manner of causal or supportive being. Portrait-making does not require a noumenal world: it is sufficient epistemically that whenever we are as knowing subjects there is for us that which lends itself to being known.

Further, portrait-making does not require—in fact it is antithetical to the very idea of—there being some singular, ideally adequate character-ization which could either encompass all perspectives informed by the aims and interests of their bearers or reduce that multiplicity foundation-ally to it. Knowing, we have argued, is irredeemably pluralistic.[9]

the satisfying of various epistemic expectations

An epistemic portrait emerges as an organized mode of knowledge when the value-laden, belief-based perspectives we bring to the givens of our experienced world are such as to fulfill adequately our cognitive explanatory interests, make possible the successful instrumental attain-ment of our various ends and purposes, and allow us to understand the meaning of our experience. Knowing is transactional: the world as it is for us is so structured that it lends itself to limited, albeit multiple, warranted readings, their warrant resting on the degree to which they fulfill the pos-itive criteria the members of communities of inquirers employ in their respective justificatory epistemic practices with their appropriate "fit" with the world. Just as we allow that different interpretations of a literary text may each yield varied degrees of rightness in expanding our under-standing of the work and appreciating its aesthetic merit—that a literary text lends itself to various non-reductive readings—so with our knowing of the things and events of our experience; several ways of describing, characterizing, conceptualizing may be warranted. And just as the literary text is indispensable to its being interpreted without its being singularly authoritative as such with regard to its readings, so an event or pattern of experience can have its own character and integrity without its calling for a one true account of its nature, meaning or value.

As an organized interpretative framework of experience, an epistemic portrait is, as already pointed out, necessarily value-bearing insofar as it reflects and encompasses diverse human interests and concerns and, we might now add, as it is informed by anticipations of achieving cognitive truth and success in action. Every portrait will thus exclude some possi-bilities of knowing and understanding while including and focusing on others. Just as in artistic portraiture, the knowing-scheme will highlight some features, subordinate others and will illuminate aspects of what is portrayed in ways that are not initially apparent as the event or object makes its appearance, as it were, to consciousness.

Further, just as in artistic portraiture, where a portrait is always ren-dered in a language (of style, form and particular materials) that places it in a given historical period, so in an epistemic portrait, at any given time, it will be articulated in various symbolic vocabularies that give it a recognizable historical location and that thereby set limits at that time to our understanding of the world. In short, a portrait, no matter how abstract its mathematical formulation might be, is always temporally laden in a cultural context. It follows then that there can be no certain or indubitable (non-analytic) positive knowing of events, and hence rational inquiry of whatever form is never a matter of securing a correct representation as such of what is taken to be purely objective. This situation ought not, however, to provoke cognitive anxiety that "anything goes"; rather it ought to stimulate strongly the ongoing development of new (and at times radically new) portraits that alter and extend our understanding of our worlds.[10]

What, though, one might very well ask, is the situation when portraits of the same kind (mainly in science) appear to be directly in conflict with one another, when they *contradict* each other? Thomas S. Kuhn is credited with arguing, at least initially in his now famous *The Structure of Scientific Revolutions*, which appeared in 1962, that in the history of science competing theories (which we may here assimilate to the concept of "portraits") often "speak different languages" and are therefore "incommensurable" with each other, which is to say that they cannot be translated conceptually into each other. Accordingly their proponents do not so much conflict with or contradict one another on the same territory, as it were, but rather they "practice their trades in different worlds. One contains constrained bodies that fall slowly, the other pendulums that repeat their motions again and again. In one, solutions are compounds, in the other mixtures. . . . Practicing in different worlds, the two groups of scientists see different things when they look from the same point in the same direction." Kuhn goes on to insist, however, "that is not to say that they can see anything they please. Both are looking at the world, and what they look at has not changed. But in some areas they see different things, and they see them in different relations one to the other. That is why a law that cannot even be demonstrated to one group of scientists may occasionally seem intuitively obvious to another."[11]

Later, however, Kuhn allowed that "In applying the term 'incommensurability' to theories, I had intended only to insist that there was no common language within which both could be fully expressed and which could therefore be used in a point-by-point comparison between them"[12]—and hence it would not seem to follow that a choice between rival paradigms was necessarily beyond adjudication by argument and that science was not, in this context, hopelessly "irrational."[13]

In any event, the recent, and at times still rather heated, discussions about incommensurability between successive theories in science do

appear to strongly support a pluralist understanding of epistemic portraits in science which disallows the possibility of there being a one, true,
purely objective explanatory account of everything or anything that
would thereby exclude all other possible accounts. An epistemic portrait
is always underdetermined insofar as in principle other epistemic portraits may be equally consistent with what is portrayed.[14] As we have
already noted, for a portrait theory of knowing, the actual world of our
experience is like a text that lends itself to various justifiable readings, and
so, in a highly restrictive manner, the same obtains for portraits themselves.

Epistemic portraits may take many forms—as theories given in mathematical signs, as systems of organizing principles set forth in metaphysical terms, as structured viewpoints expressed in the vocabularies of
everyday beliefs, and so on. Common to this rich variety of symbolic makings is the fact that they themselves require interpretation by human
knowers to secure their meaning and relevance. Epistemic portraits are
not pictures in the sense argued for in the logical atomism of Russell or
in Wittgenstein's *Tractatus*. The "elementary propositions" that constitute
or may be derived from them, if such there are, do not in portraits stand
for any "atomic facts" that a purified formal language can map onto.
There is no structural isomorphism here between language and the
world. But neither are the symbolic makings merely pragmatic in their
being essentially guides to experience based on observed consequences of
their effects, for their truth value does not rest solely upon their workabil-
ity, however this is understood, nor are the makings entirely contextual
in any deconstructive sense that disallows any authority of the portrait to
determine the rightness of its interpretation.

When we say that epistemic portraits require interpretation we are
pointing out only that even in their explanatory modality, where they
may aspire to a designative or objectively referential functionality, they
nevertheless always have to be read both correctly within the controlling
semiotic constraints of a given community of language users and rightly
within the framework of generalized patterns of significance whose
meanings emerge from a kind of negotiation between the experienced
knower and what is known.

In other words, an epistemic portrait is a live portrait only to someone
who knows how to relate the organizing perspective to the selected givens of experience and to understand the connections within that field that
yield their significance. Take, for example, the situation of a medical doctor and her patient, who is untutored in medical matters, looking at an
X-ray (as a portrait within a larger theoretical framing or background) of,
say, the patient's lungs. Whereas the patient sees only a pattern of shapes
and lines in varying degrees of black-and-white shadings with the knowl-

edge only that this refers to his lungs, the doctor reads the markings in terms of an interpretative scheme that tells her the specific condition of that to which the markings refer (say, a cancerous condition) and allows her to understand it in terms of its relations to, and implications for, the course and likely development of the patient's malady, and indeed what steps should be taken for its treatment. The X-ray needs to be read correctly before it can be interpreted rightly.

It needs also to be noted, however, that at their higher levels of generality epistemic portraits are not only objects subject to their own readings, they are places, as it were, wherein we make our cognitive homes. We dwell in our portraits insofar as they become our native presuppositions regarding what we believe the world to be, informing our expectations and anticipations of how we can be in and with that world. In other words, the more comprehensive in scope a portrait is (e.g., Darwinian evolutionary theory), the more it becomes a kind of *Weltanschauung* or framework within which much of one's experience finds its place and value. For us, an epistemic portrait with depth and scope mediates the world of which we are always a part. It becomes ingrained, as it were, into our perceptions-conceptions and gives rise to an habituated consciousness. As is our portrait, so is our apprehension of objects: every seeing *as* is determined by what we bring to it and what we presume we will receive from it. In this regard an epistemic portrait may be said to be at once a portrayal of what it is about and a kind of self-portrayal: it shapes and forms our ways of seeing and thinking. At the same time, however, we are able to stand apart from it in virtue of our ability to criticize and alter it. Although the dislocation may sometimes be rather traumatic, we do move from one house to another and make it our home.

If an objection then is raised to the effect that there are "compulsive concepts" or "pre-wirings" that are categorical in portrait-making, necessary—in a strong positive sense—to their basic structures, and hence render at some deep level the dislocations referred to not just as difficult to endure but impossible to attain, we can only point out that the very issue can be engaged only in terms of further portraiture. We do not—and cannot—come to an understanding of what a category of the mind might be independent of the ways in which we come to an understanding of any other object of inquiry, which is in and through various kinds of portraiture.

In sum: an epistemic portrait, I have argued, emerges when socially grounded human knowers, who are organically part of the environment which is sought to be known, engage the givens of the world as experienced by them in such a way that the value-laden belief-bearing organizing perspectives that they bring to that transactional situation fulfill various of their justificatory expectations. An epistemic portrait is thus not merely an abstract schema for organizing conceptually a given domain of experience from within certain standpoints, it is also a guide for our bodily actions in the world, enabling us to function with some degree of confidence in negotiating our ways with and within our natural and social environments. Our human history clearly exhibits the development of many diverse epistemic portraits, and surely there is every reason to believe that our knowing is an ongoing creative enterprise that holds forth the possibility, indeed the promise, if not the necessity, of our having in the future ever-better and richer ways of knowing our worlds— with the understanding, of course, that what we mean by "better" is itself subject to revision and alteration in the light of future experience.

NOTES

1. Hilary Putnam, "Why Reason Can't Be Naturalized," in *Realism and Reason* (Cambridge: Cambridge University Press, 1983), 230–31.

2. Ibid., 234. Something like Putnam's "transcendent" function of reason is perhaps what Karl-Otto Apel has in mind in his criticism of Gadamer to the effect that Gadamer's hermeneutics "cannot deal with the causal connections or unintended consequences of the tradition of interpretation itself; nor can it deal with systematic distortions within this tradition's self-understanding. Hermeneutic interpretation alone is incapable of breaking free of the tradition to which it belongs in order to uncover external influences in its force and direction. Hence understanding must be combined with a form of theoretical explanation . . . capable of appealing to a reference system outside the tradition's account of itself." (Translator's Introduction to Karl-Otto Apel, *Understanding and Explanation: A Transcendental-Pragmatic Conception*, trans. Georgia Warnke [Cambridge: The MIT Press, 1985], xix.)

3. *Truth and Method*, 286.

4. Ibid.

5. William James, *Principles of Psychology*, vol. I, 289.

6. *Reason, Truth and History*, 52.

7. Ibid., 54.

8. Another way of putting this would be to say that an epistemic portrait does not legislate a set of facts, rather it articulates facts within the framework of its own making which then gets legitimized, to the degree that it does, by its success in guiding action and bringing coherence to our experience.

9. In other words, there is not, nor can there be, a single ideal portrait that could adequately describe and make sense of the world as we experience it, for every portrait is by its nature selective, at once including and excluding various possible contents, and cannot thereby rightly claim a unique privileged status. Also, there is not, nor can there be, a "mother of all portraits," a master portrait from which all others might be derived and within which all would find their

appropriate place, for quite clearly the aims and interests of the cognitive users and makers that transact with the innumerable givens of our world, are multiform and subject to ongoing revisions and displacements. The fundamental differences in kind between various portraits (scientific, artistic . . .) rule out their being reduced to a single kind. When successful, a portrait of any kind will disclose only something or other of that which it portrays. Happily, our knowledge of the world is necessarily partial and incomplete.

10. And it should, of course, be understood that a kind of hierarchy of generality and specificity tends to arise from our portrait-makings insofar as we frame and accept a web of belief with its fundamental epistemic presuppositions that then accommodates diverse levels or sub-sets of representations within it. For us there are portraits within portraits: in acts of knowing, more embracing theories or modes of cognitive organization clearly may encompass narrower, more restrictive ones.

It should also be noted that the more general the portrait the greater is it a bearer of tradition, and therefore susceptible, in principle, if not easily in fact, to revolutionary *displacement*. On the other hand, the more specific the portrait—its focusing on a narrow range of experience or incorporating a highly restrictive perspective—the greater is it being a hypothesis subject to outright *rejection*.

11. Thomas S. Kuhn, *The Structure of Scientific Revolutions*, 2d ed. (Chicago: University of Chicago Press, 1970), 150.

12. Thomas S. Kuhn, "Theory-Change as Structure Change," in *Erkenntnis*, no. 10 (1976): 190–91.

13. Stephen Toulmin, for one, offers an interesting way out of this problem by looking to the nature of the human activities of the sciences rather than simply to their logical or conceptual systems as such. He writes that: "We must begin . . . by recognizing that rationality is an attribute, not of logical or conceptual systems as such, but of the human activities or enterprises of which particular sets of concepts are the temporary cross-sections: specifically, of the procedures by which the concepts, judgements, and formal systems currently accepted in those enterprises are criticized and changed." When we do so, he argues, we are not then "forced to choose between a uniformitarian account, which assumes the universal relevance of a single set of rational methods, and a revolutionary account, which treats conceptual change as a sequence of radical switches between rationally incommensurable positions." *Human Understanding*, vol. I (Oxford: Clarendon Press, 1972), 173–74.

14. This is especially the case when, in a somewhat extended sense of the term, we consider different kinds of portraits such as the artistic or religious, which do not compete with one another in any direct way, employing as they do different kinds of vocabularies with different symbolic-meaning intentions in mind. The veracity of a geologist's account of a landscape is not in contention with the significance of an artist's representation or the authenticity of a religious-minded seeing in terms of reverence and celebration.

10

Creative Rationality

A precondition for the making of epistemic portraits and for practicing any form of justificatory rationality, including the scientific explanatory, is the existence of an irreducible rational subject or human knower—"irreducible," for if a reductive explanation was put forward to explain away the subject (say, by means of some physicalist account), one could always ask, Who, then, is carrying-out this reductive explanation? and the answer to it can never be given within the reductive explanation itself: if it could, the question—which meaningfully is asked—could not have been asked in the first place. Any theory of rationality must acknowledge a creative power of human reason that allows human knowers, while being very much a part of their natural and cultural worlds, to be able to distance themselves from those worlds and carry out certain of their rational tasks in the logical (or, if you will, ontological) space that is thereby opened up.

Many postmodernist accounts of knowledge assert, to the contrary, the impossibility of our being able to step outside of our cognitive frameworks or language games; we are, it is argued, always locked in to some particular conceptual scheme or other. But the very fact of our recognizing a conceptual framework, a system of ideas, indeed even one's own society as being one among many, presupposes this rational capacity for a certain transcendence of our habitual ways of knowing and seeing. Although, as we have insisted, all acts of knowing, grounded psychologically as they are in various dimensions of one's personhood—conscious and unconscious, affective and intellectual—are intensely personal, they are not, as we have also noted, on that account private or subjectively self-centered. They bear as well, at least always potentially, the marks of publicity and impartial insightfulness. Reason, in short, can be genuinely creative in character.

Three different modalities or styles of what we may call "creative rationality" can, I believe, be identified: the *critical*, the *constructive*, and the
playful (which finds its natural home in philosophy and is in many ways,
as we will see, qualitatively different from the others). These forms of creative rationality are not, of course, sharply distinguishable in actuality
insofar as more often than not they combine and intertwine in various
obvious and subtle ways; nevertheless they exhibit distinctive features
that allow for their particular characterizations.

The *critical* form of creative rationality involves clearly the exercise of a
transcendent function of reason: it stands outside of any given rational
practice in its capacity to put any such practice, including its own, to
rational scrutiny and to make intelligible the very idea of a pluralistic
epistemology. Rational criticism is, or at least can be, non-parochial: it can
stand apart in such a way as to subject any truth-claim, form of life or
social theory to an examinination of its consistency and coherence, of its
fulfilling the positive criteria set for it by the relevant community of
inquirers, of its adequacy in accounting for and guiding our experience—
albeit such criticism is always articulated content-wise from within a particular, historical and culturally-informed rationality.

This suggests strongly that whenever reason is genuinely critical it is
itself guided by an idea of the good. Rational criticism expresses a commitment to the value of correctness and, more important, when grounded
in that sense of rightness, of taste, integral to contemplative consciousness, it carries out its tasks with the appropriate tact and dialogical openness which enables its bearers to gain that "intersubjective recognition of
criticizable validity claims" so ardently sought for by Habermas and his
followers. Criticism, in short, when it is what it ought to be, seeks precisely that hermeneutical "fusion of horizons" which seeks agreement in
the pursuit of understanding.

Rational criticism is not necessarily, then, inherently negative or
destructive in character. It can, of course, degenerate into mere dry
arguing and the aggressive putting-down of an opponent—a tendency all
too evident in so much of analytically inspired academic philosophiz-
ing—yet, while always retaining a certain contentiousness in virtue of its
very nature, criticism can quite clearly be positive or constructive as well,
seeking through dialogue to strengthen and support the development of
worthy ideas or truth-claims of whatever sort that it engages, rather than
simply confronts. It is here that its impartial character best stands
revealed, for constructive criticism assumes precisely the integrity of the
person putting forth the criticizable claim.

The critical style of creative rationality is not confined, however, to
claims put forward by others, as it is always present to some considerable
degree in all of one's own rational undertakings: rational consciousness

is always mindful of the possibility of there being better alternatives to what it initially entertains. Framing a new hypothesis, seeing novel ways to organize and integrate various otherwise disparate ideas into a coherent order, evaluating, in probabilistic terms, the correctness of a claim according to the best information available, requires that distancing of self from its own constructions in the very process of bringing them forth.

The *constructive* form of creative rationality is precisely the exercise of reason that enables positive truth-claims to be made within any of the modalities of justificatory rationality and in the framing of epistemic portraits; that articulates and examines closely the basic metaphysical presuppositions in any of its organizing activities; and that develops new vocabularies that may revolutionize at-the-time conventional models of the world and the given standards of rationality itself.

In its constructive style, creative rationality assumes that there is an order of things or a complex of relations and events in the world that is independent of language as such but which can, through arduous empirical analysis and reasoning, be structured linguistically and be communicated to another as a set of statements or claims regarding the nature of that order, of whatever kind it may happen to be, and incite another to agreement or disagreement. In the constructive form of creative rationality, language is basically a tool for persuasive communication: *what* is communicated is of paramount importance; the form, the manner, the *how* by which meaning is presented is unimportant. Constructive philosophy is thus essentially discursive. One passes over the "medium" to confront the prosaic "message."

Now it might very well be the case that there is no "logic of discovery" available to the constructive rational mind (of the sort sought for by a Descartes, a Leibniz, a Husserl), that is, a proper method of inquiry that can guarantee the correctness of a hypothesis or epistemic portrait, and it might also very well be the case that the fruits of all synthetic rational construction are probabilistic in character, without hope of any of them ever attaining a knowable certainty; nevertheless, the great constructive works in science and mathematics, indeed in literature and the arts, and in systematic and worldmaking philosophy itself, clearly testify to the creative power of the mind to bring forth new, and oftentimes, better ways in which we are able to make ourselves and our worlds intelligible. Reason here finds its proper necessity, then, not in *a priori* makings that issue completely out of its own resources and that lay claim to be coincident with the lawlike structures of the world, but in the more fallibilistic processes of actual creative discovery—which brings us to that playful style of creative rationality which finds its clearest expression in philosophy.

Philosophy is *play* when the philosopher sets aside his belief that there is an order of meaning *in* the world which can be communicated as such in speech and writing and makes rather a *philosophy-work* which is not so much a means for achieving rational agreement as for giving rise to a world of meaning and value in itself. Rationality is playful when it articulates a new order of meaning for consciousness. In philosophy as play, however, the language, the philosophy-work, is by no means a hermetic affair. When it fulfills its intention to be insightful, it does bring consciousness to reality. In philosophy as *argument*—to combine now the critical and constructive forms of creative rationality into a single philosophical kind for purposes of contrast with the playful—language remains very much within an established referential or designative order. Philosophy as argument tends to be ontologically, as it were, self-contained.

In general, then, when conceived of as argument, creative rationality in philosophy is akin to, but assuredly is not identical with, science; when conceived of as play, it tends toward art. Philosophy as argument sets out to *demonstrate* and *defend* a theory, a belief, a viewpoint; philosophy as play tries to *show* what it sees as being the case. There is an apparent Enlightenment-like reasonableness in critical and constructive rationality, as though knowledge and truth were available to everyone; in philosophy as play there is an apparent dogmatism, an assertiveness, as if (but only *as if*) truth were recognizable and understanding obtainable only by a few.

In philosophy as argument the creative philosopher thus tends to become committed to a system, position or theory, believing as she often does that she has managed to get (at least a handle on) the truth. But the commitment is not regarded as something which may fundamentally change her life. In philosophy as argument the philosopher can gain or exchange a position, can give up one theory for another; she can, in short, shift or change her commitment—for that, after all, is what "being reasonable" means.[1] From the perspective of play, on the other hand, while sharing a fallibilist understanding that no system, theory or well-argued position can lay claim to any kind of finality or to a correspondence-grounded truth taken as, or aspiring to be, timeless, philosophy here turns to a creative making which has a decisive formative affect upon the philosopher. In philosophy as play (and this discloses its kinship as well with religion) the philosopher can only change herself—and make a new philosophy-work (with often the changing occurring in the act of making).

One is thus convinced by a philosophy-work in much the same way that one is taken hold of by an artwork; its *rightness*, as distinct from any criteria of *correctness* as such, is discerned as internal to it; its depth is disclosed as it connects with, and opens up new dimensions of, our own experience. Convincement in philosophy as play, therefore, does share certain features with classical and especially contemporary rhetoric (e.g., what convinces one involves, although of course is not reduced to, the power of utterance, exhibited in the unity of its style and content); but it differs strikingly from those debased forms of rhetoric where persuasion is more the other side of the critical argumentative ideal than something qualitatively different in kind from it. When philosophy is play, the intent is not to persuade by means of appealing to a range of affective forces and private interests, but to show the rightness of its articulation in such a way as to elicit its recognition in the participant who is open to it.

Philosophy as argument presupposes (at least historically in terms of its various correspondence, coherence, pragmatic and semantic theories of truth) that propositions can, at least to some significant degree, successfully state "what is the case"; that thought can, if not absolutely at least in greater or less degree, accommodate itself to reality; that the nature of things and the categories of thought itself can in principle be discovered and communicated in language. Philosophy as play, on the other hand, turns in a rather different direction toward internal coherence and rightness of expression, seeking thereby a truth that is embedded rather than transparently designative as such.

John Searle has argued that some form of metaphysical realism is necessarily presupposed in *all* philosophy, because, "The person who denies metaphysical realism presupposes the existence of a public language, a language in which he or she communicates with other people."[2] He goes on to ask: "But what are the conditions of possibility of communication in a public language? What do I have to assume when I ask a question or make a claim that is supposed to be understood by others?" And answers: "At least this much: if we are using words *to talk about something*, in a way that we expect to be understood by others, then there must be at least the possibility of something these words can be used to talk about."

Searle then acknowledges that he is "not claiming that one can prove metaphysical realism to be true from some standpoint that exists apart from *our human linguistic practices*. What I am arguing," he states, "rather, is that those practices themselves presupposes metaphysical realism. One cannot *within those practices* deny metaphysical realism, because the meaningfulness of our public utterances already presupposes an independently existing reality to which expressions in these utterances can refer."

Well and good—which only goes further to show precisely the need to develop alternative linguistic practices which enable us to *speak with* the world and not merely *talk about* something or state of affairs. "Our human linguistic practices" need not be, and most certainly are not already, confined to just the kind of communicative discourse outlined by, and insisted upon, by Searle. Poetic speech, much of the wisdom discourse to be found in many cultures and traditions—indeed all that comes under what I have elsewhere called the "ontological power of speech"[3]—goes beyond referential, communicative discourse. The latter, with its realistic assumptions, may bind us to a world of common experience; the former, with its understanding of the nature of radical discontinuity, may make evident the possibility of many other worlds.

Rational creativity or, what might in the context of playful knowing be called "liberated creativity," is not a knowledge-gathering or speech-making activity for the achieving of something else (e.g., control over nature or over other persons); it is rather a natural expression of that powerful harmony that obtains between the creative person and his or her world. A liberated creativity, with respect to speaking, is, then, as much a listening as it is a speaking. The listening is to and with that silence of being that is realized in awakened consciousness and which becomes part and parcel of all playful knowing and speaking.

It is not so much then a matter of "whatever is knowable is sayable," as that what is known playfully is always said in a manner that is entirely appropriate to it. In fact, the manner of saying in playful knowing is part and parcel of what is known. We do not, in other words, have two distinct acts, a knowing-act and a saying-act; rather the knowing and saying are part of the same creative process. It is not that X knows Y and could then communicate/express/utter Y in a variety of different ways (as is the case to a considerable extent, but even here not fully, with simple empirical assertions); when X knows Y playfully the mode of utterance is inseparable from that which is known.

Playful knowing and speaking, then, is very much like poetry in this, that its formed-content is always a unique presentation; the particular "how" and "what" of speech being as one. It is unlike poetry, though, insofar as whereas the poet may through the power of imagination create a character-voice or adopt a uniform authorial voice that is not strictly speaking his own, the playful knower will always be present in his utterance, it will always reflect his state of being. This is the case because the utterance is part and parcel of his immediate experience. The utterance, in other words, is an integral part of the experience of the knower and will accordingly embody the degree to which he has achieved openness, sensitivity, insight. These are as much qualities of his being as they are features of his experience. Playful knowing, thus, always culminates in expressive, insightful utterance—utterance that is inseparable from the knowing and that exhibits the state of the knower. And it is this that further distinguishes playful knowing from pure intuition or awakening, which need not culminate in anything outside itself. The playful knower is centered in reality, but does not simply remain there. His knowing, his experience, his very being, calls out for articulation.

This leads, then, to an important epistemological implication, namely, that the criterion for the truth of statements originating from playful knowing has always to do, in an important way, with the quality of the personhood of the knower. This means that the more genuine the person, the greater will be the truth-value of what he or she says, relative to his playful knowing. The later qualification is needed, for it is not the case that this variable truth-value pertains to all forms of assertive utterance. If it is raining now outside, the statement "It is raining now" is not more or less true depending upon the quality of the person who utters it. Its *meaning*—many of us would now agree—might very well depend upon what the speaker intends by his utterance (one might, for example, intend it as a warning rather than as a straightforward factual claim; or it might even be used as a code for some entirely different kind of meaning); its *truth*, however, we believe is independent of the character, as it were, of who says it.

Take a Sanskrit statement like *tat tvam asi*, "Thou art that," one of the *mahāvākyas* or "great sayings" of Vedānta which asserts the identity of the self and reality (*ātman* and *brahman*). Is it not more or less true depending upon who says it to whom, when, and in what manner? If the philosopher-sage utters *tat tvam asi* from the full authority of his own experience and achieved being to a well-prepared disciple it bears a truth value very different from, for example, the response of a student when asked on an examination to give an example of one of the *mahāvākyas* of Vedānta and answered *tat tvam asi*. Her answer might be *correct*, but it would not, in any interesting existential sense, be a true statement. The uninitiated student knows not whereof she speaks.

From the hearer's side, as it were, one does not look to some alleged isolable content of playful speaking (the mere what that is said) in order to determine its truth; rather one responds to the utterance as precisely the utterance it is in the full richness of its nature—and this nature which is, as we have seen, a formed-content will necessarily embody the qualities of the being of the speaker. "Style is the man," it is often said; and the rightness of a style is grounded in the being of the person. One's "religious language" of whatever kind is thoroughly informed by who one is as a person; the manner of its utterance inescapably disclosing the personhood of the speaker—the degree to which she is a consummate person who exhibits a loving sensitivity and has achieved freedom in being and action. When one responds to playful speaking in the full richness of its nature one invariably responds as well, then, to the person who utters it. One recognizes its rightness, if it possesses it, in terms of the quality of the knower as this is made evident in the utterance. The opposite of truth in playful knowing and speaking is thus not falsity as such, but inauthenticity, pretense, insincerity.

This is a rather familiar position in Chinese philosophy. Confucianism in particular insists that moral utterance is true only insofar as it is spoken "sincerely." The concept of "sincerity" (*ch'eng/cheng*) is a very profound one in Confucian thought and points to the whole qualitative being (*jen/ren*) of a person. It is not thus reducible to simple "honesty." In the *Chung-yung/Zhongyong* or "The Doctrine of the Mean," one of the major works of ancient Confucian literature, it is said:

> Sincerity (*ch'eng/cheng*) is the Way of Heaven. To think how to be sincere is the Way of man. He who is sincere is one who hits upon what is right without effort and apprehends without thinking.[4]

Tu Wei-ming points out that the English word "sincere" does not encompass the many-leveled meanings of *ch'eng/cheng*—and that in fact the word is often translated as "true." D. C. Lau, he notes, renders *ch'eng/cheng* as "true" in his translation of *Mencius/Mengzi*. Wing-tsit Chan likewise sometimes renders *ch'eng/cheng* as "true" in his translation of *Chung-yung/Zhongyong*. In any event, as Tu Wei-ming also indicates, "Whether it is translated as 'true' or 'sincere,' *ch'eng/cheng* definitely points to a human reality which is not only the basis of self-knowledge but also the ground of man's identification with Heaven."[5]

Confucianism thus clearly recognizes the intimate relationship that obtains between the quality of the person and the truth of his or her knowing at the deepest levels of being. And further, in *Chung-yung/Zhongyong* it is said:

> As there is sincerity, there will be its expression. As it is expressed, it will become conspicuous. As it becomes conspicuous, it will become clear. As it becomes clear, it will move others. As it moves others, it changes them. As it changes them, it transforms them. Only those who are absolutely sincere can transform others.[6]

Speech that issues from a liberated creativity is thus a social or communal act. The playful knower does not know for his own sake alone but finds the consummation of his experience as that experience is taken up and embraced by others. A formed-content is always *for* someone; it does not stand isolated in a rarified, pristine space. Playful knowing and speaking intends to be shared: it fulfills itself as it "moves," "changes," and "transforms" others.

The playful philosopher, therefore, is not a skeptic. The skeptic is one who despairs of ever acquiring epistemic certainty because of the nature of human experience and the limitations of rational thought. Not finding certainty in the empirical order, where everything is subject to change and to legitimate doubt, and knowing no other place to turn, he denies the value of all knowledge-claims and theorizing. Being caught up entirely in the domain of philosophy as argument, the skeptic is one who expects to find unchanging truth and thus, disappointed and frustrated and certain in his feeling that there is no certain knowledge, closes off his sensitivities to the mystery of being. The skeptic, ironically, obliterates wonder—and is impotent thereby to create.

In philosophy as play, on the other hand, propositions, to be sure, do not tell "what is the case," except in highly qualified perspectivist and intentionalist terms, and, it is believed, there is no ready-made truth out there eager to be seized by argument as such; but, it is also believed, truth may be, and indeed must be, created—and the creation must be insightful. The inventiveness, the creativity, in philosophy as play, therefore, it must be noted, is not capricious or fanciful; for the meaning, the truth, that it seeks to bring into being by its own disciplined articulation must be grounded in that special kind of philosophical understanding which recognizes the uniqueness of its object and at the same time its manner of relating axio-noetically to that larger framework of values constitutive of awakened and contemplative experience. One understands, for example, a person—the paradigmatic subject for philosophical understanding—not when one only explains her by a set of universal laws or generalized principles, but when as well one grasps sympathetically, imaginatively what she is as the particular person she is in relation to the essential possibilities of her being human. Philosophical understanding acknowledges whatever it seeks to understand not only from some objectifying external standpoint, but from within the full integrity of the subject's own being and manner of being in the world.

In its style as play, philosophy is thus burdened with understanding and originary thinking. And it must, then, be at once a solitary achievement and a social activity. For the sake of developing the special insight which is at the core of philosophical play, it requires something of that Plotinian "flight of the alone to the alone," that quiet and alonely spiritual adventure that allows for the development of depth and sensitivity; for the sake of expressing a disciplined reflection and vision it demands sociality, a shared language and concern, the participation in a conventionally determined and learned order of articulation and belief.

When philosophy as play moves too far in the direction of the solitary without the constraint of the social it tends toward unintelligibility (a Heidegger or a Nishida, on occasion), and to the wayward subjectivism of the romantic (a Novalis or a Tagore, on occasion) who confounds his own private emotion and feeling with the nature of being; when philosophy in general moves too far in the direction of the social without the inspiration of the solitary it tends toward superficiality, to that extreme of philosophy as argument where philosophy is just dry arguing and a fruitless search for a technique or method that will produce truth like a machine.

To play is to bring about a spontaneous yet stable integration of meaning and form. And just as there are no formulae in art, the correct following of which will guarantee a good work of art, so in philosophy as play there are no methods the use of which can guarantee the right attainment and expression of truth and meaning. Again as with art, methods in rational creativity generally are primarily of negative employment; they serve exclusionary-wise more to help one avoid what one must not do (like contradict oneself) than to tell one what one must do. "To do philosophy" (as the rather barbaric expression goes), to put it baldly, cannot in any of its creative expressions be simply taught as such.

And although it may have a therapeutic value (which many of the recent "doers" of philosophy saw as the primary office or mission of philosophy) philosophy as play is not therapeutic as such. It is not, that is to say, primarily destructively critical, but originary. Most therapeutic philosophy, with its uroboric tendency to devour itself as it performs its healing function (the later Wittgenstein, Nāgārjuna), seeks to dissolve complexities, puzzles, viewpoints, theories, through various logico-linguistic analyses and to establish a meta-philosophical position or stance that goes beyond the limitations of philosophy itself. But by relying upon discursive analysis (albeit with the aim of overcoming it) therapeutic, critical philosophy remains as a special kind of philosophy as argument. It strives in its communicated form to incite agreement, to demonstrate, to prove.

The playful philosopher, on the other hand, does not so much use or build a ladder that is to be discarded as he reaches its end, as he creates a work which, while it may be acknowledged to be in a universe which extinguishes it, as it were, nevertheless seeks to function revelatory-wise at the level of philosophical understanding. Philosophy as play thus presupposes in the beginning what therapeutic, critical philosophy seeks to achieve at the end, namely a kind of enlightenment that knows where philosophy (as mere argument) properly belongs. Unlike with therapeutic philosophy, though, this knowing enables philosophy as play to be a genuine creation of meaning.

But it is not, on that account, to be confused with speculative philosophy—whether of the kind associated with the various idealisms of later Buddhist thought or with those German philosophies of the eighteenth-nineteenth centuries which were grounded so deeply in Romanticism and which seemed to encourage a free flight of the imagination to conjure up system upon system, as though philosophy were a kind of fantasy literature, or with the more hard-headed rationalist-empiricist kind typical of the Nyāya tradition in India and the Aristotelian in the West which, seeking a comprehensive account of experience, set forth the "generic features" of all modes of being. Speculative philosophy of all kinds is basically discursive: it is essentially a constructive form of creative rationality.

Although it may allow an important role to intellectual intuition and may bring consciousness to the awareness of various possibilities of freedom, speculative philosophy is not, as is philosophy as play, rooted fundamentally in insight: it tries to be demonstrative, sometimes a priori, always systematic. And while philosophy as play may contain certain speculative elements and strive for a certain comprehensiveness it calls most basically for that distinctive understanding which differs from explanation and that yields a creative articulation of new meaning.

Philosophy as play is, then, indeed like art; but unlike, say, a purely abstract work of art, a philosophy-work cannot be entirely autonomous; for philosophic understanding always puts one in relation to a world that is to be seen and understood. A philosophy-work, in short, is always symbolic; it must point to as well as partially embody a truth of being.

Philosophical play, the making of a philosophy-work, is thus somewhat paradoxical in this, that the play, while pointing to a truth of being, is necessarily to some extent illusion making. Philosophy, like art, must always be in a language and is, accordingly, unable to represent, mirror, or otherwise assimilate directly a presumed objective structure of being; it must always fashion its own world as well as struggle to be an insight into a real world. But because it is aware that it is not an adequate substitute for reality, philosophy as play is a knowing illusion making: it is a supremely innocent, but not naïve, way of being rational.

NOTES

1. Another way of putting this would be to say that because of the self-contained character of philosophy as argument *nothing happens* in the fundamental relationship between thinker and world as a result of the argument. Arguments in the context of typical legal, social, political, economic discussions and debates can certainly influence behavior in these areas, and even philosophy as argument can lead in due course, if not always immediately, to different forms of action; but the arguer is not himself touched by his or another's argument in any fundamental self-transforming way. This is the case because, it would seem, despite their so-called "cogency," arguments are accepted in a basic, vital way only when they already accord with one's deep-seated belief-system—with those values which are most basic to one's own being. And this system is changed by experience, not be argument as such.

2. John Searle, "The Storm Over the University," in *The New York Review of Books*, vol. XXXVII, no. 19 (December 6, 1990), 40 (italics mine).

3. See *The Journal of Chinese Philosophy*, vol. 12: 117–29.

4. Tu Wei-ming, *Centrality and Commonality: An Essay on Chung-yung* (Hono-

lulu: The University Press of Hawaii; Monograph no. 3 of the Society for Asian and Comparative Philosophy, 1976), 107.

5. Ibid., 109.

6. In *A Source Book of Chinese Philosophy*, ed. Wing-tsit Chan (Princeton: Princeton University Press, 1963), 108.

PART III

11

✳

On the Being of Time

We feel the pain before we perceive the wound: Or is it the other way around?

Time, I argue, *is* only as articulate temporality; otherwise we have the timeless and mere raw temporal materials. The time that is intrinsic to an activity, then, is paradigmatic for the meaning of time, with artwork time as its consummate achievement.

Time—articulate temporality—is thus at once quantitative and qualitative: it involves as agreed-on measure of change together with a structure of conscious discernment, and it is achieved in varying degrees of appropriate timing. In its consummate form as artwork time (through the play of creativity vitalized by an awareness of the timeless), articulate temporality further may bring forth the timeful—and becomes that in which we are able to rejoice.

I

To begin with, we need to distinguish between the raw materials of public time (an agreed-on measure of change) and experiential time (the structure of conscious discernment), and then see how they contribute to the time intrinsic to an activity.

Public Time

There are two interrelated aspects or dimensions of public time or what we take to be objective change: time as ordered succession marked by an agreed-on measure and organized as a series of divisible units or "nows"

185

(for us today, time as clock time); and time as generative (and degenerative) process, constituted by stages (or sometimes by cycles). In the first, change is essentially the *displacement* of an object (time as the measure of movement); in the second, change is essentially a *modification* of an object (time as the form of transformation). These interrelated aspects or dimensions of our thinking about change have served historically and traditionally as the basis for most philosophical conceptions of what time is. In the West, especially since the rise and development of modern science, a serial order of passing nows has proved most congenial for modeling an understanding of time. Other, more organic models, generally in Eastern (especially Chinese) thought but in Western as well, are most at ease with a developmental conception of time.[1]

In spite of the fact that Greek thinkers (Plato, Aristotle, Plotinus) related time to sequential movement and regular change, they were keenly aware of developmental becoming. Aristotle said explicitly that "it is the nature of all change to alter things from their former condition."[2] Time, he maintained (or *mahākāla*, as the traditional Indian thinker would call it), is "the condition for destruction": generation and degeneration inevitably belong together. Plotinus argued that time "is contained in differentiation of Life: the ceaseless forward movement of Life brings with it unending Time; and Life as it achieves its states constitutes past time."[3]

It was not in fact until the seventeenth century that change and motion were conceived of rather exclusively in geometric (and strictly quantified) terms. In both continental rationalist and British empiricist thought the idea that motion involves a linear, sequential movement of divisible units dominates, and indeed persists until today.[4] Even Kant, for example, when inveighing against "English philosophers" and "Leibniz and his School" concerning the alleged objective reality of time, does not seriously question that time means some kind of serial order or successiveness. He writes, "Those who assert the objective reality of time, conceive it in one or other of two ways. Among English philosophers especially, it is regarded as a continuous real flux, and yet apart from any existing thing—a most egregious fiction. Leibniz and his School declare it to be a real characteristic abstracted from the succession of internal states."[5] Kant then asserts, "Time is an absolutely primary, formal principle of the sensible world. For all things that are in any way sensible can be apprehended only as at the same time or in successive times."[6]

Kant's "working notion of time," it has thus been pointed out, "seems to have been Locke's 'train of ideas'; conceived along a linear analogy, the basic notion seems to have been that of the succession of discernible moments as points on a line."[7] Still, Whitehead can write, "It is an exhibition of the process of nature that each duration happens and passes. The process of nature can also be termed the passage of nature. I definitely refrain at this stage from using the word 'time,' since the measurable time of science and civilised life generally merely exhibits some aspects of the more fundamental fact of the passage of nature."[8]

Generically, our idea of time as a passage probably derives more from our awareness of becoming than from our noticing movements of objects as such in space. We see with interest that things come to be and pass away, and we see especially that living things are born, mature, grow old and die. It is the aging process, biologically speaking, rather than a mere numerical heaping-up of calendrical years that we care about. In any event, Hegel is able to say that "it is not *in* time that everything comes to be and passes away, rather time itself is the becoming."[9]

But the becoming does become for us a time that is measured: the earth rotates, there is light and darkness, and then days of a week, hours of a day, minutes of an hour, seconds of a minute—and whatever divisions that might otherwise be made. When we spatialize time and say that events or changes occur *in* time we really can only mean that events or changes are ordered by a mode of measurement—and we call that public time.[10]

This temporality associated with change, we say, is objective, by which again we can only mean objective to *us*. We assume in our daily lives that there is a temporal structure within which we regulate much of our activities. We take this temporal structure, functionally, to be universal and objective. Whether public time is objective in and of itself, utterly independent of consciousness, is perhaps impossible to ask intelligibly, as this temporality—being, as I will try to show, a condition for the identification of activities—is not some kind of substantial thing or entity itself. Further, as Aristotle noted, "we apprehend time only when we have marked motion." Insofar as we regard it as if it were an entity and as the measure of motion, (public) time is a consciousness-dependent phenomena. Without an awareness of motion and of the changes that substances undergo there would be no (public) time.[11]

But Aristotle himself realized the circularity in the proposed relationship of time to change. "Not only do we measure the movement by the time," he writes, "but also the time by the movement, because they define each other."[12] And as Plotinus pointed out in his astute criticism of Aristotle, if the before and after which are said to mark or measure motion are to be temporal then they must be in time. When a body is said to move a certain distance in a certain time, its movement is measured against some other regular agreed-on movement.[13] If time is defined in terms of motion and motion in terms of time we do not then have (and apparently can never have) a definition of what time is; we only have a sense of how we measure "it."

In his famous analysis of time, however, Augustine was not convinced that we actually do measure (public) time. The past and the future do not exist now, and so cannot be measured; the present, although measurable in principle, does not have a specified duration. What we measure then as time is that which is contained in the present, namely our memories and expectations.[14]

But in what sense is existence an attribute of time, so that it makes sense to speak of the past and the future as not now existing? Events that once occurred might not now be occurring, but this has nothing to do with the existence of the past as such. To exist means to exist temporally. In ordinary language, which Augustine otherwise accepts, the past exists as much as the present.

In somewhat the spirit, if not intent, of Augustine, J. T. E. McTaggart, in his well-known argument concerning the unreality of time, points out the circularity in the ordinary serial, objective notion of time; that we have to assume "the existence of time in order to account for the way in which moments are past, present and future." And this past-present-future scheme (the "A-series"), McTaggart further believes, "has to be assumed in order to account for time."[15]

Nevertheless, and this is sufficient for our purpose, we do meet at certain times (as well as places) and conduct our affairs within a commonly agreed-on framework of temporality. We do have a tensed way of talking (in terms of past, present and future) as well as tenseless, yet temporal speech (of earlier and later relationships). This framework is what I mean by public time. It may be said to have a unity not because "any particular time is part of time and all parts of time are temporally related to one another,"[16] but because it is a system of measurement with a distinctive identity of its own. The systemic character of public time is not, though, to be understood as being purely conventional, for, like all workable concepts it has a transactional relationship with various natural givens. The time that is measured, in fact, is done so by reference to some sequence which approximates absolute uniformity and constancy, for example, the vibration of the caesium atom. Being an abstract system of measurement does not mean, in short, that public time is an entirely arbitrary construction.

What public time is (a Leibnizian order of the dynamic relation of things to one another and to us, a Newtonian absolute coordinate, a Kantian a priori form of our sensibility, a Minkowskian fourth dimension"[17] is, as I have suggested, perhaps ultimately unaskable and thereby unanswerable if we assume public time to be some kind of entity determinable by essentialist statements, *that* it is is indisputable, for we do negotiate our daily lives in its terms. Even if it were possible to reduce all successiveness to consciousness itself, the successiveness would still be a public phenomenon once we learned how "to tell time."[18]

We say that public time is a raw temporal material, for it is a phenomenal-social given which we employ in the creation of time proper. Public time—I will try to show—is a condition for the possibility of articulate temporality.

Experiential Time

Traditionally, one of the most perplexing difficulties for a metaphysics or ontology of time arises because we apparently do not actually experience ordered change as a single series of discrete passing nows. Experiential time (durational temporality as experience) consists, as phenomenology has shown us, of past-laden presents bearing future possibilities.

We must, though, distinguish experiential time from personal temporalities. By the latter I mean all the individual variations in temporal experience that are reflective of the special interests, needs, and capacities of the individual experiencer. Personal times are, as it were, individual responses to public time. They are what certain times, periods of time, duration mean to one as actually experienced (e.g., boredom, busyness, time that seemed to have flown by; the last minutes before retirement). Experiential time, on the other hand, as I use the expression, consists of the universal dimensions of consciousness in its time-constituting phenomenality. It is a time shared by humans in virtue of the nature of perceptual consciousness.[19]

There seems to be, as we previously noted, some considerable agreement (among gestaltists and philosophers such as James, Merleau-Ponty and Husserl) that perception is more a process (with stages of attentive intensity, shifting of foregrounds and backgrounds, organic unfoldments) than an apprehension of discrete existences as such (Hume). Rather than a duration consisting of autonomous nows (Descartes), or of lapses between successive ideas in consciousness (Locke), change consists for us in whole-event relationships that are contextually defined and are apprehended relative to differing (spatial) standpoints. In short, we do not experience a mere sequential, linear train of events or ideas that is given a numerical determination as much as we apprehend relative durations in which pasts converge with futures in gestaltlike, irreducible wholes. In our specious present the past, in varying degrees of intensity, is always there and has a future in virtue of present possibilities. Temporal continuity is, then, a kind of primitive datum of experience. If our perception were confined to separate moments, we would not reach beyond simple states of awareness. As James argued, "a succession of feelings, in and of itself, is not a feeling of succession."[20] Thus Husserl is able to show that a temporal flow can be constituted as phenomena only by means of retention and that "in the undivided stream of lived experience . . . every act of memory contains intentions of expectations whose fulfillment leads to the present."[21] The perceptual field itself then excites "protensions" as well as retentions within its horizon.

And as Husserl also showed, each now of that stream of lived experience presents itself as the unity of which it is a part. When we listen to a melody (a favorite Bergsonian and gestaltist example), each and every note, as we attend to them, shows the melody. It is not that the notes are heard simply as isolated contents that are then added up at the end to constitute the whole, which would then make the melody only an act of remembrance or an ideal construction, rather the melody gets revealed, is disclosed, presents itself, in and through every moment of the temporal configuration that is part and parcel of its being.

Heidegger has nicely elaborated on this existentially when he argues that we live time rather than perceive it as some kind of objective entity. Time is the when, just as space is the where, wherein we dwell. The present is thus a "making present," one that is authentic when it reflects and embodies our freedom, in contrast to our living the present as if it were made up of determined situations and activities. We are inauthentic when we await the future as if it were just the not-yet-happened, rather than realizing it as it consists of our own possibilities. Authentically, we go towards the future; it does not just lie there waiting for us.

Experiential or lived time is thus a process of familiarizing temporalities, making them congenial to our appropriation. Whatever one engages in the present is always selected, or gets selected, according to some criteria of importance, which criteria is expressive of one's wider understanding (articulated or not) about the nature of human events—the possibility of directing them to novel ends, their movement toward a predetermined goal, the very meaningfulness of one's participating in a communal temporal order, and so on. In short, our beliefs about philosophical history inform at every turn our manner of making sense of our present.

For historical consciousness, then, the past is always occurring. Events that once have happened continue to happen insofar as they form part of some configuration (as an extended Husserlian retention) or link together with some present happening in ways that determine its significance. The past occurs whenever a present is defined and made intelligible with reference to it.

But this lived time can also be unrealized, an occasion for failure as well as success. The past gets changed when our protentions (Husserl), or the *Entwurfcharakter*, the projective character (Heidegger), of our existence, is unfulfilled or is drastically altered by some unexpected change that occurs within the temporal configuration. If, when listening to a musical composition, it were suddenly to become what appeared to be a series of disjointed sounds, the melodic past would itself be radically changed, the configuration becoming something quite different than what was anticipated. It is not that Time is the destroyer, but that time gets destroyed when activities are unfulfilled.

However experiential time is to be properly described, characterized, and understood, we do seem to have two rather disparate temporal worlds, public time and experiential time. The question of whether one can derive public from experiential time or whether physical time (public time as given in a physical theory) has some kind of priority over mind-dependent becoming (as Adolph Grünbaum would have us believe)[22] is not of particular significance to the view being developed here. Once we have learned how to tell time, we have a public time that for us is objective and universal. Once we have achieved a certain maturity of consciousness, we experience an integrated temporal field in varying durational terms relative to perceptual contents. We experience continuities and we mark divisible unities. But just as public time can be seen as a raw temporal material, so experiential time can as well be understood as a condition for the possibility of articulate temporality—or time proper. It is our ability to experience temporalities as integrated durations that makes it possible for us to apprehend activities (and not just events), which are the loci of articulate temporality.[23]

II

Consciousness (ordinarily) involves ceaseless alterations and is thus continuously active, with each individual consciousness having thereby its own temporal field. From within the horizons of that field and the structures of biological change, activities occur, each with a rhythm intrinsic to it.

I use the term "activity" rather than "action," for I want to restrict the latter term to human agents. And I use the term "activity rather than "event," to avoid any suggestion of discreteness, which in empiricist thought is so often associated with the term. Activities are history-laden happenings. Further, although we isolate them for identification and analysis, activities always link together in complex networks, so that any present activity is what it is in virtue of its connectedness to other present and past activities. Whereas an event is defined largely in terms of its (public) temporal placement, an activity defines the temporality to which it gives rise.

There is, therefore, a time intrinsic to an activity; a time that is *in* and *of* the activity, a time that contributes to the very definition of a particular activity. In every activity, I will try to show, there is an articulate temporality—the bringing to fruition, in varying degrees of qualitative achievement, of a temporality that *is* only in virtue of the activity.[24]

Let us take a running race as an example. Before there can be a race there must be public time—an agreed-on time when the action will begin and come to an end. The officials will have clocks, or the whole race might be marked by electronic measuring devices. The experience of the race, for both runners and spectators, albeit in somewhat different ways, will necessarily involve more than the measured, linear successiveness of the runner's movements: the running becomes, in virtue of the experiential time which integrates temporalities into an unified whole, a race in a larger context, against a perceived extended background. The runners warm up and are poised in high tension at the start of the race. At its conclusion they slow down to a walk and finally to a stop, duly exhausted. The race that the spectators see is thus more than an abrupt beginning, middle and end, as if there were discrete time-points being traversed; the race is seen as a continuous action with its own unique integrity.

In the race that is seen, then, there is a temporality that has its being only in virtue of the race qua race. The complex, interconnected rhythms of the runners (which might even appear as a kind of dance—one runner moving ahead of another, only later to fall back; the heightened exertion near the end) and the style of movement of each runner along with a collective style of the race itself—all this is the articulated time of the activity. As a unique temporality, the rhythm, the style, is simply part and parcel of the activity that is the race.

The time intrinsic to a race does not merely pass away upon the completion of the race. As a constituent of the activity, it is remembered whenever the race is recalled—or, through videotapes, is shown again. The passage in the time intrinsic to an activity is thus not something external to that which passes. The time *is* the activity as carried out. Time proper or articulate temporality is always *presented* in activities, it is not *represented* as such; it is not a derived abstraction but is among the essential ingredients of experience itself.

There is, then, real sense in saying that the more genuinely active a person is the greater the time there is for him or her. The less consciously active we are the more we sink (unless we move toward the timeless) into raw temporality or ennui.

If, however, the fundamental meaning of time is articulate temporality, then "empty time" as such is a nonsense locution. If there were no activities, we would not have empty time but the absence of time.

Further, and this becomes a central notion in our understanding of time, all activities are carried out in different qualitative ways. The best cooks know exactly when to raise or lower the heat; a good comedian has, we say, "perfect timing"—he knows how to control the rhythm of joke-telling so that the activity seems to have an inherent rightness or inevitability to it.

With timing, every temporality, then, carries along with it an implicit ought, the right when that something needs (ought) to be done. Time is thus laden with opportunities for success in action. Knowing the right time to do X is the temporal knowledge that really matters.[25]

A distinction must nevertheless be made between the timely (*kairos*) and timing, as I am using the term, although they are indeed closely related. The timely is what it is primarily in virtue of some set of conditions external to the activity as such. There is a time to sow and a time to reap. The right time is here a particular time within the temporal fold (*chronos*), whether the rightness be social or natural in origin.[26]

In all agrarian economies, it seems, we thus find a keen awareness of the right time for certain actions to be performed, if indeed they are to be successful. In "primitive" thinking this leads quite naturally to making sacred those crucial times that call for certain actions to be carried out that will guarantee the survival of the community. Mircea Eliade has drawn attention to the manner in which periodic regenerations of life, for primitive thought, involve the repetition of a cosmogonic act: "There is everywhere a conception of the end and the beginning of a temporal period, based on the observation of biocosmic rhythms and forming part of a larger system—the system of periodic purifications (of purges, fasting, confession of sins, etc.) and of the periodic regeneration of life."[27] And further: "On the occasion of the division of time into independent units, 'years,' we witness not only the effectual cessation of a certain temporal interval and the beginning of another, but also the abolition of the past year and of past time. And this is the meaning of ritual purifications: a combustion, an annulling of the sins and faults of the individual and of those of the community as a whole."[28] Although calling for a sharp awareness of temporal passage, the timely for primitive thinking is nevertheless unhistorical just insofar as it involves repetition, reenactment; indeed the very reversibility of time. "The primitive, by conferring a cyclic direction upon time, annuls its irreversibility. Everything begins over again at its commencement every instant."[29] Still it is precisely the sense of temporal rightness that bestows meaning on historical events. John E. Smith, with reference primarily to the Greek distinction between *chronos* and *kairos*, notes that "*kairos* is peculiarly relevant to the interpretation of historical events because it points to their significance and purpose and to the idea that there are constellations of events pregnant with a possibility or possibilities not to be met with at other times and under different circumstances."[30]

In any event, the timely is clearly that which is dependent upon, and is defined in terms of, some set of given conditions that are not intrinsic to the activity itself. "Timing," on the other hand, calls attention precisely to that which is internal to the activity. It is what the activity itself achieves temporally as native to it—within of course the various contexts in which it takes place.

Timing is a qualitative achievement. No examination of public time as such or description of experiential time will yield mechanically the right when to do something that is inherently appropriate to a particular activity. And every activity involves timing of a sort. For example, when walking down the street, one has a pace appropriate to where one is going and why. Timing is thus of central importance for the meaning of time. It is a value-bestowing feature of time; it allows for qualitative achievement.

An activity, I believe, is only as discerned (discriminated, bounded) by consciousness, but activities need not, on that account, always have conscious agents as their locus. Leaves falling from a tree, if so discerned, constitute an activity: dogs, cats, dolphins, and the like may engage in activities or happenings with their own intrinsic rhythms. But this articulated temporality, it should be noted, is for most persons of little qualitative interest, for timing is a result of conscious (albeit often unselfconscious) attentiveness and creativity. Birds sing, but, as far as we know, only humans compose choral music.

Articulate temporality, in other words, can be said to be present at a bare level of being whenever we discern an activity—human, natural or otherwise. An activity will, however, achieve an interesting qualitative degree of timing only through and in conscious participation. And certain activities, such as artworks, realize this timing in the fullest and most fundamental ways.

Artwork Time

Works of art, like everything else, exist as objects in time; they are locatable (datable) in public time and are subject to processes of change (some of which, in varying degrees with the different arts, can be anticipated and controlled).[31]

Works of art also require time for the apprehension of their form-content. Not only the so-called temporal arts (music, poetry) which clearly unfold in time, but the spatial arts (painting, architecture) as well are not simply given at once as a full aesthetic presentation. They take time to experience.[32]

Apart from the temporalities conditional for the existence of the object and for the apprehension of its form-content, there is also the temporality involved in the experiencer's recognition of the work as the result of its creative process. A work of art is perceived aesthetically not as a static completion but as a dynamic becoming. We do not, for example, see lines simply as bare perceptual qualities in a print; we see, when we see aesthetically, the lines as *of* a woodcut or an engraving and we see them in terms of our knowledge of the limitations and possibilities of the medium.

This temporal dimension in our experience of works of art show how works of art may be said to be a kind of activity (and not just the result of the artist's creativity). They embody a ceaseless becoming.

Most important among the temporal aspects of art, however, is the manner in which, in extraordinarily varied ways, works of art are formally creative of a temporality. Works of art are constituted by patterns, tempos, shifting of foregrounds and backgrounds, explicit rhythms and movements; by what Étienne Souriau has called the "artistic time inherent in the texture of a picture or statue, in their composition, in their aesthetic arrangements." This is the articulate temporality of the work, what we may call artwork time. In music, Souriau notes, "the tempo is the *qualitative* impression of slowness or of speed expressed by indications such as: *adagio, andante, presto,* etc.; and of which the slightest variations often have a great expressive value."[33]

Artwork time is thus at once quantitative and qualitative; it is analyzable formally in terms of the diverse elements that comprise it (sequences, rhythms, etc.) and it is experienceable as working aesthetically to achieve various expressive values. Timing thus becomes the dominant temporal aspect of art. Each pattern, sequence, rhythm is what it is as it contributes to the inherent rightness of the work. The articulated temporality, the time intrinsic to the work, is just what it ought to be when the artwork is a successful work. We sense the inevitability of the relations created in, through, and by the work.

Artwork time is, then, consummatory in virtue of the fact that the temporal relations created are precisely intentionally primary to the activity. They constitute the activity in a fundamental (not simply adventitious) way. The created temporality of any activity can, to be sure, achieve an excellence of its kind—that is, when the timing is just right for it. And the judgment of rightness here will always be at least partly aesthetic (formally if not expressively) in character, for timing is never a matter of mere mechanical or functional efficiency. The recognition of the perfect timing of an engine requires more than (although it probably always includes) the bare seeing that the machine is running most efficiently. But in cases such as this, with the possible exception of the automotive engineer or mechanic, the created temporality is not, as with artworks, one of the compelling, controlling features of our experience of the activity qua the particular activity that it is—and for its own sake. With artwork time we are presented with a unified organizing of a temporal field; we are given a world. Time is uniquely performed in art.

There is one last temporal mode in artwork time which is of considerable importance, and that is the realization (rare as it might be) of the timeful that is achieved in the greatest works of art, in and through their intrinsic temporality.

Augustine characterized eternity as where "nothing passes by; everything is present." Timefulness is a concentration of temporalities, experienced in art as a transcendent realization. With the achievement of the timeful we are brought into that world that seems to contain all worlds within itself.

III

As a general concept, time is thus an ideal construction, a generalization from our primary temporal experience of articulated temporalities. It is, in other words, a conceptual extension from our concrete, lived activities. This ideal concept, the world time, if it might be so called, is not at the level of our ordinary experience unreal as such, anymore than other such abstraction is. World time becomes for us conceptually the matrix *through* which (and only incorrectly *in* which) we live our lives.

In the last analysis, however, there is no time, because reality itself is changeless. Being undifferentiated, without quality, reality is a completeness, a fullness of being that knows no distinction between itself and anything else. Utter timelessness is the most fundamental truth of our temporal being.

When we are estranged from reality, the truth of our temporal being may be a terrible abyss that swallows up everything into a meaningless silence and hollow emptiness and from which we flee into our little busyness, or when we are engaged with reality it may be our most vital source for creative play.

Creativity becomes rightly real for us when we see it for what it is, as a kind of dynamic illusion. But we are deluded only when we ascribe ultimacy to what is created; we are deluded when we fail to see the illusion of all that is temporal.

Creativity is illusion making. And at its best it is carried out with that very realization. One is able to play truly only when one understands the game.

The concentrated energy of creativity is made joyful by the freedom consequent upon the realization of the timeless. Only when we are unattached to the temporal can we rightly articulate it.

In sum: there is, then, the timeless, and, in a fundamentally different way, there is articulate temporality, with its raw temporal materials—public time and experiential time. Articulate temporality, or time proper, is not a moving image of the timeless; it may, however, be a creative engagement with it. The creativity of time as play is possible because there is the timeless. Without the timeless we could not have ontologically the illusion that is essential to play.

Articulate temporality is thus neither objective nor subjective as such. It is not simply out there, as a bare feature of an external world; nor is it simply in here, as an empty form of an inner consciousness. Time *is* intrinsic to an activity discerned by consciousness.

And it is at once quantitative and qualitative. From its raw materials it is presented as native to activities in varying realizations of timing. In artwork time, the consummate achievement of articulate temporality, we may have the timeful brought forth—and therein we are able temporally to rejoice.

NOTES

1. Traditional Indian conceptions of time, on the other hand, tell a rather more complex story. In opposition to the popular view that for Indian philosophy time was either metaphysically unreal or phenomenally cyclical, J. N. Mohanty has argued convincingly that "these views, as stated, are false. As regards the first, it may suffice to point out that time is held to be unreal (in a deep metaphysical sense) only by the Advaita Vedānta system, but that too must be understood in the larger context that for Advaita Vedānta the empirical order with all its categories (space, time, causality, amongst them) are metaphysically unreal." But more centrally for our purpose, he notes that "the theory of cyclic changes (the cycle of creation and dissolution, the cycle of happiness and suffering, the cycles of birth and death, and so on, pictures of which abound in Hindu and Buddhist religious and mythological writings) should not be confused with a theory of cyclic time. If these cycles succeed each other, such succession requires a non-cyclic time. . . . The idea of *yugas* or epochs (or their larger multiples) is not *eo ipso* the idea of time cycles: it is at one level determining units of cosmic time-calculation, at another amounts to an idea of recurring valuational types—but not in any case one of 'eternal recurrence'. . . . In economic theory, one talks of economic cycles, of cycles of inflation and recession. These cycles do not imply a theory of cyclic time. The Indian philosophers did *not* hold such a theory." (*Reason and Tradition in Indian Thought: An Essay on the Nature of Indian Philosophical Thinking*, 184–185; 186–187.)

2. Aristotle, *Physics* 222[b].

3. Plotinus, *Enneads*, III. 7. 11, trans. Stephen MacKenna (New York: Pantheon, n.d.), 234.

4. Apart from phenomenological-existential notions, one important exception to this commonly accepted notion of what time is (as distinct from its ontological status) was Henri Bergson, who believed that the primary meaning of time was to

be found from an intuition into a primal, indivisible continuity or dynamic flow, which is reality itself. Real time, Bergson insisted, "has no instants." It is only by means of our habit-laden intellect that time gets converted into spatial categories and that we acquire the idea of separable moments.

5. Immanuel Kant, *Dissertation on the Form and Principles of the Sensible and Intelligible world*, in Charles M. Sherover, *The Human Experience of Time: The Development of Its Philosophical Meaning* (New York: New York University Press, 1975), 148.

6. Ibid., 149.

7. Ibid., 116.

8. A. N. Whitehead, *The Concept of Nature* (Ann Arbor: University of Michigan Press, 1957), 54.

9. G. W. F. Hegel, *The Philosophy of Nature*, trans. A. V. Miller (Oxford: Clarendon Press, 1970), 258.

10. It is interesting to note in this regard that some traditional cultures seem to have been acutely aware of this ordering process as the meaning of public time but marked the passage of events not with respect to an abstract, uniform, mathematical order but to other, significant events. The traditional Chinese, for example, it has been said "lacked a system to record the years in a linear progressive way." Rather, "in order to identify a year in the past in the traditional way, one must first identify the dynasty, the emperor, the title of the emperor . . . before one can finally settle on the year. In doing so, certain concrete historical knowledge is required. And yet even when one has this year identified, by merely looking at the description of the year, he still cannot tell exactly how many years it is from now." (Shu-hsien Liu, "Time and Temporality: The Chinese Perspective," *Philosophy East and West*, vol. 24, no. 2 [April 1974]: 145. The public time ordering for the Chinese was thus one of noting special occasions and marking others in relation to them. Time for the Chinese was essentially a complex web of happenings constituted in its shape by and through certain key points or centers within that web.

11. Aristotle, *Physics*, 219[a]. William James also emphatically stated that "awareness of change is thus the condition on which our perception of time's flow depends." (*The Principles of Psychology*, vol. 1, 620.)

12. Aristotle, *Physics*, 220[a].

13. See Plotinus, *Enneads*, III, 7.

14. See his *Confessions*, Book 11.

15. J. T. E. McTaggart, *Mind*, New Series, October 1908: 457–74. The "A-series" is contrasted by McTaggart with the tenseless "series of positions which runs from earlier to later, or conversely," which he calls the "B-series".

16. W. H. Newton Smith, *The Structure of Time* (London: Routledge & S. Kegan Paul, 1980), 79.

17. Minkowskian spacetime, however, it has been argued, does not represent some radical metaphysical break with Newtonian theory, for this spacetime "has its independent existence and structure, as space and time did before. So, for example, a spacetime totality empty of all events is perfectly intelligible on this view. And, as before, the spacetime remains totally immune in its structure to any changes due to the emplacement in it of any material events or their interactions.

As in the Newtonian theory, spacetime is still the passive arena or container of the world." (Lawrence Sklar, *Space, Time, and Spacetime* [Berkeley: University of California Press, 1974], 163.)

18. It is surely a mistake, then, to assume that whenever one asks, What is time? one is asking for a definition of a word so that it "would enable me to eliminate the word 'time' from any given context and replace it by its definiens." (Friedrich Waismann, "Analytic-Synthetic," in *The Philosophy of Time*, ed. Richard M. Gale [Garden City, New York: Anchor Books, 1967], 56.) Like most metaphysical questions, What is time? is not asking for a definition, rather the question is an invitation to organize, with discipline, our awareness of the complex temporal features of our experience and thus possibly to acquire some insight into their nature.

Also, it should be pointed out, this public time is, quite naturally, culturally informed in many ways. For example, for many of us today technological developments in information exchange seem to make all manner of events instantaneous for us; we are made aware of them as they are happening. Consciousness, in short, gets turned into a present now. In other times, when it took weeks and months for news to travel, one's sense of public time must have been considerably different. One's present awareness was more often than not of events and situations that had already occurred and were over and done with.

19. It should also be pointed out that much of the content of individual consciousness has its locus in that subwaking domain of mental life which has its own peculiar atemporality, one that is closely related to, but not to be identified with, the atemporality of the mentally deranged. The deranged (severe psychotics) are simply unable to perceive and constitute for themselves those configurations of actions and events that have an articulate temporality. Lacking the ability to "protend" (as much, if not more, than being unable to grasp public time as such) and thereby to realize themselves as future, as well as past and present, the deranged, as we have seen, lose the wholeness or integrity of an activity, and with it time proper. Madness is to be trapped in a now without transcendence. It is a dwelling in a kind of fallen time, rather than a vital experiencing of time proper.

The temporality of subwaking consciousness, on the other hand, while closely related to that of the deranged in its inability to realize a clear purposive order, is not so much a dwelling in an unconstituted now as it is a rather freewheeling roaming across the past and future possibilities, which does bring the most disparate elements of experience into some kind or other of relational order, but without timing. Subwaking temporality lacks precisely the sense of appropriateness that, as we will examine shortly, the qualitative features of time require.

20. William James, *Principles of Psychology*, 628.

21. Edmund Husserl, *The Phenomenology of Internal Time-Consciousness*, ed. Martin Heidegger, trans. James C. Churchill (Bloomington: Indian University Press, 1964), 76.

22. See Adolph Grünbaum, "The Status of Temporal Becoming," in *The Philosophy of Time*, 322–53.

23. It is quite possible that what is a condition for time proper, namely its raw materials of public and experiential time, is at the same time an abstraction from it. Logically we could not have, could not discern, the time intrinsic to an activity,

could not indeed note an activity as being such, without an agreed-on time measure and a capacity to perceive temporal gestalts; yet, taken in themselves, the raw
materials do not have an independent ontological status as substantial entities or
realities. There is only time proper, from which generically we abstract the conditions whenever we are inclined, for whatever reasons, to isolate them for consideration.

In *Being and Time*, Heidegger was concerned with this issue or derivation and
wanted to show how public time is derivative from the more originally given unified temporal field with its three *"ekstases"* of past, present, and future. The ontological ground of public time is *"Dasein's* temporality." Public time is used by us,
according to Heidegger, to order our projects so that *Dasein*, human being-there,
can have authentic being in the world.

After his "reversal," Heidegger, in his *On Time and Being*, concluded that
"Being and time determine each other reciprocally, but in such a manner that neither can the former—Being—be addressed as something temporal nor can the latter—time—be addressed as being." (*On Time and Being*, trans. Joan Stambaugh
[New York: Harper & Row, 1972], 3.)

24. One of the most interesting, but terribly obscure and elusive treatments of
time as defined in terms of activities is to be found in the work of the thirteenth-
century Japanese thinker Dōgen, founder of the Sōtō sect of Zen Buddhism.
Dōgen argued that time (*uji*, "being-time") is a product of activities and not that
in which they occur. Flowers don't bloom in spring; spring is the blooming of
flowers. "Therefore, pine trees are time. So are bamboos. You should not come to
understand that time is only flying past. . . . If time were to give itself to merely
flying past, it would have to have gaps." And thus it is, according to Dōgen, that
"each being-time is without exception entire time." Every happening is a bringing
forth of time and contains, as it were, all time within itself. (See his *Shōbōgenzō*,
trans. N. A. Waddell and Masao Abe in *The Eastern Buddhist* A more recent and
somewhat more readable translation of the "Uji" selection has been made by
Thomas Clearly in his *Shōbōgenzō: Zen Essays by Dōgen* [Honolulu: University of
Hawaii Press, 1986], 104–9.)

In the context of explicating Dōgen's notion of *uji*, Joan Stambaugh says, "if
time is not the form of going and coming, then ascending the mountain (or crossing the river, or anything else) is the right-now of being-time. Whenever I am
doing anything . . . I *am* the right-now of being-time in the transitive sense of the
verb 'to be'. . . . Instead of a supposedly permanent ego anxiously watching time
fly past or slip away, I *am* time. As long as I am time, it does not slip away." (Joan
Stambaugh, *Impermanence is Buddha-Nature: Dōgen's Understanding of Temporality*
[Honolulu: University of Hawaii Press, 1990], 36.)

25. The timely has, of course, as well to do with knowing when *not* to do something or other. To have patience is a difficult burden for most of us, for it seems to
involve only a passive waiting. In the context of the timely, however, it means
being alert to the appropriate when to act.

26. It was the ancient Chinese, though, perhaps more than the Greeks, who
emphasized the social character of the timely—although, to be sure, many of the
social rites were thought to have an ontological grounding. Liu notes that, "For

Confucius, rites and music were the two means that he heavily relied upon to educate people. And we find that timing [the timely] is really the essence of the practice of rites and music; for example the emperor must make sacrifices to Heaven only in a certain season, certain music must be played on a certain occasion. Even in a household, the practice of rites is of a seasonal nature." ("Time and Temporality: The Chinese Perspective": 149.)

27. Mircea Eliade, *Cosmos and History: The Myth of the Eternal Return* (New York: Harper & Brothers, 1959), 52.

28. Ibid., 54.

29. Ibid., 89.

30. John E. Smith, "Time and Qualitative Time," *Review of Metaphysics* 40 (September 1986): 4–5. One of the most fascinating notions of time that seems to bring together in a rather deep ontological manner the apprehension of historicity and primitive reversibility is the so-called Dreamtime which, as David Abram notes, "plays such a prominent part in the mythology of Aboriginal Australia.

It is a kind of time out of time, a time hidden beyond or even *within* the evident, manifest presence of the land, a magical temporality wherein the powers of the surrounding world first took up their current orientation with regard to one another, and hence acquired the evident shapes and forms by which we now know them. It is that time before the world itself was entirely awake (a time that still exists just below the surface of wakeful awareness)." (David Abram, *The Spell of the Sensuous*, [New York: Vintage Books, 1996], 164.) The Australian aborigine, in his Dreamtime, sings his songlines as he traverses a landscape whose significant sites record (and entomb) the names and events associated with their histories. "Each ancestor thus leaves in his wake a meandering trail of geographic sites, perceivable features in the land that are the result of particular events and encounters in that Ancestor's journey. . . .

"These meandering trails, or Dreaming tracks, are auditory as well as visible and tactile phenomena, for the Ancestors were singing the names of things and places into the land as they wandered through it." (Ibid., 165–66.)

31. An architect, for example, can select various materials according to how actual physical changes may occur in them. Certain materials weather in predictable ways (in coloring, texture) and the anticipated changes can be incorporated into the design.

32. See my "Time and the Visual Arts," in *Essays on the Nature of Art* (Albany: State University of New York Press, 1996), 37–40.

33. Étienne Souriau, "Time in the Plastic Arts," in *Reflections on Art: A Source Book of Writings by Artists, Critics & Philosophers*, ed. Susanne K. Langer (New York: Oxford University Press, 1961), 138. It is, of course, in music (and music-related arts such as poetry) that the achievement of temporal articulation is most evident. The ordering of temporal relationships is one of the dimensions in listening to music of which we are most immediately aware. But the manner in which any artwork (in painting, in architecture, as well as in music, poetry or dance) controls the discernment of its intrinsic rhythm and ordering of relationships discloses the temporality that is created uniquely by the work in a primary way.

12

✳

On the Being of Space

There is, as with time, a space proper—a space that is articulated in and through the raw spatial materials of public space (a common-sensed-based geometric or measurable space) and experiential space (a value-discriminated, activity-filled, horizon-laden space). There is also that fullness of space which results from right spacing (most notably in artwork space) and there is the spacelessness of reality.

The being of space proper, then, as with time, is at once quantitative and qualitative; it involves relations between objects or events, measurable volumes and distances, and it involves relationships between persons and their environments. Space proper is achieved always in varying degrees of right or appropriate spacing.

The fundamental meaning of the term "space," I shall argue, is that of space proper or articulate spatiality.

I

Public Space

The most enduring metaphor of space, one that still informs so much of our common everyday thinking about space, is that of a container. Space is imagined to be like an empty receptacle in which objects get placed and happenings occur. This space, then, is taken in our naive thinking about the world to be a real feature of the world, a material entity in itself, and is thought to be rendered intelligible through geometry or through any mathematical system of measurement that is able to model reality or be rightly applied to it. The pre-Socratics, although sometimes distinguishing between atoms and a void (e.g., Democritus), conceived of space generally in these material container terms, as did Plato (in the *Timaeus*). It was for Aristotle to answer Zeno's charge, that if there is such a real space, it too must be in something, by defining space qua place as an immovable vessel, the boundary or inner surface that bodies may occupy, with absolute space being the surface of that outermost heaven that cannot be contained in anything else. In his *Physics*, Aristotle points out that "the existence of place is held to be obvious from the fact of mutual replacement." Place or space exists in virtue of the fact that we perceive that where one thing now is, something else may come to be. "What now contains air formerly contained water, so that clearly the place or space into which and out of which they passed was something different from both."[1]

But can we perceive this space apart from the objects which "occupy" it? Space cannot be prior to entities—and be itself an entity of another kind—if it exists only in virtue of the possibility of a perceived (re)placement of objects.

In non-Western philosophical traditions, for example with the Nyāya school of Indian philosophy, space (*ākāśa*) is also taken as a real ubiquitous substance, but with this sophisticated twist— that it is understood at the same time to be relational in character. For Nyāya, "to say that there is one space and time is to deny that any two objects in the universe cannot be related temporally and spatially."[2]

We have also had in Buddhism Nāgārjuna's denial of the self-sufficient reality of *ākāśa* on the grounds that space cannot exist as a basic element before it is defined, and there can be no definition in the absence of that which is to be defined. In the last analysis, space is only because it gets so designated and named.[3]

Nevertheless space, qua receptacle, persists in both Western and Asian traditions and gets enshrined in Newton's system as an absolute entity. In his *Philosophiae Naturalis Principia Mathematica* of 1687, Newton expressly insists that absolute space, which is empty, "in its own nature, without relation to anything external, remains always similar and immovable"; it, together with absolute time, is God's sensorium.

Leibniz, in his famous correspondence (1715–1716) with Samuel Clarke, forcefully denies that space is some kind of (Newtonian) real entity in favor of its being a *relation*—"an order of things which exist at the same time, considered as existing together." Hence, "there is no space where there is no matter." As Bertrand Russell puts it, "Space for Leibniz is something purely ideal; it is a collection of abstract possible relations."[4]

Leibniz develops this remarkable view (which, in his time, was duly ignored in favor of Newton's position) largely from theological grounds as fortified by his principle that nothing happens without a sufficient reason. If space were absolute, a substantial something in itself, it could not have a sufficient reason, for it "is impossible that there should be a reason why God, preserving the same situation of bodies among themselves should ever have placed them in space in one certain *particular manner.*"[5]

Leibniz was perhaps right in understanding that space is not a substantial, independently existing entity, but he clearly failed to take into account those qualitative features (which we have yet to mention) that contribute so significantly to our actual spatial perceptions, and, most important, he failed to see that space as a relational category is not so much an ordering of objects as it is that which itself gets ordered in virtue of the placement of objects and events and the relations that obtain among constituent spatialities—with this space then having a character of its own.

Further Leibniz' idealization of space, as Russell and others have noted, for all its brilliance cannot make intelligible just that reality of space which so puzzled Aristotle, namely as place. "[Leibniz] is anxious to give an unambiguous meaning to *same place*, so as to be able to say definitely that the two bodies A and B either are, or are not, successively in the same place. But this, on his theory, is neither necessary nor possible."[6]

The boldest and in many ways the most revolutionary attempt to explain what (objective) space is may be found in Kant's argument that space is nothing but the form of our outer intuition. It is an a priori form, a condition for the very possibility of experience: "Space is not an empirical concept which has been derived from outer experiences. For in order that certain sensations be referred to something outside me (that is, to something in another region of space from that in which I find myself) . . . the representation of space must be presupposed."[7] Further: "Space is a necessary a priori representation, which underlies all outer intuitions. We can never represent to ourselves the absence of space, though we can quite well think it as empty of objects. It must therefore be regarded as the condition for the possibility of appearances, and not as a determination dependent upon them."[8]

From which it follows that space can never be regarded as a property of, or relation among, things in themselves, but only of their appearances. "It is, therefore," Kant says, "solely from the human standpoint that we can speak of space, of extended things, etc."[9] As Heidegger well describes it, Kant is arguing that

> Spatial relations—the relations of *beside, above,* and *in back of*—are not localized "here" or "there." Space is not just another thing in hand; it is no empirical representation, that is, nothing that can be represented empirically. In order that any given thing may be able to reveal itself as extended in accordance with definite spatial relationships, it is necessary that space be already manifest before the receptive apprehension of the thing. Space must be represented as that "within which" any actual thing can be encountered.[10]

Kant has often been criticized for assuming that Euclidian geometry is *the* geometry of that "necessary a priori representation," but this does not seem fatal to his view, for it is not evident that his general argument need presuppose any particular geometry with its apodeictic certainty. A more crucial difficulty lies in Kant's failure to appreciate the active value-bestowing and value-discerning capabilities of consciousness as they are at play in all perceptual experience so that spatialities are always experienced by us in articulated forms and are not simply given to us by means of a general form of outer intuition. We can have intuitions, according to Kant, only as we are affected by objects. Spatialities, we will try to show, do involve a contribution of consciousness to what we take to be an objective order of experience, but this contribution is much more subtle, multi-leveled and intricate, and certainly more axiological, than Kant realized.

However we understand the nature of (public or what is usually thought of as objective) space—as a real receptacle or substantial entity in which objects may be placed, a relation that orders existing things without itself being a thing among those things, a formal principle which is presupposed in all judgments of externality—it is clearly evident that, although this presumed objective space does not exhaust the meaning of space, we all have a working knowledge of what space means in terms of measured distance or measurable relations. We can all learn geography and know where one place is in relation to others. We can all use a measuring tape and mark off one hundred yards or meters. We can know what size a certain room is and what the depth of the ocean is at a certain place. We know what this presumed objective space means without our knowing its nature or without our having to presuppose that it is an entity with a nature of its own. Once we acquire various rudiments of education and socialization, a public space is simply a given of our experience. We can agree on where we will meet as well as when we will meet. We navigate in our world in and through an acceptance of socially agreed-on spatial orderings. This public space is thus a raw material for space proper or articulate spatiality.

Experiential Space

We navigate in our worlds, we have noted, in a public space constituted basically of measured distances or measurable relations. We clearly live, however, in a more integrated way among spatialities that have special significance for us. The world as a familiar dwelling place is our lived spatiality, and not a world of objects placed by indifferent modes of measurement. Space here becomes a medium, as it were, for the presencing of things, happenings and persons and not for their mere placement.

Mircea Eliade has nicely pointed out how for "archaic religious consciousness" space is not homogeneous, rather "some parts of space are qualitatively different from others." There are sacred spaces, places which become the center and locus of value, and that provide a point of reference from which to "found the world": "The sacred reveals absolute reality and at the same time makes orientation possible; hence it *founds the world* in the sense that it fixes the limits and establishes the order of the world."[11]

Phenomenologists, of a more secular bent, have also convincingly shown how in our lived-world we familiarize space as a neighborhood, a place of work, and so on and imbue various places with special values. It might even be argued that we are able to perceive one thing as its stands in relation to other things only when we first have some centered sense of belonging. We would not be able to perceive spatialities in a totally alien world. Just as an experience of spatial distortion presupposes some given objective normality, so that normality itself presupposes some essential unity of meaning or order of spatial significance.

In his *Phenomenology of Perception*, Merleau-Ponty looks for this "essence of space" in a primordial organic relation between a perceiver and his world. Rejecting from the start the main alternatives offered in the interpretation of objective space as the fundamental meaning of space, Merleau-Ponty argues that space for us is something that is always "already constituted." "Is it true," he asks, "that we are faced with the alternative of perceiving things in space [the "realist," container view], or . . . of conceiving space as the indivisible system governing the acts of unification performed by a constituting mind [the Kantian "idealist" view]? Does not," he continues, "the experience of space provide a basis for its unity by means of an entirely different kind of synthesis?"[12]

This synthesis, Merleau-Ponty believes, is to be found at a level of pre-critical experience where a primitive "spatial level" gets established. And here it is the body which "plays an essential part in the establishment of a level." But "What counts for the orientation of the spectacle is not my body as it in fact is, as a thing in objective space, but as a system of possible actions, a virtual body with its phenomenal 'place' defined by its task and situation."[13] The primordial lived space, then, is a field for the actions that may be performed by a human actor. "The constitution of a spatial level is simply one means of constituting an integrated world: my body is geared onto the world when my perception presents me with a spectacle as varied and as clearly articulated as possible, and when my motor intentions, as they unfold, receive the responses they expect from the world."[14] Hence, "Everything throws us back on to the organic relations between subject and space, to that gearing of the subject onto his world which is the origin of space."[15]

Merleau-Ponty insists that "being is synonymous with being situated" and that, accordingly, "Space has its basis in our facticity. It is neither an object, nor an act of unification on the subject's part; it can neither be observed, since it is presupposed in every observation, nor seen to emerge from a constituting operation, since it is of its essence that it is already constituted."[16]

This primordial experiential space then takes on many qualitative determinations. "Landscape," Marjorie Grene writes, "is where I dwell, as distinct from geography, which locates me, or any one or any thing, in terms of an objective framework constituted by science as well as by common sense."[17] Our most fundamental originary sense of spatiality is thus perhaps more that of enclosure than of placement, for, when enclosing we provide for ourselves just that centering and orienting that our sanity seems to demand. This suggests once again that our experiential space and time are, as Calvin Schrag argues, "ingredients within the dynamic structure of experience itself, rather than transcendental and a priori conditions for the possibility of experience."[18] Space as lived spatiality is the way I belong to a world. It "vitalizes and structures world experience, it assigns values to concrete bodily movements and historical anticipations."[19] Space, like time, has then a kind of historicity: "The now as living present never appears as an isolated and atomistic instant. Likewise, the here in which all experience is rooted partakes of breadth and thickness, vectorially connected with variant 'theres' that surround it and define it as a here-with-an-environment."[20]

And thus Schrag, like Grene, can argue that, "Markings on maps and metrical points are lifeless abstractions and arbitrary constructions for the convenience of measurement. Space as a horizon-form of world experience is presupposed by them, and first provides the living context out of which they are abstracted."[21] But the arbitrary constructions of measurement do become part of the actualities of our lived perception. Once educated into the use of a particular system of measuring distance (such as miles or kilometers) that system does become a content of our experience. We know what a certain distance is in terms of our system of measurement. This is borne out by the fact that it is very difficult for one to adapt to a different system of measurement. One is confused and irritated in not understanding by way of experience what the lived meaning of, for example, twenty kilometers versus twenty miles is.

Further, these modes of measurement that become integral to our experience of space themselves take on differing meanings relative to technological change. With new ways of transportation and almost instantaneous communication what were once understood as vast distances become something more congenial—the distances quite literally shrinking for us. Public space is not then something that is merely derivative from a more primordial experiential space; rather, as we will try to show, the two belong together as the raw materials of space proper or articulated spatiality.

What phenomenological analysis seems however clearly to disclose is that for human consciousness space is where our projects get actualized; it is a *dynamic* field of interrelated meanings. As manifest in our concrete individual experience, some spaces are filled with our warm memories; others are, and have been, sources of terror. In moods of sadness and despair spaces become empty for us and we stare into the void. This fundamental capacity (and indeed compelling need) of consciousness to be in relation to a value-determined world in its spatiality is just what is meant by experiential space. It is as much a given of our experience as is objective or public space.[22]

II

If space is as spatialities are perceived then the fundamental or primary meaning of the term "space" is articulate spatiality—with its consummate achieved form as artwork space.

Articulate spatiality is a dynamic relationship that is constituted from the raw materials of a given measurable public space and a value-bestowing experiential space. Articulate spatiality is thus the space that is intrinsic to a situation—a circumscribed interaction of a person and his or her environment. We do not first experience an empty space and then impose boundaries on it; rather first and foremost we experience volumes and lengths, depths and heights which, as value-laden, get defined as such essentially in their relations to each other. A given spatiality is obviously dependent upon whatever gives it a unique determination—whether it be gross physical configurations as in a landscape, or specific objects as in a room, or locatable sounds and smells wherever found. But it is experienced as such in its own terms as having the character that it has.

Let us take the space in a furnished room—Helen's study, for example. The room has a measurable volume that defines it as a room of a certain size; the walls, ceiling, floor in their relation to each other determining that volume. This room of a certain size is a created spatiality, and one that exists as a meaningful place in virtue of its being Helen's study. The space is as the situation of a study. The space is invested with Helen's life, with her hours of pleasant reading and joyful or anguished work. It is not simply an indifferent piece of geography marked off on a blueprint, but a privileged place filled with memories and anticipations. Further this spatiality as a meaningful volume, is made up—and is essentially defined—in terms of the intricacies of the spatialities created by the relationships of the diverse objects in the room. There is a space between the chairs and the sofa and desk that makes for the possibility of intimate conversation—a space created by the placement of these objects and existing only in virtue of their continued presence.[23] There is a space brought forth by the placement of the bookshelves on the walls and the placement of the books therein. These, and the other vital spatialities that may be present, together are the parts that constitute that gestalt that is the articulate spatiality of the room. We say gestalt, for surely one does not go about adding up piece by piece the indefinite actualities and possibilities of spatial relationships in a room in order to experience a room spatially as the room that it is; one does grasp the whole with its unique qualities.

And some rooms are certainly better than others spatially. Some rooms invite our participation, welcome us, as it were, to their presence; others make us uncomfortable—some even purposively designed to humble one (as with many kinds of totalitarian architecture). This brings us to the interesting problem of spacing—for, once an articulate spatiality takes on qualitative (aesthetic) determinations, the relative rightness of the relationships becomes an intrinsic feature of perception, and not something superadded to an otherwise bare perception as a judgment of it.

Artwork Space

Let us take dance as an illuminating example. Before the choreographer can do his work he needs an objective space, a stage of a certain size (the stage, in turn, being located in a concert hall of a certain size) and a measurable way of relating one dancer to another. And as a performance his dance is for an audience, an audience which regards the stage not just as a measurable place but as a place where a very special action is to occur. It is a locus of exciting interests and anticipations. The stage is a place for a value-laden situation to occur. The objective and lived spaces are the raw materials for the articulate spatiality that is intrinsic to the dance performance. Through the assigned movements of the dancers, the choreographer creates a spatiality that exists only in the dance. It is a dynamic spatiality constituted by the movements of the dancers in relation to each other. Charged with an inherent vitality, this articulate spatiality contributes to the very definition of the particular dance itself, in its uniqueness. And, if the dance performance succeeds as dance, a proper spacing is brought forth in its construction. The spatial relationships that together constitute the unique spatiality of the dance are perceived to be right for each other, to have the appropriate aesthetic fitness which makes for the achievement of form. Spacing is essential to the articulate spatiality of the dance. We perceive that spacing as intrinsic to the dynamic spatiality that is the dance.

Architecture, being perhaps pre-eminent among the arts of space, can also serve in making clear this phenomenon of spacing and its importance for the concept of articulate spatiality. Bruno Zevi in his *Architecture as Space* has written that "the specific property of architecture—the feature distinguishing it from other forms of art—consists in its working with a three-dimensional vocabulary which includes man."[24] He goes on to say that "the facade and walls of a house, church or palace, no matter how beautiful they may be, are only the container, the box formed by the walls; *the content is the internal space.*"[25]

This space is dynamic: it is made up of created tensions—of interrelated movements that are exciting or dull in aesthetic terms. Architects speak of flowing space, of volumes in relation to one another, of a single volume surcharged with a sense of its form. Geoffrey Scott argued some time ago that "the whole of architecture is, in fact, unconsciously invested by us with human movement and human moods. . . . *We transcribe architecture into terms of ourselves.*"[26] Scott, like Zevi, sees architecture as *the* spatial art. "Architecture," he says, "alone of the Arts can give space its full value."[27]

We can leave aside the question of whether the sense of spatial rightness in architecture has a ground in human physiology (as Scott would seem to have us believe) or reflects simply our capacity to discern quality in relationships, for the important point, for our purpose, is to note that this sense of rightness is an integral part of our perception of articulate spatiality, that aesthetic discrimination is part and parcel of our experience of space. We see spatialities in terms of proportion, of fitness to function, of gracefulness, of grandeur. This architectural vocabulary is, in varying degrees, part of the vocabulary by which we experience any articulate spatiality.

The sense of rightness is not, of course, thought the same everywhere. In fact the arts of a culture themselves contribute a great deal to the shape of perception (who has not seen natural landscapes through the work of certain painters?) and influence strongly the sense of what is right in the relationship of spatialities. Chinese landscape painting, for example, typically employs a non-perspectival spatial sense in which various depths are coordinated. George Rowley writes:

> To achieve depth, scientific perspective depended, first, upon a continuous receding ground plane which held all the verticals together, and, secondly, upon a diminution in the size of the verticals according to a vanishing point or points. Instead, the Chinese perfected the principle of the three depths, according to which spatial depth was marked by a foreground, middle distance, and far distance, each parallel to the picture plane, so that the eye left from one distance to the next through a void of space.[28]

The flat countryside of western painting with distance measured by cloud shadows or atmospheric perspective, is absent from the Chinese repertoire, in which the mountains mark off the distances.[29]

The content of the sense of rightness in articulate spatiality will thus vary from culture to culture with the sense itself nevertheless being a general feature of perception. Just as what is taken to be a proper distance between persons in conversation may vary (Middle Eastern peoples preferring rather narrow distance, Northern Europeans a greater distance) with nevertheless everyone having some sense of what is appropriate, so with the sense of right spacing. Some principle of aesthetic rightness, in varying ways, enters into everyone's perceptual experience.

Time (as articulate temporality) and space (as articulate spatiality) need, then, to be brought together conceptually, and indeed are so presented to us in our concrete engagements with the world. If time is intrinsic to an activity and space to a situation, then it becomes evident that they are together, for an activity involves a where as well as a when, and every situation, being inherently dynamic, involves changes as well as (value-laden) locations.

This union of time and space is further expressed, as we have now seen, in timing and spacing. Intrinsic to the timing of the master athlete is his working with spatialities (the tennis player must be at the right place— indeed his being at the right place is part and parcel of his timing); intrinsic to the spacing realized in a room is the room's historicity in terms of its own changeability and the retaining and portending features of the consciousness that apprehends it. Every happening is context-laden; every situation is a little history.

Dōgen writes, "Once a monk asked Priest Kempo, 'I have heard that there is only one gate, used by all the Buddhas throughout the entire universe, that leads to nirvana.' Kempo drew a large circle in the air with his staff and said, 'Here it is.' 'Here it is' is the entire universe."[30]

When articulate spatiality achieves a radiant form, as with masterworks of dance or architecture in any tradition, we have something equivalent to that timefulness which is also achieved in the greatest works where temporality gets concentrated as a transcendental realization. When spacing achieves perfection, the articulate spatiality seems to contain all spatialities in itself; to be literally full of itself, an aesthetic plenum; one in which we rejoice.

III

In boundless consciousness reality is without category of time or space. Spacelessness is of the nature of being.

This spacelessness, however, is not a mere void, a nothingness, for it is not in any way an entity in itself. Its meaning for us is as it provides the opportunity, the ground, for that creative play which is our apprehension of, and creation of, articulate spatiality.

Space proper, articulate spatiality, is thus a kind of illusion, an appearance—but it is not a delusion except insofar as we are alienated from its ground, which is spaceless reality. It is an illusion because it is set forth as appearance against that ground. And yet it is meaningful precisely to the degree that we understand it for what it is and engage it in the manner of a liberated creativity.

NOTES

1. Aristotle, *Physics*, Bk. IV, 1.

2. See Karl H. Potter, ed., *Indian Metaphysics and Epistemology: The Tradition of Nyāya-Vaiśeṣika up to Gaṅgeśa* (Princeton: Princeton University Press, 1977), 93.

3. See *Mūlamadhymakārikās*, 5.

4. Bertrand Russell, *A Critical Exposition of the Philosophy of Leibniz*, 2d ed. (London: George Allen & Unwin Ltd., 1973), 122. For a careful analysis of Newton's theory and Leibniz's response, see also Bas van Fraassen, *An Introduction to the Philosophy of Time and Space* (New York: Random House, 1970), chapter IV, "The Classical Problems of the Theory of Space."

5. Leibniz, 3rd Letter to Clarke, 5, in *Leibniz: Selections*, ed. Philip P. Weiner (New York: Charles Scribner's Sons, 1951), 224.

6. Russell, *A Critical Exposition*, 121.

7. Kant, *Critique of Pure Reason* B38, 68. Generically, however, it seems that we do experience spatialities (as young infants) in terms of our reaching out and holding things and by our awareness of the needful presence of others. Space here is more a form of activity that the form of outer intuition.

8. Ibid.

9. Ibid., 71.

10. Martin Heidegger, *Kant and the Problem of Metaphysics*, trans. James S. Churchill (Bloomington: Indiana University Press, 1962), 49.

11. Mircea Eliade, *The Sacred and the Profane: The Nature of Religion*, trans. Willard R. Trask (New York: Harper & Row, 1959), 30.

12. Maurice Merleau-Ponty, *Phenomenology of Perception*, 244.

13. Ibid., 249–50.

14. Ibid., 250.

15. Ibid., 251.

16. Ibid., 254.

17. Marjorie Grene, "Landscape," in *Phenomenology: Dialogues and Bridges*, ed. Ronald Bruzina and Bruce Wilshire (Albany: State University of New York Press, 1982), 55.

18. Calvin Schrag, *Experience and Being: Prolegomena to a Future Ontology* (Evanston: Northwestern University Press, 1969), 50.

19. Ibid., 54.

20. Ibid., 56.

21. Ibid., 55.

22. It is important to recognize that, within the framework of experiential space, we also have, in the state of subwaking consciousness, that peculiar freedom from the spatial constraints of waking consciousness. In dreams, for example, spaces get freely intertwined; they overlap, disperse, recompose and otherwise present what appear to be self-contained fantasy worlds. The extent to which this kind of spatiality enters into the matrices of lived space at the level of waking consciousness is, of course, an empirical question (and one which is no doubt extremely difficult to answer), but if depth psychology is at all correct in its belief that the unconscious does play a vital role in waking experience, one would expect that at least for many persons much of their spatial experience will bear strong influence from that nonconscious domain. It should also be pointed out that in various deviant (pathological) modes of waking consciousness we have what we might call fallen spatiality—dislocations either or both in psyche and in environment. Damaged brain states, as well as those artificial laboratory scenes set up to study the effects of radical spatial distortion, yield experiences that prevent the experiencer from enjoying that centeredness essential to spatial perception and to the discerning of the qualitative dimensions of articulate spatiality. This fallen spatiality or deconstituted space is basically unendurable in experience.

23. It might therefore be said that space (as articulate spatiality) is not so much infinite as that there are an indefinite number of possibilities for its creation. Further, human spatial perception is not a fixed, stable mode of organization; rather it is itself subject to new forms of spatial awareness, for example, as with new technological means of presenting rapidly shifting images that radically alter one's accustomed narrative way of perceiving. After repeated experience of this dynamic, apparently incoherent, bombardment of images that develop spatialities seemingly impossible of comprehension, one does become habituated to recognize a novel kind of spatiality—or at least not to be overly disturbed in failing to recognize the more familiar ordering of spatial relations.

24. Bruno Zevi, "Architecture as Space," in *Art and Philosophy: Readings in Aesthetics*, ed. W. E. Kennick (New York: St. Martin's Press, 1964), 239.

25. Ibid., 241.

26. Geoffrey Scott, from *The Architecture of Humanism* in *Problems in Aesthetics*, ed. Morris Weitz, 2d ed. (New York: The Macmillan Company, 1970), 601.

27. Ibid., 241.

28. George Rowley, *Principles of Chinese Painting* (Princeton: Princeton University Press, 1959), 64.

29. Ibid., 65.

30. Dōgen, "Jippo," *Shōbōgenzō*, trans. N. A. Waddell and Masao Abe.

13

✳

Causality, Creativity, and Freedom

M ost contemporary analyses of causation are based on, or at least take as their starting point, Hume's analysis and are thus carried out in terms of the causal relation that is thought to obtain between discrete events (one moving billiard ball hitting another), and with assumptions (about space and time) that are drawn largely from mechanistic models of science. George Henrik von Wright, in his work *Causality and Determinism*, for example, acknowledges explicitly that the "basic ontological categories" to be employed in his investigation are "those of a generic state of affairs and of an occasion."[1] He goes on to state that "in the following discussions we shall employ an extremely simple logico-atomistic model or picture of the world. The model assumes that the number of elementary states is *constant* and *finite* and that time is a *discrete* flow of successive occasions."[2]

We have already questioned—and shall want to question somewhat further—the adequacy of such a model and especially the analysis of causality related to it, but it should be noted that it is precisely this kind of model that has led over the years to the so-called problem of free will—a problem that has been formulated for several hundred years now not so much in relation to God's alleged omnipotent will and foreknowledge as against the background of a determinism that many believe is the conclusion most appropriately drawn from the alleged uniformity and universality of causality. Although he rejects traditional doctrines of determinism it is no accident that J. L. Mackie, following Hume, entitles his recent study of causation *The Cement of the Universe*.

The main question I propose to raise and explore here is: Can we understand something more about the *meaning* of causality and freedom

215

by attempting to understand the nature of one of the most complex forms of human experience, namely (artistic) creativity? I propose, in other words, to take the creative act (of artwork making) as the primary example or case to be understood in our thinking about causality (rather than one that appears to lend itself prima facie to an explanatory lawlike account, such as a match being ignited and starting a fire) and to see what features of creativity can be applied to an enriched meaning of causality. This approach to the nature of causality will undoubtedly be resisted by many thinkers, for it is customary today in studies of creativity (especially psychological ones) to approach creativity as something that is itself to be explained (reductively)—for example, as a compensatory activity that, according to Freud, feeds on wish fulfillment and substitute gratification.

It is clear to many of us, however, that this effort to reduce creativity to a mechanistic-based model of causality is rather fruitless, as it tends to miss just what we understand to be the distinctive characteristics of creativity (e.g., novelty, critical control and autogeneous development).[3] The inadequacy of applying the usual causal models to creativity, as well as the many difficulties that beset empirico-mechanistic models of causality, suggests the possibility of advancing in the other direction, namely from an analysis of creativity to the meaning of causality and freedom.

I

What is the genesis of our notion of causality? At the most general ontological level the idea of causality seems to arise from our awareness of change, from our awareness of alterations in nature, some of which we are able to initiate, and from our awareness that at least some of these alterations are regular in their occurrence. Where there is no change, or just pure change (whatever that would be),[4] there is no causality. At this level of archaic attentiveness the idea of causality also clearly derives from a cosmological or cosmogonic concern, namely a concept that can somehow account for there being a world. Creation, in most theistic traditions and mythical formulations, is essentially causal: a creator is seen as the cause (or source); the world, the created, is perceived as an effect (or product). Philosophically, then, at this level of basic experience, the term "causality" is at once descriptive and explanatory; it functions so as to describe the occurrence of change and of observed regularities and to explain in principle their origin.

Psychologically, on the other hand, it has generally been believed that causation, or the very idea of causality, arises simply as a projection from our awareness of human agency. W. R. Dennes writes, "The common view of the genesis of the notion of causation is that the child notices particularly those regular sequences in which what is experienced as pain, strain, effort, and relief, are factors; and learns as he develops, to get such sequences off and to carry them through with increasing skill. As he comes to notice regularities in areas where he supposes he feels no strain, it is commonly observed that he reads into these regularities the factors of work and force."[5] And Richard Taylor observes that "Everyone . . . *knows* what causation is—simply because everyone thinks of *himself* as an efficient cause, in the traditional and generally considered archaic sense of that term. . . . Everyone knows what it is to make something happen and to exercise such power as he has over his body and his environment."[6] Georg Henrick von Wright further notes, "There is a time-honoured idea that agency is itself a form of causation—in fact its basic or primary form. . . . Causes operating *in* nature were conceived of on the pattern of agents operating *on* nature."[7]

This "time-honored" view of the genesis of the notion of causation clearly assumes at a very early stage of development the presence of an I who, in self-conscious awareness of her own feelings and her own efficacy as an agent to initiate change, conceptualizes an idea of causal relationship that is then read into nature. This view, however, has been roundly (and probably rightly) criticized by psychologists such as Jean Piaget on the grounds that it is simply not the way in which empirically the notion of causation is acquired. Piaget states, "It would seem rather than force, while it is the result of a transposition or transference [from muscular effort], is first of all discovered in things, before being felt in the self."[8] He adds, "For everything happens as though the child began by attributing forces to all outside bodies, and as though he only ended by finding in himself the 'I' that was the cause of his own force. After all, nothing is less likely than that the feeling of the self should originate in very young children."[9]

Whatever the precise order in the development of our primitive philosophical idea of causality—although the notion that we first accumulate certain kinds of relational experiences before we have a sense of ourselves as separate I's will have some bearing on what we hope will be a more adequate account of the meaning of causality—it is clear that from either direction the idea of force or inherent power is so intermingled with that of cause as to be a primary constituent in the latter's meaning. Richard Taylor points out that "a cause was always thought of as something that exerted power, as something that originated something or brought it into being by virtue of its power to do so,"[10] and that "the idea of an efficient cause was inseparably linked with the idea of active power such that a cause was always thought of as something that *acted*, as contrasted with being acted *upon*."[11] The importance of power in causality is still very evident today in our common-sense understanding of causality. Although

Hume supposedly banished the notion of power from the concept of causality, the examples of causation that we give all the time (stones thrown into closed windows, pushing chairs, and so forth) attest to the perdurance of power in the meaning of causality.

Taylor further distinguishes four other characteristics in our "original idea," or what we post-Humeans now assume to be an "archaic idea," of causality, and whose genesis we have been discussing. These are:

Lack of uniformity or single-case causation. The original idea of an efficient cause had no necessary connection with the ideas of uniformity, constancy or law. It was always supposed that, given the cause, the effect must follow, but this was not usually understood to mean that, given the same cause, the same effect must always follow.[12]

Curt John Ducasse has argued that "causation is directly concerned with single cases, not with constant conjunction."[13] It is the case, however, that most recent thinking about causality is related very closely to nomic explanation. It has been pointed out that there is a "strong tendency in philosophy to assimilate or even to reduce analysis of the causal relation to analysis of causal explanation."[14] At least since Hume, and very much with positivists and modern-day logical empiricists, the laws of nature have come to be seen not as modes of governance—prescriptions as to what must happen—but as descriptions of what has happened and does happen. Moritz Schlick puts the matter succinctly in these words: "Laws of nature do not prescribe a certain order *to* the world, but simply describe the order *of* the world; they do not command what must happen but simply formulate what does happen."[15]

Now although many might conclude that the strict empiricist is bound to deny entirely the meaningfulness of the concept of natural law, and although some philosophers (e.g., William Kneale) and scientists (Einstein) have tried to give a somewhat more rationalistic account of the concept, it may be acknowledged that nomic generalization has come more and more to be at or near the center of philosophical notions of causality. The question we must ask, though, and will indeed ask later in our discussion, is whether this notion of law is primary for the meaning of causality. I will argue that it is not.

Cause as object or substance. An efficient cause was almost always thought of as an object or substance—typically, as a person, human or divine—rather than as an event, process, or state.[16]

This is not the case, however, of many Eastern philosophical traditions, especially Buddhistic, which were adverse to substantialist ontologies. In the West it was certainly due to the rise of science that causation came to be understood primarily in terms of a relationship between events, rather than in terms of substantial subjects initiating or undergoing some fundamental change. For Aristotle, who in many ways nicely expresses the primitive philosophical idea of causality, it was necessary to distinguish four kinds of causes to account for that fundamental change and why things are as they are. A. E. Taylor notes that

> the literal meaning of the Greek terms *aitia, aition* [is used by Aristotle] to convey the notion of cause. *Aition* is properly an adjective used substantively, and means 'that on which the legal responsibility for a given state of affairs can be laid.' Similarly *aitia*, the substantive, means the 'credit' for good or bad, the legal 'responsibility,' for an act. Now when we ask, 'what is responsible for the fact that such and such a state of things now exists?' there are four partial answers which may be given, and each of these corresponds to one of the 'causes.'[17]

Aristotle's four causes—the *material* (the relatively undifferentiated stuff from which something is made or is given form), the *formal* (the pattern, law or idea according to which the object is to be made), the *efficient* (the active agent of change), and the *final* (the end or purpose for the sake of which the thing is made; the completed result of the process)—answer then to the need to account for change in and to individual, substantial things. "It will, of course," A. E. Taylor goes on to say, "be seen that individual bearers of 'forms' are indispensable in the theory; hence the notion of *activity* is essential to the causal relation. It is a relation between things, and not between events."[18]

But the question we shall have to ask is whether either a substance or an event ontology best conforms to the facts of experience. I will argue that what is needed is a more dynamic (than the substance) and more holistic (than the event) view.

> *Necessity.* An efficient cause, it was always thought, necessitates its effect in the sense that, given the former, the latter *cannot* (and not merely does not) fail to occur.[19]

As we know, this essentially rationalistic notion of necessity in causality has been rather thoroughly undermined by Humean empiricism, which finds only constant conjunction in experience. According to Hume, and to contemporary regularity theorists, we do not perceive any necessity connecting cause and effect. The belief in necessity derives from custom alone. In order to establish their nomic character, however, particular or singular causal statements must then, for the empiricist, be logically related to general causal statements, which are themselves regarded only as contingent generalizations unrestricted in their scope. A. J. Ayer argues that "any necessity that there may be in the connection of two distinct events comes only through a law. The proposition which describes 'the initial conditions' does not by itself entail the proposition which describes the 'effect': it does so only when it is combined with a causal law. But this does not allow us to say that the law itself is necessary."[20] But "unconditionality" and generalizations which are "unrestricted in scope" go considerably beyond the sense impressions of Humean empiricism and are as little the content of experience as is the necessity of the rationalist.

It seems, then, that without some kind of necessity (albeit not necessarily the rationalist's logical kind) it is impossible to distinguish causal sequences (or nomic explanations) from accidental regularities (or mere generalizations of fact), as in Thomas Reid's example of the invariable sequential relation of day and night without one being the cause of the other. J. L. Mackie has argued that Hume was right in dismissing logical necessity from experience, but wrong in thinking that he had to find a psychological basis for our belief in it. Mackie distinguishes two kinds of necessity in his analysis of Humean regularity: "We might call *necessity*₁ whatever is the distinguishing feature of causal as opposed to non-causal sequences, and *necessity*₂ the supposed warrant for an a priori inference, for example, the power which if we found it in C would tell us at once that C would bring about E."[21] Mackie goes on to say that Hume "starts with a firm conviction that nothing can count as necessary connection unless it will somehow support a priori inference. His search for *necessity*₁ is sacrificed to his argument for *necessity*₂."[22] In short: "Hume's resort to psychology was premature. . . . He looked for a psychological explanation of a very puzzling idea of necessary connection without having properly shown that the kind of necessity which he was about to locate in the mind really was the key element in our concept of causation."[23] But then Mackie too searches for an appropriate sense of necessity and concludes that "a singular causal sequence instantiates some pure law of working which is itself a form of partial persistence; the individual sequence therefore is, perhaps unobviously, identical with some process that has some qualitative or structural continuity and that also incorporates the fixity relations which constitute the direction of causation."[24]

This need for some kind of necessity, however obscurely expressed, to distinguish nomic (or genuine causal constant conjunction) from accidental regularity is further evidenced by the attempt to analyze causality in terms of conditionship relations. It is often thought that a cause is that set of conditions (among those present) each of which is necessary and which jointly are sufficient for the occurrence of a certain effect. In somewhat more elaborate and precise terms: "A causal condition of an event is any sine qua non condition under which that event occurred or any condition which was such that, had the condition in question not obtained, that event (its effect) would not have occurred, and the *cause* of the event is the totality of those conditions. . . . Once one has enumerated all the conditions necessary for the occurrence of a given event, that totality of conditions will at once be sufficient for its occurrence or such that no further conditions will be necessary."[25]

Now it has also been pointed out by many contemporary analysts of regularity theories that on this account of conditionship it is no longer possible to distinguish cause from effect. As von Wright points out: "The fact that a certain state obtains is a sufficient condition of the fact that a certain other state obtains if, and only if, the fact that the second state does *not* obtain is a sufficient condition of the fact that the first does *not* obtain."[26] For example, "Heavy rainfall in the mountains might, under given circumstances, be a causally sufficient condition of a flood in the valley; but we are not inclined to say, at least not on that ground alone, that the fact that no flooding occurs is a *cause* of the effect that there is no heavy rain."[27] Richard Taylor also writes, "The expression 'X is sufficient for E' is exactly equivalent to 'E is necessary for X.' "[28] He adds, "The analysis of the causal relationship [in terms of necessary and sufficient conditions] has one strange consequence . . . namely, that it does not enable us to draw any distinction between cause and effect."[29] In somewhat different terms Mackie makes this same point: "On a simple regularity theory, a cause is both necessary and sufficient for its effect in such a sense that it follows automatically that the effect is equally sufficient and necessary for its cause; whenever an event of type B occurs an event of type A has preceded it and whenever an event of type A occurs an event of type B will follow."[30]

I have quoted somewhat extensively on this point to sum up some of the difficulties in Humean regularity accounts of causation, especially with regard to the question of necessity, and to prepare the way for an aesthetic approach to the question—an approach which, it is hoped, will bring us to a deeper understanding of causality.

The last feature of the primitive philosophical idea of causality that Richard Taylor distinguishes is

Temporal priority of cause. There is in this notion of causal efficacy . . . the idea that the power of an efficient cause never extends to things past. This temporal priority of an efficient cause to its effect was not, moreover, thought to result merely from conventions of speech but to be a metaphysical necessity.[31]

Likewise, on logical, if not metaphysical, grounds, with Humean regularities. According to Mackie, "Regularity theorists tend to rely on time to supply the asymmetry. . . . Causal priority is just temporal priority under a new name."[32]

He goes on to say, however,

> But this view is at variance at least with our ordinary concepts.
>
> For one thing, we seem ready to accept causes that are simultaneous with their effects—for example, Kant's leaden ball resting on a cushion and being causally responsible for a hollow. . . . We even seem able to conceive that there might be backward causation, with the effect preceding its cause in time. . . . [These possibilities of conception] show that our concept of causal order is not simply that of temporal order, that we have some notion of a relation of causal priority which can be variously directed with respect to time.[33]

Von Wright also argues that causal asymmetry need not be based on temporary priority alone: "Accounting for the cause-effect asymmetry in terms of action and interference caters, at least in some cases, also for the possibility, excluded by the temporality view, that cause and effect may occur simultaneously."[34]

Now although I welcome in some ways the accounting for causality itself in terms of action and interference, and I strongly favor the notion of mutuality in cause-effect relationships, there are, I think, good grounds for being suspicious of the notion of simultaneity of cause and effect in the examples typically given. On close analysis they turn out to be merely redescribing single events or occurrences in multiple terms—that is to say, what is causal in the leaden ball resting on the cushion was its placement there; the resting ball and the hollow as such are a single event or state of affairs. Similarly with Richard Taylor's example of a moving train with the caboose and locomotive securely attached:[35] under the circumstances given, the moving train is a single event, and the appropriate causal question would have to do with its moving and not with the moving of locomotive and the moving of caboose being a cause and an effect occurring simultaneously. In other kinds of examples given—for instance, "the absence of brain function caused death, the two occurring simultaneously"—there is a simple confounding of logical equivalence with causal simultaneity. "Death," in the example cited, *means* "absence of brain functioning."

There is one additional feature in the primitive philosophical idea of causality that Taylor does not discuss in this context and that should be mentioned, and that is the notion of final cause or *telos*, the notion that changes always occur relative to certain ends that they seek. It does seem that this notion, at least in the West, has played a highly significant role in the understanding of causality and was given, as we have seen, its clearest expression in Aristotle. Although Spinoza confidently dismissed final causes from nature as anthropomorphic fictions,[36] the question still remains whether it might be possible and meaningful to formulate a concept of purposiveness which does not call for a fixed predetermined end in view. But more of that later.

One thing that does seem rather certain in this context, however, is that what we are inclined to call the cause of an event is precisely those conditions that answer to *our* immediate (and plural) interests and purposes. For the most part we are interested in looking for the cause of an event when we are concerned either to manipulate the situation directly (e.g., fix a stalled engine) or to learn from the situation something that will be of value for future experience—and we designate as cause that which answers to these interests.

Smith and his family of campers are making a fire in the woods to prepare their evening meal. Smith ignites a match to start the fire, but due to unforeseen circumstances (the extraordinary dryness of the area, etc.) the fire spreads and shortly gives rise to a forest fire. To the physicist the cause of the forest fire is traceable in terms of a chain of efficient causes—the igniting of the match under the conditions that obtained, the spreading fire, and so on. The psychologist, on the other hand, might account for the fire in terms of various tendencies toward pyromania in Smith, tendencies, perhaps, that he had earlier observed in Smith. The park director might rightfully argue that the cause of the forest fire had to do with allowing campers to build fires in the first place: he would forbid it. In each case, and one could easily multiply the perspectives, causal accounts are given that are related to particular human interests—and each, in its proper context, may be legitimate.

J. L. Mackie has noted that, "what is said to be caused, then, is not just an event, but an event-in-a-certain-field, and some 'conditions' can be set aside as not causing this-event-in-this-field simply because they are part of the chosen field, though if a different field were chosen, in other words if a different causal question were being asked, one of these conditions might well be said to cause this-event-in-that-other-field."[37]

Hilary Putnam proffers this example:

Imagine that the escape valve on a pressure cooker sticks and the pressure cooker explodes. We say 'The stuck valve caused the pressure cooker to explode'. We do not say 'The presence of △ caused the pressure cooker to explode', where △ is, say, an arbitrary irregularly shaped piece of the surface of the cooker, 0.1 cm. in area. Yet, in the physics of the explosion, the role played by the stuck valve is exactly the same as the role of △: the absence of either would have permitted the steam to escape, bringing down the pressure and averting the explosion.

Why, then, do we speak of one of these things and not the other as 'caus-ing' the explosion? Well, we know that the valve 'should have' let the steam escape—that is its 'function,' what it was designed to do. On the other hand, the surface element △ was not doing anything 'wrong' in preventing the steam from escaping; containing the steam is the 'function' of the surface of which △ is a part. So when we ask 'Why did the explosion take place?' knowing what we know and having the interests we do have, our 'explana-tion space' consists of the alternatives:

1. Explosion taking place
2. Everything functioning as it should

What we want to know, in other words, is why 1 is what happened *as opposed to* 2. We are simply not interested in why 1 is what happened *as opposed to* such alternatives as:

3. The surface element △ is missing, and no explosion takes place.[38]

But then where does this leave us today with respect to science and its alleged objective, universal causal explanations? Bertrand Russell drew the radical conclusion that "the word 'cause' is so inextricably bound up with misleading associations as to make its complete extrusion from the philosophical vocabulary desirable."[39] Richard Taylor, however, correctly observes that "it is hardly disputable that the idea of causation is not only indispensable in the common affairs of life but in all applied science as well. Jurisprudence and law would become quite meaningless if men were not entitled to seek the causes of various unwanted events such as violent deaths, fires and accidents. . . . It is true that the concept of causa-tion is a theoretically difficult one, beset with many problems and the source of much metaphysical controversy, but the suggestion that it can be dispensed with is extreme."[40]

Let us see, then, if a new approach, based on the nature of creativity, can resolve, or at least redirect, some of the persistent problems in the idea of causality.

II

Desiring, then, that all things should be good and, so far as might be, nothing imperfect, the god took over all that is visible—not at rest, but in discordant and unordered motion—and brought it from disorder into order, since he judged that order was in every way the better.[41]

The theory of artistic creativity of a culture, it seems, is always closely related to that culture's cosmology. Under the sway of Judaeo-Christianity, romanticism saw creativity as a kind of creation ex nihilo, a spontaneous but purposive bringing forth of something new into being, with the creative artist, like the creator god, as a fit object of worship. Traditional Indian culture, on the other hand, saw divine creativity in emanational terms, as an overflow of spiritual energy, an exuberant and purposeless play. It then saw human creativity as a spontaneous but highly disciplined expression of joy and adoration. For Plato, and the Greeks generally, creativity was seen essentially in demiurgic terms, as a rearranging of existing materials so as to bring about a greater (and the greatest possible) measure of order in an otherwise chaotic world of visible becoming. The artist, like the demiurge, is a craftsman, a maker.

Today, however, we do not have a received cosmology that recommends itself axiomatically, as it were, to all educated minds—East or West. In its place we have several competing scientific theories or models, with the strong possibility that they are all (including the currently favorite "big bang" theory) seriously inadequate. Thus, although we bear the weight of historical perspectives on the matter, we can enjoy a certain freedom from the traditional dependency on cosmology in our thinking about creativity.[42]

Nevertheless we are still bound to a considerable degree to a quasi-romantic view of creation *ex nihilo*, for in ordinary language the term has come to be applied indiscriminately to any activity that bears some mark of originality. Still it is artistic creativity that serves as the model of what creativity means, and so in our analysis we will take artistic creativity, the process by which an artwork is made, as the paradigm case—realizing, of course, that it may contain some features that are not present in any significant degree in other forms of what we accept as creative activity.[43]

Before turning to some general features of artistic creativity, let us look briefly at the idea of creative imagination—an idea with a long and rather checkered history.[44]

Unlike Plato, for whom the imagination was, on the one hand, centrally the power of forming images and therefore a debased kind of, or lowest form of, cognition and, on the other hand, the demonic power (especially of the poet) to conjure images that fuel the passions and displace rational activity, Aristotle understood this image-forming power to mediate sense experience and rational cognition.

> For imagination [*phantasia*] is different from either perceiving or discursive thinking, though it is not found without sensation, or judgment without it. That this activity is not the same kind of thinking as judgment is obvious. For imagining lies within our own power whenever we wish (e.g., we can call up a picture, as in the practice of mnemonics by the use of mental images), but in forming opinions we are not free: we cannot escape the alternative of falsehood or truth. Further, when we think something to be fearful

or threatening, emotion is immediately produced and so too with what is encouraging; but when we merely imagine we remain as unaffected as persons who are looking at a painting of some dreadful or encouraging scene.[45]

Francis Sparshott thus states that Aristotle defined imagination "as the ability to formulate, frame, and consider objects of sensation and cognition other than those directly anchored in the reality presented to the participant" and then notes that "The word 'fancy' comes from the Greek *phantasia*, which was used even in Latin as a sort of catch-all term for abilities and tendencies to envisage things as other than they are; the word 'imagination' was imported into the French and English languages at an early date from Latin, where as *imaginatio* it stood for various abilities and tendencies to manipulate or succumb to images and image-thinking, becoming especially popular as a technical term in rhetoric."[46]

As noted by Schiller and others, however, imagination may also be a kind of play, a free creative activity. The processes of nature as such, it is believed, are bound to governing laws and principles or to fortuitous happenings (random selection). Human creativity, on the other hand, is not necessary or random. The process has causes and reasons and it has limits, but, when genuine, the creativity is self-determining and thereby free.[47]

Through imagination (which is always informed by intellect and a certain affectivity) one structures experience, one articulates new relationships between things, one brings forth values, and thus by its very objective character it is bound to reality. Whenever imagination is free it enjoys an obedience to reality, a being influenced by it, a partaking of its essential character.

And, at the same time, it has its own subjective nature which is also reality-oriented, for without memory, as Aristotle and Augustine knew, there is no imagination. Imagination works in the present through the past directed to what is yet to be. It demands that one bring forth past intensities of experience, especially those which are rather useless for simply adapting to, or working in, the present, and that one unite them with a vividly ordered content.

Creative imagination, on the subjective (psychological) side, therefore, involves a full, active integration of the diverse mental and feeling capacities of a person. Drawing from the entire range of appropriated experience, the creative imagination of a person is a disciplined play directly involved with reality. Creative imagination thus differs both from the kind of fantasy making that, with its wish-fulfilling dynamic, is associated most strongly with the subwaking alone, and from the rather more ordinary imagination (imagining) which is part and parcel of what we call thinking. Fantasy making is self-enclosed; it does not go beyond its own subjective contents to provide insight into reality. And the imagination associated with thinking, while primarily relational in that it involves a person with his world, whether in a mode of calculating or planning (e.g., a trip) or of constructing (e.g., a theoretical model), draws its contents by and large from waking consciousness alone. There might indeed be various subliminal relating processes going on in ordinary imagining—as when struggling with a certain problem whose solution suddenly appears after the problem has been set aside—but these unions are fortuitous convergences of otherwise disparate functions. They are not, as in creative imagination, a full active integration.

Creative imagination is, then, a kind of synthetic unity of intuition and representation. It is, we might say, an "intentional synthesis": it aims to bring forth a presentation of reality. It is thus (quasi) nontemporal. Reaching over, as it were, into timelessness, it transcends the otherwise organic attentiveness to events that we find in ordinary waking consciousness. By being grounded in subwaking experience as well, it also partakes of a (quasi) atemporality—the subwaking's total unconcern with ordered change.

Also, as part and parcel of its drive to issue forth new meaning and value, creative imagination recognizes a lack, an incompleteness. Creativity, as we will shortly see in greater detail, always strives toward unique presentations of formed content. It calls for a nonegoistic openness, a loving sensitivity that at once celebrates reality, and, for the creative person, is a rejoicing in his own power of being.

One of the most striking features of artistic creativity (which I will hereafter use synonymously with the term "creative act") is what we might call its immanent purposiveness. Aiming at the fulfillment of only those ends that it itself defines and articulates, the creative act answers to no other guiding need or external *telos*. Its purpose is developed in the process itself, that is, a sense of rightness or appropriateness, within the context of the particular creative act, governs the artist's bringing his work to fulfillment or completion.

I have argued elsewhere that when art achieves autonomy, as it assuredly has in our age, the meaning of an artwork is not to be found as such in the conventional symbols it might employ or in an independently formulated series of concepts that it may be said or seen to embody, but that its meaning is inherent in the work. A work of art is meaningful, I argue, to the degree to which it realizes the possibilities that it itself gives rise to. This means the bringing of the artwork to an appropriate conclusion and exhibiting the process by which that conclusion is achieved.[48]

A poem, a play, a musical composition sets up conditions of expectation and anticipation that call for resolution and fulfillment. The progress toward this fulfillment—the process that is in fact exhibited—is not mechanical; the artist does not put down initial words, colors, sounds, with everything else then following inevitably from this initial placement, as a conclusion might from premises in a valid deductive argument; rather the appropriateness of a conclusion or consummation of the work depends on elements of surprise or novelty as well as on a sense of inevitability. The artist is himself often surprised by the development of his work, and sometimes appears—as Plato observed some time ago—the least able to explain what he is doing. If explanation calls for lawlike generalizations and prediction, then it is not difficult to understand the artist's ignorance. Anyone else's supposed knowledge would only be a gross pretension, for the creative process, by its very nature, does not aim at a fixed, predetermined end that can confidently be predicted, and does not admit entirely of relationships that can be generalized into nomic statements or universal rules. Rather it autogeneously defines itself; its purposiveness is precisely immanent to it.

For a work of art to have the kind of integrity—of wholeness and honest use of materials—that is appropriate to it, the creative act must involve what I call cooperative control. It is a rather fancy name for the fact that the creative act involves a noncalculative, intuitive, if you will, grasp of the structure, principles or syntax of a medium, be it of concrete materials or abstract symbols, so that the act is one of working with these principles and not one of exercising force over them. Any craftsman, from the woodcarver to the auto mechanic—and all artistic creativity is craft in one of its dimensions—realizes this need to be attuned to his medium in such a way that he *contributes to*, but does not *impose* an alien will *upon*, its natural rhythm or structure. This cooperative, in contrast to coercive, control is very difficult to analyze, but it is of considerable importance, I believe, in understanding creativity in relation to causation. One of the reasons the usual models of causation apply so poorly to creativity is because they ignore just this intimacy between the creative act and its object, the agent here being effective only insofar as he works *with* the potentialities of his medium in a profoundly sympathetic and understanding way. I can push a chair around the room with only a rudimentary knowledge of practical physics acquired by experience, but I can create a work of sculpture only by a highly disciplined understanding of how to work *with* stone.

In fulfilling the purposes which it itself articulates, the artwork, through the creative act, stands then as a joint effort of its creator and the given medium. It calls for a harmonious relationship, a special reverence, a loving concern, of artist for his material so that he may indeed bring to full articulation one of the many possibilities of that which is given to him.

But this is not to suggest some one-sided passivity or abject obedience on the part of the artist. The creative act is a kind of "letting be," but at the same time it is a shaping, a formative act, that involves expressive power. Together with immanent purposiveness and cooperative control, the creative act is an infusion of power, an imparting of a felt life or vitality; it is a making of that which is alive with the very spirit of natural-spiritual life. Yet the presence of power in creativity is not, as I understand it, so much an expression of a Nietzschean will to power—with its associate romantic emotion and sense of radical achievement—as it is a manifestation of a rhythmic force spontaneously exhibited. Life is rhythm, as the poet will tell us, and the creative act is just that act that grasps this rhythm —what the classical Chinese called "spirit resonance" (*ch'i-yun shêng-tung/qiyun sheng tong*)[49]—and manifests it as expressive power. Hume might well have exorcised all powers from (efficient) causation—but to do so for creativity would be to trivialize it and render it incomprehensible.

Closely related to the feature of power in creativity is that of form—its natural complement. What often distinguishes genuine creativity from those acts of self-expression enjoyed by the ardent young lover who writes what he is pleased to call poetry, or by the amateur painter who wants to share his pleasure of pretty landscapes with others, is just this arduous task of bringing the created object to its right conclusion through the achievement of form. By the term "form" in art we do not mean some kind of independently analyzable shape or structure, but rather that blending of content and structure that appears as inevitable. Form is the artwork as a realized end that establishes those relationships that are right for itself.

Creativity is formative. It is a making, a *technē*, which when wholly successful, results in a form that is radiant by virtue of the rightness of the relations articulated and the appropriateness of the feeling and insight achieved.

No two creative acts are ever exactly alike. Although it is assuredly the case that in some important sense no two human acts of any kind are ever exactly alike insofar as any act, no matter how routine, takes place at a given time and place with all its attendant particularities, in asserting the dissimilarity of creative acts we assert something much stronger than this; we assert that a special kind of uniqueness or singularity is one of the distinguishing features of this kind of activity.

Creativity *means*, at least descriptively from the standpoint of the creative actor, precisely that fusion of chance and determination that allows of no repetition. Constrained by all the limitations of one's character, of one's history and experience and capacities and talents, and yet having this history—and present moment of insight—available to one, is the non-repeatable opportunity that is at the very essence of the creative act. Creativity thus makes for unique objects. Works of art may be similar in many ways (style, genre, and so on, and especially when from the hand of the same artist), but it is always precisely *this* realization of form infused with power that interests us—and is in some way compelling for us.

Creativity, it has often been pointed out in both East and West, is a kind of play; in Sanskrit it is designated as *līlā*, that sportive act of the god who, in creating, admits of no purpose and whose activity is thus a spontaneous overflow of his own superabundant nature. "Play," however, does not mean a lack of seriousness or intensity; it means rather a kind of innocent, but not naïve, illusion making—an innovative and hence unexpected ordering and shaping. In creativity as play there is a felt voluntariness, which paradoxically perhaps is nevertheless felt as inwardly necessary, as something that is required to be done. Play, in short, is disciplined spontaneity. It is knowledgeable and insightful, but it answers to no formula. Spontaneity in creativity is not, on the other hand, an uninhibited exhibition of emotion or feeling; it is not impulsive, a blind response to the strongest force within one at the moment; it is rather a natural extension of that harmony or that subtle tension that is there as part and parcel of the creative act. Spontaneity, in other words, is utterly continuous with all other elements or features of the creative act. Creativity is a free, self-determining act; it is singular and unpredictable, and hence, in these terms, it defies usual causal explanation, but it is also disciplined and ordered and, in these terms, is amenable to intelligent understanding. The term "discipline" means ordering relations, through experience, to achieve just that rightness in relationship that is of the essence of form. Being formative the creative act is necessarily a controlling of a medium—in play.

We have so far distinguished immanent purposiveness, cooperative control, infused power, formativeness, uniqueness or singularity, and playfulness as special features of creativity. The last feature I should like to call attention to, one that has a peculiar relevance for the theme of creativity and causality, is the special transitivity or mutuality that seems to obtain between creativity and what is created. In creativity the creative agent does not simply remain untouched by his act, as we tend to believe an efficient cause is by its effect; rather creativity, perhaps more than any other activity, is self-formative as well as formative of an object. One is changed in the process of making; one discovers oneself (more actually than one expresses oneself) in the creative act; one achieves what Albert Hofstadter calls an articulation of self as well as of work, by and through the work itself. The relation, in short, that obtains between human creator and thing created is one of mutual conditioning. Something of oneself is carried over into the work, with the work, in the process of becoming what it then is, also influencing one's own being.

Creativity, then, is that activity whose end or purpose is realized as such only in the activity; that calls for a working with, rather than coercive control over, the principles or structure of a medium; that infuses a power or vitality and is thoroughly formative in nature; that gives rise through its own singularity to objects whose uniqueness is central to their definition; and that is a kind of play or disciplined spontaneity that goes in turn to influence or condition its agent.

III

As we have observed, most contemporary analyses of causality derive from, or at least take as their starting point, Hume's analysis and thus tend to be grounded in an empiricist-oriented ontology, with its discrete existences, occasions and Newtonian temporality. There have been, however (as we know but perhaps often forget), other ontologies proffered in philosophy (both in the East and the West) which have in turn guided the development of other theories of causality and have been especially important in determining the choice of paradigmatic cases of causation.

In Brahmanic Indian thought, for example, two main kinds of theories are often distinguished: *satkāryavāda*, the theory that the effect preexists in its cause, and is thus in some way identical to it; and *asatkāryavāda*, the theory that the effect is fundamentally different from its cause. *Satkāryavāda* is associated with the Sāṁkhya system, which advocates a *pariṇāmavāda* version of the theory, that the effect is a real transformation of the cause,[50] and also with Advaita Vedānta, which expounds a *vivartavāda* version of the theory, that the effect is only an apparent change, in reality there being only the cause, Brahman. The *asatkāryavāda* is associated with the Nyāya-Vaiśeṣika school and with some schools of Buddhist thought. The main concern of the Brahmanic theories is material causality, especially as related to cosmological concerns (the status of the material world in relation to reality). And, insofar as it deals with efficient causality, one of its main problems has to do with the universality of causality.

Whereas Western thought, at least since the eighteenth century, stresses the uniformity of causation (the same or similar causes yield the same or similar effects), allowing thereby for the establishing of laws of nature, Indian philosophy stresses the universality of causality (every event has a cause), making thereby the freedom that is sought and the liberation that is achieved through the realization of Brahman all the more precious and rare. At the risk of oversimplification we might say that Western thought, for the most part, wants to allow for freedom on the empirical level and accordingly is pleased to restrict the application of causality to events in nature; Indian philosophy wants to acknowledge the possibility of a complete freedom (*mokṣa*) and accordingly is pleased to limit the uniformity of causality to special cases.

When we turn to Buddhist thought we find an even greater stress placed on the importance of the idea of causality, and rather different ontological concerns. In the very earliest sermons Buddha is said to have insisted that the suffering (*duḥkha*) that characterizes existence can be understood in causal terms. The general formula of causality enunciated in Buddhism is:

Imasya sato, idam bhavati, imasya asato idaṃ na bhavati. Imasyotpadad idam utpa-dyate, imasya nirodhād idaṃ nirudhyati

> (When this is present, that comes to be;
>   from the arising of this, that arises.
> When this is absent, that does not come to be;
>   on the cessation of this, that ceases.)[51]

Although there is a great variety in the causal thinking of Buddhists, especially as between the early Sarvastivādins and Sautrāntikas and the later Mādhyamikas and Yogācārins, they tend to affirm this general empirical, conditionship type of analysis and uphold, as we have seen, some form of the doctrine known as *pratītyasamutpāda*—"dependent co-arising" or "conditioned origination." This doctrine distinguishes twelve interrelated causes, originating in ignorance (*avidyā*) and culminating in life's suffering. Edward Conze writes:

> The word 'conditioned' is said to mean 'where this is (or becomes) then that is (or becomes)'. This rule applies to all conditioned phenomena, and defines the relation between condition and conditioned. . . . It would be misleading to say that the cause is an active agent which does something to 'produce' or 'generate' the effect. In fact, apart from 'being there' it does nothing at all, and the effect arises in functional dependence upon the conditions.[52]

Conze goes on to remark that *pratītyasamutpāda* "makes clear to us that what we call our 'experience' or 'knowledge' of the world is in fact linked to ignorance, and that the total negation of ignorance . . . is the only way out of this welter of confusion."[53]

When we turn to traditional Chinese thought, on the other hand, we come upon a radically different conception of change and process, and of the nature of causality. "The Chinese word for change, *i*," we are told by Wing-tsit Chan, "also means 'easy' "[54]—and suggests a kind of natural spontaneity informing all processes. Chung-ying Cheng sums up the Chinese model of causality in these terms: "If we may say that the Western model of causality is characterized by the atomistic, the externalistic and the mechanistic principles, the Chinese counterpart is characterized by the holistic, the internalistic and organistic principles."[55] Further, "The purpose of investigation of things is not to seek laws governing individual relationships of things, but to understand individual orders in regard to and in reference to the whole."[56]

In short, in traditional Chinese thought (and here the Taoists and Confucianists share a common heritage) the processes of nature are seen as organic wholes grounded in an ordered, natural-spiritual reality. Causation is fundamentally a description of what *is* in its dynamic interdependent development.

Georg Henrik von Wright, on the other hand, in his *Causality and Determinism*, is extremely modest in his ontological claims. He does not believe that he is in a position to articulate features of reality directly and states accordingly that it is "legitimate to ask which requirements the *facts* (the world) must satisfy in order that there shall exist a *concept*, roughly at least like ours, of nomic causation."[57] He concludes that on this basis "the world must to some degree approximate to the model of logical atomism."[58]

But suppose we follow a somewhat different path and ask what model of experience is most in accord with our understanding of creativity and with the facts of our experience, and then from this model derive our concept of causality. Rather than starting with "our notion of nomic causation" and asking what the world must be like to satisfy that concept, we start with an account of experience and see what concept of causality is best in accord with it.

We start then with perception. And we may meet the issue directly by asking, Do we actually perceive mere states of affairs and atomic events or do we experience processes, event patterns structured into organized wholes to which, for a variety of reasons, we assign beginnings and ends? Although it is not possible to elaborate here a theory of perception, it should be noted that differing psychologies of perception (gestalt, genetic) do seem to agree that our basic experience of the empirical world is an active, purposive engagement with dynamic structural unities; what we perceive, as we have previously noted, are processes and not simply things frozen in space and time. We do, of course, mark off from continuous changes those aspects that are of special interest to us and regard them as relatively isolable. We do not experience the world as a Bergsonian pure *dureé*; rather we see things and events as distinct insofar as they allow for individuality, for being identifiable ontically as particulars; and it is this kind or measure of individuality rather than Humean "distinct existences" that is the stuff of our experience. Let us look at this a bit further.

J. L. Mackie argues that distinct existences are indeed required for the meaning of causality. "For this purpose [of saying what causal statements mean]," he writes, "it is sufficient to say that someone will not be willing to say that X caused Y unless he regards X and Y as distinct existences."[59] Now if all Mackie means by "distinct existences" is that we recognize that a change has occurred in a manner that calls for our recognizing an event and other consequences taking place, then this is trivially true; in order for the claim to be of any philosophic interest his meaning must be stronger ontically and, as with von Wright, involve at least a model of the world as reducible to atomic events of the sort that can only enter into external relations as entities that are otherwise self-defined. But this account of experience neglects the fact that events are histories. What we experience are not events corresponding to (atemporal) logical entities, but events having their own direction and aim, or what might be called their normality.

By the normality of an event or process I mean its aiming to be what is natural and appropriate to it. The normality of a process is the "direction" it takes, not spatially so much as ontically; we conceive of a process as tending toward some state that is native to it. Normality, however, does not imply a final cause or even a teleological view as such. It means only that all that we perceive as process has for us, in virtue of our experience, a normal state or becoming of its being. Normality is the principle that unites the continuity of a process with what the particular process is.

What makes for the specific normality of any given process is for the sciences and other modes of inquiry to determine (the normality of a billiard ball in motion with its particular velocity and direction may be articulated by explanatory concepts of physics, perhaps even adequately for some purposes by classical mechanics); it is enough for us to acknowledge it conceptually. The reality of normality, however, is borne out by our understanding of creativity as well as by the apparent facts of perceptual experience. We saw in our discussion of cooperative control and immanent purposiveness how a creative act develops its purpose in the very process of making the artwork, that is, it does not have a fixed, predetermined end but one that emerges in the activity through the artist's sense of rightness. This rightness, we argued, was related to the nature of integrity and accordingly, to the idea of cooperative control. The creative act is with and through a medium; it demands that the artist work with the inherent structure or rhythm—the material and spiritual potentialities—of his medium. Creativity is par excellence a process of altering and bringing to realization potential normalities. As paradigmatic for an analysis of causality, creativity is that process that controls, through active, intelligent participation, the principles of a medium so as to establish an aiming of those elements which it selects, organizes, and controls.

This understanding of creativity provides a major clue, I believe, to a meaning of causality that is commensurate with the facts of our experience. We conceive of an alteration in states of affairs or events as either disrupting a present, relatively achieved state (e.g., an inanimate object at rest, whose aim is precisely to be at rest), or inhibiting the fulfillment of the natural course of an event (or, as the case may be, of preserving through counteracting force, a given state of affairs), or bringing it to a fulfillment (e.g., as when caring for—watering, trimming—a plant). Disrupting, inhibiting, and bringing to fulfillment imply an otherwise normality—what the process is in its essential character as the process that it is. As A. Michotte has pointed out,

> Psychologists of the Gestalt school (Wertheimer Köhler, Duncker, and others) have emphasized that, when certain processes are in course of taking place, they "require" to be continued in a definite way. If they are halted, or if their direction suddenly changes, this produces a feeling of deception, surprise, or displeasure. This can be seen in particular in the case of rhythmic series, melodies, the shape of the path traversed by an object, and even in the case of a simple, fairly rapid movement when the object in motion suddenly ceases to move. Conversely, when the process is continued without interruption, the result seems satisfying or normal; it seems to develop "according to plan." The same no doubt also applies to the experience of causality; and this is probably one of the characters which differentiates it in such a clear way from a simple impact in which the moving object comes to a halt. It is difficult, however to see here a genuine necessity; it is rather an "invitation," and an invitation is neither an obligation nor a decree of fate.[60]

The meaning of causation (at least as given to us initially in single-case experience)[61] is, I argue, bound up with the concept of normality. *An event A is a cause of another event (or object) B if and only if, among all other conditions present, relevant and necessary, A alters the normality of B so as to disrupt, bring to a fulfillment that would not otherwise obtain, or inhibit that normality.*

Mary throws a stone through a closed window shattering the glass. The thrown stone, the causal event, alters radically the normality of the closed window, and the causal meaning of the thrown stone is found precisely in this interference. The determination that the thrown stone is the cause, the verification of causality, might very well be had only by an analysis of conditionship relations (daylight, Mary's arm being in the right condition for throwing a stone of a certain weight, etc.) and involve the assertion of an appropriate counterfactual conditional that will ensure that the glass would not have been shattered if Mary had not thrown the stone; but the meaning of the event, as causal, is found in the radical alteration of the window's normality.

John turns on the heat under the pot of water and brings it to a boil. The boiling water is a disruption in the accepted field of normality. The heating, tested as cause, involves the counterfactual belief that the situation would have remained as it was, the water not boiling, except for the extraordinary presence of the heat.

Henry is driving along in his automobile but is suddenly disturbed by unusual sounds in the engine. He brings his car home and examines it closely, seeking to find a way to eliminate the unwanted noise. He cleans the points and then discovers that the car now drives smoothly and noiselessly. The event of cleaning is the cause of the car now running properly (just as the dirty points may be said to be the cause of the noise); the cleaning brings to a fulfillment that would not otherwise obtain in the circumstances the normality of the engine to run smoothly and noiselessly.

H. L. A. Hart and A. M. Honoré in their interesting work *Causation in the Law* write,

> So we cause one thing to move by striking it with another, glass to break by throwing stones, injuries by blows, things to get hot by putting them in fires. Here the notions of cause and effect come together with the notion of means to ends and of producing one thing by another. Cases of this exceedingly simple type are not only those where the expressions cause and effect have their most obvious application; they are also paradigms for the causal language used of very different types of cases.[62]

They go on to say,

> Human action in the simple cases, where we produce some described effect by the manipulation of an object of our environment, is an interference in the natural course of events which *makes a difference* in the way these develop. . . . Commonsense experience teaches us that, left to themselves, the things we manipulate, since they have a 'nature' or characteristic way of behaving, would persist in states or exhibit changes different from those which we have learnt to bring about in them by our manipulation. The notion that a cause is essentially something which interferes with or intervenes in the course of events which would normally take place, is central to the commonsense concept of cause, and is at least as essential as the notions of invariable or constant sequence so much stressed by Mill and Hume.[63]

Von Wright has, I believe correctly noted, "The confidence which I have that the water in the kettle would have boiled if heated is a confidence in the difference which the presence of a cause would have made to the prevailing situation. . . . Confidence of the latter kind presupposes confidence of the former kind, that is: confidence in the effects of causes (nomic connections) presuppose confidence in the causeless continuation of certain normal states of affairs."[64]

We assign priority to the sense of cause that is based on experience, then, as this sense is precisely what is involved in our usual concern with "what is the cause of" questions. Nomic generalization is experientially derivative. We know about normalities and their alterations in experience before we know the laws of nature qua laws. A young child knows what to expect when he throws a ball against the wall without his knowing the laws of trajectory and impact.[65] Also laws are not themselves causes. In the example of the boiling water, the "law" that certain liquids will boil when brought to certain temperatures is not the cause of the water's boiling; rather it expresses only the structure of normality of a given process.

P. T. Geach is thus able to write correctly that, "scientists do not describe natural events in terms of what always happens. Rather certain natural agents . . . are brought into the description, and we are told what behavior is proper to this set of bodies in these circumstances. If such behavior is not realized, the scientist looks for a new, interfering agent."[66]

Causal events of alteration (interference, inhibition, etc.) of normality as such are thus always single-case—that is, it is always a particular interference that takes place, albeit some single-case situations may be seen and explained as instances of causal uniformity or of nomic generalization. The particularity needs, I believe, to be part and parcel of our meaning of cause for this reason: a causal relation obtaining between events implies determinations that are never exactly repeatable. It may very well be that for certain kinds of physical events the factor of particularity is rather unimportant in seeking the cause(s) of certain phenomena (e.g., in medical science the search for the cause(s) of a disease is carried out with little, if any, importance attached to the fact that it is Tom or Alice or whoever, with their special physical particularities, that is suffering from the disease), yet the dimension of particularity seems evident for the meaning of causality. (Even in modern medical science there is a growing awareness that it is not enough to see a patient as merely an instance of a disease, but rather as a particular organism, whose particularity must holistically be addressed.)[67]

The idea of causation as interference with a given normality also allows us to appreciate the mutuality that often clearly obtains in cause-effect relationships—that is, the effect in turn affecting the cause or the cause simply being affected by its being a cause. Many causal relations in our experience (especially in the domain of human action) are potentially symmetrical in the sense that my doing something (talking to someone in a certain way) in turn gives rise to activities directed toward me, which affect me in a variety of ways. And all causes as events suffer some consequences of their actions as causes. Events, we have said, are histories, not logical entities. In actual experience an event occurs in a context of processes, which is to say that events do not just take place, appearing as it were out of a void, as self-sufficient, self-defined things; they occur in structures of, and are subject to, continuous change. The stone thrown into the glass window is not the same stone it was before; it too is affected by the impact. The thrown stone as event has its own little history.

This mutuality, which is exhibited to a preeminent degree in creativity, where the very being of the artist is conditioned by his act, is also becoming increasingly apparent in technology with the advent of many self-regulating (feedback) systems. Contemporary technology in many ways seems to be working from more organic models as it moves away from simple, unidirectional mechanical ones. Interdependence with intertwining histories—mutuality—become the key features of both animate and inanimate processes. This brings us to freedom in relation to causality.

IV

Most contemporary discussions of freedom vis à vis causality have taken place in the context of the so-called free will-determinism controversy. We feel ourselves to be free, to be able to do otherwise than we did, and morality (and especially legal ascriptions of responsibility) demands this freedom; and yet experience seems to support the universality of causal laws, of determinism, which means that all human as well as strictly physical behavior, in principle, is predictable.

The arguments for and against determinism and free will have, it would seem, been rather exhaustively treated by now. In the main, as it is often pointed out, the determinist faces a challenge as to the status of his own principle. That every event is causally determined so that it could not have been otherwise than it is or was is not itself something that is or can be empirically demonstrated. It suffers from overgenerality, allowing nothing to disprove it. The principle has a certain charm of simplicity, and it may be an important heuristic device of scientific inquiry, but it is not itself amenable to proof or disproof. The libertarian, on the other hand, when he frames his position as an outright denial of determinism—that is, when he asserts that there are events and actions that are not causally determined—faces the criticism (by a Hobart or an Ayer) that an event or activity so defined is not so much free as it is random or chaotic.

The recognition of these (and many other more subtle) difficulties led many philosophers to embrace a reconciliationist position (a "soft determinism") that argues that freedom and determinism are entirely compatible when freedom is understood to mean being able to act without external constraint according to one's character, and causal law or determinism to involve only a description of what does happen (regularly) and not a prescription of what must happen (necessarily). On this account causal determination, as we have seen, in no way compels a particular event to occur, it only describes observable regularities. Compulsion, it is believed, implies a tension between having to obey a law and being otherwise inclined. But, as Moritz Schlick says, "The laws of celestial mechanics do not prescribe to planets how they have to move, as though the planets would actually like to move quite otherwise, and are only forced by those burdensome laws of Kepler to move in orderly paths; no, these laws do not in any way 'compel' the planets, but express only what in fact planets do."[68] Similarly psychological laws, "are not civic laws, which compel [a person] to make certain decisions, or dictate desires to him, which he would in fact prefer not to have. They are laws of nature, merely expressing which decisions he *actually has* under given conditions."[69]

Therefore, having one's actions (or desires or motives) be caused in a lawful manner does not, according to reconciliationism, inhibit freedom; rather it becomes a necessary condition for its realization. Without determinism an agent could not control her behavior so as to act without external constraint. She could not exert the kind of power or initiative whereby her intentions are realized unless she acted in a lawful way in a lawful world.

Libertarian opponents of reconciliationism (e.g., C. A. Campbell) have, however, strongly argued that the reconciliationist solution (or dissolution of the free will-determinism conflict) does not really address itself to the crucial (moral) issue of freedom and responsibility. The reconciliationist accepts that moral responsibility is something real, but he does not accept the commonsense understanding that if a man is to be morally blameworthy he must enjoy "a freedom of a kind not compatible with unbroken causal continuity."[70] A person must always be in a position, if she is to be held morally responsible, to have been able to do otherwise than she did, while having precisely the character that she has. In those instances when a person carries on a struggle between her strongest desires or inclinations (according to her character) and her sense of moral duty, we have free will most clearly exhibited.

"We *can* meaningfully talk," Campbell therefore insists, "of an act as the self's act even though, in an important sense, it is not an expression of the self's character."[71] This act of the self, according to Campbell, is of a creative kind.

R. E. Hobart finds this "character within a self" view unintelligible, if not self-contradictory. Hobart writes,

> Indeterminism maintains that we need not be impelled to action by our wishes, that our active will need not be determined by them. Motives "incline without necessitating." We choose amongst the ideas of action

before us, but need not choose solely according to the attraction of desire, in however wide a sense that word is used. Our inmost self may rise up in its autonomy and moral dignity, independently of motives, and register its sovereign decree.

Now, *in so far* as this "interposition of the self" is undetermined, the act is not *its* act, it does not issue from any concrete continuing self; it is born at the moment, of nothing, hence it expresses no quality; it bursts into being from no source. The self does not register its decree, for the decree is not the product of just that "*it*." The self does not rise up in *its* moral dignity, for dignity is the quality of an enduring being, influencing its actions, and therefore expressed by them, and that would be determination.[72]

But is it not the case that empiricist-positivist reconciliationism in its own terms never really advances a positive notion of freedom, but rather simply confounds liberty and freedom? Being able to act without external constraint is precisely what we mean by liberty, but unless one has set for oneself one's own character and has the power to alter it we certainly do not have freedom. It is a peculiar feature of the reconciliationist position that one could be under constant inner compulsion (e.g., an obsessional gambler, a sex maniac) and still be free.[73] The positivist and Freudian centers of Vienna never seemed to have met.

More important for our discussion here, however, is the reconciliationist's view (in its positivistic mode) of causal determination. Schlick, as we have seen, argues that the laws of nature do not compel, as do civic laws; they only describe. But once inherent power or necessity is taken away from the concept of nomic causality, it is extremely difficult, as we have noted, to understand what is lawlike about descriptive regularities. The paradigm sense of law (and early scientific understanding was in accord with this) involves governance. A law of gravity, it was believed, did indeed compel objects to behave in certain predictable ways. It is a linguistic confusion to try to have the majesty of law carry over to descriptions of what does happen (in regular ways).

"Psychological laws," Schlick says, "describe the nature of the will in the same manner as the astronomical laws describe the nature of planets." But do they? Indeed, are there any such psychological laws which describe the nature of the will? Even on the positivistic understanding of law, laws of nature (astronomical laws) involve universalizability and predictability. We have considerable confidence that once we have the law we can, with amazing accuracy, tell what will happen next, before it has happened, and that under similar conditions it will happen again. Science demands repeatability—at least in principle, if not always in fact. But except perhaps in a few gross cases (you will always resent someone who is torturing you) nothing like the needed universality and predictability seems available with the will. In actual human experience there is very little indeed that testifies to the idea that X or Y (or just X at different times) will perform the same or similar acts or have the same or similar desires, motives, feelings, under the same or similar circumstances so that we can predict with any happy degree of specificity and certainty what X or Y will in fact do or say or feel. There might indeed be laws of perception, but psychological laws that describe the nature of the will do not seem to be readily forthcoming.

Now just as the meaning of causality need not be bound to traditional philosophical notions based on classical mechanics, so a conception of freedom need not be based on ideas of having a free will in relation to causally ordered (determined) events. Especially since the social sciences have increasingly shown how our behavior and our attitudes, beliefs and values are conditioned by (and subject to manipulation through) social as well as strictly environmental factors, it is imperative that we frame a richer sense of freedom that is related to the achievement of personhood. If most (or even a considerable amount) of the time our desires and activities are highly conditioned by forces that resist our immediate control or (if psychoanalytic theory is at all correct) even our awareness, then the fundamental problem of freedom is one of how, in the face of conditioning, is it possible to attain autonomy or genuine self-determination.

To be conditioned as a human being is to have one's being set for one, without creative initiative. To behave in a conditioned manner is to act entirely in terms of the conditions of one's being and one's environment. It is to act not as a person but, like things that are only products, merely as an individual. Agent-causality, as alteration of normality, is absent, which is to say, with conditioned events self-initiated processes of change have not occurred.[74] "To be able to choose otherwise than I chose" or "to be able to do otherwise than I did" is not, however, the central consideration in the problem of freedom, at least not until the issue of one's character is settled. If I cannot control or determine the general structure of my desires, thoughts and beliefs, then to be able to act in accord with them or with alternative ones within the same matrix is not a very significant freedom—or achievement. A more significant freedom, as I have already suggested, would have to do, then, initially with freedom of consciousness, rather than of will, and would have its locus in the person. I am free when I am able to attend to reality, and from that attendance to achieve rightness of action. I am free when I am able to realize the Self and become the person I ought to be. I am free in my actions (and choices), then, only when I am not bound in consciousness to a static, conditioned structure of habits and dispositions.

With this sense of freedom, we have, at the theoretical level, the possibility of a new kind of reconciliation between causality and freedom, a new compatibilist position; for without causation (understood as alteration of normality) there could be no freedom. From being conditioned to being autonomous calls for a disciplined realization of a person's being and her potentiality—what she essentially is, her spontaneity, and what she actually is, her conditioned individuality.

Causality, then, is compatible with freedom and does not imply determinism at all. From our understanding of causality, determinism would mean that everything is or acts only according to its given normality. Hobbes (who liked to think that this was a state of liberty) speaks of it as "the absence of all the impediments to action that are not contained in the nature and intrinsical quality of the agent." But this kind of activity, this determinism, although perhaps lawful, is not causative in the primary sense, which, as I have argued, is that of alteration of normality.

We have said that a person acts freely, and that one is free when one is able to attend to reality and from that attendance to achieve rightness of action. Freedom can thus become a quality inherent in an action itself as well as in the actor, or, to put it more accurately, freedom is an achievement that is always embodied as a quality of an action.

To act freely means, I think, *to act skillfully in fulfillment of the natural grace manifest in every action-related process and thereby to attain an effortless power.* To act freely is to express the achievement of personhood; it is to be fully self-expressive as a social being in action.

In order to act freely the actor must know the how and what of the action-related process so that he can perform the action, not by mere rule or method, but unselfconsciously and correctly. Skill in action means having a mastery of the appropriate technique associated with a particular kind of doing—from walking to painting a picture—in such a way that one is able to carry out the action without concerned awareness of its being carried out as such. Lacking skill, one gets calculatively involved with one's act. Incessantly making conscious decisions with respect to the act, one gets caught up in it and loses thereby that necessary attentiveness to the larger context within which the act occurs.

Skill in action, then, requires a spontaneity that is causally efficacious. The actor must be a master of the conditions of his actions, which means that he must be a master of himself. The spontaneity related to acting freely, therefore, is to be sharply distinguished from impulsiveness. Spontaneity is grounded in the deepest structures of one's being and is, accordingly, a nonegoistic expression of one's spiritual potentiality. Impulsiveness, on the other hand, is groundless. It works from the strongest force within one at the moment. It is willful and uncontrolled. Setting aside (rather than rightly integrating, disciplining and thereby transforming and transcending) our usual psychic complexity allows us nothing more than an uninhibited display of instinctual force. Instead of enlightened sensitivity, we have, with impulsiveness, a tactless outburst of crude emotion. What supposedly has been set aside has got its full revenge.

Actions that are skillful, which are performed with spontaneity, are also expressive of a loving care and concern that they be performed rightly. In every action-related process there is, I believe, a natural rhythm and inherent order that is appropriate to it. We may call this the "natural grace" in an action-related process—"natural," for it is precisely what is most native to a process; "grace," for it offers itself, as it were, for realization in action. The natural grace of a process is that controlling rhythm or informing vitality that defines a process in its particularity. Every process—from mere walking to the most intricate dance—has its own law or way, if you will, of being right for itself, and is actualized in varying degrees and ways (appropriate to the conditions of the particular actor) in each concrete instantiation of the process. When acting freely the actor takes on that controlling rhythm as his own and easefully creates his action in accord with it. A new rhythm is thus established that is right for the process-cum-actor (in his full particularity). In other words, the natural grace that is achieved is what is entirely appropriate for the action as performed by a particular actor. In action that is free, natural grace is given a specific concrete form. The natural grace manifest in, for example, a young person's dancing will be exhibited (created) concretely in a way different from that of an older person. Each person dancing may have a rightness appropriate to his action in virtue of its grounding in the natural grace of the process as this is given articulation in the particular circumstances that obtain.

We may thus speak of this realization of natural grace in much the same way we speak of artistic creativity—as the autochthonous ordering of elements under a controlling sense of rightness that results in the achievement of what, when the work is successful, appears to be inevitable. Unlike supposedly causal necessity of a logical kind (given A, then B), where an effect must or will invariably follow from a set of conditions, or logical necessity of a strictly formal kind (if A > B, and B > C, then . . .), where a given outcome cannot be other than it is under the rules of the system game, aesthetic necessity does not dictate a particular result or correct answer or solution; rather it functions (in Kantian language) as the ground for the possibility of a particular form to appear as inevitable—to be what it should be, with the should, the ought, being dynamically internal to the particular process according to its own individual conditions. There is no one (aesthetically) right way of doing anything that can be divorced from the actual ways in which right actions get performed.

Further, as with artworks, actions that are free involve a timing and spacing that is right for them. When acting freely the actor controls the raw materials of temporality and spatiality in such a way that each articulation (each movement, pause, sequence, pattern) becomes a necessary, organic part of the action qua action. A free action is properly timed and spaced; it involves an articulate temporality and spatiality that is a direct expression of the realization of the natural grace exhibited in the action-related process. It will thus be obedient to what is called for by the situation and it will reflect wholly the rhythm of the actor's own achieved persona.

The actor, in his or her skillful, spontaneous, rightly articulated action, thereby achieves and experiences a power in action, a power that is effortless—that is, it is achieved as a natural expression of that harmony and accord between actor and act, and not as something striven for, wrenched from, or otherwise imposed on the action. The power is *anarchia*; it is not for something other than itself.

Acting freely, then, means to act in such a way that nonegoistically one is able, with knowledge and insight, to act in accord with the natural grace present in an action-related process and to achieve a skillful, rightly timed and spaced action which expresses the natural power of the actor-action. Freedom, therefore, as applied to action, is a style or quality of acting; it is integral to the act, part and parcel of its being.

Acting freely is thus a kind of creative play. It is the acting out of one's achieved personhood. When acting freely the actor is most fully himself as the owner of his act. It belongs to him in virtue of its being the most natural expression of his nature.

There is no incompatibility between being a person qua persona and being and acting freely. On the contrary, it is only when the mask fits rightly—with that detachment and creativity essential for the formation of genuine personas—that the quality of freedom can be realized. This is the case because it is only in creative play that freedom as a quality of being and acting is realizable. Earnest striving is ego-bound, and actions thus get performed with obsessive concern for their results. With the absence of creative play the actor is taken over by the demands of his nature and the conditions of his action; he does not properly belong to himself. With creative play, the actor is owner of himself, being aware of the very ground of its formation, and is thereby expressive of his own being. And he thereby becomes fully responsible for his actions.

V

In sum, I have proposed that instead of taking as paradigmatic for the meaning of causality those everyday events that seem to lend themselves nicely to explanation by mechanistic causal accounts (billiard balls hitting one another, matches being ignited), we start with one of the most complex forms of human experience, creativity; and that we seek to understand that experience as far as we can in its own terms and then apply that understanding back to the question of the meaning of causality. We want, in short, to see if an understanding of creativity can enrich our understanding of causality.

We saw that creativity, as exemplified in the making of an artwork, may be characterized as that activity whose end or purpose is realized as such only in the activity; as that which calls for a working with, rather than a coercive control over, the principles or structure of a medium; as that which infuses a power or vitality and is thoroughly formative in nature; as that which gives rise through its own singularity to objects whose uniqueness is central to their definition; and as that which is a kind of play or disciplined spontaneity which goes in turn to influence or condition its agent.

In answering the question of what concept of causality best accords with the nature of creativity and the nature of experience, we found, first of all, that the notion of process must take precedence over atomic events as the content of experience. The term "process" means that events are histories; that we experience events not as corresponding to atemporal logical entities but as having their own direction and aim—their normality. A process tends in its normality toward some state appropriate to it. Causation may then be seen as an alteration of that normality. We are concerned with everyday causal explanation when an alteration occurs in what we take to be the normality of a process. Thus causal events are single-case; it is always a particular interference that takes place, although this particularity (to which insufficient attention on the whole has been paid in analyses of causality), while denying strict repeatability, does not rule out universality. When causality is understood in terms of this organic model (which itself seems more closely in accord with the self-regulating systems of contemporary science and technology) the mutuality of cause and effect, the event as a history, also becomes evident.

The meaning of causality, then, as related to creativity and our ordinary experience, is to be found in an alteration of the normality of a process. While the normality of a specific process might call for nomic categories, the meaning of (single-cased) causality nevertheless may be kept distinct from questions of what constitutes the general structure of normality.

With this understanding of causality, the problem then becomes not so much a question of free will versus determinism, but how to achieve a freedom of consciousness (in the face of various forms of conditioning) that allows for our being able to act freely. And here a new kind of reconciliationist or capatibilist position arises, for causality—when understood as alteration of normality does not imply determinism but is required, rather, for the realization of freedom. It makes acting freely possible.

To act freely, we have suggested, means to act spontaneously in accord with the natural grace inherent in the normality of every action-related process so that the act is performed rightly in its concrete particularity and is genuinely owned by the actor, it being the fullest expression of his achieved personhood.

NOTES

1. Georg Henrik von Wright, *Causality and Determinism* (New York: Columbia University Press, 1974), 13.

2. Ibid., 17. Von Wright believes that the concept of causal necessity, which is required to distinguish nomic from accidental regularities, is intelligible only with reference to counterfactual conditionality; and that the latter in turn makes sense only when seen in relation to a concept of action. "When saying that p is a causally sufficient condition of q, we are not saying *only* that, as a matter of fact, whenever p obtains, q obtains too. We also claim that on all occasions in the past, when p did in fact *not* obtain, q would *have* obtained, *had* p obtained on those occasions. Only if the proposition that p is a sufficient condition of q warrants the truth of the counterfactual conditional proposition in question, does the conditionship relation here amount to a causal relation" (18). He goes on later to ask, "Can a singular counterfactual conditional statement ever be verified?" and says: "In order to verify it, we should have to substitute for a state which obtained at a certain stage in the world's history another state which did not obtain at that very stage. In any straightforward sense of 'verification' this is certainly not possible" (37–38). He then says, "This implies that, although we cannot interfere with the past and make it different from what it *was*, we may be able to interfere with the future and make it different from what it otherwise *would be*. It is on this possibility, viz. of interfering with the 'normal' course of nature, that the possibility of distinguishing the nomic from the accidental ultimately rests. The clue to an understanding of the epistemic problem here thus lies in the logical peculiarities of the concept of an action" (39).

3. See Vincent Tomas, "Creativity in Art," *The Philosophical Review* 67, no. 1 (January 1958), and Monroe C. Beardsley, "On the Creation of Art," *The Journal of Aesthetics and Art Criticism* 23, no. 3 (1965).

4. To turn oneself over to "pure sensation" might be to experience a radical becoming that knows nothing of regularity—anything would seem capable of following upon anything else. This rather perverse dissociation of sense and intellect, this Rimbaudian derangement, is certainly not without possible aesthetic value; but its complete achievement would undoubtedly be—or at least quickly lead to—a form of madness.

5. W. R. Dennes, "Causation as Continuity and Production," in *Causality*, University of California Publications in Philosophy, vol. 15 (Berkeley: University of California Press, 1932), 164.

6. Richard Taylor, *Action and Purpose* (Englewood Cliffs, N.J.: Prentice-Hall, 1966), 21–22.

7. Von Wright, *Causality and Determinism*, 48. A. E. Taylor, in 1903, also noted that "the origin of this notion [of the power of the cause] is sufficiently obvious. . . . The 'activity' of the cause results from the ascription to it of the characteristic feeling of self-assertion and self-expression which accompanies our own voluntary interference in the cause of events." (*Elements of Metaphysics*, 169–70.)

8. Jean Piaget, *The Child's Conception of Physical Causality*, trans. Marjorie Gabain (Paterson, N.J.: Littlefield, Adams, 1975), 126.

9. Ibid., 128.

10. Taylor, *Action and Purpose*, 11.

11. Ibid., 14.

12. Ibid., 10.

13. Curt John Ducasse, *Causation and the Types of Necessity* (1924; reprint New York: Dover, 1969), 201.

14. Tom J. Beauchamp, ed., *Philosophical Problems of Causation* (Encino and Belmont, Calif.: Dickenson, 1974), 201.

15. Moritz Schlick, "Causality in Everyday Life and in Recent Science," in *Causality*, 110.

16. Taylor, *Action and Purpose*, 16.

17. A. E. Taylor, *Aristotle*, rev. ed. (New York: Dover, 1955), 50.

18. Ibid., 52.

19. Taylor, *Action and Purpose*, 11.

20. A. J. Ayer, "What is a Law of Nature?" in Beauchamp, *Philosophical Problems of Causation*, 83.

21. J. L. Mackie, *The Cement of the Universe: A Study of Causation* (Oxford: Clarendon Press, 1974), 12–13.

22. Ibid., 13.

23. Ibid., 28.

24. Ibid., 229.

25. Richard Taylor, "Causation," in *The Encyclopedia of Philosophy*, ed. Paul Edwards, vol. 2 (New York: Macmillan and The Free Press, 1967), 63.

26. Von Wright, *Causality and Determinism*, 10.

27. Ibid., 10–11.

28. Ibid., 29.

29. Ibid., 32.

30. Mackie, *Cement of the Universe*, 160.

31. Taylor, *Action and Purpose*, 11.

32. Mackie, *Cement of the Universe*, 161.

33. Ibid.

34. Von Wright, *Causality and Determinism*, 63.

35. See Taylor, "Causation," 65.

36. See Spinoza's *Ethics*, app., pt. 1.

37. Mackie, *Cement of the Universe*, 35.

38. Hilary Putnam, *The Many Faces of Realism* (LaSalle, Ill.: Open Court, 1987), 37–38.

39. Bertrand Russell, "On the Notion of Cause," Proceedings of the Aristotelian Society 13 (1912–13). Russell's problem here is partly a result of his own confusion

in speaking about causality as a law. At one point he says: "I am not concerned as yet to consider whether this law is true or false. For the present, I am merely concerned to discover what the law of causality is supposed to be." But whatever else causality is, it is not itself a law, albeit it may serve heuristically in any scientific pursuit for the "laws of nature." In other words, causality is a principle in whose terms laws might be expressed, without being a law itself.

A. E. Taylor made the point clear in these terms: "regarded as a universal principle of scientific procedure, the causal assumption must be pronounced to be neither an axiom nor an empirical truth but a *postulate*, in the strict sense of the word, i.e., an assumption which cannot be logically justified, but is made because of its practical value." (*Elements of Metaphysics*, 167.)

40. Taylor, "Causation," 56–57.

41. Plato, *Timeaus*, trans. Francis MacDonald, in *Plato's Cosmology* (London: Routledge & Kegan Paul, 1937), 33.

42. It is interesting to consider how a theory of creativity, as indeed a cosmology, might be developed if, as feminist thinkers have urged, we were to take the experience of procreation rather than "big bang" situations as paradigmatic. The fundamental relationship between "creator" and "created" would, with procreation, perhaps be seen more in intimate (nurturing) terms than in those of separation and distance, with mutuality between the creative process and what is produced rather than radical difference being stressed.

43. Also, the model of creativity we are putting forth is not, of course, intended to be universal in the sense that it could serve as an adequate description of all forms and kinds of artistic creativity. The various materials used in the different arts, the diverse styles and techniques that are part and parcel of the history of art, East and West, the differing social standings of artists and their relations to peers, indeed the manifold ends and purposes to which art has been put and commissioned, preclude the possibility of any such adequate description. Nevertheless it is expected that the main features isolated for analysis in a model of creativity do have bearing upon the rich diversity of what we call art; that they apply to our understanding of what a work of art is (descriptively and prescriptively) in terms of the process of its coming to be.

44. See Eva T. H. Brann's 810-page volume *The World of the Imagination: Sum and Substance* (Lanham, Md.: Rowman & Littlefield Publishers, 1991) for an elaborate treatment of the imagination, especially in its image-making modality. See also, Mark Johnson's brief and philosophically sophisticated account of the history of the idea in his *The Body in the Mind: The Bodily Basis of Meaning, Imagination, and Reason* (Chicago and London: The University of Chicago Press, 1987), chapter 6, "Towards a Theory of the Imagination."

45. Aristotle, *De Anima*, Bk. III: Ch. 3, trans. by J. A. Smith in *The Basic Works of Aristotle*, ed. Richard McKeon (New York: Random House, 1941).

46. Francis Sparshott, "Imagination—The Very Idea," *Journal of Aesthetics and Art Criticism*, vol. 48, no. 1 (winter 1990): 21.

47. Anthony Kenny writes: "By 'imagination' there are many things which we can mean. Let us begin by considering the imagination in the sense simply of the ability to call up mental images. . . . The imagination, in this sense, is a power that

is generally shared by members of the human race. There is another sense of the word in which imagination is a much less evenly distributed faculty. The ability to imagine the world different in significant ways; the ability to conjecture, hypothesize, invent—this is a different form of imagination, creative imagination, possessed *par excellence* by persons such as poets, story-tellers, and scientists of genius."(*The Metaphysics of Mind* [Oxford and New York: Oxford University Press, 1992], 113.)

48. See chapter one of my *On Truth: An Ontological Theory* (Honolulu: University Press of Hawaii, 1979).

49. This is the first of the famous six canons of classical Chinese painting as set down by Hsieh Ho/Xie He in the fifth century.

50. Mario Bunge, in his interesting work *Causality: The Place of the Causal Principle in Modern Science* (Cambridge: Harvard University Press, 1959), states his belief that the *satkāryavāda* of Sāṃkhya rules out any novelty in experience (205). But *satkāryavāda* does not say that only one specifiable effect is preexistent in its cause; it says only that the effect as given is so preexistent. Further it is arguable whether *satkāryavāda* has to do with ordinary empirical causation at all; it might rather have to do only with the unfolding of certain cosmic principles (*tattvas*). See Gerald J. Larson, "The Notion of *satkārya* in Sāṃkhya: Toward a Philosophical Reconstruction," *Philosophy East and West* 25, no. 1 (January 1975): 31–40.

51. See David J. Kalupahana, *Causality: The Central Philosophy of Buddhism* (Honolulu: University Press of Hawaii, 1975), 90.

52. Edward Conze, *Buddhist Thought in India* (London: George Allen & Unwin, 1962), 149.

53. Ibid., 156.

54. Wing-tsit Chan, *A Source Book of Chinese Philosophy* (Princeton: Princeton University Press, 1963), 263.

55. Chung-ying Cheng, "Model of Causality in Chinese Philosophy: A Comparative Study," *Philosophy East and West* 26, no. 1 (January 1976): 13.

56. Ibid., 14.

57. Von Wright, *Causality and Determinism*, 55.

58. Ibid.

59. Mackie, *Cement of the Universe*, 32.

60. A. Michotte, *The Perception of Causality* (London: Methuen, 1963), 261.

61. When we speak of single-case causality we do not mean that every happening (event) has a singular, identifiable cause as such, for it is obvious that not infrequently we have what Michael Scriven refers to as "compound causes" of the sort that "we need to bring about not only C but also D in order to get E (and that D is not sufficient)" "Defects of the Necessary Condition Analysis of Causation," in *Causation and Conditionals*, edited by Ernest Sosa (Oxford: Oxford University Press, 1975), 45.

62. H. L. A. Hart and A. M. Honoré, *Causation in the Law* (Oxford: Clarendon Press, 1959), 27.

63. Ibid.

64. Von Wright, *Causality and Determinism*, 43.

65. As G. E. M. Anscombe has rightly noted, "we often know a cause without

knowing whether there is an exceptionless generalization of the kind envisaged or whether there is a necessity." "Causality and Determination," in Sosa, *Causation and Conditionals*, 61. Further, "If A comes from B, this does not imply that every A-like thing comes from every B-like thing." (Ibid., 67.)

Donald Davidson has also remarked that "There is an important difference between explaining the fact that there was *an* explosion in the broom closet and explaining the occurrence of *the* explosion in the broom closet. Explanation of the second sort touches the particular event as closely as language can ever touch any particular. "Causal Relation," in ibid., 94.

66. As quoted in Mackie, *Cement of the Universe*, 75.

67. As C. J. Ducasse has noted: "the supposition of recurrence is wholly irrelevant to the meaning of cause; that supposition is relevant only to the meaning of law. And recurrence becomes relevant at all to causation only when a law is considered which happens to be a generalization of facts themselves individually causal to begin with. . . . The causal relation is essentially a relation between concrete individual events; and it is only so far as these events exhibit likeness to others, and can therefore be grouped with them into kinds, that it is possible to pass from individual causal facts to causal laws. "On the Nature and the Observability of the Causal Relation," in Sosa, *Causation and Conditionals*, 118–19.

In his discussion here Ducasse does go on to allow that "we are interested in causes and effects primarily for practical purposes, and that for such purposes causal knowledge is of direct value only so far as it has been generalized." Still, "although it is true that, as practical beings, we are not directly interested in concrete individual facts of causation [except, he should have added, when it comes to ascribing responsibility and recognizing freedom], it is not true that there are no such facts; nor . . . is it true that generality or recurrence is any part of the meaning of cause" (124).

The denial of strict repeatability in favor of particularity for the understanding of cause, in short, does not rule out universality. It is quite possible, and indeed necessary, that we recognize causal regularities in experience without having to ascribe a sameness to the particular events that constitute the regularities. The law of gravity may happily obtain even though one could never again drop the same object under identical conditions. Strict nonrepeatability and universality are logically independent.

68. Moritz Schlick, "When Is a Man Responsible?" in *Problems of Ethics*, trans. David Rynin (New York: Prentice-Hall, 1939), 147.

69. Ibid.

70. C. A. Campbell, "Is 'Freewill' a Pseudo-Problem?" *Mind* 60, no. 240 (October 1951): 446–465.

71. Ibid.

72. R. E. Hobart, "Free Will as Involving Determination and Inconceivable Without It," *Mind* 63, no. 169 (January 1934): 1–27.

73. "Freedom," writes Schlick, "means the opposite of compulsion; a man is *free* if he does not act under *compulsion*, and he is compelled or unfree when he is hindered from without in the realization of his natural desires" (Schlick, "When Is a Man Responsible?" 150).

74. Most of the time, most of us, however, do enjoy a relative freedom or voluntariness in our actions, the most convincing proof of which is perhaps to be found in our awareness, at various times, that we are acting under compulsion, that we are victims, as it were, of ourselves. We would not have this awareness if, in our various actions, we were completely unfree, that is, always subject to compulsion or impulsiveness. *It is our (occasional) awareness of bondage which provides us with a warrant for believing in our relative freedom.*

PART IV

14

✳

A Creative Morality

I

Personhood and freedom are values for us just insofar as they are in fact desired, sought for, and striven after, whether consciously or not. Personhood and freedom are not, however, absolute or ultimate values, nor can their being as (intrinsic) values be justified as such.

First of all, one of the basic understandings in a creative morality is that there are no absolute or ultimate values that are knowable by reason or are available to sense experience or are otherwise given through some kind of revelation. This is the case not because of any inherent limitations of our reason, of our senses or of our spirituality, and not because of any metaethical difficulties we might have in making sense of what an absolute or ultimate value would be but because of the character of reality, of the Self, to be a surpassing value—one that lays bare the pretension to ultimacy in any rational, empirical or revealed value scheme. With the Self all other values are ultimately empty. Reality knows nothing of our good and evil.

It is often thought that what must follow from the view that there are no absolute values or principles of conduct written into the nature of things is either nihilism (no values can be meaningful or possible) or some form of existentialism (all values must be made ex nihilo by radical choice and commitment)—but this conclusion, I think, would be a mistake. What does follow from the experiential reality of the Self as a surpassing value is the necessity for a morality that is fully aware of the Self or reality as its metaphysical ground and thereby of its own creative character that needs be brought into harmony with that ground. A creative morality lays stress on the capability of a person to realize spontaneously his or her social nature, to develop what is appropriate morally in concrete situations, to recognize that one's actions are one's own, and therefore to assume responsibility for them—in short, to incarnate the values of personhood and freedom.

Second, certain kinds of justificatory value-asking questions have the peculiarity of not being able, as it were, to get outside of themselves. If one asks, Why ought I to value personhood and freedom? a prior commitment of a sort has already been made to these values. It is like asking, Why should I be a rational being? You must already be rational before you can ask for, respond to, or even recognize something as being a reason for something or other. Any answer to Why ought I to value personhood and freedom? would have to appeal to just what is supposedly being questioned. You must already be something of a person, have achieved some measure of personhood, before you can see—or question—its value.

In any event, a creative morality is concerned with personhood and freedom as values and recognizes that these values, while lacking ultimacy, are nevertheless intrinsic, and not instrumental to the securing of something else.

Like traditional systems of normative ethics, however, a creative morality must also address itself to certain basic moral questions or ethical problematics. Apart from the fundamental value question, What ought I to value? or What is the good? it must attend to: (1) How ought I to judge my own and other's actions? or What is right? (2) What ought I to do (in X situation)? or How can I realize the good in right action? and (3) How should I be with others? or What mode or manner of social being is right for me?

The basic concerns of a creative morality will be with these (interconnected) normative problematics. It will, as well, have obvious implications for metaethics—the analysis of the meaning of such primary ethical terms as "good" and "right" and of the nature of moral reasoning and its justification, and so on—and in any event it will presuppose, and indicate a justification for, certain metaethical commitments.

II

Since at least the Middle Ages normative ethical theory has tended to the other extreme from the early Greek tendency to regard good actions simply as those which are performed by a good or noble man, and it has thus tended to neglect (and with classical utilitarianism to the point of eliminating) the actor in favor of (praising or condemning, enjoining or prohibiting) the type of action that is performed. Even the deontologists, with their (one-sided) attention to the motives and intentions of the actor, have as the primary object of judgment what is done as such, albeit judged by criteria of duty, the good will and the like. That X did or did not do Y is what stands before the moral tribunal. In a creative morality of persons we have a different situation.

To begin with, we need, I think, to do in ethics what we often do in aesthetics and that is to distinguish between subject matter and formed content. In a work of art, say a Cézanne landscape such as "La Montagne Sainte-Victoire," we have a subject matter—what the painting represents—the landscape as landscape and the particular one referred to, with its mountain and trees and house. The subject matter of an artwork (insofar as it has one) is external, as it were, to the particular work; it is what the work is *about*. In a work of art we also have an aesthetic or formed content—just the specific landscape, rendered as it is in its different tones of blue, orange, green, that is presented in the particular painting and existing only in the painting. The formed content of a work of art is its unique aesthetic realization of its own internal relations. The subject matter of a work of art is its *representation* of something or other; the formed content is the aesthetic *presentation* of the work itself.

Similarly with an action. The subject matter of an act is what the act is about, its what, its referential meaning or locutionary stuff; it is that about an action that allows it to be classified into a type—for example, an act of murder, of theft, of helping a blind person across the street, of divorce, or of generosity. Although often it is not easy to get full agreement on the proper identification of an act—especially in cross-cultural situations (try to convince a man in a society that practices the ritual eating of human beings that he is committing an act of cannibalism rather than, as he would see it, a taking on of the strength of his enemy slain in battle), for so often our descriptions of actions are thoroughly value-laden—nevertheless, at least within a given sociocultural matrix, usually there will be widespread agreement on how to identify actions as being of certain sorts.

Now one of the peculiarities of moral judgment is that it is properly directed to subject matter alone only when the judgment is negative. As I will show later in greater detail, this is the case simply because no identification of an act as being of a certain kind can guarantee its having a positive moral value. An act of generosity, for example, can arise from a mean motive which infects the manner in which the act is carried out, and it can also, quite apart from motive or intent, lead to disastrous consequences. It would only be when a complete description of an act coincided with its identification (i.e., if by the word "generosity" we meant an act performed in a certain way with a certain motive and intent that yielded certain consequences) that a positive moral judgment could be directed to its subject matter. But descriptions of actions seldom, if ever, coincide with their identifications.[1] On the other hand, whole ranges of action can properly be condemned (once they are correctly identified) as being antithetical to, incompatible with, or contradictory to the values of personhood and freedom. Acts of exploitation, of oppression and senseless violence are ruled out of possessing intrinsic moral value. They are condemned in virtue of the kinds of acts that they are. And here there is, if not universal, at least near unanimous agreement among the various moral codes of humankind.

With the negative moral judgment of what I would like, following previous usage, to call the exclusionary kind, which is directed to the subject matter of an act, it makes no difference who is doing Y; it is the doing of Y as such that is condemned.

The formed content of an action, as I use the term, is just the concrete, particular action that takes place in its full specificity as the unique occurrence that it is. And here the actor or agent can never (except by artificial abstraction) be separated or divorced from her act. The formed content of an action, in other words, is not isolable from the person performing the act: the formed content of an action is a person doing something or other in just the way that it is done.

Moral judgment proper, which assesses by way of discerning the relative moral worth of an act, is directed to the formed content of an act; it is directed to someone-doing-something, to an X-doing, and not to an agent isolated from her act or to an act taking place apart from someone in a certain situation who is doing it. Moral judgment proper, in short, is directed to the person-in-her-act, not to *what* is done in abstraction from a concrete doing. Although it may properly be directed just to the subject matter of an act (as an exclusionary judgment), negative moral judgment can, of course, also be directed to the formed content of an act, to an X-doing (something badly). By the expression "moral judgment proper" I mean the whole range of judgment of actors cum actions in their specificity.

A person, in contrast to an individual, is (albeit is not exhausted by) the way she acts. She does not claim to stand apart from—and thus be able to disown—her actions; rather she acknowledges them as her own and thus accepts full responsibility for them. A person, in contrast to an individual, welcomes moral judgment, for such judgment is an acknowledgment of her personhood and freedom.

In a creative morality of persons, moral judgment directed to formed content is a judgment of the degree to which the values of personhood and freedom are promoted, exhibited, and embodied in the act. It is to the quality of the actor cum action that moral judgment is directed. Moral judgment proper looks to discern to what extent an action is performed nonegoistically, in openness to being and to the being of others; it looks to discern the degree of skill, of disciplined spontaneity, of effortless power that is embodied in the act; it looks for the measure of personhood and freedom that is achieved in the act and its consequences. And from this kind of looking it is evident that all actions have a moral dimension.

One of the most difficult problems for much ethical theory is to delimit or mark off ethical actions—actions with ethical content—from other kinds of actions. One often hears that actions, like that of opening a door, are devoid of ethical concern while various kinds of intersubjective personal relations have obvious ethical significance. But, when moral judgment proper is understood to be directed to the formed content of an action and to be a discernment of the relative degree of personhood and freedom that is embodied therein and extended thereby, then clearly there is no need to arbitrarily mark off a special area of action for moral judgment. Moral judgment can be directed to all actions—and thereby itself contribute to the growth of human freedom and responsibility.[2]

Let us now look a little more closely at the actual process of moral judgment. From what I have indicated so far, it is clear that moral judgment involves a kind of two-stage process. First there is the admittance of the actor cum action into the arena of judgment proper in virtue of the action as such—its subject matter is properly identified and is not antithetical to, or incompatible with, the values of personhood and freedom. If an action of a certain kind incites moral indignation in us we exclude the action from the court of moral judgment proper. And we do this, not simply willy-nilly nor by the strict application of a rule or principle, but by a close attendance to whatever facts are available to us. The first-stage judgments are, then, as objective as any judgments can be. If we see (are convinced that we see) an act of wanton cruelty taking place—for example a teenage gang taunting and beating an old man—we quite properly respond with indignation. We see the act as violative of personhood.

Exclusionary moral judgment tells us, then, that it is wrong to commit certain kinds of acts—that it is morally evil to commit acts of torture, of humiliation, and so on.[3] In human experience, however, the most difficult moral choices are usually not between clear-cut cases of the morally good (or, in our terms, between those acts which have the potentiality for realizing positive moral value) and the morally evil (those which are utterly violative of the values of personhood and freedom) but between cases perceived to be of conflicting good or of conflicting evil. The former are quite commonplace (e.g., should I help X friend or Y friend, both of whom need my help, my own resources and energy being such that I can help only one), but they do not usually shake one to the moral roots, as it were; the latter, the choosing between conflicting evils, do involve the most difficult decisions we make. It sometimes happens that one is confronted with situations in which it seems that one must choose between two or more wrong courses of action—only if the terrorist is tortured will he reveal where the bomb has been placed that could destroy thousands of lives. To torture the terrorist, it is often said, is a necessary evil. But what is of special interest here is that the justification employed (that of preventing the loss of thousands of lives; or as it would probably be described, that of saving thousands of innocent persons) never deprives, if you will, the act of torture from being an evil act. With exclusionary judgment no justification on other (moral or prudential) grounds denies the inherent awfulness of the act or the responsibility that the actor bears for his act. One might indeed argue that it was necessary to choose between torturing one person and letting thousands of persons be killed—and I suppose most people would agree that it was the right thing to do to torture the terrorist—but an act has nevertheless been committed that could not possibly have an inherent moral value.

When acts do pass the exclusionary test, however, we then have moral judgment proper, which a creative morality understands to be the discernment of the relative achievement of personhood and freedom embodied in the act. This attendance to the formed content of the act requires a keen sensitivity to the inherent features of the particular actor-act in its total situation. I use the term "sensitivity" rather than the term "moral sense" to make clear that this function is first of all not a special faculty of the mind that we are said to possess as part of our native mental equipment, and secondly that it is not the approval vouchsafed by this activity as such that constitutes the moral quality of the act.[4] The moral-sense philosophers (Shaftesbury, Hutchenson and, to a considerable extent, Hume) believed that certain feeling sympathies (namely of benevolence, which was to inform moral judgment) were, in their words, a product of nature alone; that everyone was endowed with them as a given of being human. Moral sensitivity, as I understand it, is certainly not artificial; but it is nevertheless something that is cultivated and is achieved, like personhood itself, in varying degrees. Moral sensitivity is like aesthetic sensitivity; it is a full openness to the unique presentation of an action—that is, to its formed content. It is a recognition—informed by knowledge and understanding—of the qualitative achievement of an actor cum action. Unlike the case with the moral sense, then, one's approval of an act consists not in the fact that it arouses a certain required response but in one's recognition of those features that are indeed inherent in the act. Moral sensitivity discerns an actor cum action qua the loving care informing the action and the skill, the disciplined spontaneity, that it exhibits. It looks, as we said before, to the total situation. Informed by a knowledge, as best one can acquire it, of reasons and consequences, it looks, in other words, to agency as it enters into the promotion of the values of personhood and freedom.

With positive moral judgment or moral judgment proper, involving the full play of the judger's moral sensitivity, then, we do not have a simple good-bad, right-wrong dichotomous situation; we have, rather, something more subtle—we have a discernment of degrees of moral rightness; we have judgments of moral value in terms of the relative success or failure that an action exhibits vis-à-vis its realization and promotion of personhood and freedom. Just as with works of art, some action contents are richer than others, that is, some actions realize personhood and freedom in better ways than others. Just as artists rarely succeed in bringing forth masterpieces (and indeed often issue outright failures), so actors rarely succeed in performing consummate moral acts. Indeed most of the time most of us are rather awkward; we stumble along, and we deserve the relative praise and blame accorded to us.

This brings us to the important distinction that needs to be made between moral *pronouncement* and moral *discernment*. So far I have emphasized the discernment of the relative value of actions (the degree to which the values of personhood and freedom are embodied and promoted in specific actions) and not the judgment of actions as (relatively) good or bad as such. The pronouncement of relative goodness and badness (the ascription of evaluative predicates) is, of course, a common affair. Too often, though, in everyday discourse as well as in normative ethics as such, moral pronouncement is based not on the moral discernment of the formed content of an action but on its subject matter, and we then get a considerable amount of hollow moralizing. When based on moral discernment, however, moral pronouncement may serve various functions. It can provide a summing up of, and bring a certain completion to, moral discernment as such; it can strengthen one's disposition to act in certain ways and to notice certain features of actions; it can provide justification for other actions (e.g, of punishment and reward) that may have to be taken. Moral pronouncement and moral discernment, nevertheless, are sometimes empirically incommensurate and are always logically separable. With our example of torturing the terrorist, as I have said, there is no way in which a positive moral value can be discerned in the specific act of someone torturing someone else, yet it is quite possible that the judgment of the act qua moral pronouncement would not be one of condemnation. The torturer might, as we have noted before, be excused for his act on the grounds that it served a higher good, or at the very least that it was a necessary evil. What might be regarded as the morally right thing to do qua pronouncement may be incapable of having an inherent positive moral value qua discernment. These cases are the stuff of tragedy, for however he chooses and acts the actor suffers guilt and degradation.

The judgments of these cases and of our ordinary, everyday pedestrian actions, I would argue, are indeed cognitively meaningful. In contrast to

emotivists and prescriptivists—to noncognitivists in general—I maintain
that ethical discourse does something more than express a private attitude that is uttered in order to influence, guide, commend or command
someone; it gives what we might call moral information, or at least it is
meant to. In short, the moral, I believe, is delivered directly in experience.

John Searle formulated the is-ought problem of Hume—the position,
that is, to which Searle himself was opposed—in these terms: "No set of
statements of fact by themselves entails any statement of value. Put in
more contemporary terminology, no set of *descriptive* statements can
entail an evaluative statement without the addition of at least one evaluative premise."[5] In other words, evaluative predicates cannot be incorporated into statements that follow logically as conclusions from premises
which are only factual. "To believe otherwise is to commit what has been
called the naturalistic fallacy."[6] Hume's is-ought problem is instructive
regarding the nature of ethical discourse—for the whole issue rests, it
seems to me, on a serious mistake, namely (and I suppose this derives
directly out of the classical empiricist's sharp distinction between impressions and ideas) that the perception of something is carried out essentially
in bare factual terms, that the perception of objects and actions is essentially of their physical, behavioral qualities. Genuine seeing, however, as
I have indicated before, is not a matter of noticing only physical qualities
as such or receiving (to use the more passive terms of empiricism) concrete bits of sense data; it is, rather, throughout value-discerning and
value-discriminating. When I see other persons (and even various objects
in my environment) I do not just see certain shapes and sizes, colors and
forms. I see meaningfully the embodiments of various qualitative achievements as well. When I see an action occurring, I do not just see a piece of
brute behavior that I describe in mere reportorial, physicalist terms. I see,
rather, the action as it expresses, embodies, and exhibits qualities of both
an aesthetic and ethical kind. When ethical qualities are present in a situation—for example, kindness or considerateness—they are observed as
such and are as factual a part of that situation as anything can be. When
I see that an action is performed with loving care and concern, I can quite
properly utter ethical statements about what is going on. The statements
do express my attitude toward what is going on, but they also do more
than that—they communicate (i.e, give and receive information regarding) ethical qualities and values. One can, I believe, agree wholeheartedly
with W. David Ross when he says, "What we *express* when we call an
object good is our attitude towards it, but what we *mean* is something
about the object itself and not about our attitude towards it. When we call
an object good we are commending it, but to commend it is not to say that
we are commending it, but to say that it has a certain character, which we
think it would have whether we are commending it or not."[7]

Once again, noticing a parallel with the aesthetic might be useful. When an art critic, if he is a good one, describes a painting, he aims at once to express his critical judgment of it and to point out various of its features in order that others might (better) see it. He mixes together aesthetic concepts (the composition is harmonious, the lines are delicate) with the physically factual (the earth is rendered in purple) and the symbolically meaningful (the skull on the table signifies human mortality). He intends to have us share—and learn from—the close, sensitive attention he has brought to the object. Good ethical discourse, we might say, likewise functions to enable others to see better what indeed is there to be seen. But just as there are no nonaesthetic features of an artwork, the mere calling attention to which will engender an aesthetic response, so there are no simple, nonmoral features of an ethical situation the mere noticing of which will call forth an appropriate ethical response. The justification of moral judgments, in short, comes about as one succeeds in awakening another person to see. And the best that one can do when two moral judgments conflict is to discern, as best one can, which judge, which moral critic, best succeeds in enabling us to see what is there to be seen.

As one sees and judges so one is and becomes. Moral judgment is as much a direct exhibition of one's own achieved moral sensitivity as it is an engaged discernment of the achieved value of an action. And as with all engagements one is very much influenced by the what and how of one's performance—that is, moral judgment is itself a kind of action insofar as in a creative morality of persons the judger is a participant and not a spectator (ideal or otherwise); one actively engages the situation in virtue of one's attentiveness, openness and commitment to take responsibility for one's judgment. The judge acknowledge his discernment (and pronouncement) as his own and willingly accepts the consequences of his judgment, such as they may be, for his own future action.

This leads us to the problem of the universalizability of ethical judgments. J. L. Mackie (following R. M. Hare) has allowed that "moral judgments are universalizable. Anyone who says, meaning it, that a certain action (or person, or state of affairs, etc.) is morally right or wrong, good or bad . . . is thereby committed to taking the same view about any other relevantly similar action."[8] But if the right or the good is not so much something that is aimed at, or possessed by, actions of a certain type but is rather what is embodied in them as inherent qualities of their performance, then it would seem—as I have indicated before—that no action is good in itself apart from the conditions and circumstances of its concrete performance. The only moral judgments that are strictly universalizable (as part of the very logic of moral judgments) are the exclusionary ones—those that are properly directed to subject matter alone. If Y action is prohibited—that is, correctly prohibited by the criteria of personhood and freedom—then, quite obviously, all other actions of the same type are prohibited (unless, of course, there is an overriding ethical consideration regarding personhood and freedom that could properly be invoked). But this does not apply to moral judgment proper—judgments based on a discernment of the relative freedom embodied in an action. In terms of formed content no two actions are ever exactly the same (and seldom are they relevantly similar)—and not just in the trivial formal or numerical sense that they occur in different space-times. Although different actions may have many features in common, each is performed precisely in its own way.

This lack of universalizability does not mean that positive moral judgments are private or idiosyncratic. We do, as a matter of fact, get considerable agreement in our moral judgments (precisely as we do with aesthetic ones), but we get this agreement not because we employ some kind of common method of ethical reasoning whose acceptance is justified with the same force as that of formal logic but because moral sensitivity is developed along similar lines in persons and we can recognize in a public way, as it were, those moral qualities which are possessed by actors cum actions. It is, I believe, quite enough that positive moral judgments are shared without their having to be universalized.

III

A moral actor, or in older terminology a "good man," is not a specialist in morality; he does not have a hold on, is not an expert in, a special branch of knowledge or body of truths called moral. Nor does he possess a specially tuned intellect that gives him a privileged ability to reason to correct moral conclusions concerning what ought to be done. A moral actor does not require expertise in deductive logic in order to know what to do in X situation. A moral actor, according to a creative morality, incarnates the moral as part and parcel of his achieved personhood.

What ought I do (in X situation)? We already know something of the answer by way of exclusionary judgment. To the degree to which we are persons, we naturally refrain from actions that are contrary to the values of personhood and freedom. A developed person is simply not inclined to acts that are destructive of personhood and freedom. This does not mean that such acts might not nevertheless be performed out of ignorance. Aristotle, we know, was prepared to excuse actions undertaken out of ignorance, when the ignorance itself was not chosen, as it were, by the actor. Often with the best intentions, as it is said, actions occur that have devastating consequences. We are disposed to blame someone for these actions only when the person was careless in examining the situation, in attending to possible consequences, and so on. In other words, we do not ordinarily blame a person for doing something that he would never dream of doing if he were aware of certain facts, and if he made every reasonable effort to secure the facts but failed to do so—for instance, insulting a host in a foreign country through ignorance of certain unstated customs.

What, then, ought I to do (in X situation)? According to a creative morality of persons there is no rule or principle or categorical imperative that can tell one what to do and thereby guarantee a positive moral quality, yet there are prima facie duties and obligations. These duties and obligations are of considerable importance, especially as they function as rules in the educative process of social maturation. The general moral codes of humankind have resulted from the experience of many generations and must always be accorded careful consideration. Nevertheless, these rules or principles of conduct cannot, I would insist, be invoked in a way that will ensure a positive moral value to an action. They behave rather as general guidelines to the actions of a person; they are not meant to make moral automatons out of individuals.

Moral rules or imperatives (the thou shalts and shalt nots), then, serve different functions (and thus have different logical forms) relative to the stages of moral development of human actors. For someone who is not already committed to a moral life or for someone who, although committed, lacks sufficient knowledge or intelligence to know even how to begin, moral rules (insofar as they specify modes of conduct in accord with moral sensitivity) function properly as *commands*. They prescribe behavior in the most literal and direct way—and are required (justified) to establish rights and thereby to sustain a social order that is needed by all. For someone, on the other hand, who has committed himself to a moral life and possesses adequate knowledge and intelligence, moral rules function more as *guides* than as commands. Like a traveler who correctly believes that he is on the right road but frequently checks the signs to confirm that he has not made a wrong turn, the morally committed actor measures his progress by the posted rules or norms. Rather than prescribe the way for him, they describe his action. They are prescriptive only insofar as one is uncertain how to proceed. And for someone who has no reason even to question but that one is on the right road, moral rules function entirely as *verifiers*. They neither prescribe his way nor describe his action; insofar as he notices them at all they confirm his achievement. When one travels on a very familiar road one does not even know (or care) where the signs are. They are quite irrelevant.

Creativity in morality is thus not some kind of intuitionist grasp of ethical principles apart from their involvement in specific actions. It is not a seeing into any kind of preexistent rule or principle; it is rather a close attendance to the demands of a situation in its uniqueness and the doing of that which, as best it can be determined, embodies and promotes personhood and freedom.

We have said "as best it can be determined"—for it is the case that an ethical situation is never or hardly ever fully known. All actions involve agency—and one can only surmise possible consequences in limited ways. The criterion for judgment of consequences is not, however, a utilitarian one (of maximizing a general happiness); it is rather the more feasible one of looking to see the appropriateness of likely consequences to the fundamental purpose of the act (i.e., consistency of consequences and purpose); the suitability of chosen means with desired consequences (commensurability of means and ends); and most important, of course, the coherence of likely consequences with the basic values of personhood and freedom. A person does what he believes will best embody and promote personhood and freedom—and that is, I believe, quite sufficient. A further word, though, about the function of knowledge.

The moral actor is at once knowledgeable and spontaneous. One is knowledgeable insofar as one comprehends the total situation one is involved in; one is spontaneous insofar as one is creative in one's response to it. The knowledge that informs one's sensitivity is not the same thing as that which results from deliberation over principles; it concentrates rather on the immediate situation, assessing motives and consequences, and so on. We deliberate about what to do only when we are unable to be creative, to exercise fully our imagination. The moral actor relies on his ability, informed by the best available knowing of the situation, to create the right thing to do in the right manner of doing.[9]

This spontaneity, however, is not a disguised appeal to a general principle of conscience. Spontaneity is situational; it is a sensitivity to what is demanded by, and is at stake in, a particular context; it is not a reliance upon an innate sense of what is right or wrong in the abstract or upon an internalized, superego-like assimilation of an imposed rule. Spontaneity means a nonegoistic, disinterested openness: it is a direct expression of one's achieved personhood.

It is here that one must be especially careful—for the possibility of self-deception arises so readily. If one is to rely upon one's moral sensitivity and creative imagination one must be assured, as best one can, that one is genuinely open to the situation and not bound by a compelling ego need.

But then—granted this danger—one can always ask, What could be more reliable in morality than the creative imagination, allied with moral sensitivity, of someone striving for personhood and freedom? The answer, I would think, is obviously that there is nothing more reliable.

No ought, in the Kantian sense, has proved sufficient or adequate to deal with the limitless range of human actions. No specific moral acts in the richness of their content can be prescribed in advance of, or independently of, the concrete situations of human experience. Those of us who are not fully developed persons often fail to see creatively what needs to be done in a particular situation. But this inadequacy is simply a fact of life; the threat of it and of the omnipresent possibility of self-deception constitutes, one might say, the drama of the moral life.

This leads to a consideration of the so-called problem of inevitable choosing. "You choose to act or you choose not to act; in either case you make a choice"—so it is said about situations where one finds oneself confronted, for example, with someone attacking another person or with someone drowning who could possibly be saved or with someone injured in an accident and requiring immediate help. Existentialists once made much of this necessity to choose, and the need for one to bear full responsibility for one's choice. And indeed the need for inevitable choosing seems part of contemporary folk wisdom.

We often, though (and rightly most of us believe), resent having imposed upon us moral choices such as, instead of reading a book or going for a walk you should be struggling to alleviate the suffering of the poor and starving. We refuse to accept this kind of inevitable choosing, for we do not recognize it as part of our own situation, as something determined by ourselves; not having assimilated it as our own, we do not think it reasonable to be confronted at every moment of our lives with having to choose between our own possible (work and leisure) satisfactions and self-sacrificing actions. We try to avoid the inevitable choosing our moral imposer would place upon us by refusing to acknowledge its force or reality.

We do seem, however, to have a different matter with those situations in which one finds oneself immediately and directly confronted with either acting or not acting (i.e., evading doing certain things), for here the imposition is not something entertained as a mere possibility but is confronted as a pressing actuality. It seems impossible to avoid helping someone who is being attacked without in fact choosing to evade taking certain actions. But let us suppose that, as in the other cases of moral impositions, one refuses to accept the situation as one of inevitable choosing, that one brackets the alternatives which appear to be exhaustive (rushing to intervene and save the victim of the attack or turning away) while recognizing the situation as such (i.e., the attack as taking place), with this bracketing then opening the way for one to see other possible responses that are entirely in accord with who one is. The bracketing allows one to assimilate the situation of inevitable choosing as one's own rather than as something simply imposed on one and thus allows one the opportunity to exercise one's creative imagination (e.g., I might be able to present myself in a nonviolent way that alters the terms of the situation). If the imagination fails, then one is simply cast back on the horns of the dilemma, which is where one began.

The important point, though, is that even in extreme situations where immediate decisions seem to be imperative, creative imagination still has an important and indeed crucial role. We certainly do not, in these situations, engage in moral reasoning, seeking to find the right thing to do as a deduction from some general rule or principle. Most of the time most of us would act impulsively; we ought, I am suggesting, to act spontaneously.

Thus, a creative morality of persons—especially in contrast to traditional normative systems—is liberating. Kurt Baier, in his *The Moral Point of View: A Rational Basis of Ethics*, states that "it is an outstanding characteristic of morality that it demands substantial sacrifices." Morality arises for Baier out of conflicts between inclination and duty. One of "the fundamental questions of ethics," he asserts, is "should anyone do what is right when doing so is not to his advantage and if so why?"[10] A creative morality of persons would start at the point where such conflicts have been overcome by virtue of one's finding the moral to be the most natural expression of one's being with others. It calls for, and constantly reinforces, both the acknowledgment of the ownership of one's acts and one's acting with the full dignity and measure of one's achieved personhood.

NOTES

1. We are, of course, predisposed to commend certain actions in virtue of their value-laden (subject matter) identifications even though we lack their complete description—for example, an act of heroism. The important point still holds, however, that no identification of an act as being of a certain kind can ensure its having a positive moral value unless that identification conveys an accurate description of a particular actor acting in a certain manner in a certain context (with its consequences). What may be called an act of heroism—an unselfish sacrifice of oneself for someone else or for some cause—might nevertheless wreak consequential havoc (re the values of personhood and freedom) and would not have been carried out by an actor who paid due respect to the likely consequences of her act.

2. This, of course, does not imply that all moral judgments are of the same weight, or that all actions carry the same degree of moral consideration. This is obviously not the case in ordinary experience and need not be the case for a creative morality. From the assertion that all actions have contents subject to moral discernment, it does not follow that one is unable to discriminate between the important and the rather insignificant in human doings.

3. With exclusionary acts it is necessary to stress again the problem of their

proper identification. The identification of acts qua their subject matter is always, as we have indicated, value-laden. To call an act of premeditated killing "murder" rather than "a contribution to solving the population problem" reflects certain prior value commitments regarding human life, and these values are not universal. No doubt one would always like to have one's primary values be universal; and when one feels confident enough about them one does not hesitate to measure another person's or another culture's values against them; yet the empirical fact remains that differences between primary values may always be present and influence fundamentally the way in which various acts are identified.

4. Hume, for example, writes, "Any action, or sentiment, or character, is virtuous or vicious; Why? because its view causes a pleasure or uneasiness of a particular kind. In giving a reason, therefore, for the pleasure or uneasiness, we sufficiently explain the vice or virtue. To have the sense of virtue is nothing but to *feel* a satisfaction of a particular kind from the contemplation of a character. The very *feeling* constitutes our praise or admiration" (*Treatise*, 3.1.2).

5. John Searle, in *The Is/Ought Question*, ed. W. D. Hudson (London: Macmillan, 1965), 120.

6. Ibid.

7. W. David Ross, *Foundations of Ethics* (Oxford: Clarendon Press, 1939), 255.

8. J. L. Mackie, *Ethics: Inventing Right and Wrong* (Harmondsworth, England: Penguin, 1977), 83.

9. A creative morality that tries to go beyond a rationalistic ethic of principles does not, of course, deny that there is a large and highly important arena of ethical controversy to which the best practical reason, or what I would prefer to call simply informed intelligence, must be applied. With many of the topical issues in medical ethics, for example, such as abortion, euthanasia and so on, it is clear that various public policy positions must be taken (for answers to these issues, within the political system, call for codification in law). It is nevertheless obvious, I think, that although ethical thinkers might aspire here to reach some overarching rational principle, what they in fact do when addressing these issues is to carry out just those intelligent activities which enter most fully into developed creative imagination. They look for the promotion of certain values; they determine, as best they can, the likely consequences (social as well as individual) of various alternative possibilities; they examine carefully what might be the implications of one adopted policy upon other aspects of ethical value and judgment. They do not—unless they believe they already have some absolutistic (theological or whatever) ethic—simply deduce the position from a set of clear premises, an exercise any schoolboy could as well perform.

10. Kurt Baier, *The Moral Point of View: A Rational Basis of Ethics* (Ithaca, N.Y.: Cornell University Press, 1958), 1.

15

Creative Anarchism

Personhood, we have argued, is an achievement concept. A human being is a person to the degree to which he or she becomes an integrated, creative, freely acting, social and moral being. If human beings are more or less persons, should not some human beings then count for more than others and enjoy special privileges and be accorded exceptional rights? The answer, I believe, is that when one achieves personhood and freedom, one has precisely the nonegoistic, loving sensitivity and concern that carries along with it the recognition of a nondiscriminatory spiritual worth obtaining throughout life. A person affirms quite spontaneously and naturally the intrinsic worth, the dignity, of every human being—and it is this recognition, this affirmation, which makes possible a political-social understanding that is commensurate with the spiritual potentialities of humankind.

Traditionally, at least in Western experience, the notion of the intrinsic worth of every human being has been grounded, for the most part, in some form or other of theism. It is because we are equal in the eye of God as His creatures, made in His image, that we are granted equal spiritual value. Some theologians would on this basis even go so far as to extend the concept of dignity to the inorganic as well as to the living. Paul Tillich, for example, writes, "Self-transcendence in the sense of greatness implies self-transcendence in the sense of dignity. It might seem that this term belongs exclusively to the personal-communal realm because it presupposes complete centeredness and freedom. But one element of dignity is inviolability, which is a valid element of all reality, giving dignity to the inorganic as well as the personal."[1]

For some considerable time now (at least since the Enlightenment and the French revolution), however, most philosophers, and indeed some theologians, have not appealed to theism to ground their ethical and political beliefs in dignity and equality; rather they have struggled to find other strictly rationalistic, pragmatic or utilitarian justifications. One need not, I think, strain moral sensitivity in this way, for, as I will try to show, it is sufficient for upholding the intrinsic worth of everyone that it is the natural expression of a person to so perceive others in those terms. The fact that a person recognizes spontaneously the inherent dignity of others provides the best warrant for asserting that dignity and for exploring the ways in which it can best be expressed in our political and social experience. Inherent or intrinsic dignity rests on the solid foundation that it is spirit that sees spirit.[2]

In his *Foundations of the Metaphysics of Morals*, and elsewhere, Kant—a paradigm of one who seeks a strictly rational justification for morality—sets a sharp opposition between duty and inclination and goes so far as to disallow moral value to those actions or states that incline spontaneously toward the good. "[M]any persons [are] so sympathetically constituted that without any motive of vanity or selfishness they find an inner satisfaction in spreading joy, and rejoice in the contentment of others which they have made possible. But I say that . . . that kind of action has no true moral worth."[3] For an action to have "true moral worth," according to Kant, it must be done not from inclination, but entirely from duty. It must be carried out as an act of rational obedience to the moral law (expressed as a categorical imperative), as an act of will totally independent of what and who one is as a person. "Thus everything empirical," Kant goes on to say, "is not only unworthy to be an ingredient in the principle of morality but is even highly prejudicial to the purity of moral practices themselves."[4]

It is thus entirely conceivable that we could have a perfectly wretched human being, filled with all manner of hate and resentment, who nevertheless would be supremely moral if he acted rationally according to the principle of duty. There is indeed something ludicrous in divorcing morality from the qualities of a person—what he inclines toward—and in seeking a purely rational ground for morality, especially one that can support the principles necessary for a just and fulfilling social and political order.

One formulation of Kant's categorical imperative, however, declares that one must always treat others as ends and never merely as means, which is to say that one must act towards others with the recognition of their intrinsic worth and inviolability. This recognition cannot itself, as Kant unwittingly showed, be grounded in a purely rational will; rather it is presupposed in the very possibility of such a will. With Kant, this presupposition of a primal human dignity no doubt derived from his own rich theistic background. The inherent dignity of every human being may, however, be affirmed, and on a stronger, unshakable footing, as it is the natural, spontaneous way in which a genuine person—one whose inclinations are, as it were, in order—regards others.

The intrinsic dignity of a person shows the person as inviolate. Violence, in all its many forms, is in essence the effort to destroy dignity.

The sense a person has of her own dignity always communicates readily to another and awakens the other's feeling of respect.

Intrinsic dignity is thus one of the value conditions constituting the individual—and as such can be cultivated, albeit never as a mere act of will.

It would be inherently contradictory for a person who has realized to the full his own dignity to act immorally; that is, to willfully deprive another of his or her personhood and freedom or, given the opportunity, to fail to enhance the personhood of the other.

Dignity becomes a manner of one's standing in the world. It is thus a fundamental state or quality of a human being as well as a source of one's judgment and action. To rob a person of dignity is to reduce the person precisely to a mere thing. We rightfully call inhumane any treatment of another which is designed to deprive one of one's dignity.

Intrinsic dignity, we affirm, belongs to individuals as a primal condition of their being, and yet, at the same time, it is a social phenomenon, for it demands recognition and acknowledgment in order for it to become a living force and for it to be sustained by the love it affords to others. With its insistence upon qualitative differentiation among human beings (between "the herd" and those endowed with a privileged "beautiful soul") romantic individualism (with which the view here being articulated is so often confounded) was entirely ego based. It recognized the social only as it was a field upon which one's own dignity could be acted out and not as that which informs one's dignity at its very core.

To realize and cultivate one's dignity is an act of freedom—a spontaneous recognition of the spiritual ground of one's being.

The awareness of one's own primal dignity, we have said, brings with it a natural extension of that awareness to others. There is, in short, a native tendency—let us call it an inner logic—to recognize and acknowledge the worth of others the moment that one recognizes and claims it for oneself.

One who successfully cultivates one's dignity does not think of oneself as superior but as worthy—and it is precisely that which is affirmed as well in others.

Evil exists. Evildoers exist. The evil that human beings are capable of inflicting upon each other and upon the world seems without boundary:

the Holocaust, genocide, torture—and the little acts that are calculated to hurt, to humiliate, to violate and degrade.

Evil is the betrayal of dignity. It is thus a spiritual sickness, a disease of the soul. Lacking the self-esteem that flows from the awareness of their own inherent dignity, the doers of evil, while bringing about immense harm and suffering, in fact destroy themselves. Evildoers are self-haters: they know nothing of the joy of being.

Evil is ignorance—if we understand by the term "ignorance" not a mere lack of knowing something or other (as if evil could be dispelled if only one had a certain piece of knowledge) but the failure to achieve a state of spiritual knowing; a state that renders one incapable of intentionally harming or degrading others. Evil does not disappear in knowledge, as though it never existed in the first place: it is seen as it is and is inwardly transformed and transfigured.

Theistic religion usually sees evil as sin, one which is overcome through redemption, however this may get understood. Evil is something over which one must triumph. As Nicolas Berdayev notes: "The genesis of evil shows that we must both recognize its positive significance, which will be turned to account in heavenly life, and condemn it, waging an unwearying struggle against it. The positive meaning of evil lies solely in the enrichment of life brought about by the heroic struggle against it and the victory over it."[5]

One must indeed struggle with the tendencies toward evil whenever they appear within oneself and in others, but a victory over evil is possible only when evil is radically denied. As the Augustinian side of Christian theology recognized, evil is the absence of what is truly significant (the good); it can have no positive meaning of its own.

Now this is certainly more than a logical quibble over the definition (meaning) of terms; and it extends as well beyond any concern to develop a theodicy (the reconciliation of evil with God's omnipotence and goodness), for to give positive meaning to evil, if only of an instrumental sort, is to allow some value to that intense degradation of the spiritual quality of life. Evil is utter nonsense. It needs to be understood; it needs to be explained; it needs to be addressed socially and politically; it does not need to be, and it cannot be, justified.

There is an impersonal, universal love, an "intellectual love of God" (Spinoza), which encompasses all being and, on some readings, discloses one's essential kinship with all living and nonliving things. There is also an interpersonal love, a caring for, an attachment to, a concern about, other particular beings in their own unique particularity. The Self is a state of universal loving being. A person, grounded in that love, loves other particular beings, but, unlike the love that individuals as such might have for one another, a person loves another person playfully, with concern for the other but not obsessively in such a way that he is caring primarily for himself. One fails as a person whenever in one's attachment to another person one becomes possessive and thereby obsessive about satisfying one's own needs.

Particularized person love might, however, seem destined always to fall into some kind of obsession, and hence be inherently flawed and inadequate. But this is so only when that love is grounded in the conditions of individuality and not in the Self. When person love is playful, it necessarily extends itself and makes itself available, as it were, to other persons and things. Partiality, as Confucius wisely recognized, does not so much become a limitation as an opportunity to deepen the activity of love: partiality (in Confucianism's case by being focused initially on the family) becomes educative in the achievement of the right performance of love.

Men, women, children need, and therefore oftentimes desperately seek, to be able to effectuate change, to control others and themselves, to influence events, to acquire some degree of mastery over their lives—in short, to have power. Power takes many forms—from a crude display of physical force exercised against another to a spontaneous expression of authoritative competency. There are also subtle manipulations of others and legitimated modes of compulsion and there are triumphant self-overcomings and acts of beauty and grace.

We need then to distinguish broadly at least between coercive power and creative power. Coercive power demands the obedience of the other (be it person, event, situation) to one's own will. It is ego based. It assumes struggle, engagement, victory or defeat. Creative power, on the other hand, seeks the realization of a harmony that is constituted in and through diverse and oftentimes otherwise conflicting elements. Creative power is an expression of freedom in action. It is exercised in celebration and joy.

As Nietzsche recognized so well in his (rather metaphysically fanciful) "will to power," nothing is more pathetic than the destructive ways in which those who feel powerless seek to acquire (coercive) power through spoiling the success and status of others. In human relations the powerless who want power are oftentimes more dangerous than the powerful, for they mistakenly believe that it is something they ought to have, as it were, for the asking (by demanding, scheming, or calculating), rather than by a self-disciplined achievement. The truly (creatively) powerful, on the other hand, are not driven by a will to power at all insofar as the term "will" means a striving for something that one lacks, a deficiency. One does not strive for that which one already has or is.

Aggression, then, is not so much an exercise of real power as it is a sign of its absence. The need to dominate another person (socially, sexually, or in work relations) betrays frustration and inadequacy rather than indicating strength.

There are those who, out of fear, or gross ineptitude, or simple perversity, or whatever, remove themselves from competition (from the whole coercive scene), but without striving to achieve something (namely, creative power) in its place. Having opted out of the entire field, they are not powerless, but will-less. The powerless person is one who wants power, strives for it, but for whatever reason does not possess it.

Subordination—either a breaking of the will to power or the practicing of a discipline to redirect that will to an altogether different end—the cult and the monastic order, the blind follower, the bold ascetic.

Power (*potentia*)—the acting out, through discipline, with skill, of one's deepest form-giving capacities.

Creative power is not, however, an imposition of order upon chaos, a therapeutic overcoming of the forces of darkness, or a simple overflow of exuberant feeling which is expressive of its bearer's personality (as has sometimes been thought); rather it is just that mastery, that skillful acting, which is grounded in an essential understanding of things and of being, and is realized concretely in consummate forms of acting freely. Creative power, unlike coercive power, aims to promote fulfillment and harmony in particular situations.

Creative power translates into the political arena as the authority which issues from competency: the authoritative in sharp contrast to the authoritarian. Creative political power strives, while seeking to attain its immediate ends, to enhance the dignity of persons.

How then does a realized person conduct herself politically? What manner or style of being politically is appropriate to an individual who has achieved personhood?

We ask the question not in the form of looking for a political theory that will call for, or justify, a particular kind of government, but in the form of seeking the right political attitude and mode of conduct for a developed person—a style of political behavior that may inform the politics of government, of work and social relations.

There are, it seems, two general, primary ways in which political (power) relations have been and can be ordered, be they in state government, work governance or in other kinds of group and interpersonal social relations. These are the authoritarian and the democratic ways. In actuality, these are not of course pure forms which are sharply separated from one another; rather they are types of political organization and behavior that overlap, intertwine and tend to be emphasized in one or another political situation. Complete authoritarian (totalitarian) ways seldom endure; no pure democratic society, as far as we know, has ever existed. An authoritarian way of centralized coercive power and rule by command could be justified only if all of the participants (the ruled) were driven on their own, in their relations to one another, solely by a narrow self-interest which took no cognizance whatsoever of others and were determined to disallow any other higher standard or possibility. In these circumstances the parties would rightly believe that only a dictatorial power with coercive control, behavioristic reward and punishment (in the governmental realm, from Western-style fascism to Chinese legalism) would be the only way that life would not be altogether short and brutish.

One can safely conclude, however, that strict authoritarianism of whatever kind is, in actuality, never justifiable, for there have always been, and no doubt there always will be, men and women who have achieved significant degrees of personhood and will thus seek quite spontaneously to enhance their own and other person's dignity in and through their political relationships. In any event strict authoritarianism, under whatever circumstances, cannot be maintained for long by sheer force. Power, even of the most coercive kind, seeks legitimacy and so will include at least some elements of the democratic, even if only in debased form (show elections and the like).

The democratic, it is often observed, is a reaction to the authoritarian and is also a compromise with it, but aspires nevertheless to something very much beyond it. Based as it is on the assumption that individuals are able to recognize that their own interest requires that they adjust to and accommodate the interests of others, the democratic allows for the dignity of each individual; indeed it proclaims its legitimacy and superiority as a form of government and manner of governance precisely on its pronouncement of concern for individual rights and individual human worth. And it advances this libertarian ideal as a rational or reasonable (enlightenment) norm rather than as it may be a natural expression of a sensitive, caring person. Democracy values both competition and cooperation, both society and community, and appeals to a self-interested reason that must be evoked to deal with the otherwise natural inclinations of human beings to pursue their own happiness at the expense of others. In short, the democratic assumes that we are inclined to a state of nature, aspire to liberty, and that we can realize that liberty only when we rationally recognize everyone's inalienable rights and interests and regulate our behavior accordingly.[6] Democracy hopes to achieve consensus, but lacking that (which is more often than not the case) is pleased to settle for some kind of negotiation between the competing interests of so-called "men of good will."

The democratic is indeed an enormous advance over the authoritarian, and is not to be dismissed philosophically because of its accommodation to what it perceives as both the glorious potentialities and unhappy limitations of human beings. The democratic ideal and practice of legitimated authority is, when we reflect upon it, and not merely take it for granted, quite remarkable. It calls for a continuing agreement, implicit if not always explicit, among the political players in the rightness of the system—even when, and one should say especially when, those who occupy positions of authority are, or seem to be, of modest competency. More often than not, legislators, judges, presidents, majors and governors—let alone foremen, heads of families, and so on—are not paragons of intelligence or virtue, yet their authority, if it is properly acquired within the rules of the system (by election, appointment or custom) is freely acknowledged.

There is surely a sense, however, in which within a democratic polity a citizen is simply placed there historically and, as so placed, can only consent to it or suffer rather dreadful consequences (e.g., prison or exile). An individual citizen does not have the liberty to accept only those acts of authority that are exercised by persons one approves of. The rule of law is indifferent to who makes the law, so long as it is promulgated properly.

A person who finds himself to be a citizen in a liberal democracy ought nevertheless to strive to be a model for a higher (what we will call a creative anarchist) ideal, while engaging the democratic process. This is an extremely difficult task, for the temptation to announce one's own rights and interests when everyone else is so doing is very strong indeed; in fact, it often appears that if one does not do so one runs the risk of being trampled upon—and in that position one can hardly be a model for a higher ideal. To be a model requires that someone is looking.

The democratic is a fragile and vulnerable achievement. There are always altogether too many of us who are willing to acquiesce to illegitimate authority or to the authoritarian when we think that there might be some immediate benefit in our doing so—especially in times of economic disarray. When the liberal democratic tradition in state government as well as in other political contexts is so precarious, it might seem, then, like an idle, if not pernicious, luxury to hold forth other higher possibilities, for, when the democratic is undermined, we usually get one form or other of the authoritarian in its place. One must agree that a narrow and vulnerable line often separates civil behavior from the storm troopers, and that historically democracy in state government in particular is still an experiment that might prove to be too demanding; however, as we have suggested before, we do not look upon anarchism (at least the creative anarchist ideal we will set forth) as one form of (anti-) government or political theory among others but as it is a style of political behavior that may inform the politics of government (primarily the democratic, as the ideal is incommensurable with the authoritarian) and the politics of work and social relations.

Historically, anarchism has often understood itself as an alternative political system and theory, one that has served as a standing critique of all existing forms of government (including the liberal democratic) that it sees as promoting violence, external and internal, as it is a primary source, and not a means of ameliorating, all manner of human misery. To this end, traditional anarchism has been intimately involved with revolutionary programs to liberate the oppressed (e.g., Bakunin, Kropotkin, even Proudhon and Godwin, in their own ways) and to give workers control over the conditions and structures in which they labor—but like most revolutionary programs it becomes primarily negative, insofar as it has as its main goal the undermining and undercutting of existing coercive powers. Important as this undermining might be in rectifying grievous forms of oppression, it cannot, however, because of its grounding in resentment, provide the basis for a genuine anarchism of persons. The creative anarchism advocated here certainly has some affinities with traditional anarchist thought (of both an individualist and collectivist sort)—namely with its aversion to coercive power, its emphasis upon voluntary association and compact, cooperation instead of competition—but differs from that thought in a number of essential ways. Creative anarchism is not, first of all, a revolutionary political program; it does not seek the violent or even peaceful overthrow of democratic institutions in favor of some kind of proletarian rule—for it understands anarchism as a style of political action that can be carried out effectively only by persons as such, whether worker or professor, male or female, rich or poor, and not by mass action. Secondly, creative anarchism does not call for the abolition of government; it asks only that the ideals that it announces serve as the standard for political relations and that the political relations within a society be informed by the concern to enhance dignity through the exercise of creative, not coercive, power.

The Chinese *wu wei/wuwei* (nonaction of the ruler) is perhaps closest in spirit to what I am talking about, namely anarchism as a spiritual condition, a creative style of acting politically, rather than a concern with the power of government as such.

Wu wei/wuwei, like the *niṣkāma karman* (action without desire for its fruits) of Hindu thought, holds that action—in this context political action—needs to be performed always in a spirit of care and devotion (following the *tao/dao*) noncoercively, the political actor thus seeking in whatever situation might obtain to contribute to the harmony of that situation without imposing an alien will upon it (hence nonaction). In Confucian terms a person in authority should possess that authority in virtue of his competency, the authority consisting then in orchestrating the talents and achievements of others. *Wu wei/wuwei* does not mean that a person in authority simply does not do anything; *wu wei/wuwei* means that political action is to be carried out spontaneously so as to exhibit one's authoritativeness in being able to enhance the welfare of all.[7]

Creative anarchists are by nature classless, which is to say that they do not regard themselves as belonging to any special group that has interests to be defended or promoted in opposition to, or at the expense of, another group.

Creative anarchists strive to bring about self-regulating governmental situations, the resultant autonomy of the whole reflecting that of its individual participants.

Creative anarchism thus stands in stark contrast to the authoritarian. As Hannah Arendt showed, a totalitarian system (the epitome of the authoritarian) demands the complete subjugation of the individual. "Totalitarian movements," she writes, "are mass organizations of atomized, isolated individuals. Compared with all other parties and movements, their most conspicuous external characteristic is their demand for total, unrestricted, unconditional, and unalterable loyalty of the individual member."[8] The loyalty associated with creative anarchism, as we will see, is of an entirely different kind, as is its conception of the individual that, as we have seen, has to do with the achievement of personhood. For creative anarchism, a human being is most assuredly not an object to be manipulated, made submissive and conformist, conditioned to believe that his only value lies in the dutiful subordinate relation he holds to a particular leader or group, with that belief informing all other dimensions of his or her political behavior.

With respect to the democratic, creative anarchists do recognize the value in the operative principle of consensus (and its superiority to that of mere compromise) insofar as it might involve the transformation of a private interest to a community good, but it recognizes as well that consensus still functions within a rights and interests mandate and is thus to be distinguished from that spontaneity which sees oneself and other in potential harmony of purpose and action.

Government without law, and the power to enforce law, would appear to be a contradiction in terms, as indeed it is when the creative anarchist spirit is absent. When that spirit is fully present, however, law is superfluous. The creative anarchist does, or tries to do, what is right without calculation or fear of punishment; he does, or tries to do, what is right not simply because he is socialized to do so, but because he spontaneously strives to promote welfare and harmony in concrete particular situations. The creative anarchist does not need law, albeit he can see its importance and acknowledge its justification when and where the anarchist spirit is missing or otherwise fails to get exercised.

There is then the style of those who are in positions of authority that, according to creative anarchism, is one of authoritative leadership, of orchestrating the necessary involvements of other men and women, of harmonizing contributions in order to advance the welfare and dignity of all concerned. There is also, in the same spirit, the style of those who are participant subjects in the governmental political arena that, according to creative anarchism, calss for spontaneously acting in accord with others in imaginative ways to satisfy common needs, striving always to enhance human autonomy and dignity.

Paul Ricoeur argues that,

> Work calls into play the power relations of man over man within the context of the relations of force between man and nature. Indeed, through work, human resistance takes on the character of a rationally organized battle against nature that makes nature appear as a reservoir of forces to be conquered. . . . Now, the force of man's work also figures among the forces to be mastered. The rational organization of the battle against nature also implies an organization of human efforts in projects, plans, and programs. In this way man ranks among the number of resistances to be overcome by man. His work is a productive force to be organized: by means of his work he enters into relations of subordination.[9]

And thus that "Authority is not bad in itself. Control is a necessary 'differentiation' between man and is implied in the essence of the political sphere."[10]

Insufficient attention, it seems, has been paid in political thought to the politics of work, which is somewhat surprising insofar as the vast majority of power relationships (and aspirations and frustrations) for most persons, especially in a liberal democratic society, occur in the workplace, rather than in the governmental arena. Day to day power situations arise more as we are workers than as we are citizens (of a state).

Given unlimited leisure, which is mistakingly taken as the opposite of work, most persons would go mad—or they would impose upon themselves all manner of new tasks. It is not so much the flight from boredom as such, however, that drives people to work, as the need to accept challenges, to have an appropriate field to engender and play out their energies and talents (let alone "to make a living"). Within the socioeconomic structures that have developed, this means institutionalized, organized productivity of one sort or another where labor is offered, money is given, power is acquired.

Let us draw a distinction between *working at* something or other and *working to*: with the former we have action, which is not inherently satisfying, carried out primarily for the sake of the end to be achieved; with the latter tasks are undertaken for their intrinsic value as well as for a purpose to be fulfilled. In other words, to work *at* something is to employ (what one takes to be) the most efficient means to realize a purpose that is strictly consummatory of the action, with the reason for the action being defined in terms of its anticipated consequences. To work *to* achieve some end is to employ means appropriate to realizing a purpose that is justified in terms of the alleged value of the process itself. Working to thus exhibits, and contributes to, a person's autonomy and dignity. The worker sees the constraints of the tasks as opportunities and not as restraints on his time and energy. He works for a reason that is entirely commensurate with the process; the result of the work is an end in itself. Working to is nonalienating; it is not part of a battle to be waged with nature, a battle requiring resistances to be overcome both with nature and with fellow workers. Working to is joyous work: it is playful skill in action.

Now most work that is carried out or tasks undertaken are not, by their very nature and character, able to be done by a single person working alone; most work requires some degree of group participation and always implies a social context—and hence becomes political. And it is here that the creative anarchist ideal can be seen to be clearly superior to any other political style, insofar as it allows for, indeed calls for, autonomy and respect for individual dignity. It makes for work to be a working to, a kind of creative play.

Authoritarian models of work relations obtain whenever one is compelled to assume a subordinate or superior role as part of a system that places power (to hire, to fire) in a very few and legitimates their being able to tell others what to do unquestioningly. In authoritarian work relations power often seems to get exercised as much for its own sake as for the goal to be attained, for the system when carried to its near extreme usually proves to be highly inefficient and counterproductive in the end. Within the authoritarian model, the worker is a mere instrument or thing, a piece of a larger whole and is thus regarded as utterly replaceable. He is discouraged, indeed often prevented, from acquiring distinctive skills of a sort that would command a measure of autonomy (and hence the traditional difficulty authoritarian structures have when dealing with craftsmen and peasants). Where initiative and pride of work are denied, however, not only are human beings degraded, but the productive purpose or goal is certain to be unrealized.

Democratic models or styles of work relations usually contain a large dose of the authoritarian, certainly within corporate or state capitalist economies (especially historically, in their early stages of exploitation and growth), but strive over time, at least within the framework of liberal political democracy, to safeguard individual rights (with laws and regulations governing safety, minimum wages, child labor and the like) and allow the promotion of the worker's welfare through collective actions (e.g., union bargaining). The democratic-capitalistic encourages the full rationalization of the productive process, whether in factory or in office, through specialization of skills and wage differentials. It remains, however, dedicated to work in the spirit of working at—work being essentially instrumental to the end product of profit for the company or for the individual, and hence will always be alienating to some highly significant degree.

Democratic work models are to be found, of course, not only in capitalist economies but in socialist ones as well, but oftentimes with this ironic peculiarity, that the worker, while not being easily replaced, is often regarded, and regards himself ever more keenly, as superfluous, as inessential. Where everybody must work, jobs having to be provided for all, most work becomes meaningless. Numerous people are called upon to do what could be done better by only a few.

Nevertheless, insofar as the democratic model of work relations does call upon worker initiatives—where by the term "worker" we mean all who are involved in the productive system of goods and services, the clerk as well as the surgeon—and their participation in various and diverse decisions involving their work, we have an important advance from the authoritarian model, and one which points in the direction of the creative anarchist ideal, where in actuality some essential aspects of the democratic are retained.

The creative anarchist work ideal draws in many ways from both a traditional master-apprentice form (to which initially it might seem to be opposed) and the kind of work structures that are often associated with monastic orders and utopian communities—but very much in its own way.

The creative anarchist honors skill and excellence, for he recognizes that mastery of an activity provides one of the strongest basis for freedom and autonomy. Mastery, no matter in what area, requires a firm willingness to learn, which in turn means disciplining one's immediate inclinations and desire for individual self-expression and subordinating oneself to the demands of the task and of the teacher. In the master-apprentice relationship, which is freely constituted, the apprentice does what he is told to do, not because of a hierarchical, wage-structured authority, as if the master were a boss, but because the apprentice recognizes the master's superior competency, from which he hopes to learn and eventually to emulate. The whole purpose of being an apprentice is to become a master.

The creative anarchist ideal is one that seeks to harmonize various competencies—in a spirit in which what appears to be necessary (e.g., the having of food and shelter) is seen as an opportunity for genuine play. Work, in the creative anarchist model, is a devout service, an offering of one's skill as a kind of ritual participation or contribution. Creative anarchists are able to serve one another without being servile. They organize a task to be carried out in ways wherein each person recognizes for himself—and is so recognized by the others—how best to contribute the appropriate skill, the leaders being granted the obligation to lead, to orchestrate the action, through the recognition of their superior ability to do so. Power is thus turned to imaginative ways of sharing responsibility and to the mutual satisfaction in what is achieved.

Now the creative anarchist ideal clearly is most readily actualized in small-scale, cooperative enterprises and work situations. When planning, designing, building an airport, many features of the democratic style of organization will no doubt have to be incorporated. Under any circumstances, though, the anarchist ideal ought to inform large-scale productive enterprises so that work can be carried out with the aim of promoting personhood and freedom, the enhancement of human dignity.

Any discussion of the politics of work relations must address the question as to "whether, in an ideal society, certain roles should be assigned to females and others to males."[11] Now the question as framed assumes roles and their assignment, nevertheless its intent is clear and the question needs to be addressed within the framework of creative anarchism. How should sex and gender differences be taken into account in the politics of work-relations? Do men and women have special, distinctive capacities for different kinds of skills or competencies?

In Joseph R. Lucas's essay "Because You Are a Woman," which in many ways is not a model for clear thinking, one reads:

> There are no conclusive arguments about feminine abilities and attitudes. But the discoveries of the scientists, so far as they go, lend some support to traditional views. It could well be the case that intellectual and psychological characteristics are, like physical ones, influenced by genetic factors. If this is so, the way in which a particular pair of genes in an individual genotype will be manifested in the phenotype will depend on the other genes in the genotype, and may depend greatly on whether there are two X chromosomes or one X and one Y. It could be that the masculine mind is typically more vigorous and combative, and the feminine mind typically more intuitive and responsive, with correspondingly different ranges of interests and inclinations.[12]

We take the customary to be what is typical and then go on to assume, as Mill showed, that it is what is most natural. "So true is it," Mill writes, "that unnatural generally means only uncustomary, and that everything which is usual appears natural. The subjection of women to men being a universal custom, any departure from it quite naturally appears unnatural.''[13]

In the last analysis it may be simply impossible to disentangle the genetic from the social in accounting for whatever differences (other than the obvious biological ones) might obtain between men and women. In any case, the central question has to do with what importance is to be ascribed to whatever those differences might be. Obviously some differences between human beings (male or female) might be relevant in some work contexts (e.g., physical strength in some forms of construction labor) but not in others (e.g., in computer programming); some differences (e.g., in one's eye color) might hardly ever be relevant; some other differences might always or nearly always be relevant (e.g., with our present technology we would not have blind persons be airplane pilots). The significance of differences in human beings in work relations is always contextual—and subject to change.

If the (appropriated) body does become an essential part of a person's identity (contributing to one's repertoire of actions and manner of acting) and if a person's identity has some bearing on the work-roles that are most appropriate to the person, then sex differences have to make some kind of difference in work roles, but precisely what kind of difference still remains the question.

Quite clearly much of what traditionally has passed for what is appropriate in sex roles is more a matter of socialization and history than of personal identity based on somatic considerations. There does not seem to be anything in somatic-grounded personal identity, for instance, that would require that women do the cooking.

Assuming that it is possible to know what is typical in sex differentiation with any degree of precision (which is of course doubtful), we still have the question about how the exceptional are to be treated. And the answer seems obvious. Every person should have the opportunity (the liberty) to act freely, to have an artful destiny within the conditions of his or her being. This means that there ought not to be any compulsory sex-role differentiation (the determination of occupation by sex) either by legal or social coercion—although it may in fact turn out that, for whatever psychological, genetic, or social-historical reasons or causes, in various contexts most men or most women might choose one or another kind of role (as being most in accord with what they understand their own nature to be).

A person's body, mental functions, emotions, language and culture are, we have seen, social as well as individual in character. Persons are social beings. An isolated, totally solitary person would be a contradiction in terms. A person sees another person, however, not just as necessary to herself, but as that other person—whether man or woman—may be part of a relationship that can mutually enhance human dignity. A person does not seek to dominate another person, although individuals as such indeed oftentimes do. Throughout the realm of social relations, nondominance, as a positive, creative anarchist attitude or style, is the political stance of a mature person.

Nondominance is essentially the translation of creative power into the politics of social relations. It is both a training in self-cultivation, in the achievement of personhood, and the fruit of that training. The more one is a person the more natural it is for one to act with and towards others nondominantly. Without effort, one extends oneself to the other, man or woman.

The exercise of nondominance nevertheless has perhaps its harshest challenge in the relationships between men and women. In almost all societies, for whatever reasons, there has been (at least on the part of males) an assumption of male superiority, and a corresponding exploitation of women, with much of that getting internalized and tacitly accepted by women.

Woman the tempter; the denial of the spiritual in man. Woman the frail blossom needing protection. Woman the nurturing, caring, earth-bound body alone able to procreate. Woman the emotional, self-indulgent child; yet the amazon, fearsome and strong; the witch, the deceiver, the wicked one—and most notably the object of intense desire.

Nietzsche has Zarathustra urge a man to bring his whip when encountering a woman. "Thou goest to woman? Remember thy whip!" And remarks in his *Beyond Good and Evil* that "Men have so far treated women like birds who have strayed to them from some height: as something more refined and vulnerable, wilder, stranger, sweeter, and more soulful—but as something one has to lock up lest it fly away." He goes on to say that "To go wrong on the fundamental problem of 'man and woman,' to deny the most abysmal antagonism between them and the necessity of an eternally hostile tension, to dream perhaps of equal rights, equal education, equal claims and obligations—that is the typical sign of shallowness."[14]

But why this need (albeit expressed perhaps ironically by Nietzsche) for a subjugation which deprives both the oppressed and the oppressor of the fullness of their personhood? The psychologist in us will assuredly say "fear." But fear of what? Is it because women make evident in some deep way men's own helplessness? Is it because, as some feminist writers would have it, men having been compelled historically to reject and repress much of their own gentle and sympathetic nature project that femininity on to women in order to keep it at a distance?[15]

It might even be argued that nondominance is itself merely a soft, feminine ideal, which is best left to women; that men need a more robust ideal of striving and triumphing that will produce strength and fortitude.

The answer to this, of course, is that there is nothing weak or submissive in nondominance; on the contrary, it exhibits the greatest strength and self-confidence, and lies within the capability of all persons, male or female.

Nondominance is liberated play; domination betrays need, and is always, in the long run, self-defeating.

The harmony that is obtained through the exercise of nondominance is not some low-level reconciling of differences, rather it has all the tensions and contrasts of life itself. What gets harmonized retains its particular character within the transformed situation. In short, patterns of social relations that develop from the creative anarchist ideal of nondominance will have all the excitement and vitality we associate with, and find within, works of art.

Let us remark on this with respect to sexuality. Persons, grounded in the conditions of individuality, are sexual beings—and are so, as Freud and others have convincingly shown, from early childhood to the waning years of old age. Sexuality is at once body based, as an organic drive, an energy, a force, and psychically constituted as a need for enhancement, intimacy, and recognition. It clearly assumes different meanings and is expressed with varying intensities during the different stages (biological and social) of one's life, for both men and women. And as Foucault has demonstrated, sexuality has a history in its diverse cultural manifestations and representations.

What does a creative anarchist style or attitude tell us about the spiritual possibilities of sexuality?

Let us call the sexuality that is a given of one's biological nature (albeit as always socialized through various cultural forms) "primitive sexuality"; primitive in virtue of its originary or primal status. Primitive sexuality is the raw physical drive for release and completion; it is the basic source of attraction (and repulsion); it is the energy, the libido, that excites and yields pleasure of a uniquely poignant intensity. Everyone knows, because everyone enjoys or suffers, this primitive sexuality. Few know what to do with it; many allow it to assume degrading or what we might call fallen forms.

Fallen sexuality is a kind of moral madness, a turning of oneself over to the object-body in such a way as to focus every strain of resentment and rage through it and on another who is reduced to that same body. Fallen sexuality is the pornographic, the hateful, and the violent. It is a deprivation of human dignity.

The sexual life of most persons is however happily carried out in more democratic frameworks that accord equal rights to the partners (for women this is only now being partially realized) and that call for the negotiating of various need and wants with some degree of mutuality established. The ideal liberal form is that of the sexual being a natural extension of an abiding love between two persons (most often between a man and a woman) that sustains their intimacy. It is a moral domesticating, as it were, of the primitive—a respectable eroticism which allows the sexual to retain something (often a good deal) of its original nature while bringing it into the structure of care and concern, of intimacy and love.

The passionate *bhakta*, the devout medieval mistress of the Lord, the bearer of agape cum eros, exhibit the sublimation of the primitive, redirecting its energy toward a divine being. Then the sexual is conquered so that the spirit can realize itself completely apart from the body, the flesh. The celibate ascetic is, however, engaged in what often appears to be a hopeless struggle, for he requires the very energy derived from the sexual in order to overcome it. Being obsessed with the temptations of the sexual, he is only plunged ever deeper into its power.

There is a mode of sexuality, a style of being sexual, which is certainly not fallen and goes considerably beyond liberal mutuality and traditional religiously grounded sublimated divine-love forms and ascetic renunciation. It is a sexuality based on ritual play, a style that we associate with the creative anarchistic.

As ritualized, sex means the participation of the partners in a spirit of devout offering, but not so much to each other as such but to and within a spiritual power that is itself made manifest in and through the activity. Sex here becomes a genuine performance—that is, it becomes an acting out of the raw energy of the sexual, giving that energy both aesthetic form and transformative meaning. As play, then, sex requires that the participants turn themselves over to the union, each giving to it a concentrated, nonegocentric attentiveness. Playful sexuality retains to the full the raw power of the primitive while transforming it into a spiritual achievement. Sexuality here becomes ecstatic in virtue of its transcending quality. It is a way of acting freely in a creative togetherness that generates, like all ritual activity, the very conditions for its fulfillment.

The creative anarchist ideal for social relations differs, then, not only from all forms of authoritarianism but from the democratic as well. In social relations, the democratic is exhibited as the attitude of adjustment, compromise, negotiation of different, and oftentimes incompatible, interests, wants and needs. I want this; you want that—ideally after failing to convince one another of the rightness of our respective desires, we look for a third thing that might be compatible with both. As with government and the politics of work relations, the democratic does aspire, one might say, to the anarchist ideal, but remains enmeshed in authoritarian tendencies toward dominance. The democratic is dominance tempered by respect for the interests of others. It is not the nondominance, the spontaneous striving for a vital harmony, of the creative anarchist.

The politics of social relations is not, of course, carried out only in the more intimate or close relationships between individual human beings. There is also the larger social setting, the society in which persons live and to which they bear continuing political relations.

We need, then, when extending the politics of social relations into the larger social setting, to distinguish sharply an anarchist ideal of community from the reality of society. Social relations no doubt occur within both forms or structures, but whereas a society is something that everyone (unless raised by animals in a wilderness) is born into and is nurtured by through education and culture, a community is something that is created by persons (within various societies). An individual is necessarily a part of (some) society (or other); a person participates in a community. A society, then, is a preexistent (for the individual) impersonal structure of socioeconomic, cultural relationships of which a person is simply a part in virtue of his or her historical being in the world. A community, on the other hand, comes into being in virtue of the voluntary participation of its members. For the individual, a society is a given; for a person, a community is an achievement. The creative anarchist is concerned to transform as far as possible the actuality of societies into the ideality of communities.

We have said that persons participate in communities. Participation, as we have seen with the sexual, is involved in ritual. It requires a certain openness and sensitivity on the part of the participant, a willingness to contribute to the evoking of a special atmosphere or presence that becomes the basis for further personal involvement.

Participation is thus not so much a relationship between an individual and a group, as it is a mode of being together with others in such a way that something new is engendered. A relationship implies the preexistence of that which is related; participation gives rise to that in which one participates.

There is thus a kind of communion present in all genuine community: a coming-together in an attitude of celebrative harmony.

There is an aesthetic, a form-giving dimension to a community: for participation means a sensing of what is right and appropriate for a given situation. A wholeness is created that tends then, like a work of art, to have a life of its own. A community, further like a work of art, expresses that quality of freedom which we associate with self-determination.

The term "community," however, connotes more than a transient encounter between persons, no matter how intense that encounter might be. It suggests something enduring for a considerable period of time; it suggests a tradition. Communities need not, to be sure, extend over many generations, as perhaps full-bodied traditions require; in any event there is a traditional dimension to a community that gives it what appears to be a life of its own. Although a community is only in virtue of the participation of its members, it nevertheless endures in a way that allows it to accommodate new involvements and to accept old resignations. A community thus becomes the ongoing repository, as it were, of the participation of those who who constitute it.

Participation in a community does not mean that a person loses herself in a group, or simply turns herself over to another. There is a fundamental difference between a community and a cult. A cult tends to reduce persons to their individuality, with the relationships they bear to each other, and especially to the leader, diminishing their humanity. A community is constituted by autonomous persons, each of whom is enhanced as a person in virtue of his or her participation.

There is, of course, always the risk that a community will degenerate into a cult, especially if there are strong personalities involved, and this points up the further risk in communitarian participation that the openness and sensitivity that is called for does make the participant vulnerable. But there is a peculiarity in this vulnerability, this exposure of personhood, which is that real openness (as distinct from superficial good fellowship) comes from a strength of spirit, from that special nonegocentricity that transcends potentially destructive egotism.

By nonegocentricity, as indicated before, we do not mean the utter annihilation of the ego. We mean rather the attainment of that spiritual indifference that shows a person as having a quiet confidence, a firm self-assurance and that allows her to be fully sensitive to the other. Nonegocentricity is characteristic of the person who is free. When one acts out of integrated personhood, unselfconsciously one is involved in one's activity. The little I is simply not there to be destroyed.

Returning to the ritual character of communitarian participation: there is one further feature which links up closely with these questions of risk and vulnerability, and that is once again power. In community there is power, but not the coercive power of dominance, rather the creative power which we associate with freedom. Just as a person's actions are free to the degree to which they are masterful and carried out in a certain spirit, freedom thereby becoming a quality of the action itself, with the actor both enjoying and engendering a power of concentrated being, so in community—where persons freely participate—a power of presence is brought forth and is experienced as an inherent quality of the community. It is a power that is there for itself, the participants partaking of it as well as engendering it. Being for itself, communitarian power binds participants in deep fellowship.

A community is thus similar in many ways to a family. A family in fact may be—and ought always to aspire to be—a community. A family, though, does tend to become more like a society than a community because of, in most societies, the unequal roles of its members and the need, at various stages of a child's growth, for some kind of authoritarian-like leadership, no matter how benevolent its intent. For an individual, her family is something like a society. She finds herself a part of it and is expected to fulfill various functions within it. She is dependent upon it for the satisfaction of basic material and emotional needs.

A community in the creative anarchist mode, on the other hand, is not, and can never properly be, hierarchical in the political sense of an unequal distribution of power. Just as those who participate in an elaborate ritual will contribute to the performance in different degrees, so participants in a community will be involved in varying ways, but no involvement is coercive.

What then, it might be asked, is the common interest or cement that, apart from individual ends to be attained, holds a community together? Members of a society are held together by their recognition and acceptance of the fact that their membership is necessary for their survival and growth; participants in a community by their loyalty to it.

By the term "loyalty" I do not mean blind, uncritical support. The demand for this kind of loyalty is a calling for a deprivation of the loyalist's being. It is an insulting claim to make upon another that he should support me even if he believes that what I am doing or propose to do, what I am saying, and so on, is wrong or possibly injurious to another. This is servitude, not loyalty as a creative anarchist wants to understand the term in a communitarian context.

Loyalty is a noncalculating, open-ended offer to contribute of oneself whatever is required to sustain that presence of the belonging together that is the community. Participants in a community undertake that kind of tacit commitment. They will be loyal to the community because they place a special value upon it and are willing to give of their being to it. Loyalty is a serving of oneself as an act of love.

When, as persons who are free, we participate with love in a community we give rise to those very conditions that allow personhood to be fulfilled. The fact that a community is an achievement, not a given, does not imply then that it is something artificial, that it is some way unnatural. Quite the opposite: there is nothing more natural than that persons should strive to achieve community, for in that achievement there is an enduring enrichment of their being.

NOTES

1. Paul Tillich, *Systematic Theology* (Chicago: University of Chicago Press, 1963), vol. III, 89.

2. Even John Stuart Mill in his classic essay *Utilitarianism* has indirect recourse to the notion of intrinsic dignity when he allows, in spite of his initial claim that the utilitarian creed "holds that actions are right in proportion as they tend to promote happiness, wrong as they tend to produce the reverse of happiness. By 'happiness' is intended pleasure and the absence of pain . . . ," that "In the golden rule of Jesus of Nazareth, we read the complete spirit of the ethics of utility. To do as you would be done by, and to love your neighbor as yourself, constitute the ideal perfection of utilitarian morality." One can love one's neighbor as oneself, however, only insofar as one can, from the standpoint of one's own achieved personhood, recognize the dignity of that other person or neighbor—and this has nothing to do as such with degrees of pleasure and pain.

3. Immanuel Kant, *Foundations of the Metaphysics of Moral*, trans. Lewis White Beck (New York: The Liberal Arts Press, 1959), 14.

4. Ibid., 44.

5. Nicolas Berdayev, *The Destiny of Man* (New York: Harper & Brothers, 1960), 297.

6. John Locke, from whom much democratic thinking derives, writes that "The freedom then of man, and liberty of acting according to his will, is grounded in his having reason, which is able to instruct him in that law he is to govern himself by, and make him know how far he is left to the freedom of his own will." *Concerning Civil Government*, (63).

7. See, for example, Lao Tzu, *Tao Te Ching*, III, 9–10; Confucius, *The Analects*, II, 3.20; XV, 5. Admittedly, in actual practice, Confucian rulers often served others only after first serving themselves quite handsomely, claiming in the process all manner of privileges as their due.

8. Hannah Arendt, *The Origins of Totalitarianism* (New York: Harcourt, Brace and Company, 1951), 316. Unfortunately, there is also a strong tendency in those of a highly rationalistic, principled and resentment-motivated (but not spiritually grounded) anarchist bent to revert to the authoritarian in its totalitarian form when their anarchist program fails to get realized, circumventing entirely the democratic. Those most resentful of authority, and impatient with human weakness, so often become authoritarian the moment they acquire power over others.

9. Paul Ricoeur, *Fallible Man*, trans. Charles A. Kelbley (New York: Fordham University Press, 1986), 116.

10. Ibid., 118.

11. Joyce Trebilcot, "Sex Roles: The Argument From Nature," in *Philosophy of Woman*, ed. Mary Briody Mahowald, 2d ed. (Indianapolis: Hackett Publishing Company, 1983), 376.

12. In Ibid., 389.

13. John Stuart Mill, "The Subjection of Women," in ibid., 47–48.

14. Nietzsche, *Beyond Good and Evil*, 237a and 238.

15. See, for example, Rosemary Radford Ruether, *Sexism and God-Talk: Toward a Feminist Theology* (Boston: Beacon Press, 1983).

16

Destiny and Death

Amor fati: Freedom in love with necessity.

Ideas of fate and destiny that rest on some notion of an external, divine agency have been put forward in many different cultures, with the ideas themselves being subject to considerable change and development in any one of them. With the Greeks, for example, fate or *moria* was taken in the beginning (by Homer) to be superior oftentimes to the gods themselves, for they were subject to its power. Sometimes *moria* was morally neutral, othertimes it embodied or represented the very principle of justice. In any event, fate everywhere was understood to mean the determination of a person's destiny—the distinction between the two concepts having to do primarily with universality (fate) and particularly (destiny); that is, destiny is fate operating in particular cases.

In Hasting's venerable *Encyclopaedia of Religion and Ethics* we read,

> Fate . . . is transcended whenever dependence upon God becomes the spring of free action, all things being then regarded as necessarily subservient to man's highest interests, and man himself as capable of so utilizing them. Such is ideally at least, the view held by Christianity, and, accordingly, Christianity repudiates *in principle* all belief in fate.[1]

Mircea Eliade, however, states that,

> whether history was governed by the movements of the heavenly bodies or purely and simply by the cosmic process, . . . whether again, it was subject to the will of God . . . the result was the same: none of the catastrophes manifested in history was arbitrary. Empires rose and fell; wars caused innumerable sufferings; immorality, dissoluteness, social injustice, steadily increase— because all this was necessary, that is, was willed by the cosmic rhythm, by the demiurge, by the constellations, or by the will of God.[2]

Traditional ideas of fate or of cosmic necessity (e.g., the Stoic's *ananke*, perhaps the Chinese *ming*, Islam's *hadith*, the Hindu-Buddhist *karman* on some readings, and so on) would appear then to be part of an ontology of misery—a search for meaning in the face of utter existential absurdity. It is as though nothing were more unendurable than random suffering. To believe that life could deal with one badly in an entirely fortuitous way is more unbearable than to believe that one's situation, however terrible, was determined, no matter how mysterious and unknowable the source of that determination might be.

One is never directly aware, however, that the givens of one's individuality and life have a predetermined order of relations among them. There is no experience as such that yields fate as a determinate order that produces personal destinies. Nor is there any compelling rational ground for the idea; it being a valid conclusion from some set or other of warranted premises. The idea might cohere with some general conceptual scheme that is congenial to one, but it does not have, as far as we know, any empirical or straight-forward rational justification. And it would take a very special intuitive eye to see fate.

The concept of destiny does presuppose in our ordinary language usage some kind of freedom. Destiny is more the belief that events *conspire* than that they *compel*. The phrase, "we were destined to meet" means, for most persons, that the conditions of their lives were such that, by some hidden design, they were to or should have or were supposed to meet; it does not mean that some deterministic causal chains as such were at work and necessitated their meeting.

The idea of destiny also clearly presupposes the existence of a unified self capable of bearing an identity over time. A person must be able to have a coherent narrative history before she can have a destiny. If one were to lack unity (numerical identity) and some kind of sameness over time (personal identity) one would be at best a collection of short stories.

What is primary for our experience, then, and hence for what ought to be the primary meaning of personal destiny, is the realization that we can make things happen as well as have things happen to us—within the framework of specific givens and events which suggest, and then need to be brought fully into, a design. Destiny ought to mean artful play.

And thus another kind of necessity needs to be, although it seldom is, identified: let us call it, as we have before, the "aesthetic." The aesthetically necessary, grounded as it is in contemplative consciousness, is what appears to be inevitable in the right forming of relationships between the elements that constitute a given whole. In art, the aesthetically necessary, as we have seen, is dynamic and emergent—and is always contextual. The rightly formed—the appropriate resolution of tensions, development of contrasts—is always presented in a specific, concrete work. For the observer, it is realized during the experience of the work; for the maker, it is immanent throughout his activity. The aesthetically necessary is based on a freedom to bring a vital form to realization. It does not, however, involve a single obvious course of action to be carried out; rather what appears to be necessary emerges in the process of its realization; it is not a given in the first place. It is only when the music, the dance, the drama, the novel, or the poem is happening that we find its meaningful direction and, if it succeeds as a work of art, have the awareness of its rightness—its authenticity as the concrete, unique work that it is.

The aesthetically necessary, I maintain, is the proper basis for the concept of destiny.

The (relatively) fulfilled person finds a kind of inevitability in her life in terms of having been able to act out, as it were, her character with the various (otherwise fortuitous) circumstances of life being regarded as opportunities that were appropriately seized. The (relatively) unfulfilled person, on the other hand, finds a causal inevitability in her life with the circumstances of life being regarded as imposed and fixed.

To achieve an artful destiny oftentimes requires abrupt discontinuities and dislocations (alienation)—for it is these that present the challenge to imagination to realize a design.

Destiny presupposes not only a freedom of consciousness but a degree of (social and political) liberty sufficient to allow one the opportunity to give shape to the events of one's life. The destitute, the oppressed, the starving, do not have a destiny; they have only a pressing actuality—raw materials of destiny that cannot be appropriated.

Destiny is the recognition that there are certain structures (biologic, social, environmental) at work in the growth and decline that is one's life and over which one does not have direct control and to which, in the last analysis, one can only offer one's assent, the structures then appearing nonetheless as material for creativity. Personal destiny requires imagination: it is not properly an acknowledgement of helplessness.

The (apparent) chance events that change one's life dramatically (most often having to do with encountering another person) provide the dynamic stage for the performance of one's destiny rather than constituting that destiny as such. If not that event (that chance meeting, that unexpected happening) then some other event would have provided a way of acting out one's character—playfully in freedom.

For many persons destiny is a burden not because it is something externally imposed upon them, but because it does require an active making (*karman*)—for which one is responsible.

To have a destiny, however, does not mean that one's life is free from suffering, from pain, disappointment, failure, or frustration. It means only that one has succeeded in taking up that suffering, that pain, in such a way as to make it a deepening, transformative feature of an integrated life.

Unfortunately, when the older idea of fate, as an inexorable power molding individual lives, is abandoned we often get the radical opposite, namely some kind of existentialist demand for total freedom, the affirmation that there is nothing given in human nature, everything remains to be done by us. This romantic dream of free being—that I am what I do as a result of my own choice and commitment without restraint—turns out always to be what it is, a chimera. For there are givens to human being and to human lives, and the richest freedom finds its expression, indeed its only way of being, within those structures.

Destiny is thus the appropriation of the givens of one's individuality and specific events of one's life in an appropriate way; in a way that has the feel of rightness about it. Appropriation is more than a resigned acceptance, a passive assent to what is, it involves rather a transformation of the merely given, in freedom of consciousness and action.

Destiny, then, is not a matter of taking a certain attitude towards the givens but is a creative taking up of them as raw materials to be shaped and formed within the patterns suggested by them. Destiny requires a kind of self-cultivation or crafting and the acting out, within the happenings of one's life, of that cultivation.

Just as an artist recognizes and has a profound respect for the limits of his medium, seeing these constraints not as obstacles but as opportunities for bringing forth a vital formed content, so in fulfilling one's destiny one acknowledges the given conditions and events of one's life as indicating a design, but one that is capable of being realized dynamically. Personal destiny ought to be the way a fulfilled life and living appears to be (aesthetically) necessary.

Despair, where everything becomes meaningless, is the enemy of destiny. In despair, nothing is seen as an opportunity, only as an indifferent, oppressive given. Our destiny ceases when we are in despair.

The freedom that we recognize as possessing in the shaping of our destiny is at the same time a recognition of spirit. It is an acknowledgement of the creative power of being in which we share and participate. And, like all creativity, it thus involves as well a celebration of life.

In old age destiny often runs its course insofar as one's capabilities to realize a design are diminished, oftentimes to the point of childlike dependency and helplessness.

Destiny should not be conceived, however, in strictly atomic, individualistic terms, for it is throughout a social concept. I have a destiny only as a social being. The socially based givens of my birth, family life, education and the rest, together with the happenings and events of the world that become part of my experience, are as real as the physical and mental givens of my individual (biologic) being. Destiny is realized interpersonally, or not at all.

A person has a destiny, then, to the degree to which she is able to realize a design that seems (aesthetically) necessary. An unachieved destiny would be a contradiction in terms. To have a destiny means to have the lively conviction that one is and is becoming what was meant for one to be. Destiny is a creative performance: an acting out in freedom of what seems entirely right for one—until the very end.

A free man thinks of nothing less than of death, and his wisdom is not a meditation upon death but upon life.[3]

The knowing self is never born, nor does he die at any time. . . . He is unborn, eternal, abiding and primeval. He is not slain when the body is slain.[4]

The opposite of death is birth. Between death and life, dying and living, there is a strict correlation. Taoism recognizes this and accordingly regards death as just the other side, as it were, of life. There is the oft-cited account of the Taoist master Chuang Tzu who upon the death of his wife initially suffers grief, but then realizing that her death is part of the Tao spontaneously expresses in song a celebration of the joy of being and of natural becoming.

Chuang Tzu's wife died and Hui Tzu went to offer his condolence. He found Chuang Tzu squatting on the ground and singing, beating on an earthen bowl. He said, "Someone has lived with you, raised children for you and now she has aged and died. Is it not enough that you not shed any tear? But now you sing and beat the bowl. Is this not too much?"

"No," replied Chuang Tzu. "When she died, how could I help being affected? But as I think the matter over, I realize that originally she had no life; and not only no life, she had no form; not only no form, she had no material force (*ch'i*). In the limbo of existence and non-existence, there was transformation and the material force was evolved. The material force was transformed to be form, form was transformed to become life, and now birth has transformed to become death. This is like the rotation of the four seasons, spring, summer, fall and winter. Now she lies asleep in the great house (the universe). For me to go about weeping and wailing would be to show my ignorance of destiny. Therefore I desist."[5]

What happens, then, to the unfree upon death? The answer must be that, quite literally, nothing happens—and it is the dim awareness of this fact that no doubt contributes to our fear of dying.

Gods of death, like Yama—who have a special place of their own. The underworlds peopled by mythic consciousness tell us about living hells not about afterlives.

The powerful and the oppressed, it seems, both yearn for some kind of personal immortality. For the one it offers the opportunity to maintain one's privileged position (Pharaohs buried with their things in order to endure with them); for the other, the chance to get even (or, as Kant would put it, to ensure a just universe).

Persephone and Hades; the ancient Egyptian bull of Amanti; Charun, the winged Etruscan guide of the dead—ready always to take others to the place of the dead and to receive them there. Freud (and indeed Epicurus) allowed that "death is what happens to others"; that one cannot think positively one's own death, for thinking is necessarily an existing activity about something or other.

Is it existing or dying, then, that is the meaning of life? Socrates (Plato) thought that the genuine thinker, the philosopher of vision, lived his life as a preparation for dying, for upon death, with the purity of a disembodied soul, he could realize the proper end of living, the contemplation of the good. Gabriel Marcel has argued, "As long as death plays no further role than that of providing man with an incentive to evade it, man behaves as a mere living being, not as an existing being."[6]

But is it not the case that the philosopher, like everyone else, behaves in fact "as a mere living being"? Kierkegaard says, "We wish to know what it means to prepare for death, since here again one must distinguish between its actual presence and the thought of it."[7] One must indeed prepare for death (namely by living rightly) but not because of some distinction between its actual presence and the thought of it, rather because it provides the occasion to fulfill one's destiny.

Dying should be an acknowledgment of *māyā*, with a profound and liberating sense of the spiritually absurd. It ought not to be a loud moaning about finitude, or about something that ought to be conquered.

A meaningless life: when one's obituary is a mere chronicle of one's individuality.

If time-space is as articulate temporality and spatiality, then upon death there could not be a when or a where for a person to reside. Personal immortality is without sense.

Being a psychosomatic unity, a person vanishes upon death. For if personal identity is as much body-based as it is bound up with memory and the like, then upon the loss of bodily being one's consciousness could not involve that of an I or a me. It could, however, be of that which is "unborn, eternal, abiding and primeval"—a nonpersonal, boundless consciousness, a state of being that is an ever-present reality to be realized.

With death the person game is over. Only various silences remain.

NOTES

1. James Hasting, ed. *Encyclopaedia of Religion and Ethics*, vol. 5 (New York: Charles Scribner's Sons, 1924), 774.

2. *Cosmos and History: The Myth of Eternal Return*, trans. Willard R. Trask (New York: Harper Brothers, 1959), 133.

3. Spinoza, *The Ethics*, prop. LXVII.

4. *Kaṭha Upaniṣad*, I, 2, 18 in *The Principle Upaniṣads*, ed. and trans. S. Radhakrishnan (New York: Harper, 1953), 616.

5. Chuang Tzu, *The Chuang Tzu* (*Nan-hua chen-ching*), trans. Wing-tsit Chan, in *A Source Book of Chinese Philosophy*, 209.

6. Gabriel Marcel, *Creative Fidelity*, trans. Robert Rosthal (New York: The Noonday Press, 1964), 241.

7. Søren Kierkegaard, *Concluding Unscientific Postscript*, trans. David F. Swenson and Walter Lowrie (Princeton: Princeton University Press, 1941), 151.

Index

Abram, David, 201n30
action: and determinism 238–41; and effortless power, 244; and freedom, 241–44; natural grace in, 243; quality of, 242; skill in, 242–43
Ames, Roger T., 33n34, 130
Anscombe, G. E. M., 249n65
Apel, Karl-Otto, 169n1
appropriation: agent of, 75; of the body, 73; and the emotions, 61–62; of individuality, 21; process of, 62
Aquinas, Thomas, 117
Arendt, Hannah, 180
Aristotle, 30n6, 115, 116, 127, 133, 152, 187, 205, 219, 223, 225, 226, 264
artistic creativity: Chinese understanding of, 229; and cooperative control, 228; and cosmology, 224–25; as a formative act, 229; its immanent purposiveness, 227–28; as infused power, 229; as *līlā*, 230; and meaning, 227–28; and mutuality, 230; as play, 230; singularity of, 229; and spontaneity, 230
Audi, Robert, 38
Augustine, 96, 187–88, 196
Ayer, A. J., 9, 219

Bacon, Francis, 145
Barnes, Barry, 127, 135
beliefs: credible and incredible, 137; formation of, 137; justification of, 137–40; as open to revision and defeat, 137–38; positive criteria for, 139; role of authority in justifying,

143n41; role of exclusionary principles in as shareable, 138; social character of, 139
Bergson, Henri, 197n4
Bhagavadgītā, 48, 115, 118
Blanshard, Brand, 116, 117
Bloor, David, 127, 135
body, the: as an achievement, 69; as appropriated, 73–77; and bodily sensations, 83n23; instrumental metaphor of, 71; as lived-body, 78; machine metaphor of, 71; ontological contingency of object-body, 82n15; ownership of, 76; primary meaning of, 72–73; prison-house metaphor of, 70; as subject-body, 79–80; temple metaphor of, 70–71; as thing-body, 78–79
Boethius, 19
Brann, Eva T., 248n44
Brooks, Peter, 70
Buddhism: and causality, 232; empiricist tendency in, 29n3; "no self" (*anātman*) doctrine in, 4, 29n5; Śaṃkara's argument against, 14; theory of momentariness (*kṣaṇa*) in, 5
Bunge, Mario, 249n50
Butler, Joseph, 17

Campbell, C. A., 239
causality: archaic idea of, 218–22; Aristotle's theory of, 219; Brahmanic Indian theories of, 231–32; Buddhist theories of, 232; Chinese conceptions of, 232–33; as conditionship

301

About the Author

Eliot Deutsch is professor and chair of the Department of Philosophy, University of Hawai'i, Mānoa. He is a former editor (1967–1987) of the international journal *Philosophy East and West,* director of the Sixth East-West Philosophers' Conference, and a former president of the Society for Asian and Comparative Philosophy. Deutsch received his Ph.D. from Columbia University and has been a visiting professor at the University of Chicago and Harvard University, and a visiting fellow and life member at the University of Cambridge. He has been an invited lecturer at numerous universities and colleges in Asia, Europe, and the Americas, and is the author of fourteen books, including *On Truth: An Ontological Theory; Advaita Vedānta: A Philosophical Reconstruction; Studies in Comparative Aesthetics; Religion and Spirituality;* and *Essays on the Nature of Art.*